Born in Brooklyn, New York, Rudolph W. Giuliani was elected the 107th mayor of the City of New York in 1993. Prior to becoming mayor, he had been Associate Attorney General, the third highest position in the United States Department of Justice, a position he left in 1983 to become US Attorney for the Southern District of New York. He was voted *Time* 2001 Person of the Year.

Rudolph W. Giuliani founded Giuliani Partners, a consulting firm, in January 2002, and is based in New York.

Ken Kurson, who worked on the book with Rudolph Giuliani, is editor-at-large at *Money*, a contributing editor for *Esquire* and author of *The Green Magazine Guide to Personal Finance*. He lives in the New York metropolitan area.

RUDOLPH W. GIULIANI

with Ken Kurson

LEADERSHIP

timewarner
paperbacks

A *Time Warner* Paperback
First published in the United States of America by Hyperion in 2002
First published in Great Britain by Little, Brown in 2002
This edition published by Time Warner Paperbacks in 2003
Reprinted 2004, 2005

A CIP catalogue record for this book
is available from the British Library.

ISBN 0 7515 3333 5

Printed and bound in Great Britain by
Clays Ltd, St Ives plc

Time Warner Paperbacks
An imprint of
Time Warner Book Group UK
Brettenham House
Lancaster Place
London WC2E 7EN

www.twbg.co.uk

This book is dedicated to all the people
described in these pages, whom I leaned on and learned from—
it was from them that I derived the strength to lead.

Contents

Preface

I have always loved to write. As a trial lawyer, I found that my favorite part of the work—and the part I was probably best at—was the final summation. In a way, that's what writing a book is: bringing together the threads of a complicated theme and weaving them into a clear, convincing story. I have also always loved to research. Mastering a subject and persuading an audience to interpret it as you do is akin to the art of politics. As I entered 2001, my last year as mayor of New York City, I still had much to learn about leadership. That's why I had long resisted offers to write a book like this. But I thought that the experiences I had accrued and the strategies I had developed had provided enough material to offer valuable insight to readers about leadership. I had no idea that I would soon face the greatest leadership challenge of my life.

During the spring and summer of 2001, I worked on this book alongside my official duties as mayor, taking voluminous notes on a trusty legal pad. I spent countless hours with Ken Kurson and had him observe what I do, then we'd discuss why I did it. By summer's end, the structure of the book had taken shape. One of the reasons I found this process so satisfying was that it was not simply the passive activity of transcribing foregone conclusions: it was an active pursuit. Putting this book together forced me to consider my ideas more deeply, to challenge them in my own mind.

By September 11, I had been working on the book for months. It had become almost a seminar for me, a self-imposed program on how to run an organization. It was as if God had provided an opportunity to design a course in leadership just when I needed it most. By the time of the horrible events of September 11, because of all that I'd been working on, the elements were fresh in my mind, which gave me more confidence.

Every single principle that follows was summoned within hours of the attack on the World Trade Center. Surround yourself with great people. Have beliefs and communicate them. See things for yourself. Set an example. Stand up to bullies. Deal with first things first. Loyalty is the vital virtue. Prepare relentlessly. Underpromise and overdeliver. Don't assume a damn thing. And, of course, the importance of funerals. It was ironic, prophetic, and very useful that all these principles had been discussed and analyzed so recently.

The events of September 11 affected me more deeply than anything I have ever experienced; but the idea that I somehow became a different person on that day—that there was a pre–September 11 Rudy and a wholly other post–September 11 Rudy—is not true. I was prepared to handle September 11 precisely because I was the same person who had been doing his best to take on challenges my whole career. I didn't dust off some secret book reserved only for national emergencies, but did my best to implement the same leadership I used throughout my two terms as mayor, five years as U.S. Attorney, and two stints in the Justice Department, as well as my bout with cancer and other battles and roles in which I learned valuable lessons.

What I have not included are details from my personal life. The dissolution of my marriage, for example, had nothing to do with my public performance and never affected it in any way. While it certainly generated attention, I don't believe the public was as interested in it as the media. There's little enough private life left for public figures. It may be a counsel of perfection, but if we as a nation expect to attract real people to public life, we have to do what we can not to intrude on matters that don't affect a public figure's duties and performance.

Throughout this book, I seek to demonstrate the effectiveness of the lessons I have learned with hard evidence. I believe in proof more than theories, results more than rhetoric, so I have included a range of before-and-after examples. For instance, in the year I first ran for mayor, 1989, there were 1,905 murders in New York City. I lost that election, and in the subsequent year, 1990, the city set an infamous record of 2,245 homicides. I became mayor on January 1, 1994. In that year, murders were reduced from 1993's 1,946 by almost 20 percent—to 1,561. By 1996, the number was under 1,000. In my last year, 2001, there were 642 murders in New York City—a reduction of 67 percent in just eight years.

Similar success was enjoyed in many areas of civic life. How these results were achieved is detailed in the chapters that follow, and in the book's appendix. On top of the mountain of before-and-after data, one element is not captured by the numbers. The hopelessness and despair in New York City were just as painful as any crime statistic or joblessness figure. A literal sign of the city's malaise were the ubiquitous "No Radio" flags drivers would hang in the windows of their cars. This was essentially a negotiation with the worst members of society, a plea to thieves: "Don't victimize me—that other car doesn't have a sign, go take his radio."

In September 1990, the cover of *Time* displayed the familiar "I Love New York," but the picture with it showed a broken heart. The headline read "The Rotting of the Big Apple," and the story described out-of-control violence, vanishing jobs, crumbling infrastructure, and a pervasive dread of the future. New York City was the crime and welfare capital of America, a city that had seen its best days and held no hope for recovery. The *Time* story—picked up by the *Daily News* and other local papers—went on to report that 59 percent of New Yorkers said they would move out of the city if they could.

To me, an incident that encapsulated the city's condition occurred during a 1990 trip to London. I was giving a lecture on securities law and white-collar crime. In the question-and-answer period, someone asked how bad crime really was in New York. This person called to my attention a brochure that contained tips on how a visitor to New York might steer clear of crime. One of the suggestions was, "Avoid making eye contact." All of a sudden, the depth of my city's problems came into stark focus. Why would anyone visit a city in which you can't look at people? Why would anyone live in a city in which you can't make eye contact? What a crazy, sad proposition— yet probably good advice.

Ten years later, after many of the principles in this book had been deployed, the cover of *Time* once again featured New York. It showed Times Square at midnight, January 1, 2000. The Big Apple was aglow with activity. It had become the safest large city in America. It bustled with economic activity throughout virtually every neighborhood. Small businesses were growing in every borough, and corporations were relocating their headquarters—and thousands of jobs—to New York. Young families were raising their children here. Tourists and conventioneers were setting records for visitors. New York City had once again become a place where it was okay to make eye contact.

Leadership does not simply happen. It can be taught, learned, developed. Those who influenced me—everyone from Judge Lloyd MacMahon, my first real boss, to my parents to Ronald Reagan to Attorney General William French Smith to U.S. Attorneys Paul Curran and Mike Seymour to my five uncles who were members of New York City's Police and Fire Departments—all contributed valuable elements to my philosophy.

There are many ways to lead. Some people, like Franklin Roosevelt, inspired with stirring speeches. Others, like Joe DiMaggio, led by example. Winston Churchill and Douglas MacArthur were both exceptionally brave and excellent speakers. Ronald Reagan led through the strength and consistency of his character—people followed him because they believed in him.

Ultimately, you'll know what techniques and approaches work best—those you hope to lead will tell you. Much of your ability to get people to do what they have to do is going to depend on what they perceive when they look at you and listen to you. They need to see someone who is stronger than they are, but human, too.

Leaders have to control their emotions under pressure. While I was mayor, on the few occasions someone who worked for me used "panic" to describe their state during some crisis in their bailiwick, I made it clear that it would be the last time they'd employ that word. "Concerned" is the attitude I wanted. If it turned out that an excess of caution had made us more concerned than we needed to be, that was acceptable, but panic was not. You can't let yourself be paralyzed by any situation. It's about balance.

Some of the rules and concepts in this book are entirely mine—drawn from my thoughts and life experience. Others are ideas developed by academics that had never been tested in the real world, or at least not in a laboratory as large and complicated as New York City. James Q. Wilson and George L. Kelling's "Broken Windows" theory of crime-fighting convinced me that paying attention to "minor" infractions like aggressive panhandling, graffiti, and turnstile-jumping would greatly reduce all crime, including major felonies. The ideas about "reinventing government" found in the book of the same name by David Osborne and Ted Gaebler proved extremely useful: as much as possible, I tried to run the city as a business, using business principles to impose accountability on government. Objective, measurable indicators of success allow governments to be accountable, and I relentlessly pursued that idea.

I am not above using good ideas that originated from places one might not expect me to mine. My predecessor as mayor and opponent in two elections, David Dinkins, implemented a program called "Beacon Schools," which used schools as neighborhood centers. It was a good idea, and when I became mayor I expanded it. Similarly, I instituted an Adopt-A-Highway program that eventually covered the vast majority of the city's highways, an idea I borrowed from Mayor Richard Riordan of Los Angeles.

All my life, I have been thinking about how to be a leader—whether it was when I was running the Corruption Unit of the U.S. Attorney's office in the Southern District of New York, then the Narcotics Unit, or turning around a bankrupt Kentucky coal company after being appointed as receiver, or watching Ronald Reagan, Judge MacMahon, and others. I realized later that much of what I was doing in studying these people so closely was preparing. Unconsciously, I was learning how to run things.

All leaders are influenced by those they admire. Reading about them and studying their development inevitably allows an aspiring leader to grow his own leadership traits. If he's lucky, he'll be able to learn from leaders in his own life—ask them questions, observe them in private, determine which of that leader's methods work well and would complement his own burgeoning style. But as critical as it is to learn from others, much of a leader's approach must be formed from the raw material of his or her own life.

There's no substitute for personal experience when it comes to dealing with problems. That's particularly true in times of crisis, when there's less time to develop ideas and plans. Wisdom gained from one's own history provides a head start. After September 11, people would tell me that it was brave to go to the scene of the attacks. It was actually just carrying out my usual practice for any significant emergency. Two of the lessons in this book involve the importance of seeing things with your own eyes and of setting an example. These lessons didn't appear out of thin air, nor were they the product of a book.

To take an example: on Thursday, December 10, 1992, I had finished lunch and was walking by myself back to my office at Anderson Kill, the law firm where I was a partner. As I came across 43rd Street, I noticed smoke coming from the historic Church of St. Agnes. St. Agnes was one of the nicest buildings in the entire city, an island of tranquillity amid the bustle of its next-door neighbor, Grand Central

Station. I realized the smoke was too heavy and black to be from a furnace, but there were no firefighters around, so I made my way into the rectory.

The ladies there were a little concerned, but not much more. "Have you called 911?" I asked.

They said, "Yes, the Fire Department is on the way."

I said, "Have you gotten everybody out of the rectory and the church?"

"We don't know. We think the church is evacuated, but Father is still upstairs."

"Get out of here," I told them. "Go outside and wait for the Fire Department. I'll go upstairs to make sure everybody has left the rectory." At this point, I saw one of the doormen from my office building and asked him to come with me. We quickly climbed up the stairs, and as I got near his room I saw the father through the open door gathering his possessions. He poked his head out and I told him, "There's a fire in the church. The Fire Department is on its way. We need to get out of here. Is anyone else in the building?" He said probably not, but that we should check. Together, we three walked up the floors, looked around, then went downstairs and saw there was still one person left in the office. We told him he'd better leave the building.

Now that we'd cleared the rectory, I asked if anyone remained in the church itself. The priest wasn't sure, so we hurried from the rectory to the altar side of the church. As we entered, we noticed two opportunistic thieves about to steal the candelabra from the altar. I yelled in my most authoritative voice, "Put that fucking stuff down and get out of here!" I immediately regretted my language, suddenly remembering that I was in a church, next to a priest. But it worked, and the would-be looters dropped them back on the altar and ran out of the church. It was then that I saw the fire for the first time, and it was raging. I stood transfixed by the flames for a moment, then realized we had to move fast. Somebody said, "I think we'd better get the hell out of here." By the time we were on the sidewalk, the Fire Department had arrived.

When I got back to my office, my longtime executive assistant Beth Petrone was waiting for me. Someone from the office had noticed me going into the burning building, and that was the last they'd seen or heard. Beth was understandably worried. I had a camel hair jacket on and she said, "Look at your coat." It was completely black and covered in soot. I later sent that coat to be cleaned but it came back shrunken. To this day, I refuse to part with it. For the events of that afternoon, the Fire Department gave me a medal and I treasure that medal, along with my coat, as reminders of the St. Agnes fire.

Many signs of America's extraordinary humanity emerged from the horror of the September 11 attacks. One was the emergence of a newfound respect for the police and fire professionals, who daily risk their lives. This was especially heartening in New York City, where the efforts of the uniformed services are often taken for granted. One factor that created this appreciation was that the firefighters and police officers who rushed into the World Trade Center never hesitated to risk their lives. They didn't wonder whether the people in those buildings were black or white, young or old, Muslim or Christian or Jew. They simply rushed in and accomplished the greatest rescue in the history of this country.

In the days and months following the attacks, people often asked me about the source of whatever ideas, strength, energy, or courage they perceived me to have. I do my best to answer those questions in the pages that follow. I begin with a detailed account of the events of September 11, as I personally experienced them. The next fourteen chapters are the heart of the book, in which I describe my precepts in full, using stories from my own life. The final chapter shows all these rules in action as I sought to lead the recovery of the city in the months following September 11. The truth is, however, that a big part of leadership is mysterious. Inspiration must be taken wherever and whenever it comes, and sources of strength appear in unexpected places.

In my final days as mayor, I often thought about what made America a special place. When my grandfather Rodolfo Giuliani, for whom I am named, left Italy, over a hundred years ago, he set sail for America with only $20 in his pocket. He left his family, his home, everything that was familiar and safe. He saw the obstacles that faced him: a treacherous journey across a dangerous ocean, coming to a place whose language he didn't understand. And yet Rodolfo and his wife and my other grandfather and grandmother all made the same choice to come here.

How did he do it—overcome all the fears he must have felt? It's simple. Rodolfo and millions of others were able to answer the call because they were guided by an idea. America, the land of the free and the home of the brave, this very special place. It was an idealized vision, undoubtedly romanticized. But by coming here, my forebears and so many others gave something back to America, making it even more special, because they worked hard to make this country better, fairer, more prosperous for themselves and their children.

Abraham Lincoln used to say that the test of one's Americanism was not one's family tree; the test was how much one believed in America. Because we're like a religion, really. A secular religion. We believe in ideas and ideals. We're not one race, we're many; we're not one ethnic group, we're everyone; we don't speak only one language, we're all of these people. We're tied together by our belief in political democracy, in religious freedom, in capitalism, a free economy where people make their own choices about the spending of their money. We're tied together because we respect human life, and because we respect the rule of law.

Those are the ideas that make us Americans. And those are the ideas that I leaned on when it was time to lead, both after September 11 and long before.

PART

I

1

September 11, 2001

It was an exceptionally clear summer morning. The skyline was surreally beautiful against a backdrop of the purest blue. No matter what day it is, New York City is a unique place, but on mornings like September 11 it was truly special.

I was at the Peninsula Hotel on 55th Street with Denny Young, my counsel and longtime friend, having breakfast with my former assistant U.S. Attorney, Bill Simon, and discussing Bill's upcoming primary race to be California's governor. We were saying our good-byes in the entrance hall when at about a quarter to nine,[1] Detective Patti

---

[1] These times are extremely difficult to pinpoint. Even the times that should be objective and definitive, such as the moments the planes hit, have not yet yielded to complete agreement. For example, the first plane to hit (American Airlines Flight 11 out of Boston, Massachusetts) has been listed as striking Tower 1 at 8:45, 8:46, and 8:48. While everyone seems to agree that the second plane to hit (United Airlines Flight 175, also from Boston) struck Tower 2 at exactly 9:03, there's no agreement on when the towers fell. Tower 2 went down first, at around 10:05, and Tower 1 collapsed at around 10:28. And naturally, the precise times I was at different places are impossible to know.

Varrone, one of the NYPD in my security detail, got a call from Joe Lhota, my Deputy Mayor for Operations. "How near are you to the Mayor?" he asked. Patti said she was five feet away, and it was then that Joe told her that a plane had hit the World Trade Center. It might be a Cessna, he said, but no one had any idea whether it was intentional or an accident. I was still chatting with Bill, but I could see Denny talking to Patti out of the corner of my eye. Denny came over and in his trademark low-key style said, "There's a fire at the World Trade Center. They think a twin-engine plane hit the building." Without knowing the enormity of what had happened, Bill said to me, "God bless you." It was the first of many prayers that day, and in the days to come. As we stepped outside onto Fifth Avenue, I looked up at the clear blue sky and thought, "It's such a beautiful day. A plane doesn't just hit the World Trade Center by accident."

While mayor, I made it my policy to see with my own eyes the scene of every crisis so I could evaluate it firsthand. It was a lesson I learned from a detective named Carl Bogan. Back when I was a young assistant U.S. Attorney, Detective Bogan investigated many of the cases for our office. He always underlined the importance of see-ing things with your own eyes, saying that all kinds of things would suggest themselves—the alibi witness could not possibly have slammed the door of the red building because the red building had a revolving door, and so on.

As shocking as this crash was, we had actually planned for just such a catastrophe. My administration had built a state-of-the-art command center, from which we handled the emergencies that in-evitably befall a city like New York, such as the West Nile virus, black-outs, heat waves, hurricanes, snowstorms, and Y2K (the year 2000). It was packed with computers and television screens to monitor condi-tions all over the city and beyond. It had generators in case the power failed, sleeping accommodations in case we had to stay overnight, storage tanks with water and fuel, and stockpiles of various antidotes. It was located on the 23rd floor of 7 World Trade Center, just north of the twin towers. So that's where Denny and I headed, with Richie Godfrey at the wheel and Patti next to him.

The mobile phones in the van, as well as our personal cell phones, were ringing incessantly. We went west along 42nd Street, then south onto Seventh Avenue. By bending down in the backseat, I could see the very top of the north tower. There were flames coming from the upper floors. At that distance, it looked bad but not unmanageable. I asked Patti to put calls in to the Police Commissioner, the Fire Commissioner, and the director of the Office of Emergency Management, as well as to the Governor and to the White House. My first assumption was that it was some nut flying a small plane.

The streets were fairly clear for that time of morning and we had the lights and sirens going, so by nine A.M. our car was in Greenwich Village, near St. Vincent's, one of the hospitals closest to the crash site. Doctors and nurses were bustling about outside in operating gowns, preparing for triage. Seeing the medical personnel on the street like that made me begin to understand the depth of the situation. It had to be even worse than I thought.

Then the second plane hit. All I saw was a big flash of fire. By that point we were at Canal Street, which marks the beginning of Manhattan's southern tip. Initially, I thought it was the first tower experiencing a secondary explosion, but Patti got a call from Police Command saying the south tower, Tower 2, had also been struck, by what turned out to be United Airlines Flight 175, a 767 en route from Boston to LA. This convinced us it was terrorism. We redoubled calls to the White House switchboard but cell phone service was now becoming difficult. We continued rushing south toward the scene. Driving by, I could see the stunned expression on every face as people stared up at the nightmare unfolding before their eyes.

Now that the second plane had hit, the command center was being evacuated—it was too near to the attacked buildings and could itself be a target. After he called me about the first plane, Joe Lhota and the director of the Office of Emergency Management, Richie Sheirer, had gone to the command center, still assuming it was a terrible accident. Police Commissioner Bernie Kerik had told Patti where our car should meet him. A minute later, I arrived at Barclay Street, which formed the northern border of the World Trade Center complex. Joe, Bernie, Bernie's First Deputy Joe Dunne, and the Chief of the Police Department, Joe Esposito, were all running toward me.

I immediately devised two priorities. We had to set up a new command center. And we had to find a way to communicate with people in the city. Bernie and his staff had already identified a building at 75 Barclay Street, just northeast of 7 World Trade Center, as a possible site. "The security guy here was on the job," said Bernie, meaning a former cop, "and he's got phones for us. We commandeered the place." Down the block, I saw that news trucks were already arriving, and told Sunny Mindel, my Communications Director, to start organizing the press so we could brief them outside, at Church Street and Park Place. As Bernie and I walked, he told me that they'd set up the fire command post between the Merrill Lynch and American Express buildings on West Street, the western border of the World Trade Center site. I decided that we'd go there to figure out what instructions we should give people in or near the towers, both of which by then had flames shooting out from their upper floors.

At that point, I wasn't sure how bad the conditions were. I followed my usual practice of going directly to the scene to see it myself so I could discuss it intelligently. I also wanted the fire commander to talk to me face-to-face—to look into my eyes and give me an undiluted assessment. I hurried down West Street, to the fire command post, and on the way there saw something that made me realize that we were in a new world.

Joe Lhota had told me people were jumping, but I had assumed— "hoped" is probably the better word—that he was mistaken. I looked up and saw what I took to be debris falling from the building. When we turned onto West Street, John Huvane, another of my security detail, told everyone to try to look up to avoid being hit. I did and saw more waste and rubble coming down. Then all of a sudden, I focused on a man leaning out of a window of what must have been about the 102nd floor of Tower 1. I saw him jump and followed his whole trajectory as he plummeted onto the roof of 6 World Trade Center, the building just north of Tower 1. That someone would choose certain death brought home the reality of what was unfolding on the floors above where the planes had hit. I grabbed Bernie's arm and said, "We're in uncharted waters now. We're going to have to make up our response." I looked up again and saw other people jumping. Some appeared to be holding hands as they plummeted. They were not blown out of the building. They were making the conscious decision that it was better to die that way than to face the 2,000-degree heat of the blazing jet fuel.

Within minutes of the first plane hitting the towers, the decision was made to establish two command posts—one for the Fire Department and one for the Police Department. The reason for this is that the departments were going to perform different tasks and had different requirements. The Fire Department had to lead the rescue and evacuation. The Police Department had to protect the rest of the city. As the team leading the rescue, the Fire Department immediately became the incident commander. They set up their command post so that they had the buildings in their line of sight. The Police Department had already begun setting up at 75 Barclay and securing the hardlines that were needed to communicate with the Defense Department and the White House, as well as Albany and the Governor. Cell phone service was sporadic and unreliable.

Had the Police Department established its command post on West Street with the Fire Department, it would have been impossible for them to access the hardlines and necessary communications for the defense of the city. Had the Fire Department put its command post with the Police Department at 75 Barclay, it would have been impossible to observe the buildings and fight the fire. It was absolutely necessary to have two command posts—one to observe the fire and the other to permit communication via hardline. Having the police commissioner, the fire commissioner and Director of OEM together with me ensured coordination of the emergency rescue recovery and provided for the security of both the site and the city.

We got to the Fire Department's command post and I saw Pete Ganci, the department's highest-ranking uniformed officer, working the board that the department used to plan its response, and next to him First Deputy Commissioner Bill Feehan. Battalion Chief Ray Downey, in charge of special operations, was about 100 feet away, standing with a number of his men. Being there alongside these men meant I would get the answers I wanted. Thinking of the people I saw jumping from the top of the tower, I asked Pete if there was any chance of using helicopters to lift people to safety. Impossible, he told me—the smoke and swirling matter wouldn't let the choppers get that close. He said, "We can save everybody below the fire. Our guys are in the building, about halfway up the first tower." I knew that he was actually saying something else: "We can't do much above the fire except hope that there's still a staircase."

I asked Pete how bad the situation was. He told me they'd evacuated about half of Tower 1, heading up to the point of impact, which was above the 94th floor. They were also making their way up Tower 2, each firefighter carrying some 60 pounds of equipment, as well as coping with the thousands of occupants descending the same stairs the firefighters ascended. Next I said, "Tell me what I should tell people."

"To get out of the building," Pete replied. "We have enough men there to help them." The stairways were smokeproof and fireproof, and if the doors were kept closed they would stay safe. Looking up at the falling debris and swirling smoke, Pete added that all survivors should head north as soon as they were outside. He also wanted to move as many people as possible from the vicinity so we could get fire equipment and ambulances in and out.

With pieces of the towers falling down around us, I told Pete, "I think you should move this command post." They were going to, he said—they planned to relocate farther north. We shook hands. "God bless you," I said. "Thanks. God bless you." Then I turned north and headed back up West Street to the Police Department command post.

Meanwhile, Tony Carbonetti, my Chief of Staff, had called the White House. He spoke to his counterpart there, Andy Card, but didn't realize Andy was in Florida with the President and that the call had been patched through. Andy confirmed that it was definitely a terrorist attack. At the time, they thought there were seven planes missing. Knowing that I'd want to speak to the President, Andy told Tony to reach him through the White House's Situation Room and gave him the number.

As soon as Tony heard that this was the intentional work of terrorists, he asked the Police Department to evacuate City Hall and seal it shut. Tony set out to find me, heading for 7 World Trade Center, where he assumed I'd be. He had Garry McCarthy, the NYPD's Deputy Commissioner for Operations, with him, and as they hurried west on Barclay toward 7 World, all these people were streaming east. Garry stopped somebody and asked why everyone was running, since elsewhere the evacuation had been surprisingly orderly. There were men and women "falling out of the building," he was told. Tony and Garry looked up and were stunned by the sight of jumper after jumper. They found me on West Street at the Fire Department post and joined the group that was making its way to Barclay. I wanted the Police and Fire Commissioners and the Director of the Office of Emergency Management together to maximize communication between agencies. I also needed them to advise me on what to tell the public.

I then told the firemen that I wanted Fire Commissioner Tom Von Essen to join my group. Tom had rushed to the lobby of Tower 1 after it was hit and wanted to stay there with his men, but I needed him to tell people how to evacuate. As Bernie and I were leaving the fire command post, we said good-bye to Bill and Pete and waved to Ray and wished them all luck. Father Mychal Judge, the chaplain to the Fire Department, rushed by. I said, "Father, pray for us." He smiled at me—we had to stretch to reach each other's hand—and replied, "I always do. I always pray for you."

I had known these men—Bill and Pete and Ray and Father Judge—for many years, had looked up to them and pinned medals on them. I loved these men. I did not realize that this would be the last time I'd ever see them. All four died that day.

I had been at the scene for about forty minutes. The group of people with me had grown to about twenty-five—Joe Lhota, Bob Harding, and Tony Coles (three of my deputy mayors), Tony Carbonetti, Denny Young, Senior Advisor Geoff Hess, Sunny Mindel, Bernie Kerik, Health Commissioner Neal Cohen, Richie Sheirer, Criminal Justice Coordinator Steve Fishner, Director of the Mayor's Office of Operations Mike Carpinello, Joe Dunne, Joe Esposito; the cops on my detail, Patti Varrone and John Huvane; Bernie's Chief of Staff, John Picciano; and several other policemen there to help set up the new location.

At about 9:50 A.M., we commandeered the offices at 75 Barclay Street—a nondescript building that Merrill Lynch had used for back-office functions—and worked to establish phone communications. Tony Carbonetti went to one office to reach the White House, while Joe Lhota took another to phone the Governor. As awful as things were at this point, no one imagined that the towers would actually collapse. The World Trade Center had already survived the terrorist attack of 1993—a bomb that blasted a hundred-foot hole through four floors, knocking out all the electricity and communications systems—and none of the towers had come close to falling.

Once in 75 Barclay, we got through to the White House. I asked a question I never thought I'd have to ask: "Do we have air cover?" I was speaking to Chris Henick, Deputy Assistant to the President. He told me they had dispatched jets twelve minutes before, and that they would arrive any minute.

I asked whether it was true that the Pentagon had been attacked, an idea so outrageous I hoped someone had misheard the radio reports amid all the confusion. Henick said, "Confirmed." Could I talk to the President? Henick told me they were evacuating the White House and that the Vice President would call me back soon on the hardline I was using. At that time, I still didn't know that the President was in Florida, and assumed that the crash into the Pentagon must have meant precautions were being taken against additional attacks. Those around the President have an obligation to protect him. Especially after the third plane crashed, it was reasonable to assume that more could be on the way.

I was acting Associate Attorney General when John Hinckley attempted to assassinate Ronald Reagan. I thought about that and about all the evacuation plans they used to have during the Cold War, and I wondered if the Vice President was now in charge. Dick Cheney was President Ford's Chief of Staff when I first served in the Justice Department; I knew him and had great confidence in him, so I was relieved to hear a woman's voice on the telephone say, "Mr. Mayor, the Vice President will be on the line." My intention was to speak to the Vice President and then immediately relay what he told me to the people of New York through the press, who were being assembled outside by members of Sunny's staff. Within a second or two, the line went dead. For the moment, re-establishing that phone link took up all my attention. So it took some time for me to realize why the phone line was disconnected.

A few minutes after ten o'clock, we felt and heard a thunderous roar but did not know what had actually occurred. Some thought the sound was a new attack, and the way the ground shook made it feel like that. I was still on the telephone, hoping to be reconnected, when Joe Esposito yelled, "It's coming down—everybody down!" Those who could see out the south-facing windows all hit the floor or ducked under furniture. From beneath a desk, Tony Carbonetti said what we were all thinking: "What the hell is happening?" The south tower—2 World Trade Center—had collapsed, thrusting an enormous cloud of acrid smoke and building material throughout the area.

Since I was still in a back cubicle trying to speak to the Vice President, I didn't hit the deck. In fact, when I heard the words "tower" and "down," I imagined that the radio tower atop the World Trade Center had fallen off. Even surrounded by smoke and objects flying through the air outside, we could not conceive of the entire tower collapsing. I stayed by that phone for a minute or two, hoping the Vice President would be able to ring through again.

All of a sudden John Huvane grabbed my arm and said, "Boss, we've got to get out of here." Although we couldn't know exactly what was going on, it was clear that more and more people were not going to survive. I decided we had to evacuate. That was no easy task—the entrance was impassable. All kinds of objects, including crushed concrete and tangled steel, had hit the front of the building, knocking out every single south-facing window and piling rubble and ash throughout the offices. Outside was darkness as the tidal wave of the fallen tower snuffed out the same sun that had lit the sky only a couple hours earlier.

Our whole group marched downstairs into the basement in search of an escape route. We went to the first exit door, and a cop pushed at it. Locked. We tried a second door, which also wouldn't open, then a third. Impasse. I decided that we should go back the way we had come. We tried a back exit upstairs, but that was chained shut as well. I saw through the windows on the ground floor how bad it was getting outside—the ash and smoke formed a completely opaque haze.

All of a sudden, two men materialized. They appeared to be maintenance men, and one of them told us that there was another exit downstairs that led directly underground into 100 Church Street, an adjacent building I knew well because it housed the city's law department. I said that was perfect because we'd emerge facing north—the direction Chief Ganci had told us to follow. Nobody knew who this guy was, but he seemed to know where he was going, so we returned to the basement. I was thinking we were just going to hit another locked exit—why should this one be different from the others we'd tried? We went downstairs in a line, everyone concerned but not showing it, each of us focused on what needed to be done. Joe Dunne had severed his Achilles tendon several weeks before and was still on crutches. He is a big, strong career cop, and seeing him shuffle on his broken foot as we filed toward the door made me realize both the gravity of our situation and also how brave everyone was being. We finally reached the door. One of the maintenance guys calmly gave the knob a twist and—*boop*—it opened. We felt an immediate wave of relief, quickly replaced by the feeling that we were going from bad to worse.

We emerged from the basement into the lobby of 100 Church, and all hell was breaking loose. The lobby was surrounded by windows, and all we could see was an impenetrable cloud of white—we couldn't make out anything beyond the glass. Stuff was blowing through the streets like the tornado scene from *The Wizard of Oz*. One of Bernie's deputy commissioners (and a close friend of mine), Tibor Kerekes, walked in completely covered in white soot and bleeding. Even his trademark psychedelic tie was covered with white dust. After the first tower collapse, Tibor had been sprinting from the cloud but was overtaken before he could make it around the corner. He was staggering a bit and almost unrecognizable. In a stunned voice, Tibor said, "It's terrible out there." It was sobering to see such a confident man so shaken. Bernie ran to embrace him. He and Tibor had served in the military together, had studied martial arts together, and had worked in Korea and Saudi Arabia. Pictures from that day show Bernie with blood on his shirt—that blood was Tibor's.

We huddled in the lobby of 100 Church as Tibor described what was going on outside. I sat him down on a ledge in the lobby, and John Huvane came in from the outside with a first aid bag while someone found some water. We stayed there for a couple of minutes, then I made the decision to move out. If we were inside and the building collapsed, a big portion of city government would be eliminated. Outside, there was a better chance that we could re-establish city government. I had a fleeting thought that I'd rather be hurt on the street than crushed within the building, but I had to put that thought out of my mind. I had to focus on finding the press and communicating with people to give them advice.

After we emerged from 100 Church, we saw reporters who had rushed to the scene to cover the disaster. I was determined to communicate with people both the fact that they should head north and also that the leaders of the city were alive and in control. In the midst of this walking press conference, I grabbed Andrew Kirtzman by the arm (he's a reporter from all-news channel New York 1) and said to him and to other members of the press, "Come with us. We'll talk as we walk."

Just then, the cops started yelling, "Another plane's coming, scatter!" John Huvane shouted, "The second building just came down." In fact, it hadn't yet, but he had been outside with Tibor when the first building toppled and heard a similar noise.

Our group kept growing as we strode toward Canal Street. I looked back at the hundreds of people walking alongside us and saw Patti Varrone. She is a former major-case squad detective and willful enough to root for the Mets in my presence. Her red hair was caked with the walls of what an hour earlier had been New York's tallest building. She looked stunned, but also focused. We saw a man on crutches intoning, "I need to get out of here." I went up to him and said, "We'll put you in one of the cars." Bernie motioned to his car, which was right behind us, and Bernie and I helped him into it.

My objective was to re-establish city government. The Police Department—which housed our back-up command center—lost its telephone service. It was also a potential target. We considered the firehouse on Duane Street, which has plenty of extra space because it formerly contained the fire museum. Tony noted that it was in the shadow of the Federal Building, which could be a target. The next choice was the First Precinct, but following up on Tony's advice I thought that was too close to the AT&T Building, also a possible target. John Huvane suggested the Tribeca Grand Hotel. By this time, Tom Von Essen had joined us. We had almost reached Murray Street, four blocks north of the World Trade Center, when Tower 1 really did fall, at about 10:28.

John Huvane jumped on me to protect me, and pushed me forward for about a third of a block. I could feel him behind me. I stopped for a moment and looked at the cloud coming up the cavern of Lower Manhattan, then heard another plane. Richie yelled out, "It's one of ours." How strange, I thought—New York City had become a battlefield. Once again I had to shut out the thought and focus.

Our cell phones were all but dead. The landlines throughout Lower Manhattan were dead. Every entrance to the city was closed. No subways or buses were running, and there wasn't a taxi in sight. There was no way to find out what was going on—the World Trade

Center towers held many of the antennae that broadcast cellular phone and television signals, both of which were reduced to minimal capacity. It was primitive, shocking, surreal. And above the dust and soot and glass that still rained down was the same perfect blue sky.

Our government no longer had a place to work. Not only was City Hall a likely target, but it was only about a quarter mile from the World Trade Center. Covered in ash, it was nearly invisible. Bernie had sent a couple of his guys ahead to the Tribeca Grand to set up phone lines and clear the place out, like a scouting party in an old Western. As soon as I walked into the main lobby I rejected it—the entire building was sheathed in windows. I'd seen more than my share of raining glass over the last two hours. Under different circumstances, it might have been funny to see about twenty people from city government march into the hotel, turn around, and march right out.

Somebody mentioned Engine Company 24, a firehouse at Houston Street and Sixth Avenue. We made our way the few blocks north. I had strong memories of that particular building. A fire on March 28, 1994, just three months after I became mayor, killed three brave men—firefighters James Young, Chris Siedenburg, and Captain John Drennan. That tragedy marked the first occasion I ever spent substantial time with Father Judge, and I brought President Clinton to visit Engine 24 after Captain Drennan had died following a valiant forty-day fight to stay alive.

When we got there, the firemen were all at the World Trade Center, so it was empty and the door locked. It was that kind of day. The entire city government—mayor, deputy mayors, commissioners—spent several minutes trying to get into the firehouse, but the door was made of unbreakable Plexiglas. John Huvane grabbed a fire extinguisher and repeatedly tried to throw it through the door until someone pointed out that the tank itself could explode. We had been surrounded by breaking glass all morning, and here was this glass door that wouldn't give. Finally, we jimmied the lock and got inside. Having evacuated City Hall, my executive assistants Beth Petrone, Janna Mancini, and Kate Anson arrived, accompanied by my friend Bobbie Waldman, who had been in a meeting at City Hall with their Rolodexes, filled with the numbers we needed to reach the White House and Albany and everyone else. We found a couple of working phones and soon I was speaking to the Governor, George Pataki. He told me he'd been concerned that I was missing and asked if I was all right. He offered to call in the National Guard, which I accepted. I had resisted in the past, fearing that without being trained in the peculiarities of New York City, they could potentially find themselves in difficulty. It was obvious that we'd need all the help we could get. George and I agreed as soon as we relocated city government, he'd meet us there.

It was unclear how much of my "walking press conferences" had been broadcast. To ensure the widest distribution of information, Sunny insisted that all footage be declared "pool," which meant that every media outlet had to share what they shot with everyone else. Now, a few minutes before eleven A.M., I was able to attempt an actual press conference. I talked to the television channel New York 1 on the telephone and asked everyone to remain calm and do what they could to evacuate Lower Manhattan. I assured people that I had spoken to the Governor and the White House, that the city was being protected by our military, and that I'd observed the jets. Then I just said what I was thinking.

"My heart goes out to all of you. I've never seen anything like this. I was there shortly after it happened and saw people jumping out of the World Trade Center. It's a horrible, horrible situation, and all that I can tell you is that every resource that we have is attempting to rescue as many people as possible. The end result is going to be some horrendous number of lives lost. I don't think we know yet, but right now we have to focus on saving as many people as possible."

I divided my mission into three parts. First, I had to communicate with the public, to do whatever I could to calm people down and contribute to an orderly and safe evacuation. Second, I wanted to prepare for the injured. At that point, I thought we would be taking survivors out for a couple of days and that the number of injured would overwhelm the four nearest hospitals—St. Vincent's, Bellevue/

NYU, NYU Downtown, and Beth Israel. So I wanted to coordinate a system for all of the city's medical centers, public and private. The third track I was considering was, "What will happen next?"

I tried to get inside the heads of the terrorists. What were they going to attack next? Would they try to hit the Statue of Liberty, the Empire State Building, the United Nations? Or would it be a completely different type of attack—mortar bombs or hostage-taking? Biological weapons? We knew that there was a fascination with our tunnels and bridges. Bernie and I decided which buildings to cover, analyzed our intelligence, and planned a strategy to provide personal security for anyone who might be snatched. Might they attack the Stock Exchange? I called Dick Grasso, the CEO of the New York Stock Exchange, to see how things were going. He didn't want to add to the congestion in Lower Manhattan and wanted time to send home the thousands of brokers and traders to secure their safety and orderly exit. I told him to sit tight for now and promised I'd call him back after the police said it was okay to release everyone. I spoke to Dick again at about 1:00 and agreed that it made sense to send everyone home.

Something that hasn't been focused on in the immense amount of coverage following the attacks is that they occurred only one day before the scheduled sentencing—at the Federal Court just blocks from the site—of Mohamed Rashed Daoud al-'Owhali, an associate of Osama Bin Laden. He was convicted of murdering 213 people in the terrorist bombing of the U.S. Embassy in Kenya.

I turned my attention to my loved ones. As we walked in the street, I asked the police to provide extra security for my family. I called Donna to tell her I already had sent extra security to evacuate Gracie Mansion (which we knew from prior intelligence reports was a possible target), and we agreed that she would stay overnight in New Jersey with the children.

Then I called Judith Nathan, who had been by my side for two difficult years. Our relationship at that point was very public, and she, too, had received threats. I thought those attacking our city might go after her, and I wanted to make sure she was safe. Normally, when I call

Judith, it's my voice she hears—either I dial the number or someone else does and hands the phone to me before she answers. Making sure to speak to her myself, even regarding minor details such as when we'd meet for dinner, had become our own private ritual. As soon as the first plane hit, Judith knew I'd head down to the site. With the second plane and both towers collapsing, she was extremely worried. Patti had finally reached her, and Judith said, "I need to hear Rudy's voice." Patti told her that was not possible because I was on the other line.

When I finally got on the phone, I told Judith I loved her and that she must stay in her apartment—that she'd be safest there and that security was already on its way. But Judith insisted on joining me, saying, "I need to see that you are okay because I thought you were missing." I agreed to allow her to join me at the firehouse, since we hadn't yet decided where to set up our provisional government. Driving south on Lexington Avenue, on her way to meet me, Judith saw a large crowd gathered around a boom box—teenagers, senior citizens, all sorts of New Yorkers. She could hear my voice coming from the radio, telling everyone to head north. Her reaction was mixed. On the one hand, I was alive and well enough to be doing what I should be doing—guiding people through the crisis. On the other hand, I was telling them to go north. But I was still south.

Bernie had heard back from his scouts and suggested the Police Academy on 20th Street for an interim City Hall. Knowing the rivalry between the FDNY and NYPD, I asked Tom whether that was okay, and he said it wouldn't be a problem. Even so, getting everyone over there was a logistical challenge. There were now more than twenty of us, plus a press contingent, and we had only a few working vehicles. Tony's driver, Eddie Kalanz, known as something of a maverick, had been a repossession man before he started to work for the city. He approached Sergio Conde, another member of the security detail, and began pointing at cars that had been abandoned on the street, saying, "I can hotwire that one, that one, probably that one . . ." Luckily, it didn't come to that. I waited outside until everyone had piled into cars, and we all drove to the Police Academy.

We arrived about noon, and nearly every member of my administration crammed into the small administrative offices. Soon we were at
work, planning our response. Each time a member of the city's government showed up safely, we would hug and kiss the new arrival. It
had taken me seven years to put this team together, to fine-tune it to
the point where we could handle even the biggest challenge. I wasn't
yet sure we could tackle what lay ahead, but I knew that if we were to
have even a fighting chance the whole team would need to be in place.

Beth Petrone came up to me and said, "I was worried about you.
They said you were trapped." It was eerily reminiscent of the fire at St.
Agnes. Beth has worked with me for eighteen years. She is a lovely
person and I thought how nice it was to have worked with her so
closely for so long. It was my great honor to marry her to a fine man at
Gracie Mansion in May 1998. Her husband, Captain Terry Hatton,
commanded the Fire Department's elite Rescue 1, perhaps the country's most innovative specialized fire fighting and rescue squad. He
had been awarded nineteen medals and commendations in twenty-
one years with the FDNY. As Beth began to walk away, I suddenly put
it all together and realized that Terry would be in the towers. I looked
at Beth and said, "Was Terry working?" Beth replied, "Yes." I could see
tears in her eyes. I hugged her, and noticed that for the first time I also
had a tear in my eye. Beth said to me very quietly, "He's gone." I said,
"You don't know that yet. We will do everything to find him."

Terry Hatton, of course, was not the only one. Geoff Hess was my
Senior Advisor, as well as the son of Corporation Counsel Mike Hess,
who headed the city's 600-attorney Legal Department. Mike and I
had been assistant U.S. Attorneys together in the early 1970s. Geoff
was with the group that set up in 75 Barclay, then walked together to
Engine 24 while Tower 1 collapsed. At the firehouse, Geoff got word
from Kate Anson that his father was on his way to the Trade Center
to look for his son. Mike in fact arrived at 7 World Trade before it was
evacuated, but seeing that we weren't there, he phoned back to City
Hall to ask where we were. He had reached Kate, who at that point
didn't know that we were at 75 Barclay. By the time she saw Geoff at

the firehouse, all she knew was that Mike had called her from the "Trade Center"—amid the chaos, she didn't know whether he meant 7 World Trade or if he'd actually gone into one of the towers.

Geoff had been at City Hall when the first plane hit. He had called his father on the phone and told him that he was going down to the scene. Mike and Geoff were not just father and son—they were best friends. And now Geoff felt responsible for Mike being missing: had Geoff not called him, Mike would presumably have stayed somewhere safe, awaiting further instructions. The only reason he went to the site was to search for his son. And now, nobody knew where Mike was. With communications completely out, there was no way to reach him.

At that precise moment, Mike was in 7 World Trade Center, itself a 47-story building. He had gone to the 23rd floor to search for us. Everyone else in the building had already evacuated, and the elevators were inoperable, so Mike began walking down the stairs. When he got to the 8th floor, Tower 1—the north tower—collapsed, part of it falling on top of the southern part of 7 World Trade Center. Luckily, Mike was in the northern section of the building. Unluckily, he was now trapped, as the stairs impassable.

Mike went into an office on the 8th floor, joined only by a fellow from the Housing Authority. The building was filling up with smoke and dust from the collapsed towers, but since the men were facing north they had no way of knowing the towers had fallen. They couldn't breathe, but the windows were not designed to be opened—the panes were specially reinforced, since that building housed the command center. In an odd coincidence, considering our experience getting into the firehouse, Mike's companion threw a fire extinguisher at the window. It broke the first pane but bounced back. A second throw did the trick. Together, the men stood at that window for two hours yelling to the firefighters below. The firemen kept shouting up instructions but told them they couldn't get up to rescue them, which puzzled Mike and his companion because they didn't know about the towers' collapse.

Amazingly, a television reporter captured Mike leaning out the window, flames everywhere, screaming, "Help! Help!" We knew that 7 WTC had also eventually collapsed. So we were stunned—and overjoyed—when Mike walked through the doors, covered in soot and glass and blood from the jagged edges of the window through which my 60-year-old friend had thrown the fire extinguisher. He looked like someone who had walked through a snowstorm.

Sometimes, it's a blessing not to have time to dwell on the tragedies around you. If I had stopped to think about Terry and Beth and Mike and Geoff and the thousands of other families I was already sure would be devastated by this disaster, I don't know how I would have continued. Seeing Mike walk in, I hugged and kissed him, then got back to business while Mike and Geoff greeted each other in a way befitting a father and son who had both survived life-threatening peril. Months later, we'd all joke with him: "Mike, didn't you suspect something was amiss when you got up to the 23rd floor and the only person manning the 260 terminals was some guy from Housing? Didn't you and the other guy wonder where the hell everyone was, instead of sitting there for hours?"

By the time I arrived at the Police Academy, Judith was already there, comforting and consoling. She was not only an important part of my personal life, she had become part of the family at City Hall. I was looking at her at the Police Academy and thinking, "Okay, she's here—now what?" I knew I was going to take care of her, but what was I going to *do* with her? How could she contribute?

Meanwhile, Judith kept telling us all to wash our faces. A paste of building materials and assorted dust caked everyone. Even now, thinking about it, my eyes burn from the memory, but I didn't want to take a minute to wash my face. Then I remembered Judith had been a nurse for many years, and afterward a pharmaceutical executive; she had managed a team of people and had many organizational skills. Further, she had wide-ranging scientific knowledge and research expertise, as I discovered when she helped me through my fight with cancer.

I thought, "Okay, she just got a job," and put her to work helping me organize the hospitals. Every single one of those nearest the site

had been a client of Judith's. She knew the doctors and the adminis-
trators, how large the emergency rooms were, and where they were
located within each hospital. She spent part of the day confirming
beds would be available at St. Vincent's and NYU Downtown Hospital for those injured in the attacks.

By late afternoon at the Police Academy, I met with New York
City's Medical Examiner, Dr. Charles S. Hirsch. He was still covered
in dust and debris from the site, where he had rushed after the first
building fell. As soon as he'd heard of the first crash, he drove down
there to observe and make decisions on how his office would handle
it. I saw cuts all over his face and noticed Frankenstein-looking
stitches all over the back of his hand. I asked him what had happened
and he said that he got pelted as pieces of the building rained down
on him. To avoid diverting doctors who were needed elsewhere, Dr.
Hirsch stitched his own wounds with a cross-hatch of dark black
thread. He was the first to tell me it was unlikely that we would recover anyone alive. He said, "Most of the bodies will be vaporized.
We're going to end up with biological stains, where the tissue has become shapeless, amorphous masses of matter." He also was the first to
explain the massive heat, correctly estimating it at 2,000 degrees.
I went to Ground Zero five more times that day. On my first trip
there, I felt tremendous anger. I kept wondering aloud, "What kind
of human beings could do this to other human beings?" There's
never been a time that I've gone there without feeling that rage. That
first time back, I just let it wash over me.

I needed to see with my own eyes the disaster site and our rescue
operation and get a sense of what we'd be dealing with in the months
to come. I always kept a pair of boots in my van, in case there was a
fire or some other disaster. I put them on and got out of the car. I am
an optimist by nature. I think things will get better, that the good people of America and New York City will overcome any challenge
thrown our way. So in the face of this overwhelming disaster, standing amid sixteen acres of smoldering ruins, I felt a mixture of disbe-
lief and confidence that we would soon be rescuing survivors.

Furthermore, there was no time to spend actually experiencing an emotion. There were moments of anger, fear, and sorrow, but with so much to do it was impossible to dwell on those feelings. During that first day, I can think of only three times I allowed myself to feel any sharp sense of personal loss. One was the exchange with Beth about Terry. Another occurred at the firehouse, when I was notified that Mychal Judge was dead, followed a few minutes later by the news that Feehan and Ganci had been killed. I said, "Are you sure? I just saw them." I realized that if we had lost them, who I knew had been outside the buildings, our losses inside must be devastating.

When I was going through my worst personal problems, and stories were appearing in the newspapers that were embarrassing and humiliating, Father Judge would always find a way to make me feel better. He'd write a note or call to say he was thinking about me. I remember Easter 2000. He didn't know this, but I was preparing for my prostate cancer biopsy to take place two days later. In the midst of the problems with my marriage and my worry about cancer, Father Judge wrote me a beautiful letter. He reminded me of all the time we had spent together in hospitals with injured firefighters and told me that I had a talent for comforting people in distress. He would leave notes at the gate at Gracie Mansion whenever he would see something in the newspaper about my situation, always reminding me that everybody made mistakes, nobody was perfect, and that I had done things to help people. That came from a good heart, he said, and it came from somebody God loved. So I was crushed when I found out he was gone. Later, the photo of him being carried out of the building, his body limp underneath his white hair and gentle face . . . it was hard to see. I realized that when Father Judge died, I lost somebody who would have helped me get through this crisis—somebody who would have helped the whole city get through it.

The third time I felt a personal sense of loss on that first day was when I found out that Barbara Olson had been on the plane that crashed into the Pentagon. I was at the second press conference, and had finished my part of the briefing, and the Police, Fire, and Emergency commissioners were doing theirs. Then we got to the question-and-answer session. A reporter from the local CBS affiliate, Marcia Kramer, asked whether we'd heard a tape of a woman on Flight 77 talking to her husband, the Solicitor General, and explaining that the hijackers were slitting throats with box cutters. I did not hear the question completely but was slowly processing what I thought I heard, and asked Marcia to repeat what she had said. "She was talking to her husband, the Solicitor General . . ." It was then I realized she was referring to the Olsons.

Barbara and Ted were my friends. One can only guess why a certain image appears when confronted with news like that, but what I recalled was the long blue dress Barbara had worn a few months earlier on April 23, when she and Ted dropped by City Hall on the way to a dinner at the Women's National Republican Club. A month later, they came by again and spent a long time, enough for us to relax and talk about old times and enjoy one another's company.

I felt like crying right there at the press conference but couldn't, with so many people present. I walked quickly to the makeshift office I was using at the Police Academy, which was hardly private. I spoke to Ted, and that was the only occasion I allowed myself to cry. The rest of the day, there was no time.

Even those three moments lasted no more than a minute. I would immediately have to focus, turn around, and face a thousand decisions: was Grand Central Station covered? Were there reports of any more attacks? How would the construction equipment get into the city and where would it come from?

For example, I made the immediate decision that we would work at the site all night, twenty-four hours a day. I knew the odds of anyone surviving under the rubble would diminish the longer we waited, and therefore wanted to light the whole area so work at the site could continue, rather than stopping at eight at night and resuming at eight in the morning. Those twelve hours of activity could be critical; but the site was gigantic. How could we find enough lights to illuminate an area that size, let alone find people to set them up and run electricity to them, especially since the roads and access points were strewn with abandoned cars and parts of buildings? I assigned Deputy Mayor Rudy Washington to gather the heavy equipment and bring it to the site, and put Richie Sheirer in charge of finding lights. At the same time, I was concerned that we might be attacked overnight. If this were some kind of a coordinated effort to destroy the city, the terrorists might wait till nightfall to blow up more buildings. So I made sure that the police were deployed throughout the hours of darkness.

There was also immediate pressure to place a figure on the casualties. The media demanded an official estimate, pushing me for a specific number. Some members of my staff argued that if we didn't provide it the press would say we didn't know enough about the situation. I decided right away not to play guessing games with lost lives. I told them the truth: "When we get the final number, it will be more than we can bear."

I returned to the Police Academy by about eleven that evening. I went over the preparations for the next day and told everyone that they should get some rest because this would be a sustained, long-term effort. I walked out with Judith and sent her home, but not before she had extracted a promise that I would go home, too. But I just couldn't. I went back down to Ground Zero. As I walked around the site, I had a thought that was repeated endlessly by nearly everyone who witnessed the disaster and its aftermath: it was like a movie, not real. By that time, we had the floodlights up and rescue workers were digging through the mounds of rubble. Men emerged from murky clouds of dust, fires and smoke dotted the entire scene, and chunks of cement or office equipment were still falling off the hulks of the buildings. I met Bernie there and we walked on in silence. Several times, I closed my eyes and expected to open them and see the twin towers still standing. *This is not real. This is not real. This is not real.* Then I'd shake myself. *Damn right it's real, and I had better figure out what I'm going to do about it.*

In the space of less than two hours, New York City lost thousands of lives, hundreds of firefighters and police and other rescue workers, and a defining piece of the most famous skyline in the world. New Yorkers had lost the sense that their city was a place in which good people could venture out with a reasonable expectation of returning home in one piece. Only this time the threat wasn't a purse-snatcher or a mugger or a knife-wielding junkie. This was the handiwork of vicious terrorists, lunatics who were somehow convinced that the men, women, and children killed in this catastrophe had something to do with whatever "cause" they represented.

That night I got back to the apartment of my good friend Howard Koeppel, where I'd been staying for the last few months, at about 2:30 A.M. Howard had the television on, and for the first time I saw how the towers actually collapsed and understood how dangerous and chaotic everything was. Judith had told me to take a shower as soon as I got home, to rinse the soot off of my skin. I was too tired. I kept the television on, with the sound turned down, in case something else happened and the news media learned of it before the police. Then I took off all my clothes and arranged a different set so that I could jump into them if something happened during the night. I remembered reading somewhere that Mayor La Guardia had made a habit of that, and so did I for the next two weeks. It was a strange feeling, being on the 32nd floor. I had the Roy Jenkins biography of Winston Churchill on my nightstand, which I had been reading for the previous week or so. For a while I read the chapters describing his becoming Prime Minister in 1940. I thought about the people of London enduring relentless bombing and continuing to lead their lives. I thought about how people in present-day Israel do the same. It reaffirmed a strong feeling I had that Americans would rise to this challenge. I fell asleep at around 4:30. I woke less than an hour later and waited for the sun to come up: I wasn't sure it would. When first I saw it rise I was relieved. Now it was our turn to fight back.

PART

II

2

First Things First

Every morning, at exactly eight o'clock, I make my mother very happy. Throughout my childhood, she would lecture me on the virtues of finishing my schoolwork before I went outside to play. It used up a lot of daylight, which always annoyed me, but as with almost everything she taught me, she turned out to be right.

That's why I've begun every single morning since 1981 with a meeting of my top staff. The importance of the "morning meeting" cannot be overstated. In all my time as mayor, I missed very few such meetings, and then only when another commitment absolutely prevented my attendance. I consider it the cornerstone to efficient functioning within any system, especially a complex one.

When I became mayor, I realized that the job could overwhelm me. Without a system for processing the day's challenges, the sheer number of issues needing my attention could easily have dictated the agenda. The main purpose of the morning meeting was to get control of the day and prevent that from happening. We could accomplish a great deal during that first hour, in large part because the lines of communication were so clear. The people who needed to reach me—like the members of any large organization who need to convey information to the chief executive—knew that their concerns could be funneled in an orderly way through their representatives at the meeting; and I could ensure that my deputies and commissioners were working off the same page and could carry a coherent message back to their staffs.

Paul Crotty, my first Corporation Counsel, knew Mayor Wagner, Mayor Lindsay, and Mayor Beame, and had worked for Mayor Koch before working in my administration. According to Paul, ours was the only administration that got all the commissioners to speak with one voice. He attributed that to the eight o'clock meeting. He once recounted how, in the Koch administration, a number of commissioners thought that they were empowered to make their own policy statements. After the budget was adopted, certain commissioners would go to the media during the City Council review process in an attempt to raise their department's budget, saying, "Well, if you give me some more money I can do such and such . . ." In my administration, commissioners did their bargaining with the Office of Management and Budget. They could always appeal to me, but I wanted disputes settled within the family, not in the press.

Early in my first term, some staff would try to skirt the scrutiny of other members of the administration by approaching me in private. It was one thing to have your initiative shot down by the mayor, quite another to have your peers suggesting a reason why a pet idea might not work, or a better way to go about it. Those suggestions and debunkings were often best for the city, though, and thus worth hearing. I insisted that all such plans be brought up at the morning meeting. More often than not, the others there had valuable information to contribute and could enhance the plan's chances of gaining my approval.

The only exception to the rule about skirting the group and bringing matters directly to my attention was Denny Young, officially

"Counsel to the Mayor." At every morning meeting, when his turn round the table arrived, Denny would intone the same comment, "I'll talk to you later." He performed a function different from anyone else at the table; rather than managing his own portfolio of agencies and advocating for budgets and projects, he had a single concern: protecting all of us.

The idea was to get as much work as possible out of the way in the first hour of the day. As mayor—as with the head of any large organization—I had many people trying to reach me. I may have had thousands of employees and millions of constituents, but I had to communicate with them. Obviously, I couldn't do that directly. What I tried to do was to have at the meeting the staff through whom I could communicate to all of those people, or through whom they could communicate to me.

Here's how the morning meeting worked. At eight o'clock, my top staff—between fifteen and twenty people—convened around a table, ready to discuss the events of the day before and to plan for the one ahead. For forty-five to ninety minutes, we proceeded clockwise around the table, each participant sharing any pertinent news regarding the departments or agencies they represented.

There would be the four deputy mayors, who among them had responsibility for most of the agencies of city government; the commissioners of the agencies that reported directly to me, such as the Police Department, Fire Department, and the Administration for Children's Services; Personal Counsel, Senior Advisor, the Corporation Counsel (who knew the status of all the city's lawsuits and cases); the Budget Director; the Communications Director; the Director of OEM; my Chief of Staff; the Director of Scheduling; and the Chairman of the City Planning Commission.

In addition to those regulars, we would be joined by any commissioner or other agency representative with particular issues to discuss. During the West Nile virus emergency or the anthrax scare, for example, Health Commissioner Neal Cohen frequently attended.

Although the Health Department fell under the purview of the Deputy Mayor for Operations, the specific expertise of a medical doctor was needed rather than his explanation as filtered through the Deputy Mayor. Even without specific issues brewing, I liked the commissioners to be present about once a month on a rotating basis—the better to keep everyone abreast of their departments, and just to show their faces.

Examples of the effectiveness of the morning meeting are endless. Because I organized the entire city government during these sessions, countless decisions were made there—a dozen or more for each day I was mayor. Here are a couple of items from a representative day, Tuesday, August 7, 2001. The meeting that day was held on Staten Island, since we were scheduled to be at the monthly cabinet meeting with the heads of all the agencies immediately afterward (these cabinet meetings would be held at a different borough each month, a reminder to myself and my commissioners that we served all parts of the city).

On Saturday, a superintendent at the Sanitation Department named Michael Gennardo had been murdered at work. I had been to the hospital after it happened and now we were discussing the aftermath. Bernie Kerik explained that the Police Department had confirmed the make of wristwatch Gennardo had been wearing, a clue that would allow his staff to tell their people to keep an eye out for it. Having spent some time with Gennardo's grieving family, and taking into consideration that he had been killed at work, I proposed that we double the reward to $20,000. My deputy counsel, Larry Levy, reminded us that $10,000 was the statutory limit, so I suggested asking the Sanitation Department to put up the extra $10,000. If they agreed, I could then announce the doubled reward at the press conference later in the day, as well as the fact that Gennardo had a habit of writing his initials on the larger bills he carried. That fact had been kept a secret up till then in the hope that we might find the money on someone, but with no results so far, Bernie and I thought it might be more productive to have the public on the lookout for the bills.

Bernie got on the phone and arranged to have a poster made of the distinctive insignia Gennardo put on the money, while the rest of us moved to the next order of business—a strip club that planned to open in Midland Beach right there in Staten Island on the coming Friday night.

Sunny Mindel read from that morning's *Staten Island Advance*, noting that the community was lining up against it. A dissenting voice gave the idea of a new club two thumbs up. Deputy Mayor Bob Harding responded with a wisecrack: "Are you sure that was his thumb?"

I asked whether the Buildings Department had confirmed whether the club conformed to all applicable building codes and permits. The Buildings Department spokesman quoted in the *Advance* claimed that the city could not do anything until it opened, which I considered ridiculous. I asked Joe Rose, chairman of the City Planning Commission, to discover not only who was listed as the owner but who really owned the place. My years as a prosecutor had taught me that the name on the paperwork did not always tally with the full story.

Once we'd gone all the way around the table—ending, as always, with the Deputy Mayor for Operations on my right—I'd say, "Okay, that's it," and the meeting adjourned, with some staffers breaking into smaller groups to follow up on what we'd discussed.

Different groups have different dynamics, naturally. In the beginning of my first term, my staff and I had some of the most stimulating meetings that any of us had been involved in, mostly because we were arguing basic premises and establishing the philosophies that would guide us into the future.

I had several long-term friends and colleagues around me, including lawyers from the Justice Department and the U.S. Attorney's office. It was a combative group, not afraid to mix it up with me and with each other. By the third year, the team moved from debating fundamental principles to operating on them, and the heat of the debates cooled a little. After re-election in 1997, the cycle then repeated itself with my second term. By *that* fourth year, we were more congenial than ever. New York City limits its mayors to two terms, so there was no question of campaigning. We had established the working rhythm of any team that's played together for a long time—our no-look passes and hit-and-run combinations focused on accomplishing as much as possible in the time remaining. Then, just as the twilight of the administration loomed . . .

After the World Trade Center towers were attacked, the morning meeting became even more critical. Overnight, it was transformed into the platform from which the entire response and recovery would be planned. The meeting was expanded to include many people from outside my administration, such as Governor Pataki's staff, members of the CDC; representatives from utilities, FEMA, and many from my own administration who hadn't typically attended the meetings. There were frequent appearances by others who had special expertise, or simply offered additional perspective.

The morning meeting was the core of my approach to managing. It served numerous purposes—decision-making, communicating, even socializing—but most of all it kept me accountable. The morning meeting was where the chief executive was responsible, and could hold everybody else responsible. Those present could go back to their agencies and act in a similar way. Instead of trying to protect themselves against the risk of a bad decision, they were willing to make decisions knowing that a few might end up being wrong but at least things got done, and in reasonable time.

In any large organization, meetings are often derided as roadblocks to progress, set up by bureaucrats who would rather talk than act. In fact, my morning meetings have been extremely helpful to the reform agenda I set out to accomplish. Nevertheless, I have taken steps to guard against the gridlock that is sometimes associated with the word "meeting."

My mayoral staff knew that they would see me at a specific time and place every day. Executives of all types, even the mayor of New York City, have been known to hide behind a phalanx of secretaries and assistants, leaving underlings twisting in the wind. A daily meeting, in which everyone is entitled to air concerns, meant my staff knew that they could get a yes or no from the boss. They knew they could tell whoever was waiting for that yes or no that they would definitely see me by the next day. And even if the issue could not be decided in twenty-four hours—perhaps it needed more deliberation or additional research—the staff member at least knew the issue had been brought to my attention and could truthfully explain to whoever awaited a decision that it was under consideration.

This access worked both ways. My staff knew that I would be seeing them just as surely as they saw me. This inspired them to have answers ready for any questions I might ask about their areas of responsibility. If some issue arose, say, about the cleanliness of the streets—maybe our tracking system had picked up an increase in overflowing trash cans or a newspaper had run an article claiming that a neighborhood was dirty—the Deputy Mayor for Operations, responsible for the Sanitation Department, could not simply lie low, hoping that he wouldn't see me until he'd had time to address the problem. He knew I'd be asking him about it first thing in the morning, and would expect a summary of the specifics and some ideas about a solution.

It's not always easy to get people to admit that they don't have all the answers. Any chief executive should expect his top staff to be experienced, successful individuals. Sometimes these aren't the type of people accustomed to admitting in front of a group that they don't know everything, especially when that group setting includes the rivalries and jockeying for position that are signs of healthy competition. The boss should counter that reluctance early and often. One of the best lessons a leader can communicate to his or her staff is that encountering problems is to be expected. But failing to mention problems—or, worse, covering them up—should not be tolerated.

Another way to avoid the pitfalls of "meeting drag" is to keep them moving quickly. A drawn-out meeting each day could easily have become a burden. To ensure a good pace I would make it clear why the participants were at the meeting—not to display mastery of the details of their areas of responsibility, but to share and receive information that would be useful to the entire group. Each participant should be aware that he or she was always *welcome* to speak, but never *required* to do so.

This threatened to become an issue in the weeks following the World Trade Center disaster. In those first few weeks of September we followed our regular morning meeting with a larger nine o'clock meeting, which included commissioners and others from agencies that suddenly played a more public role, such as the coroner and the Commissioner of Transportation, and the people in charge of clearing the debris. All these were important people in my administration, and I came to rely on them heavily.

But with so much to do and so many in need of assistance, I feared that the addition of another meeting could eat up valuable time, especially if the new participants thought that they would seem unimportant if they didn't contribute each day. I told my top staff to let the attendees who reported to them know that they were expected to speak up when they had something to say, but not to feel that they would be disappointing me if they remained silent. At his sit-down with Sollozzo in the first *Godfather* movie, Don Corleone says, "I have a sentimental weakness for my children, and I spoil them, as you can see; they talk when they should listen." I, too, do not give points to those who talk to hear their own voices. Time was too scarce to waste, especially during those first weeks. Beyond that, with so much information and even emotion to handle, the quicker, more-focused exchanges kept all of us, including me, from experiencing the fatigue that could easily have resulted.

The morning meeting produced several other positive results. Typically, the meetings would begin with a few minutes of joking around. As I have said, with any high-achieving staff, rivalries and turf wars can be expected. The socializing and simple daily contact helped prevent resentments from festering. Not every commissioner I had has adored all his or her colleagues. Of course not. There was the occasional internecine skirmish. But I was confident that the daily contact I insisted on kept those battles from becoming wars — wars that could ultimately have harmed the city.

That was another reason to hold such meetings on a daily basis: frequency allowed constant follow-through. Too often, especially in politics, bold initiatives are announced only to wither on the vine. With the morning meeting, my staff knew that if I decided on a Monday that something needed to be done about a problem, I would be asking the relevant commissioner for a plan on Tuesday and eager to hear how the plan was going by Wednesday. If the lapse between those stages were two weeks instead of two days, it was likely the commissioner would take the whole two weeks — not out of laziness but because that was how long it would have taken to get approval of the plan. Parkinson's Law about "work expanding to fill the time available" definitely applies in government work — but only if it is allowed to do so.

SET THE TONE

The principle of taking care of first things first extended beyond the morning meeting. So did the concept of taking control early. I believed in learning as much as I could about a challenge as soon as I could. Often that meant before the challenge even manifested itself. The point was not just to get a head start on the task at hand, but to set a tone — for myself and for those who looked to me for leadership.

On the day after I won my first term in November 1993, my predecessor, David Dinkins, invited me to City Hall. I had never explored the building before. I'd been in the Blue Room, where press conferences are held, and in the mayor's private office, and one time I'd had lunch downstairs with Ed Koch. (City Hall used to house a city jail in its basement, and to get downstairs one went down a forbidding spiral staircase.)

Looking around that day with Mayor Dinkins, I became concerned that space would be a problem. When I worked in Washington and was in and around the White House, I witnessed the constant struggles over the limited space, and realized that we, too, would have a problem if we showed up at City Hall and left people to grab desks wherever they could. So on December 26, 1993, Peter Powers, my campaign manager, soon-to-be deputy mayor and life-long friend, and I went down to City Hall. It was a Sunday and the office was nearly deserted. We walked through the whole office for two hours, taking notes on the floor plan and how it was organized. By the time my staff moved in the following week, I had already decided where everybody should sit—before we got off on the wrong note by bickering over who sat where.

Even more than most old buildings, City Hall was not designed to run a $40 billion operation. I don't refer to the lack of plush quarters, but simply to having enough space to do all that needed to be done. After that initial survey, Peter and I headed to the Tweed Courthouse, one block north of City Hall, to see if we could secure some extra space there. It eventually dawned on us that one of the items we were missing was a conference room. I don't know what previous administrations had done, but given the importance I attached to meetings, I needed a large conference room.

On the second floor of City Hall sits a gorgeous room called the Committee of the Whole—where a large portrait of James Monroe[1]

---

[1]When I became mayor, I hung a portrait of Mayor Fiorello La Guardia behind my desk and looked to it for inspiration. In the Blue Room, where press conferences were held, I hung a portrait of Thomas Jefferson, because I wanted the image of him to appear in photographs looking over our shoulder. I think of President Jefferson as America's philosopher. I've read his papers, the superb Dumas Malone biography, *Jefferson and His Time*, and most of the biographies of Jefferson, and believe Jefferson articulated our nation's ideals. So there was clear purpose to the hanging of those two paintings. The James Monroe portrait, on the other hand, while large and very beautiful, was chosen for a more practical reason—the carpet on which President Monroe stands in the painting matched that in the Committee of the Whole.

hangs opposite a magnificent grandfather clock. The room had traditionally been used by the City Council, which shares the building with the mayor's office. So we came up with a deal—we'd share the hearing chamber (where large public gatherings such as town hall meetings were held) with the City Council if they'd let us use the Committee of the Whole.

Just before midnight on New Year's Day, 1994, my friend Michael Mukasey, by then a federal judge in the Southern District of New York, swore me in at his house. I delayed the inauguration ceremony, planned for later that day, because it was the Jewish Sabbath and I wanted members of the Orthodox community to be able to attend, since I had enjoyed such strong support in the religious Jewish community. Bruce Teitelbaum, who had worked to organize support for me there, called the matter to my attention and we discussed whether we were legally clear if we delayed the ceremony. We realized that as long as I took the official oath before January 1, I didn't have to be officially inaugurated, so we planned the ceremony for the following day—Sunday. Somebody suggested that Cardinal O'Connor might be upset with that decision. I said, "Here's what I'm going to do. I'm going to invite the Cardinal to give the invocation. I'll explain to him what I'm trying to accomplish, and if he has an objection I'll put it off until Monday." I called the Cardinal, and he not only approved but even suggested pushing the time back so that churchgoers could attend. Just like that, we'd solved the problem.

Shortly after Mike Mukasey swore me in—but before the inauguration ceremony—I swore in my deputies and commissioners at a party at the Museum of Natural History. Afterward, I was on my way home—this was before I'd moved into Gracie Mansion—when I was informed that two police officers had been shot at a housing project in the Bronx. So came about my first hospital visit as mayor—Westchester Square Hospital in the Bronx, at about three in the morning. I didn't realize then how many there would be.

Beginning early that same Saturday, I visited all five boroughs, bringing cookies with me to the people who were working over the New Year's holiday. I went to a Transit Police station in the Bronx, Elmhurst Hospital in Queens, a firehouse and a hospital in Manhattan, the Jackie Gleason bus depot in Brooklyn, and another firehouse in Staten Island. From that time on, delivering cookies on New Year's Day became something of a tradition for me—I've gone to Rikers Island twice, as well as police precincts, firehouses, hospitals, and other city institutions. I don't even remember the genesis of that idea, whether it was my own or if it came from one of my advisors. But it set a tone.

I made my cookie run around the city the first day I was the mayor, before I was even ceremonially sworn in, because I thought it vital to go out of my way as many times as possible to thank the people who were doing so much work for New York City. As mayor, I tried to be as involved as I could. But I had to rely on others to pull somebody out of a building, or interrupt a robbery or make an arrest to prevent it happening in the first place, or keep the streets passable, or find homes for orphans. City workers did that. It was essential to keep their morale up, to keep finding ways to thank them. Four of my uncles were police officers and one was a firefighter. Growing up, I admired their bravery and dedication so much. One of the best parts of being mayor—really, of any leadership role—is getting the chance to let people know how much their work means to you. Setting that tone early and often was not only good for my employees and for the organization—it did me good, too.

START SMALL WITH SUCCESS

Whenever I started a new endeavor, I looked to have a clear, decisive victory as early as I could. It needn't have been a large initiative, and in fact was usually better if the problem was small enough so that it was easily understood and yielded an unambiguous solution. This gave people hope, and let one's constituents, employees, and even critics know that action and positive change were more than just rhetoric.

This was particularly important when I became mayor, because I was dealing with a failing operation. In Appendix A, I detail some of the distressing statistical realities at the time I was elected, so I won't belabor the point here. Suffice it to say that even devoted Gotham-boosters had started to regard their hometown as ungovernable. It was an attitude summarized by an October 1993 joint *New York Times* and WCBS poll in which 62 percent of New Yorkers said life had worsened over the previous four years (9 percent said it had improved). More troubling, on each of the issues, those surveyed said they didn't expect any significant improvement no matter who was elected. One citizen characterized her despondency with the claim that the best any mayor could do was cheer people on. "It's a bigger job than anyone can handle . . . [It's] more of a moral support kind of thing."

It was against that backdrop that I took office. Many elements of the city required dramatic change. Because I had run on a platform of increasing public safety, and because that's where my background was strongest, I decided that the first problem I'd tackle would be in that arena. The goal was to turn around the view people had of New York City as a dangerous place. But I couldn't do that all at once. I couldn't go from 2,000 murders a year to none, nor wave a magic wand to transform people walking the streets in terror to people whistling happy tunes.

We attacked crime immediately, but we knew that it would take time to show results. And reducing the number of crimes wouldn't be enough: people had to see an improvement, not just hear about it. If crime went down but the existing amount of pushing and shoving, urinating on the streets, and other quality-of-life issues remained the same, we would never have a convincing case that life was better. We had to get people to be safe and to *feel* safe.

That's how the idea for addressing the squeegee man problem first appeared. At that time, there were men who would wander up to a car stopped at a red light or in traffic, spray the windshield, and wipe it down with a dirty rag or a newspaper or the stick wrapped in cloth that earned them their sobriquet "squeegee men." After the unsolicited "cleaning," the squeegee man would approach the driver and "request" payment with varying degrees of menace. Drivers who refused might have their windshields spat on or their car doors kicked.

What made this form of intimidation a particularly tempting first target was that the squeegee operators were notably aggressive near bridges and tunnels. It was one of the first and last impressions of New York for anyone visiting the city—hardly an image that inspired confidence.

Banishing the squeegee operators was something I suspected we could accomplish fairly easily—and that would have an immediate and measurable impact. I called in Police Commissioner Bill Bratton and Denny Young, who played an important role in all quality-of-life initiatives. Bratton, who shared my belief in treating small crimes as a way to establish lawful, civil behavior and a feeling of safety, came back in a couple of days and told me that the Police Department said that getting rid of the squeegee men couldn't be done. He wanted to do it, but had been told that so long as they were not physically threatening drivers or "demanding" money, we lacked a legal basis to move the operators along or arrest them if they refused.

This is an example of how being a lawyer and former prosecutor could be helpful. I said, "How about the fact that they're jaywalking?" I told him to forget about whether they were asking for money or not. When they stepped off the curb and walked out onto the street they had just violated the law. You could give every single one of them a ticket immediately. Then, in giving them that ticket, you could investigate who they were, whether there were outstanding warrants, and so on. If they became intimidating you could arrest them.

About a week later Bratton came back and said not only could we do this, but it was going to be easier than we thought. He conducted a survey, and discovered there were only about 180 squeegee men in the whole city. Nobody could believe it—estimates usually said that there were at least a couple of thousand. So we started writing summonses for these guys, and found that a certain percentage already had warrants for violent and property crimes. In under a month, we were able to reduce the problem dramatically. Things had visibly improved. New Yorkers loved it, and so did all the visitors, who brought money into the city and provided jobs for its inhabitants. That was our first success.

If someone had told me, at a time when we were celebrating making so much headway against 180 squeegee men, that we would end up reducing crime by some 5,000 felonies per week, I would have strongly doubted it. I would have thought 2,000, maybe even 3,000; but that's the power of starting small with success—by combining several small victories we could achieve the larger result.

Tax-cutting was another area where we garnered a similar "start small" victory. When I was first elected, taxes on hotel rooms in New York City were the highest in America, perhaps the world. At 21.25 percent on rooms priced at $100 a night and up, the burden was about triple the average of the country's busiest cities, and 50 percent higher than the rest of the five highest-taxed cities: Chicago, Atlanta, Dallas, and Houston. This was devastating for tourism, one of the city's key industries. Business staged 50 percent fewer conventions in New York in 1993 than it had five years previously, and that same year the professional convention management association actually boycotted the city.

On my very first day as mayor, I sent a letter to Governor Mario M. Cuomo, also signed by the executives of several neighboring counties, asking for a repeal of the state's 5 percent tax (on top of the 8.25 percent sales tax), which had been enacted during the first year of my predecessor's administration. And I pulled back the New York City tax from 6 percent to 5 percent. This was a small step, but important symbolically. No one in New York City could remember any tax ever being *reduced*, and I wanted to send a powerful message that I believed that lower taxes would stimulate more than enough business to offset any immediate loss in revenue. That's exactly what happened. With more visitors, net revenue from the hotel tax was actually higher at 5 percent than it had been at 6 percent.

Economists could have a great deal of fun calculating how much of the rise in visitors was attributable to the tax cut. How much of the increased hotel occupancy came from the drop in crime, how much from the improved quality of life? How much from the positive publicity New York got from those two factors? How much from the dynamics in different economies—factors way beyond the control of any mayor? The exact proportions are impossible to know.

Small successes can in themselves boost the morale of anyone in an organization who might be feeling left out. A *New York Times* poll taken in November 1993 showed that 60 percent of Staten Islanders wanted to secede from New York City. Snubbed by previous administrations, Staten Island had reached boiling point. I wanted to send a message that all of New York City was important. Since Staten Island is home to a large percentage of the city's uniformed personnel, I found it particularly important that the borough not feel overlooked.

I met with Guy Molinari, Staten Island's Borough President and a supporter of mine, and asked him to suggest visible initiatives that my administration could accomplish quickly, to show his locals— and the rest of the city—that Staten Island mattered. Without hesitating, Guy replied, "Let cars back on the ferries." After a fire at the Whitehall terminal in 1991, Mayor Dinkins had banned cars on the island ferry. Within a few weeks, we restored cars to the ferry service. A side benefit was that it kept about a thousand cars a day off the Gowanus Expressway.

This approach shouldn't be limited only to one's own initiatives. Part of good leadership is giving others under your authority the same tools you'd expect. When Nick Scoppetta took over as commissioner of the newly created Administration for Children's Services, he conducted a tour of his field locations—one or two in each borough. He notified me that child welfare workers didn't have sufficient file cabinets. Files were piled on the floor next to the desks of the caseworkers. These were all handwritten, confidential case histories. If those files fell over and were put back together, maybe the papers got back to the right file, maybe they didn't. A caseworker going to court to demonstrate why a child could be at risk if returned to an abusive home might find herself standing in front of a judge without the crucial piece of evidence. Yet children's lives relied on this material.

Nick recognized the need to put in place a computerized management information system at ACS, but that couldn't be accomplished overnight. Because he was going to start asking much more from the caseworkers in terms of training and performance accountability, Nick was determined to show them early on that he could get things done. In other words, he wanted to start small with success.

Until Nick and I made ACS its own agency, children's welfare services had been under the umbrella of the Human Resources Administration. Caseworkers were extremely dispirited by the lack of attention they'd received as a part of a much bigger unit, and Nick wanted to send a message that their work was important.

He came up with the idea of buying 4,000 file cabinets for the caseworkers, as well as professional office chairs, since many employees were using makeshift ones unsuitable for working behind desks. He wanted these people to take their jobs seriously, so he decided to send a message that he took their needs seriously. Buying all those cabinets and chairs may not seem like a complicated task, but it required real determination and planning to get the money, actually purchase them, get rid of the old ones, and coordinate the delivery and installation of the new equipment. It was a test of the will of the leader, which is why it hadn't been done for so long. In little over a week, we began installing the new equipment.

These early successes, while not of major significance on their own, provided critical evidence that plans could be put into action, and that I expected results. Each subsequent initiative became easier to enact because people started to accept the premise that things could be done—that progress was possible.

ALWAYS SWEAT THE SMALL STUFF

In 1959, the architect Ludwig Mies van der Rohe said in the *New York Herald Tribune* that "God is in the details." Amen to that. Knowing the "small" details of a large system leaves a leader open to charges of micromanaging. But understanding how something works is not only a leader's responsibility; it also makes him or her better able to let people do their jobs. If they don't have to explain the basics of what they need and why they need it every time they request more funds or different resources, then they are freer to pursue strategies beyond simply spending what they're given.

No leader can know everything about a system. A confident one won't hesitate to seek advice—publicly and privately—from those more expert in an area affecting the enterprise. When several cases of anthrax broke out in New York a few weeks after the city had already been hit hard by the World Trade Center attack, the threat was grave—not just from the disease itself but from the fear, which could have paralyzed people. I sought constant counsel from medical and public health experts to learn as much as I could as quickly as possible. Far from micromanaging, I took their advice and heard many opinions as we forged a strategy. Part of that procedure—part of sweating the small stuff—meant understanding that the way citizens would perceive the information they were getting would be as important as the information itself. When in 1998 I appointed Dr. Neal Cohen as my Health Commissioner, there was some criticism over the fact that he was a psychiatrist. It was suggested I should have chosen a commissioner with a background in public health. As it turned out his understanding not just of the medical information but of the emotional and psychological impact of crisis was critical to our handling of West Nile virus, September 11, and the threatened anthrax epidemic.

"Sweat the small stuff" is the essence of the Broken Windows theory that I embraced to fight crime. The theory holds that a seemingly minor matter like broken windows in abandoned buildings leads directly to a more serious deterioration of neighborhoods. Someone who wouldn't normally throw a rock at an intact building is less reluctant to break a second window in a building that already has one broken. And someone emboldened by all the second broken windows may do even worse damage if he senses that no one is around to prevent lawlessness.

On June 4, 1996, a man named John Royster, Jr., grabbed a piano teacher from behind and smashed her head on the ground repeatedly, leaving her for dead some 100 feet from a crowded playground in Central Park. The next night, Royster tackled a jogger, Shelby Evans Schrader, while she ran along an East River path. Holding her head by the ears, he smashed her face into the asphalt until a passerby's shouts scared him off. The woman spent three days in the hospital. Then, on June 11, Royster beat to death 65-year-old Evelyn Alvarez when she arrived to open her Park Avenue dry cleaning shop.

No one knows how long this rampage might have continued, but the reason it finally stopped was that Royster had been apprehended a few months earlier for a so-called small crime. After jumping a turnstile, he was arrested and fingerprinted, rather than simply given a summons, as he would have been in the past. When a fingerprint was lifted at Mrs. Alvarez's shop, and a match made, the NYPD had its man and future victims were spared.

The idea of sweating the small stuff applies not only to crime but to every challenge a manager faces. Graffiti provides another good illustration of the concept. Watch any movie set in New York during the 1970s and 1980s and you'll see a city covered in scrawls. The subways and buses were particularly blanketed. In New York City, the mayor doesn't control the Transit Authority, which is run by an amalgam of state and city representatives. Yet we knew that the average citizen, in New York and elsewhere, saw the graffiti on subway cars and buses and associated it with the city.

Faced with a problem for which we were blamed but over which we did not have complete control, I decided that we'd put together a task force involving about twenty agencies. We explained to them that graffiti was a challenge for the whole city, not just the Police or the Transportation Department. So the Sanitation Department, for example, was made to understand that their trucks, which were covered in graffiti, could not be sent out until the graffiti was completely removed. We also made the police aware that patrolling the yards in which the sanitation trucks were kept was a priority. We'd go out and organize community groups and provide paint to those willing to cooperate with shop owners whose walls and windows had been defaced.

This way, when we began to show progress on the fronts we did control, we were prepared to be involved when the MTA asked us to help out with getting rid of graffiti. They had begun their own initiatives and we shared information about cleaning fluids and the new "scratching" technique that the vandals were deploying. And we helped patrol the yards where the MTA kept their trains and buses.

One might suppose that attending to the details would assume less importance during times of crisis, but the reverse is true. The best way to assure that your staff, and others who rely on you at such times, feel that someone is leading the way is to show that you're as focused as ever on the details. During the weeks following September 11, I remained as committed to the details as ever.

It was the morning meeting that helped me to organize. The aftermath of September 11 saw a blizzard of details presented and decisions made. On Monday, September 17, for instance, Rosemarie O'Keefe, commissioner of the Mayor's Community Assistance Unit (and already putting in some eighteen hours a day running the Family Assistance Center), asked what we should do about the street fairs that were scheduled for the coming weeks. Again, this might seem like "small stuff," but in fact two competing needs were at stake. We wanted to reinforce the message that normal life should be restored, but there were good arguments against mounting street fairs during that period. I made my decision: "Cancel all street fairs in Manhattan, for three reasons. One, it lessens demand for police, who have better things to do right now. Two, it'll increase traffic in stores, which provide permanent jobs. Three, it reduces traffic while we've got these big vehicles coming in and out. Allow all the street fairs scheduled in the other four boroughs to go on as planned."

I spent perhaps one minute on this "small" issue, and it was worth it. We managed to resolve the issues raised by the prospect of Manhattan street fairs while preserving the normalcy of the events in the other boroughs. Moreover, with the entire top staff hearing this mini-debate, they were more likely to impress on their own people the double imperatives of keeping life as normal as possible, so long as it didn't siphon off resources from the recovery effort.

Another example following the World Trade Center disaster combined sweating the small stuff and the Broken Windows theory. I went down to Ground Zero to visit the rescue and recovery workers, as I'd been doing every day. I noticed a disturbing phenomenon— hundreds of people carrying disposable cameras and handheld video cameras. I understood the impulse—this was a historic event, and experiencing it up close had enormous impact. At the same time, this was a crime scene, and a dangerous one. I did not want anyone to get hurt, or to damage evidence as they scouted out the best angle for their snapshots.

If we didn't do something about it immediately, it would soon be out of control, a voyeur's paradise, and we risked the site developing a distasteful freak show aspect. There had been incidents in which tourists snapped photos of relatives grieving for lost loved ones, and there were reports of people selling artifacts and photographs from the site.

Credentials were already being checked around the perimeter of the disaster site, but with so many different agencies involved in the cleanup, when someone did slip through there was no procedure for asking who they were or what they were doing there. At the morning meeting that same Monday, September 17, I asked Richie Sheirer to assemble a team specifically to inspect credentials. They would patrol the site and explain to people—including those who were there to do legitimate recovery work—that use of cameras should be confined to those who had permission.

The idea of sweating the small stuff as a way of not allowing minor issues to spiral into major disasters brings to mind a quotation from Thomas De Quincey. "If once a man indulges himself in murder," it ran, "very soon he comes to think little of robbing; and from robbing, he comes next to drinking and Sabbath-breaking, and from that to incivility and procrastination." It's all connected, and it goes both ways. That quotation appears in the movie version of *Prince of the City*, the terrific Sidney Lumet film about New York City police corruption in the 1960s and 1970s. I was a young prosecutor in the U.S. Attorney's office during the events that the movie portrays, and I developed a close relationship with the primary "prince" of that story—Bob Leuci, the detective whose undercover tapes and testimony exposed the wrongdoings in his unit.

The film itself benefits from paying attention to small stuff. I was briefly consulted on the movie with Lumet. I did not choose "Mario" as the name they used for my character (real names were used in the book but not the movie), but I did make one small contribution. I was asked whether I wore the same clothes when working over the weekend as I'd wear during the week. Mike Seymour, the U.S. Attorney at that time, required his assistant U.S. Attorneys to wear a suit with a white shirt to court. I told the filmmakers that on the weekends I liked to wear corduroy pants. Sure enough, I went to the premiere of the movie, and there's Mario—working in corduroys.

3

Prepare Relentlessly

One of my predecessors as United States Attorney in the Southern District of New York was J. Edward Lumbard. Appointed by President Eisenhower, he was a terrific lawyer—a partner at Donovan, Leisure, Newton & Lumbard, he later served with distinction for many years on the United States Court of Appeals. When Ed was U.S. Attorney, his chief assistant was Lloyd MacMahon, my first boss. Lloyd learned a lot from Judge Lumbard and I in turn from Lloyd. One of Judge Lumbard's rules has served me particularly well ever since: don't assume a damn thing.

When I was a clerk to Judge MacMahon, he would frequently repeat that dictum in explaining how errors arise. Dissecting a blown cross-examination, he'd show how the lawyer failed to ask the right question. Untangling a failed argument, he'd point out where someone had forgotten to insert a critical point. The biggest mistake that good lawyers made, he said, was assuming too much—that the jury would make inferences, that the opposing counsel would raise specific issues, that their own clients wouldn't say ludicrous things or behave in some ridiculous way. Judge MacMahon observed that really bad lawyers made so many mistakes they never even reached a level of error that involved assumptions. As my own career progressed, I realized that preparation—thus eliminating the need to make assumptions—was the single most important key to success, no matter what the field. Leaders may possess brilliance, extraordinary vision, fate, even luck. Those help; but no one, no matter how gifted, can perform without careful preparation, thoughtful experiment, and determined follow-through.

An example of the value of preparation (and not assuming a damn thing) occurred during the 2000 presidential election and the vote-counting fiasco that followed. I thought it so important that George W. Bush defeat Al Gore that I campaigned for Bush even during the course of my radiation treatment for cancer. The week before the election I offered to do whatever I could to help. I went out to events in Philadelphia and Chicago. On the Thursday before the election, I was set to spend some of the weekend campaigning in nearby New England. Then Tony Carbonetti got a call from the Bush office. "We want Rudy to change his plans. We need him in Florida. If he can do it, we want him to give speeches in Fort Lauderdale and Palm Beach on Saturday, then meet Bush at a rally in Palm Beach on Sunday, followed by a rally in Miami."

I wasn't sure I could handle such a timetable, because, not to be indelicate, at that time I had to urinate frequently, a consequence of the seed implantation operation that I had had a month or so earlier. I was worried about how it might interrupt the schedule, and I was in some degree of pain. However, the pollsters had already marked Florida as a key battleground and I wanted to do whatever I could to help. We got on the plane and spent Saturday campaigning.

The first speech I gave when I got to Florida was at a synagogue for morning services. I spoke about the importance of voting for George Bush. The congregation was very respectful, and asked a few good questions. Then, as I was leaving, several of the men who had been listening came running up and gathered all around me. I thought they wanted to question me about issues in the campaign, but instead they started peppering me with: "So, how are your treatments going?" "How many times do you pee at night? I've got it down to two or three times a night." "Do you use Lupron?" "Do you think radiation is better than the operation?" "Have you tried Viagra?" The discussion focused entirely on urinary symptoms and prostate cancer, without a political question in sight. It gave me a sense of the different things people concentrate on and reinforced the old Tip O'Neill saying "all politics is local." In this case, it was very local.

Then, on Sunday, I greeted President Bush's plane at West Palm Beach Airport and, along with Bo Derek, Wayne Newton, and others, helped introduce him to the crowd. I flew with George, Laura, and Jeb Bush from Palm Beach to Miami, where we were to do a rally in the Cuban community. The two brothers kept monitoring the NFL scores. I thought to myself, "How healthy—that they can spend time checking the scores of football games." It showed that both men had perspective, and another life, and could take some time out from the election to keep tabs on sports.

I was known in Miami from my days in the Justice Department and then became better known when I refused to allow Fidel Castro to attend the UN 50 celebration in 1995. There is also a host of former New Yorkers in Florida who credit me with improving their hometown, a city about which they remain passionate for years after they've moved away. Many are traditional Democratic voters, and I was hoping that their positive feelings about a Republican mayor would make them more comfortable voting for a Republican presidential candidate.

We knew going in that the election was going to be close, but no one knew it would be *that* close. In 1993, my margin of mayoral victory had been about 2.5 percent. I remember thinking of about twenty to thirty things that were critical. Had any of them gone the other way, the outcome could have been different. For example, a ballot initiative on whether Staten Island should secede from New York City brought to the polls an unusually high number of voters from that borough. I won 84 percent of the vote on Staten Island—109,000 votes in a race decided by fewer than 50,000. Yet that victory was a landslide compared to the 2000 presidential election, where the entire result turned on just a few hundred votes. The Bush campaign demonstrated the importance of preparation when it made last-minute strategic decisions such as having me and others switch our campaigning to Florida.

In its own way, my trip to Miami was even encouraging from a personal perspective. I was still fighting the effects of my cancer treatment, but it felt good to be helping. After the election, but before the Florida recount saga was resolved, the lesson of not assuming anything was hammered home. I had to spend much of my time lying down, often unable to concentrate on reading because of the discomfort. My routine was to go into City Hall to hold the morning meeting, then work for three to four hours. By one or two in the afternoon, I would hit a wall and have to lie down, so I'd put on the television and watch the news coverage of the very places where I had been campaigning, taking in the moves and countermoves of each side's lawyers in great detail.

Ted Olson, who argued the case in the Supreme Court for President Bush, was a colleague of mine in the Justice Department in the early 1980s, and, as mentioned in my opening chapter, we remain good friends. The media made quite a bit of hoopla over the invincibility of Gore's "Dream Team," and Bush's group was relatively less well known. But Ted is one of the best lawyers I've ever worked with, anywhere. There are few people better suited to argue a case before the United States Supreme Court, which is why he became a perfect choice for Bush as Solicitor General.

When the debate finally hit the Supreme Court, I listened to Ted's argument in great detail, then read the transcript. A lawyer who comes before an appellate court typically faces three judges on a federal appellate panel and four or five in a state court. If you're before a five-judge panel, you have to work out how to get your three votes. If you're facing the nine justices on the Supreme Court, you need to concentrate on securing five votes. So sometimes you need several layers of argument. If you're looking to land five votes, you might have an argument that three judges will buy; but you need another to pick up the other two, or maybe even two additional arguments—one each for the remaining votes you need.

That's exactly how Ted structured his presentation. He created different arguments for different coalitions of justices. Reading the opinions, I saw that he gave the justices exactly what they needed. Some justices agreed with the argument that the Supreme Court of Florida acted lawlessly, and were therefore willing to overturn the Florida ruling. Other justices found the equal protection argument appealing, the idea that you can't count votes differently in different parts of the state.

There are few lawyers who can really do this well. It requires a great deal of insight into the court you're arguing before, a wealth of knowledge of the law, and a mind that can work on several different levels. Most important, it requires masterful preparation—and a refusal to assume a damn thing.

I lost the race for mayor in 1989 by about 40,000 votes out of almost two million cast. It was a razor-thin margin and a more than respectable showing for a first-time candidate, especially in New York, with its strong Democratic bias. Just as an election victory needs a dozen little things to go right, a defeat can be blamed on any number of separate bad breaks. In 1989, my whole team assumed I'd be facing Ed Koch. We hadn't anticipated Dinkins defeating the three-term mayor in a Democratic primary, and my preparation had been geared toward a race against the incumbent. I came awfully close that year. By the time I decided to run again in 1993, I made sure I'd be ready for anything.

I decided to learn everything I possibly could about the workings of New York City's government. Unfortunately, there's no book that tells you how to be mayor. Naturally, I'd read widely about municipal politics and picked up a lot over the course of my first bid for office. But what I wanted—an all-out academic program that explored the best new ideas and taught the nuts and bolts of city government— didn't exist.

So I created one. I put together what can best be described as a course in being mayor. It started informally with my own reading and asking questions of authors, professors, and elected officials for seven or eight months on my own. I decided to formalize the program, and hired Richard Schwartz, who would become my first senior advisor and later the editorial page editor of the *Daily News*. He arranged a series of seminars designed to explore and develop ideas for reinventing the city of New York. We'd bring in an expert and say, "If I were the mayor, what would you tell me to do?" We began the seminars on January 25, 1992, with Robert Wagner, Jr., son of the former mayor of New York City, giving a lecture on the structure of city government. He spoke for two and a half hours, to a spellbound audience.

Thus began a series of talks on every aspect of being mayor. At that time I was in private law practice at Anderson Kill, and the guest speaker would hold forth in the conference room. We brought in a range of viewpoints, from very conservative to very liberal—everyone from Andrew Cuomo, on homelessness, to Larry Lindsay (now an advisor to President Bush), who gave a lecture on welfare, to Professor Kelling, who talked to us about the Broken Windows theory. Ninfa Segarra, Joe Rose, Bill Bratton, and Henry Stern, all of whom later joined my administration, came in to talk, as did others from previous administrations. The lectures lasted between one and three hours and would be followed by a question-and-answer session. Richard Schwartz tape-recorded every meeting (with the exception of those who requested to speak off the record), and later we'd review the tapes.

When we started, we assumed we'd run to a dozen or so lectures in specialized areas like housing, health insurance, tax policies, and economic development, but it became so interesting that the series extended to about fifty lectures over a year and a half period. It was almost like being back at NYU.

At first, I wasn't sure we'd be able to convince established experts to conduct such small seminars, but Richard said, "You're a potential mayor and you're interested in their area of expertise—they'll come." He was right; we found that people were eager to help. This "mayor school" was enormously valuable to me. Any leader will know some parts of his enterprise better than others. As the chief executive of the city, I would arrive with plenty of experience in law enforcement. Having investigated corruption trials, I knew about the structure of government and how to discourage and detect crookedness. But I didn't know housing. Or taxation. The seminars not only taught me about those areas, they gave me the opportunity to think through how I would handle them.

Several programs that I implemented owe their origins to those seminars. The lectures on welfare and homelessness, for example, led me to America Works, a company that develops jobs and job skills for those on welfare. We invited its founders to participate in one of the seminars, and I visited their organization. After I became mayor we implemented the country's most ambitious scheme to find work for welfare recipients.

There came a point in the summer of 1993 when I felt confident that I was going to be elected. There were ups and downs, to be sure, and we had to overcome a few setbacks. When I ran in 1989, there was a sitting Republican president. By the time I ran again, a Democrat was in the White House. That was a tremendous asset for David Dinkins, starting in 1992 when the Democratic Convention was held in New York City. Still, I felt sure that the elements were there for me to win.

Were I to be elected on November 2, 1993, I'd be expected to start running the fourth largest government in the country on January 1, 1994. The federal government has three weeks more than that for transition. So I approached Denny Young and said, "Very secretly, without telling anybody else in the campaign except Peter [Powers], I'd like you to devote some of your time to organizing a transition." I asked him to talk to people who had overseen presidential and mayoral transitions before, like E. Pendleton "Pen" James, who organized the Reagan transition that I had experienced when I rejoined the Justice Department, and come up with a plan and a timetable. The only guidance I provided was that I wanted at least three choices for every important job that I had to fill, which is also what I usually requested when we selected assistant U.S. Attorneys.

I knew Denny would keep his research project quiet. This was important, because I didn't want to jinx anything, and I tried to know as little about the process as possible. The day after the election, Denny showed me the mammoth book in which he detailed all his interviews and job candidates.

I was almost comatose by that point, having had less than an hour's sleep on election night, then spending the entire next day on a post-election whirlwind and an appearance on *Seinfeld*. Even so, it was clear that Denny had organized an amazing transition. The next day I sat down with the book and saw what he had done. First, he clustered the agencies by type, as in social services and public safety. That way, if an outstanding candidate didn't quite fit, say, the Department of Probation, he or she could still be considered for the Department of Juvenile Justice. Denny had quietly approached about forty or fifty people to see whether they'd be willing to serve on subcommittees that would be expert on all these different clusters.

Each cluster had a subcommittee, and Denny had a timetable for recommending at least three commissioners for every position. They would evaluate any current incumbent interested in continuing in their job, and would help to develop candidates from all over the country. By New Year's Eve, almost every one of the fifty-plus top commissioners were ready to be sworn in. The transition had involved over 800 people and countless hours, but it was worth it. The next day, we hit the ground running. Denny had organized a seamless transition, and preparation was the key.

I gave my first budget presentation as mayor on February 2, 1994. At the time, the city's budget was $31.7 billion. I detailed work-rules concessions and productivity gains totaling $500 million, dozens of specific cuts, revenue projections, tax cuts, and privatization projects (a single example explains a lot about New York—one of my proposals was to sell eighty-five of the *five hundred* gas stations owned by the city!).

I gave the whole presentation entirely without a script. Beginning with that first speech, I've always done budgets without a prepared text. A few years later, as my confidence and knowledge grew, I began giving my State of the City address the same way. I viewed it as an opportunity to organize my goals for the coming year. The discipline of preparing for the speech forced me and my administration to keep things moving.

Because I viewed the State of the City speech as a way to establish my agenda, I'd begin preparing it in October, even though it wasn't delivered until January. First, Deputy Mayor Tony Coles would sit down with the deputy mayors, then the commissioners, and ask for their ideas and for new projects. Tony and I would go through those projects and prioritize them. I'd add my own initiatives to what was now a long list, then invite my deputy mayors to weigh in. Finally, I'd show the list to the Budget Director to see what we could afford. What remained formed the basis of my speech. The time spent preparing, getting the information into my bloodstream, paid off. By the time I presented it, I did so from my own head and heart, not from a page that someone else had prepared.

That level of preparation—learning something so thoroughly that it was part of my history—had already served me well as a prosecutor. As an assistant U.S. Attorney in the early seventies, I was assigned to the Corruption Unit, a new division established by the U.S. Attorney, Whitney North Seymour, Jr., to investigate corruption in government.

I got my first taste of management at the same time as I was developing a case against Bertram L. Podell, a three-term Brooklyn congressman who had been given illegal payments to obtain a route for an airline. I prepared for that case religiously, but by the time the case came to trial I had been given a further promotion, put in charge of the Narcotics Division, the largest—and trickiest—unit in the Criminal Division. I went from managing five assistant U.S. Attorneys to thirteen, but I carried the Podell case with me because I had put so much work into it.

It is not a casual thing to prosecute a congressman, and we were determined to dot every *i* and cross every *t*. As we approached the fall 1974 trial, we rehearsed the key cross-examination for days. Mike Mukasey, then one of my assistants and now the Chief Judge for the United States District Court in the Southern District of New York, played Podell, while I experimented with every line of questioning I could think up. Cross-examining Mukasey was much more difficult than cross-examining Podell himself. We were preparing for the brightest, most knowledgeable witness possible. When Podell turned out to be normal, our preparation paid off.

One strategy had to do with payments Podell had received under the guise of legitimate legal work. I asked him about the payment for legal services and got him to say that it was to so-and-so law firm. Once he committed himself to the bogus firm's name, I handed him a copy of the gigantic Martindale-Hubbell reference book, which lists every law firm in the country, and ask Podell to point out this firm, which of course he couldn't. This ploy turned out to be dead on, the element of surprise proving invaluable. The cross-examination reached its climax when the real-life Podell, distressed and unsettled, dropped his own glasses, poking out a lens. The next day, withering under continued cross-examination, he asked for a recess, during which his lawyer told us he had decided to plead guilty.

That evening, I went out to buy the late-night edition of *The New York Times*, as I always did back in the days when there were evening editions of the papers. I was shocked to see my name on the front page.[1] What struck me the most about the article was that it described me as having the style of a boxer in the way I moved in and out during the cross-examination. It struck me that the writer, Arnie Lubasch, had noticed something about my background. Few people knew that my father had taught me to box when I was four or five. I made copies of that story and sent them to my dad.

VISUALIZE THINGS FOR YOURSELF

One technique I used in preparing for the city budget illustrates another principle of preparation I've always espoused—visualize things in your own mind.

I can still picture the nun who taught my class in grammar school about how a bill becomes a law. She used to make little diagrams showing how a revenue bill could emanate only from the House of Representatives, then would have to pass both houses before going to the President, where, if it were vetoed, it could proceed only with a two-thirds overriding vote, and so on.

I knew that the way bills were developed in New York City was similar to the way the federal government functions, but I also knew there were important differences. I also anticipated that my philosophy of smaller government and tax cuts might antagonize the City Council, where 90 percent of the members were Democrats, and

[1] Wednesday, October 2, 1974.

realized that I needed expertise in this critical area. I wanted to know what legal powers I'd have and to learn it on my own, not from some expert's summary.

I read the entire city charter, paying particular attention to the chapters about how spending bills proceed. And I actually did that a few more times over the course of my two terms. Even in my last year, knowing the city was going into an election, I wanted to make sure the City Council didn't curry favor with voters by irresponsibly spending $500 million of the taxpayers' money. I went through the whole charter again so that I had it fresh in my mind, then, not assuming anything, had my staff prepare a contingency plan in case we'd have to fight. As it turned out, the City Council Speaker, Peter Vallone, was on a similar page. But thorough preparation is never a waste of time. Sometimes, you have to know the material as well as the experts who work for you. That's the only way to develop an independent view and not be held captive by the people around you, who may want to spin in one direction or the other.

You don't want to micromanage or undermine the authority of the good people you've hired, but on occasion there's no substitute for firsthand experience.

Whenever I tried a case, either as a prosecutor or in private practice, I went to the scene where the events took place. I frequently did the same when supervising investigations and trials. As much as I love charts and pictures, it's dangerous to rely on second-hand depictions. When you actually go to the scene, all manner of things can emerge about what actually took place.

After September 11, I was frequently asked about staying calm in the face of crisis. As I have already discussed, it comes down to preparation. Throughout my time as mayor, we conducted tabletop exercises designed to rehearse our response to a wide variety of contingencies. We'd blueprint what each person in each agency would do if the city faced, say, a chemical attack or a biomedical attack. We went through how we'd act in the event of a plane crash or a terrorist attack on a political gathering. We didn't just choreograph our response on paper, either, but did trial runs in the streets, to test how long the plans took in practice. We even simulated an airplane crash in Queens and a sarin gas attack in Manhattan, eerily in the shadow of the twin towers.

We used to take pictures of these trial runs, and they were so realistic that people who saw them would ask when the event shown in the photograph had occurred. Several of them, for example, show the simulated airplane crash in Queens, which had fire and white foam and looked like a real crash even to people who witnessed it. Those photos used to hang at the Office of Emergency Management in 7 World Trade Center on a wall we called the "Hall of Horribles." I can still picture those photos in that hall, though both no longer exist—they were destroyed in the attacks on the World Trade Center. We did not anticipate that airliners would be commandeered and turned into guided missiles; but the fact that we practiced for other kinds of disasters made us far more prepared to handle a catastrophe that nobody envisioned.

The goal was to build a rational construct for myself, and for the people around me. I wanted them ready to make decisions when they couldn't check with me. The more planning we did, the more we could be ready for surprises. Before September 11, there were those who said we were being overly concerned. We didn't hear that afterward.

Speaking of preparedness, something eerie happened in the course of writing this book. On August 7, 2001, I was driving through New Jersey on my way to a campaign appearance on behalf of the Republican candidate for New Jersey governor. I was explaining my ideas about preparation to Ken Kurson, and I specifically cited recent cases of false reports of anthrax and the awareness that it gave us of how to handle that emergency should it actually occur. A little over a month later, anthrax sent through the postal system terrified the entire country. New York City might have been brought to a standstill had our team not practiced for precisely that contingency. Later that day, I was talking about using the media as a means of communicating with the public during an emergency. The example I cited? The February 1993 bombing of the World Trade Center. I explained that if such a thing were to happen again, I'd use radio and television to communicate evacuation plans and calm fears.

Relentless preparation means not just preparing for disasters but anticipating potential trouble. A lesson I learned in trying cases was to prepare for everything I could think of so that I'd be prepared for the thing I hadn't thought of. In a trial, surprises are going to happen. A new fact will arise, a witness will say something out of the blue, a new witness will come forward. If I'd thought of every contingency, and planned for them, the best way to deal with the unexpected would emerge from that preparation.

So I put in place systems that would identify potential trouble and start dealing with it before it happened, even if I didn't know exactly what might occur. For example, we implemented a procedure called the Syndromic Surveillance System to check with the hospitals on a daily basis to note any elevated levels of symptoms: careful data analysis could predict when certain statistical patterns showed something was about to erupt. Even if we didn't know exactly what it was, we could begin preparing ourselves with extra personnel near the expected hot spot.

To a similar end, I'd meet every week with the commissioners of the Police and Fire Departments. Those meetings were devoted to the problems of the day, but we always made time to try to look into the future. If I was meeting with the Police Commissioner in May, for example, we might discuss a gathering of world officials at the United Nations scheduled for September. We'd begin gathering intelligence four or five months in advance.

In 1994, the West Indian–American Day Parade fell on Monday, September 5. The parade, held on Labor Day each year, runs through Crown Heights, Brooklyn, a community ripped apart three years earlier by an anti-Semitic race riot. For the first time in the twenty-seven-year history of the parade, which draws over a million Caribbean Americans and many others, Labor Day coincided with Rosh Hashanah, the start of the Jewish New Year, a holiday that could attract as many as 40,000 more people to Crown Heights.

Many in the Jewish community wanted the West Indian–American Day Parade re-routed. It might have been easy to honor that request. After all, I had been heavily supported by Jewish voters and soundly outpolled in the West Indian–American community. There was lingering anger that I had defeated David Dinkins less than a year before.

Instead, I sought to build a strong relationship with the people who ran the parade. As early as March, I initiated meetings. Richard Green, one of the organizers, helped make the introductions, and we sought out community leaders like Carlos Lezama who were more interested in throwing a successful event than in using the parade as a focus for racial division and scoring political points. Little by little, I worked to convince them that together we could have a festive, safe carnival. As we made progress, I brought in leaders of the Hasidic community, people like Rabbi Shea Hecht and Rabbi Yehuda Krinsky. They forged a compromise on the route and schedule, then we spent the summer meeting with representatives from both sides and selling the compromise to both communities. It all culminated in a party at Gracie Mansion at which everyone involved attended to prepare for the parade (that party was then repeated for seven straight years). Instead of experiencing disturbances, Crown Heights remained peaceful for that parade and throughout my entire administration.

INSTILL PREPAREDNESS IN OTHERS

Creating reasons for those who work for you to establish their own culture of preparedness is part of being a good leader. One of the reasons I always held the monthly town meetings in different parts of the city was that it forced the agencies to learn about the problems and concerns of places that might not get as much attention if we weren't going to be there.

I believe in creating a culture that values preparation, and in passing that ethic from the top down. When Bruce Teitelbaum came to my campaign in 1992, he was a young and eager 28-year-old concerned about the direction of the city. He had no particular interest in politics and was a lawyer in private practice. He was obviously bright and energetic, but more than that we could see he was thorough. We hired him to help with general office duties part-time—stuffing envelopes, basically. This was about twenty months before the election, when there wasn't all that much happening.

The following week, I attended a meeting in the garment industry—about seventy workers who made socks. For some reason, Bruce was assigned to that appearance. He showed up in my car on the way back to campaign headquarters and asked me if I knew who he was. I laughed and reminded him that we'd met a few days earlier, and that I didn't forget people who had helped me.

A couple of days later, I arrived at an event at which I was scheduled to speak, and there was no one there to greet me or tell me what room to go to, and to deal with all the small details a good advance team handles. The whole scene was very disorganized and I was not pleased. After the event, I spoke to Peter Powers and Denny Young back at campaign headquarters, and made my displeasure plain.

I left, and Peter and Denny held a meeting. Denny said, "The candidate is upset. We've got to tighten things up. And there are some people here who are not going to be here if these things don't improve." Denny looked at Bruce Teitelbaum and said, "You. Kid. You're now going to be doing advance work for the Mayor. Don't screw up." Bruce said, "Yes, sir," but to himself, he was thinking, "What the hell is 'advance work'?"

By this time he had left his job to work for my campaign full-time. His first assignment was a dinner at the Grand Hyatt Hotel that

I was attending with my wife. It wasn't itself a campaign event, but practically everything a candidate does is in some way campaign-related, and I was going to be greeting people there before a play. The Grand Hyatt is a tricky place at which to do advance work, because it's a huge building with many different entrances. In addition, it was raining hard, with a gale force wind. On top of that, there was a picket line around the hotel.

Bruce reached the Grand Hyatt two hours before I was due to arrive and took stock. He couldn't reach me by phone, because back in 1992 we weren't all carrying cell phones. He was positively apoplectic, thinking, "I quit my job for this. I don't even know this Rudy guy, and now he's going to get here and I won't know where to meet him or be there to tell him where to go. And what if he's photographed near this union picket? He's going to be furious. Why, oh why did I give up my job for this?"

Bruce went to the hotel gift shop, changed six dollars into coins, and found a phone. He called campaign headquarters every ten minutes to tell whoever answered that if my driver called in, he should be told to bring me to such-and-such door and how best to avoid both the rain and the picket line. He got so nervous that he began counting the steps from the curb to the door. Then he counted the steps from the door to the men's room. For good measure, he counted the steps to the ladies' room. Then he actually wrote that information down and diagrammed it on a little Hyatt Hotel napkin. Finally, it occurred to him that I might have forgotten to bring an umbrella. And if I had forgotten, maybe my wife had too . . . He needed two umbrellas—but wait, with such a strong wind they could easily break. He bought four.

I got out of the car exactly where Bruce had told my driver to drop me, and there Bruce was, waiting. Sure enough, we needed the umbrellas (two of them, anyway). He handed them to us and walked us to the door: "Hello, sir. There are forty-three steps to the entrance. Once inside, there's a men's room immediately to the left and a ladies' room fifty-five steps beyond that. If those are occupied, there's another on the second level." He told us exactly where our seats were, having checked them out himself. During the play, he said, he'd wait directly in front of the second door; if we needed anything, he'd be there.

Denny Young called Bruce into his office the next day and congratulated him. Bruce started doing a lot more advance work and traveling with me, and he was always scrupulously prepared. If we planned a campaign walk in Queens, Bruce would, without being asked, visit the street every day for a week at the same time that the walk was scheduled, to judge how many people were likely to be there. He'd visit each store along the route, tell them I was coming, and ask if they'd put up a poster. Then we'd do the walk and Bruce would say, "There are fifteen stores on this block—three pizza shops, a kosher butcher, and a fish store. Predominantly Jews and Italians shop here." Judging from the types of stores, I probably would have guessed the ethnicity of the shoppers on my own. But that's the point: Bruce wasn't going to assume a damn thing.

4

Everyone's Accountable,
All of the Time

A lot of leaders have catchy slogans on their desk; many believe in them. The two-word sign on my desk genuinely summarizes my whole philosophy: I'M RESPONSIBLE. During my time at City Hall I did my best to make those words a signature theme for every employee, starting with myself. Throughout my career, I've maintained that accountability—the idea that the people who work for me are answerable to those we work for—is the cornerstone. And this principle starts with me.

The social contract is a two-way street. It was a privilege for me to work for the government. In exchange, I had an obligation to perform honestly and effectively. For instance, during my two terms, we held a town hall meeting every month, rotating to different boroughs. I'd bring the entire city government with me to the dais—the commissioner of every agency, each of my deputies, and several others from my administration. I would talk for a couple of minutes, then turn the discussion over to the public, who would take turns asking questions. Many of these boiled down to complaints about broken streetlights or zoning issues that seemed unfair. Rather than promise "someone will get back to you," I would lead the questioner to the commissioner responsible for the issue raised.

If a questioner's complaint was that some nightclub was making too much noise in their area, I'd say, "Please come up here and speak to Deputy Mayor Rudy Washington, who enjoys nothing more than closing down noisy clubs." He'd take the questioner's name and number, the particulars of the club, then investigate and decide whether further action was warranted. My aim was to solve the problem directly, to send the message that government could accomplish things. But there was a more profound message as well. I didn't want my administration to get lazy about the "small stuff," thinking that items like park cleanliness or garbage pickup didn't matter. A fellow New Yorker who took the time to come to a town hall meeting and stand up in front of his neighbors to air a problem deserved a proper hearing.

More than anyone, leaders should welcome being held accountable. Nothing builds confidence in a leader more than a willingness to take responsibility for what happens during his watch. One might add that nothing builds a stronger case for holding employees to a high standard than a boss who holds himself to even higher ones. This is true in any organization, but it's particularly important in government.

In the private sector, there's a bottom line. The mission is clear: profits. The path to that goal may be difficult, and one faction might favor building market share while the other prefers growing margins, but generally determining the health of a for-profit corporation is much the same for everyone—the company's directors, employees, investors, and competitors all know that profits are desirable, losses are not.

In government, one is operating with other people's money. The leader of a corporation with sinking revenues cannot order his customers to pay more. He can raise prices, but his customers can respond by buying less or selecting a competitor's products. In government, however, the temptation to cover shortfalls by increasing taxes can make political leaders lazy. Worse, the "customers" of government—citizens—can and will eventually do just what any dissatisfied customer does—go elsewhere, and eventually vote elsewhere too. To a city, the effects of that impulse are devastating. High property taxes force people to move, high sales taxes provoke them to shop elsewhere, high taxes on business make companies build and hire somewhere else, and high income taxes undermine the will to work.

Nearly all the frauds that occur in the business world involve using somebody else's money less responsibly than one would use one's own. People are looser with other people's money—a problem afflicting government from top to bottom, which is why it's so important to devise accountability measures. In corporate America, compensation should be tied to performance. The best performers generally get paid more and the worst risk losing their jobs. Too often in government, all an employee has to do is show up and go through the motions. If employees have been given any objective targets at all, they often have little to do with actual goals. I wanted to change that mindset, and decided to start with the highest-profile agency, one whose performance could be measured not just in the saving of dollars, but in the saving of lives.

MANAGING CRIME REDUCTION: COMPSTAT

When I ran for mayor in 1993, I promised to do something about the out-of-control crime rates that were holding the city hostage. As a prosecutor, I had been in law enforcement my whole career. I also studied the specifics of policing New York City, especially during the years between 1989 and 1993. We were looking at 9,000 to 10,000 felonies a week, and anywhere from 1,800 to 2,200 murders a year. I didn't want to tinker with the Police Department. I wanted to revolutionize it.

Along with Bill Bratton, my first Police Commissioner, and Jack Maple, the NYPD's First Deputy, I wanted to challenge every single assumption about urban policing, issue a "Why not?" to every single "That's not how it's done." We began by assembling about

500 people into twelve teams, each assigned to envision a police force with no preconceptions. We implemented the great majority of their ideas, from ditching the wispy powder-blue police uniforms of the past to installing fairer, performance-based systems for evaluating job performance. The very fact that we were acting on the suggestions of people who worked in the department sent a message to everyone that it was not business as usual.

The centerpiece of our efforts was a process called Compstat. This combined two techniques, neither of which had previously been implemented. First, crime statistics were collected and analyzed every single day, to recognize patterns and potential trouble before it spread. At the Compstat meetings, we used that data to hold each borough command's feet to the fire—a hundred police at a time, from brass to officers, joined by others from throughout the criminal justice system, would be convened in a big room in which every one of that command's statistics faced scrutiny.

Next, we set about determining who bought into the idea of accountability and who didn't. Bureaucracies sometimes resist change because they think large ships can't be turned around; but even the biggest organization is made up of people, and those individuals either bought into Compstat or were told to find another line of work. Even in a highly unionized workforce like the NYPD, there's plenty of leverage available. Anyone above the rank of captain—deputy inspector, inspector, assistant chief, deputy chief, bureau chief, and chief of the department—can be demoted: not only a knock to morale, but to the pension. And those below the management ranks could be reassigned—a police officer who lived in Westchester might find himself stationed in Staten Island. Any manager who didn't have their heart in the new system was made to understand that it was time to retire or face a demotion. Those on the force who realized that Compstat would not only improve their city but actually make their jobs more rewarding were promoted and entrusted with leadership roles.

At the same time, we set our sights on clarifying the purpose of the Police Department and crafting indicators to tell us whether our goals were being met: accountability again. Crimes occur for a dauntingly complex set of reasons, sometimes for no reason at all. It is simply not possible to predict where and when every crime will occur, but in order to try, one has at least to know what is going on.

For years, the statistics in the Police Department that drew the most attention were the number of arrests and the reaction times to emergency calls. In fact, neither is the ultimate goal of a police force: public safety and reducing crime. Usually, a crime has already occurred by the time a 911 call is made. If one is lucky enough to make an arrest, that only puts a dent in future crimes the perpetrator might have committed rather than protecting the immediate victim. Furthermore, we needed reliable data. Arrest numbers, for example, are susceptible to manipulation.

We knew we had to come up with criteria besides arrests and response time. Each year the FBI reported for all the cities in America with populations over 100,000 the total number of crimes in each of seven categories—murder, rape, robbery, felonious assault, burglary, grand larceny, and grand larceny auto.

A main frustration with the state of policing was that each set of statistics was already obsolete by the time it was available. Examining the numbers annually or even quarterly wasn't accomplishing anything in real time. By the time a pattern of crime was noticed, it would have changed; and when the statistics finally did come in, even for huge numbers of crimes, they didn't reflect the actual volume. The reason was simple. In order for a crime to register, somebody had to report it, or the police had to find out about it. If someone walking down the street was shot at and didn't tell anyone, there was no crime statistic. Likewise, if a woman was raped and chose not to report it, or if my property was stolen and I figured, "I'm not insured, and the cops did nothing the last three times I was robbed," a crime went unrecorded. Statistics cover only the crimes that the police know have occurred. Also, as crime escalates, a smaller percentage of it is reported, because any victim must have confidence that the authorities can and will respond in an effective way.

When Jack Maple first assured me we could access statistics on a *daily* basis, I thought he was exaggerating. No Police Department anywhere was gathering data with that frequency, and I felt that it would take two or three years to implement. It was an ambitious goal, but three weeks later the first numbers rolled out of the station houses.

It works this way. The police officer in the street makes a report and enters it into his precinct's On-Line Complaint System (OLCS). The report is transmitted to the Compstat mainframe and entered in two places: 1) on a map that shows geographical concentrations of criminal activity and sorts them by hour of day, type of crime, and day of week; and 2) on a weekly summary of crime complaints that displays trends over a variety of periods, such as week-to-date, month-to-date, and year-to-date, and compares the current year's total with the prior year's and shows percentage change. The data can only result in meaningful response if it's accurate. We implemented an auditing system that resembled the Stock Watch system I was familiar with from when I prosecuted insider trading cases. It would flag statistically unrealistic performance, allowing us to dig deeper into its accuracy. There were even commanders removed for tinkering with the numbers.

Precinct commanders rely on these reports to identify patterns and allocate resources. Before Compstat, it was anyone's guess whether, say, a pattern of three A.M. gas-station robberies was emerging. A sharp-eyed policeman might notice his own activity concentrating in certain areas at certain times, but he would have no way of knowing whether his colleagues were fielding the same type of incident at the same time and place. Even if an astute commander recognized a pattern, he couldn't know whether it was occurring in a neighboring precinct, and thus wouldn't think to seek intelligence from that commander. Using Compstat, the goal of preventing crime rather than reacting to it was fulfilled. With patterns identified early, the commander deploys officers to probable targets and arrests the criminals before they have robbed their garage, instead of hoping the 911 call arrives in time to catch the fleeing villains.

The Compstat reports are distributed departmentwide. Everyone from the mayor and the police commissioner to the commander one precinct over can see whose numbers are improving and whose aren't. Successful precincts can be asked for advice; those in need can be offered remedies. Then comes the heart of the Compstat process: the weekly meeting.

The NYPD is divided into eight borough commands—one for Staten Island, one for the Bronx, and two each for Manhattan, Queens, and Brooklyn. Almost every Thursday and Friday at seven A.M., a different one of those eight commands stands before their peers and the Police Department brass at One Police Plaza and defends that command's performance over the previous four to eight weeks. This assembly—the twice-weekly Compstat meeting—is truly extraordinary. *The New York Times* commented that "the regular Compstat meetings are probably the most powerful control device ever devised for police." In 1996, Compstat won Harvard's Innovations in Government Award.

From the very start of these meetings, the NYPD realized that something special was taking shape. In those days, the colorful, bow-tied Jack Maple would pepper the precinct commander with: "Why are car thefts down twenty percent citywide, but up ten percent in your area?" Or: "Explain how assaults have been falling for six straight months until last month, then started rising." We made it difficult to pass the buck by requiring that the precinct commander's entire staff be present. It's much tougher to say, for example, that you don't have fresh numbers because "the computer guy" hasn't updated the software when the computer guy in question is standing right next to you. Other forms of accountability emerge as well. Recent photographs of panhandlers blocking traffic and harassing drivers at a particular intersection might be projected onto the large screens at the front of the room. That precinct's commander could hardly claim that he didn't have a problem with panhandlers.

Jack Maple and Louis Anemone, Chief of Patrol, were masters at both carrot and stick. Sure, there were times when someone needed to be called on the carpet. This was not to humiliate the person concerned, but to ensure that he would know people were paying attention and expected him to improve. Maple and Anemone would grill the commanders and point out areas of concern. If muggings were up on Friday nights yet arrests on that day of the week were steady, Maple or Anemone would project a chart so the whole room could see that. They'd growl, "Let's not let the bad guys think they won't be collared on Fridays."

Pointing out underperformance might clear the way for that commander to ask for help; maybe he wasn't bringing it up so no one would notice he needed it. Judging how deeply a commander accepted responsibility told his bosses a lot about how committed he was to the principle of accountability. There were also plenty of opportunities to throw compliments around, and to recognize superior bravery or insight. One of the benefits of Compstat was that commanders had objective proof of their good performance.

More than anything, the meetings reminded me of appellate arguments—putting people on the spot and requiring them to have answers. Think of the Socratic exchanges in *The Paper Chase*, but instead of Ivy League law school professors cast it with some of the most colorful New York City personalities imaginable. Overall, Compstat meetings were not prosecutions or tribunals, nor were they lovefests. They were as much about planning as accountability. Sure, someone whose numbers were ominous was expected to provide an explanation and a plan for improvement; but then someone who knew he was going to have to stand in front of his peers and defend his performance would usually do whatever he could to improve that performance *before* it embarrassed him. The mere fact that one knew that one was going to be called to account provided the motivation to try new strategies. So in a sense Compstat had already performed one of its main functions before the borough commanders even got to their feet.

The meeting's other main function was to serve as a brainstorming session. The commanders of particular units, such as the narcotics or undercover task forces, were on hand to share techniques, and other policemen shared intelligence they'd gathered in their own precincts that might help elsewhere. This could be entertaining. In the early days, a certain amount of performance anxiety could get to those who were expected to defend their precinct's performance. On one occasion a fistfight nearly erupted between Anemone and a precinct commander who took exception to the tone of the grilling he received. Another time, a precinct commander arrived at the seven A.M. meeting drunk. He was persuaded that this was a good point in his career to retire.

The impact of Compstat was immediate and revolutionary. Major felonies fell 12.3 percent from 1993 to 1994. In two of the most serious categories—murder and robbery—the city's reductions were the largest one-year drops ever—17.9 percent and 15.5 percent, respectively. While it was true that crime was falling nationwide, New York's rate of reduction was three to six times the national average. To anyone with even a casual understanding of mathematics, the evidence was indisputable—New York's crime reduction far surpassed that of any other American city. And we not only brought down the crime rate, we kept it down.

There were those who would look at the crime reductions achieved and trip over themselves to credit anything but Compstat. "In the eyes of many police chiefs and criminologists, San Diego and Boston have become the national models of policing," wrote Fox Butterfield in *The New York Times* of March 4, 2000. "While New York's accomplishments are also studied and admired, there is a sense of sadness that a great opportunity has been squandered."

Fortunately for New York, Butterfield was wrong. The city's

declines in crime over the next two years not only continued but were some of the largest ever, just as other cities saw their own crime rates start to climb. In 2001, according to the last set of statistics put out by the FBI during my term as mayor, Boston led the nation in homicide increase, with a 67 percent rise. Homicides were up 22 percent in St. Louis, 15 percent in San Antonio, 12 percent in Atlanta, 9 percent in Los Angeles, and 5 percent in Chicago. (In 2001, the Windy City, with 2.9 million people, had 20 more murders than New York City, which has a population of 8 million.) And San Diego? Sixteen percent more crime than New York, with an increase of 3.9 percent over the last six months of the year, while New York City's figure fell by 7.6 percent.

Northwestern University criminologist Wesley Skogan explained that while a number of cities had some success during the nineties in reducing crime, New York was alone in both the scope of its reduction and its ability to hold and even improve on those reductions. As he told *The Washington Post*, "What's different is New York City. The real story is the New York decline and not the Chicago increase." On December 21, 2001, to his credit, Fox Butterfield corrected his earlier prediction and was writing again, noting that Boston, the city whose crime-fighting techniques he praised only twenty-one months earlier, was now "the city with the largest percentage increase" in homicides. Meanwhile, "New York is an exception to the big cities with rising homicides."

For any system to remain effective, it must continually challenge itself. Compstat's success was so conspicuous, it would have been easy to sit around congratulating ourselves. But a leader's role is to raise the bar. If the NYPD were successful in reducing the seven major crime categories, it was reasonable to expect the department to implement similar systems in other areas. That's how Compstat evolved into a much more sophisticated tool. When we broadened the idea to include arrest warrant enforcement, for example, we had unprecedented success in getting habitual offenders off the street.

Every time we'd add a performance indicator, we'd see a similar pattern of improvement. For example, when we first started tracking graffiti arrests in 1995, the NYPD made a total of 475 collars. By 2001, that number was 1,485. In 1997, we incorporated statistics about police behavior. That year 419 uniformed officers fired shots. Every year since, the number has shrunk, down to 175 in 2001, the lowest since records started being kept in 1973 (there were 761 that year). If we could count it, we could Compstat it.

Many more performance indicators were added, such as those measuring officer misconduct (bribery, and civilian complaints of discourtesy and excessive force), while others measured the operating efficacy of the precinct itself, like staff overtime. Other indicators aimed at officer morale were built in, with the specific goal of demonstrating that just as the officers would answer to their commanders about increased criminal activity, those same officers knew that their bosses were keeping an eye on what improved conditions for police.

Some New Yorkers, in the habit of reflexively criticizing everything the NYPD did, assumed that by emphasizing crime reduction Compstat would somehow lead to a more violent Police Department. It was the opposite. In 2001, there were .26 fatal police shootings per 1,000 officers in New York City, compared to .7 in Philadelphia, 1.42 in Detroit, and 1.61 in Los Angeles. There were 81 people shot by the NYPD in 1992, 25 of them fatally. In 2001, 26 people were shot, 10 fatally.

Even after eight years, I remain electrified by how effective those Compstat meetings could be. It became the crown jewel of my administration's push for accountability—yet it had been resisted by many who did not want their performance to be measured. Until Compstat's introduction, anyone suspected of poor performance could simply shrug and say, "What are you gonna do, the city's ungovernable." There was no accountability. With a system that proved results could be achieved, that excuse would no longer fly. Compstat was true culture shock.

Eight years later, when murders were cut by almost 70 percent and overall crime was down by about 65 percent, the doubters had all but disappeared. They were too busy implementing their own versions of Compstat in other cities throughout the nation, from Chicago to Los Angeles. As the success of our approach grew from arguable to indisputable, more visitors wanted to observe the meeting, looking to copy it in their own city or observe a force that had revitalized urban life.

On a summer morning in 2001, the Compstat meeting covered the Bronx, for example. Police Commissioner Kerik and I were seated alongside Chief of Department Joe Esposito, who undertook the majority of questioning. The commanding officer of a precinct in the Bronx was up first. He and his deputies stepped to the podium prepared to defend and explain what was going on in this part of town. Espo noted that although murders decreased in the precinct by over 60 percent during the eight years of Compstat, there had been a recent increase. "What the hell's going on up there?"

The C.O. pointed out that the precinct was home to eleven Methadone clinics, including four in a notorious area. Walking the chief through the most recent murder, the C.O. described a dice game going on outside a locked park at three A.M. The perp said he acted in self-defense. However, witnesses described the victim hitting him with a bottle only after being stabbed.

Chief Esposito made it clear that he wanted to see a lot more quality-of-life C summonses issued. They could have been written for dice and drinking. Looking at his own Compstat sheet Espo continued, "Forty-eight C's is a good number, but more should be given." It was a clear application of the Broken Windows theory.

The discussion turned to a new initiative to break up fencing operations. The idea was to apply extra pressure to anyone arrested for burglary and robbery to name their accomplices. One of the first to be caught had been a chain-snatcher, the C.O. reported. The chief asked if he had given anyone up. The C.O. replied that he had not because he had received such light sentences for past convictions.

The meeting continued, with another commander noting that some barbershops in his precinct had evolved into fronts for drug dealing. Everyone was urged to keep an eye on "barbers" working unusually long hours or servicing patrons who never seemed to emerge with shorter hair. Another cop mentioned that Hector Camacho, Jr., was scheduled to fight Jesse James Leija that weekend. I was particularly interested—besides my personal interest in boxing, this was to be the first bout on Coney Island in fifty years, held at KeySpan ballpark, which no one thought we could build. I was planning to bring my son, Andrew, and several friends. The cops recommended keeping an eye on bars that televised fights and letting them know in advance that they would be patrolling the area. A young uniformed officer was then brought forward, and his commander announced that his persistent work in developing a confidential informant had broken up a gang bent on violence.

Another recent crime was described, this one a shooting. It seemed that a known drug user was on a four-day crack binge. The weather got hot and he started to stink, so his companions, knowing him to carry an ATM card, urged him to take a shower. These so-called friends then stole his pants, assuming his ATM card would be in them, and further reasoning that he'd be slowed in chasing them by having no clothes. They were wrong on both counts. The guy came running out with no pants, but he'd removed his ATM card before entering the shower— apparently he had some notion about the kind of people he was associating with. One of them, frustrated by the failure of their scam, lost his temper and shot and wounded the pants-free drug user. The police caught another of the friends, who gave up the shooter, but admitted to nothing himself—except the theft of the pants.

And so it went, for about two hours. Eventually I took the opportunity to thank the assembled police. Crime in the Bronx had dropped 62.4 percent since I became mayor, including a remarkable 16.36 percent decline to that point in 2001. The Compstat meeting is the ultimate expression of how much success relies on acting as a

team, sharing ideas, holding each other accountable, relying on one
another for support.

ACCOUNTABILITY ACROSS THE BOARD

The overwhelming success of Compstat in the Police Department
convinced me that true accountability could improve the performance and morale of any organization. I made the decision to introduce a version of Compstat to every mayoral agency in the city.
Which department should come next? I wanted to pick an agency
likely to benefit in similarly dramatic fashion—that would help silence critics who argued that the accountability approach worked
only in the NYPD.

The New York City Department of Correction had a 100-year
history of chaos. The system was averaging 120 to 150 slashings and
stabbings a month and had the worst public profile of any city
agency—it was a symbol of government failure and helplessness. In
December 1991 Mike Wallace visited Rikers Island for CBS's *60
Minutes*. He described a system out of control, where, before his own
eyes, "this inmate was cut in the eye and stabbed in the back while
being robbed of his jewelry."

Meanwhile, one of the consequences of the increased effectiveness of the Police Department was to increase the strain on the city's
sixteen jails, fifteen holding facilities, and four hospital prison wards.
I had pushed the prison population up by about 1,800 inmates in
1995, my first year as mayor. At the same time, the $2.3 billion
budget shortfall I'd inherited forced me to reduce the number of correction officers, from just over 11,000 to about 10,500.

Because of the budget crunch I had selected as my second Commissioner Michael Jacobson, who had been in the Office of Management and Budget. With his background in finance and statistics, he
needed a forceful hands-on manager and we had just the guy. Bernard
B. Kerik had a lot of new ideas and the strength of character to

implement them. We had appointed Bernie first Deputy Commissioner of the Correction Department in January 1995. His career was unusual. Abandoned as a child, he entered the military as a young man, joined an all-army martial arts team, and spent three years stationed in Korea. After that, he became the warden of New Jersey's largest prison. He left the job in 1986, taking a large cut in pay to enter on the ground level of the NYPD. He served there for eight years, winning thirty decorations. One of his most memorable achievements was heading a narcotics investigation that resulted in the conviction of more than sixty members of the notorious and brutal Cali drug cartel.

I met Bernie in 1990 at a meeting to organize the annual Buczek Foundation Dinner, held in memory of Police Officer Michael Buczek, killed in the line of duty in 1988 by drug dealers who thought they could avoid prosecution in the Dominican Republic (Bernie went to the airport in New Jersey personally to take custody of one of the killers when he was extradited). I was immediately impressed with his organizational skills, and was delighted when two years later he joined my campaign. I remember our talking one day about *Reinventing Government,* by David Osborne and Ted Gaebler, and his "borrowing" my copy out of my car, until he finally bought his own. As an outsider and a risk-taker, Bernie was someone who wouldn't accept "That's not the way we do things" as a reason new strategies couldn't be tried. I knew that the people at the top had to buy into the system and that Bernie, a black belt who'd trained Special Forces personnel at Fort Bragg in North Carolina, would be a convincing salesman.

The Department of Correction, with 125,000 inmate admissions a year, was the perfect choice for the next accountability experiment. If the Compstat model could fix New York's prisons, it could fix anything.

Kerik acted swiftly to create the Total Efficiency Accountability Management System—TEAMS (acronyms are what people in government get in lieu of stock options)—in 1995. He assigned a lot of the organization and implementation to Debbie Kurtz, who later worked with Geoff Hess to bring accountability programs system wide. TEAMS was based on the same principles as Compstat—data collection, performance indicators, and regular meetings at which the results were probed. Bernie scared the hell out of every manager, explaining that the choice was simple: embrace the TEAMS concept or be fired. He realized that some wardens would resist providing all the information we wanted, that there'd be deputies who didn't feel like mapping and analyzing and meeting. True to his word, there was major turnover in senior staff until that culture started to change. But he also supported the people who performed well, giving them the resources to build on their success. By August 2000, when Bernie left the prison service to become the city's fortieth Police Commissioner, every single correction bureau chief, and even the correction commissioner who replaced Bernie, Bill Fraser, was a deputy warden or lower when Bernie first joined the Correction Department. Inmate-on-inmate violence had been reduced by a miraculous 93 percent over the previous five years. Overtime expenditures fell by 44 percent and sick leave by 31 percent.

Part of enforcing accountability included applying it to the inmates themselves. New York City had a long history of extending all kinds of privileges to its prisoners. Inmates on Rikers Island wore their own clothes, including the jewelry that inmates would regularly steal from one another. They were entitled to a phone call every day, and correction officers could carry weapons only when responding to an emergency.

Under Kerik, the inmates learned that they'd answer for crimes committed in jail, in addition to the ones that put them there. Bernie tells a story about arriving at Rikers and seeing photos of inmates who had been held down by other inmates and had initials carved into their backs with a razor. He asked, "What happened to the inmates who did this?" Nothing. "This is jail, that's what happens in jail."

An inmate who believes nothing can happen to him feels free to behave like a lunatic. We changed that. If an inmate gave somebody a few stitches, we'd arrest him and charge him with a violent assault. Virtually overnight, the inmates received fewer injuries and committed fewer acts of violence. It's not hard to understand why—even someone serving twenty years doesn't want another five added on. And yet, when I said that even with all the problems New York City faced in those days I was going to make sure violent inmates were arrested and prosecuted, people looked at me as if I had two heads. Until they saw the results—139 slashings and stabbings in July 1995; 1 in September 2001.

That's a perfect example of how everyone benefits from accountability. Virtually every innovation we imposed on the Department of Correction was met with resistance, from the City Council to the courts to the members of the Board of Correction, who fancied themselves "concerned" about the conditions of the inmates. But who benefits when inmate-on-inmate violence falls from 1,093 incidents in 1995 to 70 in 2000? Everyone.

As with Compstat, the idea with TEAMS was to *anticipate* problems. For example, in fiscal 1995, the average uniformed correction officer was absent twenty days. Part of that high total was attributable to the culture of violence in the prisons, part to low morale from working in a dysfunctional agency. The department formed a unit to visit the homes of employees who frequently called in sick. The TEAMS program identified chronic sick-leave abusers, and managers who had several under their purview. Reining in those who abused the system and those who allowed it freed more resources for everyone else.

One of my favorite indicators started under Kerik was one in which those visiting prisoners would have their names and social security numbers checked for active arrest warrants. Not only did that get undesirables off the street, it also helped reduce the violence that would occur when a visitor from a gang ran into someone he had wronged. The fact that people with active warrants felt perfectly free to saunter up to a city jail and write down their name and social security number was a sad commentary on how the department had functioned for a long time. The message was, "This is a decrepit system, in which criminals are free to visit other criminals, and nobody does anything about it. Come and take advantage of us." Before long, the criminal community learned that when they showed up at Rikers Island and were wanted for a crime, they'd get arrested. If they'd committed a crime while in jail, they'd get arrested. The idea was re-established that society expects a certain standard of behavior from all its members, all the time. The policy even had its marketing side. Advertisers always want to reach the right market—they run ads for acne medications on MTV and for diapers in parenting magazines. What better place than a prison for the city to advertise that offensive behavior had consequences?

By the time Bernie left Correction, they were using TEAMS as a full management tool, making it the focal point around which they managed the agency. Everything from use-of-force incidents to average daily inmate population to inmate grievances to sick time and absenteeism—a total of 592 indicators—was tracked and analyzed and defended at the accountability sessions. There's a case to be made that a system can have too many indicators. Making it so complicated that only a few people understand it defeats the purpose of getting everyone on the same page. But that's the beauty of decentralizing control—each department was allowed to create its own system, and so could decide how best to solve its problems. As mayor, I didn't say, "Each agency must have 350 indicators." If 592 worked for the Correction Department—and obviously it did—I wasn't going to interfere.

Such a policy has proven useful in many unexpected ways. The best indicators don't simply measure performance, they improve it. For example, TEAMS tracks commissary sales in its jails. If sales of cigarettes and candy suddenly double, a riot may be in the planning stages. Inmates know that the first act after a prison uprising is a lockdown that confines them to their cells, so hoarded supplies can be a sign of a coming incident. Getting a jump on that allows the guards to separate the likely leaders of such an action and to prepare, which reduces the chance of violence to themselves and to the inmates. As the system grew more sophisticated, the TEAMS system was modified to track individuals' purchases, which proved enormously effective. If some inmate bought two Hershey's bars then turned up the next day with fifty, we'd know he was a leader and was extorting from his unit. We would confiscate everything he couldn't prove that he had bought—an effective, nonviolent way of exerting control and discouraging stealing.

While some indicators might seem esoteric to those not intimate with the department, the people who run it have to be trusted. For example, one of the 592 indicators the Department of Correction tracked was the number of religious service visits. This helped break up a meeting of the Latin Kings that had begun to take place during the weekly Mass. That was the beauty of the TEAMS system. The indicator that alerted managers to the sudden jump in Mass attendance might have proven utterly benign. Asked about the increase, the warden might have said, "I noticed that, too, and it turns out that the new priest we have here is very charismatic," or some other reasonable explanation. But the fact that TEAMS caught the spike meant that the warden could then be asked to explain it, and he knew that he would be expected to have an explanation.

One of the strongest proofs that the model works is that it continues to do so even after whoever implements it moves on. After Bill Bratton left as Police Commissioner, no one expected Howard Safir to be able to continue the reductions in crime. In fact, they accelerated. When Safir left, Kerik reduced crime even further. On the day he sat at Gracie Mansion and accepted the job, Bernie maintained that things like fleet management were perfectly suited to the Compstat method and would not only improve officer morale but also reduce response times—in the sixteen months Bernie was commissioner, these times were cut in half.

The same evolution occurred when Bill Fraser replaced Kerik as commissioner of the Department of Correction. The numbers got even better. The system wasn't about any of these individual officers or even the mayor. So long as the person on top believed in the system and made sure everyone beneath him bought into it and had the necessary support and resources, no one person was irreplaceable. I maintained that if my successors bought into the system as wholeheartedly as I did, they'd have just as much success. That's exactly what has happened. Mike Bloomberg and his Police Commissioner Ray Kelly have continued using Compstat and are having success with it.

With Compstat and TEAMS functioning so well (and also Job-Stat, our program for finding jobs for welfare recipients, launched by the Human Resources Administration in 1998), the approach had proven it could work anywhere. In January 2001, I set about implementing it in as many of the thirty-eight mayoral agencies as possible.

We called it the Citywide Accountability Program (CAP). Under CapStat, the agencies themselves were asked to create their own programs. They knew the problems and specifics of their departments better than anyone. And since the whole idea was to take responsibility and feel invested in the process, involving the commissioners and top staff created a program that didn't feel as though it were imposed from the top. We set four parameters that the commissioners had to submit to me:

- Data had to be collected regularly and reliably—preferably on a daily basis, but at least once a week—at a set time.
- Twenty to forty performance indicators that got at the core mission of the agency had to be established.
- A regular meeting must be convened—with a minimum frequency of once a week—including a floor plan that demonstrated exactly which agency leaders were required to be present at each meeting.

- Ten or more representative performance indicators that the agency wanted on its page of the city's web site must be submitted.

Putting the information online held the department's feet even closer to the fire. The citizens and the media could hold the agency accountable at the same time as the agency did. There was another motive behind my drive to put the numbers on the Internet. I was to retire in a year. At the time, I did not know—and it did not appear likely—that Mike Bloomberg (someone who also understood the need to run New York City as a business) would replace me. As someone who cares deeply about New York City, I knew that I, for one, would want to know how well it was doing, and that it would be hard for whoever replaced me to remove the indicators once they were up there, lest he appeared to be covering up. That reinforced the idea that it was not only about answering to whoever was above you on the organizational chart, but about answering to the public as well.

By the time I left office, twenty city agencies had an accountability system along the Compstat model. Every one of them benefited from its implementation. And that's not just my opinion—I have the numbers! And because they're on the Internet, so does everyone else.

At the Department of Citywide Administrative Services (the agency responsible for procuring everything the city needs and managing its buildings), the Agency Internal Management System (AIMS) started up in March 2001. After the World Trade Center attacks, DCAS used its new meeting model to address the crisis. Because they could share information and knew where each other's initiatives stood, this sprawling agency was able to meet the city's myriad of needs—from umbrellas to fire trucks—with unprecedented speed, all the while keeping on top of every contract.

As with Compstat, the meetings were not held to tell everyone what a great job the participants were doing. At one meeting of the

Department of Transportation's MOVE system (Management Owner-ship Vision Empowerment—I swear I'm not making these acronyms up), Commissioner Iris Weinshall asked about the cleanliness of the ferries. "Oh, they're pretty good, Commissioner, real clean." Iris then projected one photo after another, showing litter all over the boats. The department established a baseline for acceptable conditions. Within one month, each ferry was cleaner by 10 to 62 percent.

Creating indicators that have real bite is one of the toughest chal-lenges of implementing a Compstat-style accountability system. A small city without much violent crime won't have much success if it emphasizes the murder rate. Of course it must pay attention to mur-ders; but a town that goes from three in one year to two the next should not celebrate its 33 percent drop too jubilantly. So a smaller town should use its system to measure the offenses that are frequent enough to track reliably, such as traffic infractions and the speed with which complaints are addressed. By the same token, a five-person company will consider different performance measures from those considered by a 500-person company, even if they're in the same industry.

CapStat's emphasis on numbers gives some critics the impression that it is a coldly analytical way to go about achieving a goal. In fact, the opposite is true. By emphasizing results rather than methods, commissioners hold their managers responsible for improvements on their performance indicators but also give them considerable latitude to experiment with achieving those improvements. What works in one area may not be the best method elsewhere. The Police Depart-ment's Compstat, for example, completely decentralized decision-making. Each precinct commander developed and implemented strategies designed to produce the best results in his particular neigh-borhood.

This dynamic also created a marketplace for ideas, in which the best strategies got adopted through true competition. Say the com-mander of the 44th Precinct in the Bronx had reduced shootings by placing more undercover officers on quality-of-life duty. It was only a matter of time before other commanders, eager to outperform their buddy in the 44th, would implement his strategy, often adding improvements. At the open airing of these techniques and their results at the twice-weekly meetings, other commanders were free to crib from each other and tailor strategies that would be effective in their own precincts.

In all this, the overall leader must identify and install the right managers. Under a smoothly functioning accountability system, such figures wield considerable power and enjoy plenty of creative maneuvering space. Those who need their hands held and want every move to originate at headquarters will never succeed. The leader's job is to set the tone and agenda, including specific targets for managers in the field, and to supply whatever advice, encouragement, and resources are needed to meet those targets.

All enterprises benefit from increased accountability. Naturally, there are differences in the way agencies achieve it. A corporation might not want to share its internal performance numbers widely, lest people who leave take that information to a competing firm. In corporate America, at the core of many recent high-profile business collapses was a failure of accountability throughout top management. There will be endless debate over the specifics of "what went wrong" at these companies. What they share in common, however, is a refusal at the top to accept responsibility for mistakes. "I don't understand this or that accounting procedure" is not a valid excuse—it's the duty of a leader to understand. If a chief executive cannot understand his own enterprise, he must become better informed, or consider the very real possibility that the accounting technique really is too complicated and ought to be replaced by one that's more transparent.

Every leader, whether in government or business or elsewhere, needs to internalize the idea that being open and honest about the enterprise is always the best course. Whenever there's doubt about whether to make public a damaging fact, err on the side of the disclosure. That disclosure may have a momentary negative effect. But there are two compelling reasons to disclose it. First, it's eventually going to get out anyway, and will be worse because people rightfully will wonder what else one is hiding. Second, over time, honest and forthright leaders build faith with investors and constituents, which is valuable when one eventually does require the public's confidence in the face of bad news.

The best advice for a CEO is to disclose bad news sooner rather than later. Whenever a convoluted explanation is offered in favor of not disclosing, overrule the advice and disclose.

The experience of a prosecutor can be very helpful here. Whenever I needed to present a witness with significant credibility problems—dishonesty or crimes in his past, for example—it was my practice to bring out those damaging facts in my direct examination. With those disclosures out of the way, I could rebuild the reputation of the witness while not leaving the jury feeling misled.

Despite the failures of some very high-profile American businesses and the alleged "corporate greed" that caused them, the reality is that they reflect only a small percentage of the business community. And all of these collapses actually demonstrate that America's economic system is a very healthy one. It provides a mechanism for uncovering wrongdoing, which might well remain secret in other systems. Furthermore, the system is self-correcting. Whenever major wrongdoing is uncovered we seek methods to prevent it in the future. The system is imperfect, to be sure, but functions better than any other. Moreover, accountability works to improve all systems.

My experience with the many agencies that came under the Cap-Stat umbrella—and the character of the Parks Department is as different from the Correction Department as any two enterprises could be—proves that any organization is better off when everyone answers to each other.

Much of what CapStat measured were the ordinary things that make life more livable. I realize that "potholes repaired within thirty days" and "summonses for off-leash dogs" are not matters of life and death. However, creating a culture where employees feel responsible is momentous. And the reality is that some of these charts and graphs and performance indicators really are matters of life and death.

DO WHAT'S POSSIBLE, TRY WHAT'S NOT

In New York City, as in any big city, some parents neglect their children, and a certain number of monsters do awful things. Government cannot substitute for the parent, or replace the family and neighborhood groups that need to protect their most vulnerable members. There is a danger in giving the false impression that the city is primarily responsible. That relieves people of their obligations.

Even so, we still have to try our best. As a leader, you have to begin with the proposition that you're responsible, then analyze whether there was something you could have done to prevent a disaster or prevent future disasters. We applied this approach to protecting the most vulnerable children. In 1994, $209 million in child support was collected in New York City; in 2001, $447 million. In 1996, the average child protective specialist was handling 28 cases. By 2001, that number was 13.2 cases. In 1991, there were 49,000 New York children in foster care. In 2001, there were 29,000. That is because the 21,189 adoptions completed during the last six years of my administration were 66 percent more than in the previous six years.

Nick Scoppetta, the Commissioner of the Administration for Children's Services, achieved these results not only by holding accountable those who worked in his agency but also those who wished to do business with it. One of those programs—the one that tracked the performance of foster care—provides a telling illustration of how management accountability ought to work.

Beginning in 2000, ACS began issuing numerical grades for all agencies that contract for foster services, on a scale from 1 to 100. The indicators included how quickly families were reunited, frequency of caseworker visits to foster children, and percentage of children who needed medical care. When the results came in, the scores were measured against the numbers actually being achieved, rather than against some absolute that might be impossible to reach. Those scores were then made public so each foster parent could see who was above average and who below. We intentionally made the grading scale demanding, so that an 85 indicated exceptional performance against an average around 70 percent. We knew the media would have fun pointing out all the 70s, as though they were English composition scores, but I didn't believe in social promotion or artificially inflated results.

After the grades came out, the ACS placed more children with high performers, fewer with low. Once we had completed the first scoring review, the top four providers received 95 percent of their maximum allocations, while the bottom four got only 60 percent, and were assigned extensive corrective action plans. The worst-performing agencies would have the fewest children, and if they didn't raise their scores we'd eventually stop contracting with them. It wasn't an idle threat. In August 2001, an office that ran foster homes in Manhattan and Staten Island scored a 50—nine points lower than the next lowest. We closed it and transferred responsibility for its 280 children to a better-performing agency (the children themselves stayed in their current foster homes).

Strangely enough, this kind of capacity management had never been done in New York. While there had been evaluation systems, they had never been sophisticated enough to measure real performance, and the consequence of a bad score was never that the agency lost capacity. Whatever their contracted capacity was, that's essentially what they had—the contracts hadn't included performance incentives and punishments.

The reason for that was that there were so many children in foster care. One doesn't want to think of children as inventory, but the fact that no one wanted to look critically at a problem lest they be labeled insensitive meant that the actual conditions for these children declined. The old saying around the Child Welfare Administration was that nobility of intention was enough. Because there were no performance criteria, there were no outcome measures. The bottom line for the 280 children removed from the worst-performing contractor was that they ended up with an agency that had objectively fared much better.

The foster care system was a per diem, per capita system—the contracting agency received an administrative fee for each day a child was under its care. When the child was adopted or reunified with his or her family, the payment for that child stopped. When there were many children coming into foster care, staying for inordinate periods of time, the contracting agencies always had enough children and plenty of income: we couldn't be choosy about punishing the worst agencies because we were desperate for capacity. This problem shows how important it is to pursue initiatives as part of a larger framework. We realized that to provide better service we had to shrink the total foster care population by getting more children adopted or reunified. As we did that—through more preventive and after-care programs, to make sure children were safely at home—we were able to put pressure on lagging providers and reward those that deserved better.

We implemented management information systems to track items like historical norms for the number of days a child stays in foster care. We accounted for variables—little children tend to stay in the system longer than adolescents, and so on. We used that information to predict the total number of care days that an agency was likely to have. We could then say to that agency, "Based on the number of children we expect you to handle, we are going to give you $5 million. If you are efficient at achieving permanency, via adoption or reunification, you'll reduce your number of care days and thus won't have spent your full $5 million. Instead of taking it back, the way the city traditionally does when someone underspends, we'll let you keep those savings, and you can use it in other programs that we approve."

The objection here would be that we might have encouraged contractors to lower the standards for when a child could be returned to his or her family, or placed in a different permanent situation. We guarded against that by penalizing an agency when a child came back into our care system within a certain period of time. In other words, it had to be a reunification or adoption that worked. In fact, the adoptions were rarely disruptive—it is a long process, with a lot of supervision in the Family Court, so it screens itself. But if an agency reunified too quickly and the children came back in, it didn't get paid for that discharge, and might also have faced sanctions.

The carrots and sticks were both in place. More important, they were organized around the core purpose of the agency—to protect children and place them in safe, permanent homes. STAR (Safe and Timely Adoption and Reunification) did exactly that. In the first year of the program, the best-performing agencies reinvested over $3 million while reducing the foster care population to levels not seen in thirteen years.

The Administration for Children's Services has been a success. It's the ultimate proof of the versatility of accountability. No matter what you're tracking, comparing results to previous indicators, then demanding improvement, is the best way to achieve anything. These accountability measures led not only to better accountability but to better morale. As each agency became more efficient and more effective, people felt more positive. Everybody likes to play for a winning team.

At the beginning of this chapter, I describe the sign on my desk that proclaimed, "I'm Responsible." I don't deserve all the credit I received for what went right while I was mayor, or all the blame for what went wrong, but I do deserve to be held accountable for the results of my office. I expect the same from everyone who works for me.

Something else in my office at City Hall is worth mentioning. Almost buried among the Yankees memorabilia and photos and books are prints of a pair of frescoes from the Palazzo Publico of Siena, painted by Ambrogio Lorenzetti in the 1330s. One is called "Effects of Bad Government on the City Life," and features the chaos and violence one might expect from its title, with Satan jubilant amid the turmoil. In the other, "Effects of Good Government on the City Life," the citizens are happily and safely going about their day, carrying out commerce and chatting with their neighbors. It is uncanny how strongly those pictures resemble the before and after shots of Times Square seven centuries later.

5

Surround Yourself with Great People

Looking back, I believe that the skill I developed better than any other was surrounding myself with great people. The group in place on September 11 proved to be exceptionally strong—especially since so much of what we had to do in the light of the disaster had no precedent.

The axiom about good teamwork making each member of a team better really proved true. I can barely describe what it meant to me to know that I could turn something over to someone and know that it would get done, without having to hector or micromanage. On the first night, for example, we weren't sure how to get all the equipment into the city. Additionally, some of the roads we would normally have used were completely destroyed. Complicating matters, abandoned cars were blocking everything. Rudy Washington organized the entire system for getting the construction equipment in and out, so when I began reassuring New Yorkers that the city would recover and prosper if we showed resolve, it was more than hollow bravado. People could see that within hours of the attacks we were already accomplishing things, and they felt that they, too, could be strong and determined. Each member of my staff saw their team-mates acting bravely, so they in turn did.

Faced with the worst disaster New York had ever seen, it might have been understandable (but not acceptable) for some people in my administration to go through the motions. After all, there were only three months remaining in my final term. Many of them had been placed in great danger themselves and people were genuinely shell-shocked. Instead, without exception, my staff distinguished themselves. That did not come about by chance.

As U.S. Attorney, I hired more than150 lawyers for my office in the Southern District of New York, and when I was in private prac-tice I participated in hiring numerous lawyers. In the Justice Depart-ment, I helped hire ninety U.S. Marshals and was intimately involved in the selection of U.S. Attorneys.

I always tried to set a simple standard that I expected everyone I hired to follow when doing their own hiring: find the person best suited for the job. Period. A criticism directed at many politicians re-volves around the issue of patronage. Patronage does not mean giving a job to someone who supported you politically. It means giving a job to someone only because he supported you politically. Of course I hired people who supported my campaigns. After all, the reason they did so was because they shared my beliefs—and I wanted my staff to carry out and believe in what I value, all that I promised the voters I'd work for when they elected me. But I did not hire people simply be-cause they worked for my campaign or made a donation.

The same pressure is brought to bear on business leaders. A board member has a child who needs a job or an old friend is look-ing for a sinecure. Just as elected officials have an obligation to the voters, leaders of corporations owe their shareholders an honest ef-fort to hire the best-qualified staff. If that happens to include the board member's kid, fine. Because my sole criterion is employee performance, I would no more refuse the best person because of a relationship than I would hire the worst person because of a relationship. Even those who work for nonpublic companies will do well to follow that principle. You might think you're being a nice guy by finding a job for someone who doesn't measure up. In fact, you're not helping anyone when your enterprise stumbles or fails because the people working for it are in over their heads.

ANALYZE STRENGTHS AND WEAKNESSES (INCLUDING YOUR OWN)

In Chapter 3, I detail the nuts and bolts of the transition committee that Denny Young oversaw; but there was more to it than assembling a top-notch list of contenders for every major job. I tried to visualize who would be at my meetings, to picture who I would like to have around me and how those people would interact with one another. I wanted amiable team builders and ornery contrarians, people I'd known for years and people I'd never met, experts in the arcana of municipal government and those who'd never even considered such a world. Above all, I sought to match the best person available to the job best suited for that person.

Judge MacMahon used to say, "All federal judges have something in common: they're either Democrats or Republicans." His point was that every judge, no matter how talented and fair-minded, got where he was through the filter of compromise. Only, once they were on the bench, many began to think they were selected by God not the President. Leaders of all kinds—CEOs, coaches, even the occasional mayor—run the risk of thinking they are where they are because of divine intervention. Psalm 19 says, "Above all, keep your servant from presumptuous sins; let them not get dominion over me." When selected for a position of leadership, do not believe you were selected by God. That's exactly when humility should be applied. What are my weaknesses? How can I balance them?

When I first came into office, having so much experience working with police—and so many friends and family members who were either firefighters or cops—I was confident that I could run the uniformed agencies effectively. From managing large organizations in the past, I also felt that I'd have an intuitive ability to handle crises ranging from snowstorms to labor strikes. The intricacies of economic development and the budget, however, were examples of two particular areas in which I really required help. In those areas I had weaknesses, I needed to balance with the strengths of other people.

The first part of choosing great people is to analyze your own strengths and weaknesses. That gives you an idea of where your needs are the greatest. The goal is to balance your weaknesses with the strengths of others, then to evaluate the team overall. Even though I probably knew more about city government than I realized, it didn't compare well with what I'd typically known about the cases I tried. As a lawyer, I would feel insecure unless I knew everything possible about a case. So when I put together my original staff, I tried to compensate for that deficiency.

A leader wants all his managers to be strong. He doesn't want yes-men leading any departments, including the ones the leader himself knows well. If you look at the people I picked to head, for example, the Police Department, I chose three outspoken leaders, even though that was the area I knew best. So it's not a matter of hiring strong leaders only for the agencies you haven't yet mastered. But because the leaders of these agencies will have both the responsibility of heading their department and teaching you the intricacies, you need even more expertise in those positions. At the same time, that person must understand that, although you haven't mastered the details of his department just yet, it is your philosophy that is to be implemented.

For all these reasons—plus the fact that I was inheriting a $2.3 billion budget gap—I put a lot of care into selecting my first Budget Director. Mike Hess, who had worked with me in the U.S. Attorney's office, and had then been my law partner, was put in charge of finding appropriate candidates. I interviewed six different people for this key position. That's a high number to make it past the initial process-ing stage, particularly when we were hiring hundreds of people in just a couple of months. After much consideration, it boiled down to two candidates—Abe Lackman and Marc Shaw.

Lackman had worked for a long time for the State Senate. He was a budget theorist and had been based in New York City before going to Albany, so he understood the city's finances. Shaw had stronger knowledge of the current balance sheet because he had been budget director for the City Council at the time I was elected. He had also worked with Abe up in Albany, and they were friends. But when I asked whether they could successfully work together with one as Budget Director and the other as deputy, I found that whoever was deputy would have felt as though he had "lost." Given that, I was leaning toward Abe. He was philosophically Republican, and shared my passion for reducing the size of government and cutting taxes. New York City was the only place in the country where reducing taxes was unpopular, and I needed a Budget Director who believed in it as strongly as I did. Still, I felt that I needed both Abe and Marc. I had already decided to make John Dyson, an economist, the Deputy Mayor for Economic Development, and I felt that adding Abe and Marc would give me well-rounded strength.

I came up with the following idea. I offered Abe the position of Budget Director and Marc the job of Finance Commissioner, which made him a commissioner, not a deputy. Then I set up a group to consider the budget, rather like a cabinet committee. It included the Deputy Mayor for Economic Development, the Deputy Mayor for Operations, the Budget Director, the Finance Commissioner, the Commissioner for Labor Relations, and me. This way, I had both Marc Shaw and Abe Lackman considering all the budget decisions I was making. To my delight, both men said yes.

Establishing a dynamic that brings out the best in each player is one of the toughest facets of leadership. It's not enough to identify and attract great parts. Making sure they add up to more than their sum is partially conscious and partially unconscious. I like to create unexpected personnel marriages. Telling someone who's quantitatively oriented that he's not qualitatively oriented makes him feel bad. Having him work with someone who is qualitatively oriented will often create better results. Any high-achievement environment attracts people who are relatively independent. They're used to calling the shots. Forcing them to work together creates tension, and tension breeds creative solutions, with each person striving to push the project further.

One of the best examples of balancing personalities and skills involved the most complicated, intense personnel decision I ever made.

Being the Commissioner of the New York Police Department is a major responsibility. With over 40,000 officers, the NYPD is the biggest, most famous, most complicated municipal police force in the world. When in the summer of 2000 Howard Safir stepped down as Commissioner, I faced a tough decision.

Howard had left a strong legacy. Crime was drastically reduced, as he built on the gains made by my first Police Commissioner, Bill Bratton. Major felonies fell during Howard's years from 293,874 in 1996 to 202,106 in 1999, Safir's last full year, with murders dropping by over 40 percent.

Howard strongly favored Joe Dunne, at that time the Chief of the Department (the highest ranking uniformed officer). A big bear of a guy, Joe was seen as a warm, healing presence. At that point, he'd been on the force thirty-one years, had served in some of the city's most challenging precincts, and was universally respected and loved.

His principal rival was Bernie Kerik, who had compiled a superb record managing the Correction Department. In just two and a half years, he had improved on the amazing advances he'd participated in as First Deputy Commissioner, reducing violence by 80 percent from 1998 through 2000, while simultaneously reining in overtime costs and decreasing sick days. He ran an exceptionally tight ship.

As usual, I consulted my top staff, as well as others whose judgment I trusted. Half were in favor of Joe, half Bernie. One day, I followed my morning meeting with a smaller gathering in my office at City Hall. I asked everyone to speak freely about whom I should choose and why. At that time, we had about a year and a half remaining in my final term. We had experienced extraordinary success in the Police Department, but my concern was that it would become increasingly hard to sustain. There had to come a point when the numbers can't get any lower. You can never eliminate crime entirely, although we always proceeded as if we could. So I wanted to find someone who would never be complacent or satisfied.

Joe Dunne was a cop's cop who had risen through the ranks. On the other hand, Bernie was this innovative guy. Appointing him might create a disruption in the department because, even though he'd been a cop, he'd spent the last several years in the Correction Department. There was another reason why Bernie would be an unorthodox choice: he had been a detective when he left the NYPD, rather than a borough commander or deputy commissioner. Finally, although he was exceptionally bright and creative, he didn't have a college degree.

The advocacy grew increasingly ardent, my advisors arguing back and forth over several days, which is what I'd hoped for. But then something happened that I hadn't anticipated. An article appeared in *The New York Times* outlining what everybody had been saying. Although it had a few inaccuracies and had misidentified the favored candidate of a couple of attendees, it was clear that the unthinkable had happened. Someone had leaked.

This was enormously destructive. One of these two men was going to become Police Commissioner. Now, whoever I picked would have to carry the burden of knowing who opposed him, and would have to work with those he knew had preferred someone else. At the same time, the man who wasn't chosen would doubtlessly resent the people who had sided against him.

At the morning meeting on the day that the *Times* story came out, Denny Young lost his temper. You'd have to know how controlled

Denny is to understand what a cataclysmic event it was for him to express such anger. He asked that whoever was responsible do the right thing and resign. We never did find out who leaked. As we thought about it, what probably happened was that someone at the meeting described it to a staff member, and that person either related it directly to the *Times* or to someone else who did, which would account for why at least two of the positions were reversed. Regardless, I became very angry. This kind of thing had never happened before, and it was treacherous to the people whose lives hung in the balance.

I did something I had never done before or since. I cut everyone off from the decision, to protect my advisors and the two candidates. I told everyone that from that point on, this was a decision I'd make on my own. I would meet with both candidates, then decide by myself. I knew both men well already, but I wanted to interview them one-on-one for a few hours each. The article correctly stated that I had remained neutral, so both Joe and Bernie would know I was genuinely undecided.

I spent a lot of time with each man, then, on Thursday, August 17, I turned to my Chief of Staff and said, "Record this for historical interest—I've decided." I didn't tell him who it was, nor when I was going to make an announcement. The next day, I let both Joe and Bernie know that I would be calling them that night. I was going to announce it on Saturday. But I still didn't share whose name it was I'd be announcing. I did not want it to leak, or appear to be the favored candidate of a particular person.

I waited until about eleven P.M., late enough so that the papers wouldn't be able to get a story into Saturday's edition. I was at Club Macanudo and had both phone numbers with me. I asked Tony to secure the manager's office. The only one left at the table was Judith. I leaned over to her and said, "I picked Bernie," before joining Tony in the manager's office and asking him to get Joe Dunne on the phone. I told Joe that I was going to offer Bernie the job, that I thought very highly of him, and wanted him to be Bernie's First

Deputy. Then I called Bernie and offered him the job, and told him that as soon as we got off the phone I wanted him to call Joe and offer him First Deputy. Bernie did so, and Joe accepted. After that, I talked once more to both men and asked them to come in the following morning so that we could announce the news as a team.

Normally I don't select deputies, preferring that commissioners choose their own top staff, but I had asked Bernie and Joe during the interviewing process whether each would accept the other as a deputy. They both had said they would be willing to work for the other. A lot of lesser people couldn't have worked that out. I had an instinct that if I could get the two of them to work together, I'd get the best out of both men.

The reasons I picked Bernie are complicated, and boil down to factors of chemistry and feel. As I told Joe, if I had known him as long as I'd known Bernie, it could easily have been him. Also, I saw the years Bernie spent away from the NYPD as an advantage. The force can be very insular. It helps to have someone who feels that their loyalty is not just to the department, but also to the mayor and the citizens of New York.

The safer decision would have been Joe. Bernie had more downside if he didn't work out, because he was the unconventional choice; but I thought he also had more upside, in terms of taking an organization that had been pushed really far and being able to get even more out of it. I thought Bernie stood a better chance of connecting with the police officers, having been a detective in the field and not part of the brass at police headquarters. Although even I didn't realize how good he was at conveying that feeling of being one of them, of coming across as if he were still a cop on the beat.

One day I was talking to him on the phone, and I was having a hard time hearing him. I asked, "Where the hell are you?" He had walked all the way to the top of the Brooklyn Bridge (where the police sometimes had to rescue would-be suicides), just as my uncle used to do with the Emergency Service Unit. (He later told me he'd been challenged by Joe Vigiano, who lost his life on September 11, and members of the Emergency Service Unit, to go with them as part of a training exercise to rescue would-be jumpers.) That leadership filters throughout the department, a willingness to do the tougher jobs of whatever you're leading.

Bernie arrested people. He went out in the middle of the night and watched his men to make sure they were safe when they did a raid. He didn't do it for publicity, he just did it.

LEARN FROM GREAT TEAMS

Sports have played a substantial role in the development of my thinking. I am a passionate baseball fan and have studied it all my life. Baseball—and also football, golf, basketball, and boxing—have provided not just enormous enjoyment but a laboratory for seeing what leadership ideas and strategies work.

For example, the idea of teamwork, and the balance it provides, was always with me as U.S. Attorney, during my campaigns, and later as mayor. Successful sports teams are never built on only one person. Even transcendent stars like Michael Jordan or Babe Ruth need strong supporting casts—and the proof that they're true leaders is that those other players were better around Jordan or Ruth than they would have been otherwise.

There are also issues of psychological conditioning. When a trial I was prosecuting went wrong, or when some strategy failed while I was mayor, or somebody made a mistake, or I said something people misunderstood, I would think of baseball, and how even the best hitters fail two out of three times. The greatest pitchers lose some games, and lose badly. There are important skills to be learned from picking yourself up after something goes wrong, to keep moving ahead without letting it throw you off course.

When I lost my first race for mayor, I felt that it was like losing the World Series. I came within three percentage points, and to be that close but still lose was both exhilarating and devastating. On the night of the election, I was reminded of the Yankees in 1976. It was their first trip to the World Series since 1964, so they were thrilled to be back on the big stage, but they were swept, losing four straight to the Cincinnati Reds, the last of the great Big Red Machine teams. In 1977 and 1978, the Yankees came back to win two years in a row, with essentially the same team, plus Reggie Jackson. All these players, like Thurman Munson, Lou Piniella, and Willie Randolph — many of whom had never been in a World Series before — gained exposure to the World Series in 1976. Battle experience is invaluable, and difficult to replicate. It's tough to know in advance whether those around you will handle pressure. Many good teams, particularly the Yankees over the years, will trade for a playoff-tested ballplayer, even one who's not having a great season.

When I think back to September 11, I see that much of my team's readiness came from the rules I detail in this book. But some of it came from the fact that the attacks happened after I'd had more than seven and a half years to get my team where I wanted it; we'd had time to test our mettle and learn from previous crises.

Any leader will have team members with more seasoning than others. The effective leader will encourage such people to impart their wisdom to those less experienced. Talking and sharing advice can do that, but it can be done even more effectively by example.

Phil Rizzuto once told me a story about Joe DiMaggio. The Scooter recalled trotting out to his shortstop position in the top of the ninth inning at Yankee Stadium. The Yankees were losing 9–0, with one more at-bat after the visitors took their turn. Dejected, Phil turned his back to the plate as the warm-up tosses were going around. He noticed Joe D. in center field and immediately felt, "We're going to win." Whenever he thought they were mired in a losing cause, he would look at DiMaggio, just watch him standing there, and think, "I know we can win this game." That was DiMaggio's leadership ability.

Leadership and balance are easier to see in teams — to see whether the coaches, owners, veteran players are producing the desired results. The business of a convenience store or a bank is less transparent. The Enron debacle proved that even publicly traded companies—whose earnings, cash flow, and revenues are supposed to be open to all—can easily obscure their "results." Sports teams win or lose on a given day and acquire records, so theoretically the results of their leadership or lack of leadership are there to see.

The Yankees, starting from 1996 through 2001, provide a textbook lesson in leadership. The combination of George Steinbrenner and Joe Torre produced far greater success than either enjoyed with others. It's a classic dynamic. I'm not sure that even they realize how much each does to make the other better.

George is the taskmaster. In an era of high salaries and player power, George may be the last owner who can still impose his set of standards on his players. His style is decidedly old-school. Vince Lombardi motivated his team by fear and then respect, in that order. His players weren't even sure why they were afraid of him, but they were, and they respected him too. The same applies with George. What people forget is that he played football and coached at Purdue and Northwestern, so his style is not unexpected. He annoys people and he sometimes gets sportswriters crazy, but it all works. Then there's the other side—the guy who tries to keep Darryl Strawberry out of trouble, who gives Dwight Gooden a platform for a comeback, who makes sure his ballplayers are taken care of years later. Even the players he's feuded with can generally count on his generosity and loyalty later on. Like George, in a different way, all his players feel his loyalty to them. He sticks with them through difficult times.

Then you have Joe Torre. Even though I know Joe personally and his brother and sisters, too, until I read Joe's book, I didn't know about the background of abuse in his family. Joe's ability to instill calm comes from not wanting to produce arguments, because of his childhood. Joe looks for consensus, for the positive in his players. The team members who are afraid of George or angry at him can go to Joe for support. He is also an exceptional baseball tactician, so the players know he will have a plan they can follow. The players get both the demanding boss and the nurturing manager. Equally critical is that each of them is a particularly able representative of his style of leadership.

To see how powerful the combination is, one need only look at the track record of each man without the other. As a manager, Joe had a losing record when he came to the Yankees. He was doing essentially the same things as he had with the Braves, Mets, and Cardinals, but with the Yankees it was working. Although George had been successful early in his Yankees career, winning the pennant in 1976 and 1981 and the World Series in 1977 and 1978, the team entered an unprecedented drought from 1982 through 1995. That's even worse than the difficult period in the 1960s and 1970s I had to endure. Put Joe and George together, however, and the results speak for themselves—from 1996 to 2001, the Yankees won four World Series, and came a couple of outs from making it five of six.

That's similar to the way I functioned as U.S. Attorney—I was the person who held people accountable, while Denny Young was everybody's big brother. If I was too tough on someone, he or she would talk to Denny, and he would calm them down, and sometimes tell me to take it easy. In the U.S. Attorney's office, the challenge wasn't so much to motivate people to work hard—the Southern District of New York already had highly motivated people with a strong work ethic—it was more a question of directing, focusing, and assisting, while figuring out where to deploy each assistant.

Some bosses hire only those of like mind. A leader has to surround himself with a complementary staff. As mayor, I had many Democrats in top positions, such as Deputy Mayors John Dyson and Ninfa Segarra and Transportation Commissioner Iris Weinshall, wife of Democratic New York Senator Charles Schumer. Style is as important as belief, and being objective about one's own personality, including flaws, is critical. I know my desire to keep initiatives moving sometimes exposes me to acting hastily. One of the reasons I've worked so successfully with Denny for about twenty years now is that he takes precisely the opposite course, always considering every contingency before pulling the trigger on an initiative. If I were more like Denny I'd probably do well to hire someone more like me.

Part of what I love about managing is that you can't totally predict who will get along and who will work well together. Sometimes very different people will form a harmonious unit, while those with a lot in common can't be in a room together. As mayor, I found that one relationship that was entertaining to watch blossom was that between Denny and Tony Carbonetti. Tony is gregarious and boisterous, a young, high-energy guy who's always looking for a way to put a deal together. Denny is quiet and very careful about everything he says or does. Although they appeared very different, their personalities were wonderfully complementary, with Denny providing a check to Tony's exuberance and Tony providing a spark to Denny's sure-handedness.

Matching the person to the job is not only a matter of what position is right for them, but also what is right for you. After I was elected for the first time, many people urged me to pick Paul Crotty to be my Deputy Mayor for Operations. In addition to being my friend for twenty-five years, Paul had been Housing Commissioner and Finance Commissioner in the Koch administration. People like political consultant David Garth insisted that I didn't have experience in city government and needed a right-hand man, like Paul, who did. I wanted Paul in government with me, but I wanted Peter Powers in that job because Peter was a Republican, like me, and understood the changes I wanted to put in place. I was convinced that knowing too much about city government would inhibit creativity in finding new ways to do things, although it was important in carrying out our agenda once it was set.

The Deputy Mayor for Operations has the most wide-ranging role of all the mayor's staff. He is responsible for more agencies and more people than anyone else, a dizzying array including the departments of Buildings, Health, Probation, Sanitation, and a dozen others. I had more confidence in Peter than he had in himself. I knew he could do it, and I was right. I selected Paul Crotty to be Corporation Counsel, then organized city government so that the Corporation Counsel would participate every day; thus Paul was there to get us through our learning curve.

Peter was involved in another of the most important decisions I ever made about matching a person to a job. It illustrates the principle of not allowing someone's alleged strengths to decide how you use him or her.

I began organizing my first mayoral campaign on February 1, 1989. We met at Peter's law office and I brought together my friends and told them I wanted to run for mayor. It was pretty clear that Peter would more or less be the chairman, Ken Caruso would be Peter's deputy, Denny would act as the counsel, and because John Gross arrived late to the meeting he would have to be treasurer, which no one ever wants to be. Staten Island Borough President Guy Molinari, who was the first to raise my name as a possible candidate for mayor, became the political advisor. We knew we didn't really know what we were doing, and were already off to a late start. But our early polls showed we were well ahead of Ed Koch, the incumbent and presumed eventual opponent. So we were excited but thought we needed more professionals in the operation.

Russ Schriefer and Rich Bond had recently been part of George H.W. Bush, successful presidential campaign. Guy knew them well and they were good people, so we hired them. But for a variety of reasons, including my inadequacies as a first-time candidate, we soon went from being ahead to being behind.

On a warm night in late June, we met at the Sutton Place apartment of Arnie Burns, who was at that point campaign chairman. Most of the group advised me to fire Bond and Schriefer, and recommended we ask Roger Ailes to be campaign consultant. I had found myself at several dinners with Roger, including at his house, and each time we would wind up talking about how much we liked Ronald Reagan, and how much we agreed with his policies. He had been part of Reagan's campaign team and I had worked with Reagan in Washington, so that was a connection.

However, my sense of loyalty makes it tough for me to remove people who haven't done anything wrong. I realized a lot of it had to do with me. Instead, I sat down with them and explained that I wanted Bond to be in New York more. He was traveling and would come in once a week to oversee things. I kept it that way for three or four weeks, but the campaign continued to deteriorate. We had no coherent message, we were slow to fill key positions, and we wasted money on items that didn't suit me or the spirit of the campaign, such as an elaborate headquarters.

Finally, I decided that my staff was right. I had to make a change.

I came up with a new idea, one based on advice that I had been given much earlier. I hadn't followed it, but all of a sudden it kicked in, becoming a turning point in my campaign, and even in my thinking about management. The advice I got was that a campaign manager cannot be somebody from the outside. It has to be somebody you trust implicitly, someone who knows and understands you. Once I had that model in place, Peter Powers immediately came to mind. The trust and understanding were obviously there in abundance. Beyond that, I had the sense that he would intuitively grow into being a politician. We had run political campaigns together in high school and college. He enjoyed politics, and had a real sense of organization.

Several people told me I was crazy. Running for mayor of New York City is exceptionally complicated. Peter had never run anything near that magnitude. In fact, he liked being on his own. He had his own law practice. We used to spend hours over meals talking, and he would explain how much he loved creating his own thing, not answering to anyone. There was nothing in his background to suggest he was ready to run a large organization. Except that I knew him, and was sure that he was perfect for the job.

So I made Peter campaign manager. Arnie Burns became chairman, with increased responsibility, since we needed an older, wiser head around, and Arnie was also a phenomenal fundraiser. Ray Harding moved into our campaign office, where his trademark line — "It's amateur hour at the Bijou around here" — was repeated with slightly less frequency. Together, we hired Roger Ailes as campaign consultant.

So that was the core of my campaign organization, and it was enormously effective. Although the months it took to form this nucleus might have cost us the 1989 election, the team proved its effectiveness in 1993. Four years later I ran with exactly the same team, except that David Garth took the place of Roger Ailes, who had retired from campaigns to create a television network. That one change also provided an interesting lesson in putting people in positions that make the most sense for them. Garth and Ailes shared a common attribute: total dedication. Garth lives, breathes, sleeps, and dreams a campaign while it's running. We used to work until three or four in the morning, then he'd call me up at six. There was never anything the candidate knew that Garth didn't, but there were quite a few things that he knew that the candidate didn't. Garth didn't work for whoever wanted to hire him — the chemistry had to work. In our case, luckily for me, it did.

One difficulty with Garth was that he wanted nobody between him and me. I was told by all the people who had worked with him that I had to insist that there be one. I put Peter in between us, explaining that David and I were obviously going to have a lot of direct communication. But the ultimate decision — what commercial to play, how much money to spend, where we were going to spend the money — would have to include Peter. Garth resisted that, and it created some friction, but it was necessary — and it worked.

RÉSUMÉS AREN'T EVERYTHING

Hiring Peter Powers to manage one of the most difficult campaigns imaginable is an example of a strong belief I have — a person's résumé won't tell you the full story. Education, for example, is crucial: I consider books and the knowledge that comes from study a critical part of the process of developing ideas, as I make clear in a later chapter of this book. But that doesn't mean that someone whose parents shipped them to a particularly impressive university is as impressive as someone who built his knowledge through his wits and life experience.

Paul Curran was one of my predecessors as U.S. Attorney of the Southern District of New York and my boss. When I was an assistant U.S. Attorney I eventually became his executive assistant. He was always on the lookout for lawyers who had demonstrated grit in the face of adversity. He'd say, "A kid who did well going to law school at night is worth three Harvard degrees." That wasn't to knock the Ivy League, which produces great people, but part of surrounding yourself with such people means drilling beneath the surface of those you hire.

Too many leaders overlook candidates with unusual résumés because of a failure of nerve. It's safer to hire someone with pedigree than one without—if the former screws up, you can always say, "Didn't see that coming—the old boy went to Princeton." But leaders who stand by their employees, even those who make mistakes, can enjoy the benefits of hiring the absolute best person for the job.

Early in one's career, academic performance may be worth noting because there's little else to measure; but that cannot compare to looking at what a person has accomplished elsewhere in his or her life. That's why criticism of Bernie Kerik for not having a college degree was so off base. Here was someone who had trained Special Forces personnel at Fort Bragg, been on some of the most important narcotics busts in the history of the NYPD, run the biggest jail in New Jersey, and in five years as commissioner of New York's Correction Department reduced inmate violence by 93 percent. It was an amazing list of accomplishments. Yet there were still those who wanted to harp on the fact that he hadn't gone to college twenty years earlier. By the time I appointed Bernie Kerik, I had hired so many people that I was immune to such criticisms. A leader must have confidence in his own decision-making about people. He has to know he'll make the right decision eight or nine times out of ten, and be willing to accept responsibility for getting it wrong a few times.

Not placing too much emphasis on a résumé sometimes means not being prejudiced the other way—not holding an impressive pedigree against someone. I hired Bill Simon as an assistant U.S. Attorney in 1985. His father, William E. Simon, Sr., was the Secretary of the Treasury when I worked for the Ford administration, and was truly amazing. As though serving two U.S. presidents wasn't enough, he also founded a highly successful investment firm, essentially invented the leveraged buyout, gave hundreds of millions to charity, wrote two bestsellers, and for thirty years served on the U.S. Olympic Committee.

I respect someone from a poor family who has worked his way through college and law school and had to make it on his own. At the same time, I respect someone with highly successful parents and a privileged background who still works hard. Someone born with a $10 million trust fund that'll provide a million or so in income every year doesn't have to earn a cent for the rest of his life. He could just watch baseball games. Heck, I might have done that if I had had a trust fund.

When I interviewed Bill, I got the feeling that I was talking to a young man who really wanted to prove himself. Sure enough, Bill came through for me big-time in the U.S. Attorney's office. I would see him there at 11:00 at night and on weekends. Anytime I was there, so was he. He was always volunteering to handle extra cases. He turned out to be one of the hardest-working people in the office, as well as a good guy. I was proud to be among his earliest supporters when he entered the Republican primary for the California governorship, which he won after trailing by a large margin.

MOTIVATE

In a perfect world, everyone you hire would show up every day eager to work as hard as possible, viewing a job well done as its own reward.

This isn't a perfect world. No matter how much success a leader has in hiring, it is still necessary to stoke the fires. That can be accomplished in a variety of ways, and I use all of them.

There were 629 murders in New York City during 1998—the lowest total since 1963's 548 (for comparison, in 1993 there were 1,946 homicides). When Bernie Kerik became Police Commissioner, he used that number as his goalpost. For all the right reasons, he wanted as few murders in the city as possible. But there was an extra incentive: he wanted to outdo his predecessor, Howard Safir. (The same had been true of Safir, who had been keenly aware of the statistics of Bill Bratton.) In July, down 11.7 percent from 2000, the city was one murder below the same point in time in 1998. We ended up with 642 in 2001. That's still an amazing number—29 fewer than the year before, and 24 fewer than Chicago, which has five million fewer people. As that year came to an end, it was so close that I almost expected Bernie to sell New Yorkers on the virtues of a quiet New Year's Eve at home.

Continued competition is one reason why a certain amount of turnover is a good thing. Putting aside the various disputes I had and was alleged to have had with Bill Bratton, had there been no change atop the Police Department we would not have achieved the reductions in crime that we did. The change from Bratton to Safir and from Safir to Kerik required each man to look at his predecessor's success and work out ways to improve on it. Even before Safir took over, the newspapers were running stories about how the crime decline was flattening out, and had fallen as low as it could go. Of the three Police Commissioners, Howard Safir was the most competitive. He read those same stories and would constantly try to come up with new strategies for bringing the figures down even further.

In general, this kind of competitiveness is friendly and gentlemanly, but life can get rancorous. This is not always a bad thing, so long as the good of the organization is the priority for those involved. Babe Ruth and Lou Gehrig reportedly didn't talk to each other for years but shared one of the most productive partnerships in baseball history—and eventually patched things up for the famous "luckiest man on the face of the earth"[2] tribute day to Gehrig. My administration had its share of jealousies and animosities, as will any institution, particularly one filled with high achievers. Then it becomes the job of the leader to control that competition and direct it toward a good result.

Allowing employees to encounter challenges on a regular basis accomplishes two important goals. First, it provides experience—both for the employee and for me. Not surprisingly, employees who are exposed to challenges and allowed to use their heads to respond to them become better at it. Some managers choose to shelter their staff from all aspects of decision-making—keeping them outside the room as the big issues are discussed and emerging to say how the situation will be resolved without explaining how the decision was reached. These are the same managers who then wonder why their employees make so many "bad decisions" or don't respond to situations the way the boss would.

Second, regular challenge invigorates the staff. Many at City Hall had worked with, for, alongside, and even above me at various other jobs. Their personalities and approach to their work varied widely, but one quality every effective performer shared was a sense that their job was more than a simple transaction of time for money. Managers ask a lot from their employees. They want and should expect their staff to feel they're part of something bigger than themselves, something worthwhile, maybe even important.

---

[2]July 4, 1939, was the last day Lou Gehrig wore the Yankee uniform, less than a month after he learned he had amyotrophic lateral sclerosis, in a Lou Gehrig Appreciation Day in front of 61,808 fans. Surrounded by current and former Yankee teammates, Gehrig trembled with emotion as he told the hushed crowd: "For the past two weeks you have been reading about the bad break I got. Yet today I consider myself the luckiest man on the face of the earth."

I considered it part of my job as a manager to create a stimulating and attractive workplace. The only way to lure and retain bright, energetic self-starters was to fashion an environment that allowed them to shine. I learned firsthand how quickly even the most motivated personnel could rebel against an environment that prevented them from demonstrating the very qualities that inspired me to hire them in the first place.

After the 1989 campaign, I joined White & Case, a venerable law firm founded in 1901. Packed with excellent lawyers laboring on behalf of high-profile clients like the New York Jets, the firm was married to the particular ways in which they'd done business for decades. Forms had to be completed just so, and jackets were required any time a lawyer left his office (even for visits to the bathroom).

Beth Petrone, who has been my executive assistant for eighteen years, accompanying me from the U.S. Attorney's office to private practice, felt the rules were particularly restrictive. It wasn't any fun for her and it wasn't fulfilling for me. Part of the reason people remain with me is because it's an adventure. The need to create that sense of adventure is even more critical when managing employees who can't be compensated in great amounts.

So we left for Anderson Kill. Once there, we tackled all sorts of interesting legal work. We handled two antitrust cases for AT&T. I represented Willie Mays in a civil case in which he was having trouble with the company for whom he signed autographs, and we resolved it. I represented the quarterback Jim Kelly in a lawsuit that he brought against a former financial advisor with whom he had a dispute, and was able to settle it.

Alongside excitement and fun there's something that goes a long way toward motivating: loading on responsibility. When I wanted the best associates to work with me at my private law practices, I would give them added responsibility. Young lawyers rarely get to go to court. I encouraged my first law firm, Patterson Belknap, to join a program with the District Attorney's office and with the Legal Aid

Society to argue appeals pro bono; that way, young lawyers got experience and also liked working for us.

There's a particular challenge for office cultures that attract the best and brightest. The U.S. Attorney's office in the Southern District of New York is the preeminent prosecutor's office in the country, the one that everybody who graduates at the top of his or her class wants to work for. They regard themselves highly because they've been successful in law school, and they think they're always right. The secret to keeping such people interested is continually to challenge them. Make them prove that they're as smart as they believe themselves to be.

Institutions with high esprit de corps, and high morale, can be enormously productive; but if the leader's not careful there are pitfalls. If highly driven people are not sufficiently challenged, they can surrender to self-satisfaction and arrogance, a sense of "we're better than you are." When performance deteriorates and staff start to coast, they often don't realize they're no longer operating at the previous high level. Thus the need to push them to master new things, climb new mountains. It can be a delicate balancing act. You want your people to realize there's something special about being associated with the NYPD or the FBI or playing for Notre Dame. At the same time, you don't want them feeling that because they've made it to any of those places, they can rest on their laurels. A leader has to be a part of the organization but also feel that it exists for another purpose, not just the satisfaction of those who work in it. Morale isn't an end in itself, it's designed to create better performance. It can't be an afterthought—it has to be central to everything you do as a leader.

When Jimmy Carter was President, the prevailing mood was malaise. Nobody could run the country, you just did the best you could not to make it worse. When Ronald Reagan became President, all of a sudden people started to believe that things could be accomplished. The Soviet Union could be stared down and spoken about in plain language, unions could be forced to behave responsibly, taxes could be reduced in the hope that individuals would make smarter decisions for their dollars than the federal government. The feeling in the country was that the President was very much in charge. Reagan understood that much of that was optimism. It didn't mean that leaders ran around cheerful all the time, but that they found ways to build morale. That was part of their job.

Although the people that I hired worked twice as hard as before and were paid much less, they did it because it was fulfilling work. There is a certain kind of fulfillment from government work that is not available elsewhere.

Good people act from a combination of altruism and self-interest. The altruistic part comes from the feeling that you're helping people, that your talents are being used to do good. That's how New York's police and firefighters feel, how much of my staff felt. The second part is that, especially at the highest levels—deputy mayors, commissioners, deputy commissioners, senior advisors—there's an exhilaration in doing something important, which other people pay attention to and respect. As mayor, I realized that it was critical to understand those two motivations.

Whenever a city worker accomplished something brave or noteworthy—saving a baby, or finding Placido Domingo's hand-marked score from Wagner's *Die Walküre* in a taxi, and returning it—I would invite them to my daily press conference and force the media to cover the positive stories about those who work for city government. It creates perspective—another aspect of maintaining the right morale. At the same time as we're communicating to the public, the police officers themselves are at home with their families watching the same television coverage of the good job done by their fellow cops.

One of my early press conferences was with Commissioner Bratton in East Harlem to honor police officers who went into a fire to save someone. Half an hour later I got a call from Howard Safir, who was then the Fire Commissioner, complaining that police officers shouldn't be running into fires—they didn't have the right equipment. When Howard became Police Commissioner, we had several ceremonies congratulating police officers for doing the very same thing. I didn't let these occasions go by without comment.

I'm fond of Mafia movies and television shows like *The Godfather* and *The Sopranos*, but having listened to thousands of hours of actual gangsters I believe that the strong leadership often depicted is entirely fictional.

I never got a complete enough picture of John Gotti to judge his effectiveness as a leader in the perverse area he chose for his life's work. But there's no question that Gotti, although even more violent than most mobsters, understood some of the principles of leadership. Once, as I was driving the writer Gail Sheehy through Little Italy, we got caught up in a traffic jam on Mulberry Street, and I noticed Gotti sitting outside at a little café. The table was not up against the building but out by the curb. He was sitting there with two of his associates. He saw me and gave his famous confident smile and made the "shame on you" sign with his forefingers, to say, "You're spying on me." I waved to him and asked Gail if she realized what was going on. A day or so before, someone had shot at Gotti near his other social club. Now he had positioned himself in broad daylight to show everybody that he wasn't afraid. It reminded me of a scene in *MacArthur*, in which Gregory Peck, playing the general, makes his long-awaited return to the Philippines and is driven out to the front lines. One of his aides says, "Does he really think he can't get hurt?" Another guy replies, "Damn it, of course he does."

MacArthur, in the pursuit of good, and Gotti, the follower of evil, were making the same statement: I'm not afraid, so you shouldn't be. That's also the reason I would go to scenes of fires and building collapses. I knew that it would motivate the people who worked for the city. It would say, "Hey, I understand what you're going through. And if you have to be here, so can I."

6

Reflect, Then Decide

Making the right choices is the most important part of leadership. Every other element—from developing and communicating ideas to surrounding oneself with great people—relies on making good decisions.

One of the trickiest elements of decision-making is working out not what, but when. Regardless of how much time exists before a decision must be made, I never make up my mind until I have to.

Faced with any important decision, I always envision how each alternative will play out before I make it. During this process, I'm not afraid to change my mind a few times. Many are tempted to decide an issue simply to end the discomfort of indecision. However, the longer you have to make a decision, the more mature and well-reasoned that decision should be.

As explained in Chapter 2, I used the morning meeting as a way to drive decisions. Because I forced my top staff to see me every day, decisions couldn't be avoided. Some mayors tended to hide in the mayor's office, with a chief of staff or first deputy mayor shielding them. You'd have to talk to that person before the mayor, and the stand-in would know what issues the mayor didn't want to face.

The same is true in many large corporations. Instead of rolling up his sleeves and saying, "Okay, I'm here to make a decision," some CEOs hide behind a phalanx of vice presidents who protect them against the risk of making a bad decision. Procrastination becomes a state of mind, and filters through the entire organization. But a readiness to make decisions has a positive effect. Without my even asking most of them to do so, my deputy mayors and commissioners implemented their own versions of my morning meeting, and so established their own willingness to hear problems, make decisions, and risk suggesting unpopular proposals.

A chief executive is often called upon to communicate directly to the public. Although it's best if that's handled by the leader himself, a CEO in the private sector who does not communicate well can get away with hiring someone to do it for him. In government, however, the chief executive is the public face, whether he likes it or not. As mayor, I was sometimes criticized for running too much of a one-man show. Actually, the opposite was true. My administration was structured around committees. It was extremely collegial—which is not to say we had no battles. But I always considered everybody's opinion before I made up my mind, and doing so actually sped the implementation of programs.

Here's an example. New York City's parks were a major focus of my administration. Nearly all my principal concerns—quality of life, economic redevelopment, child protection, even crime reduction— were enhanced by well-tended, safe, beautiful parks. During the eight years of my administration, New York City gained 2,038 acres of new parkland (by way of comparison, 372 acres were acquired during the four-year administration of my predecessor, and only 1,744 acres during the twelve years of the Koch administration). When I was sworn in, 69 percent of the parks were graded acceptably clean. When I left, the figure was 91 percent. We created dozens of parks in all five boroughs, including the Hudson River Park from Battery Park to 59th Street in Manhattan, the Brooklyn Bridge Park, which will eventually extend 1.3 miles along the East River waterfront, and the seven-mile Bronx River Greenway.

In 2001, I announced the renovation and renaming of the park on the Manhattan side of the East River to honor former New York City Mayor John Lindsay, who died in December 2000. The park needed some repairs because the retaining wall along the river was beginning to crumble. There were different views on how to accomplish this, so we met to sort it out.

The engineers issued a report saying we should close the park immediately. My Parks Commissioner, Henry Stern, said the engineers were exaggerating and that we could easily keep the park open for five to ten years before the wall began to sag. He felt that people who wanted to enjoy the park should at least have until the end of the summer, if not longer.

In many organizations a decision would have been deferred. That's the way it works when the model is designed to protect the chief executive. Other top executives will do anything to avoid a fight—they're reluctant to allow their staff to argue with them, or each other. The reluctant CEO would have asked everyone to write a memo, then they'd conduct more studies. By that time, action would happen by inaction—either people would be using the park in a dangerous way or it would have been shut down and no work would have been started.

That particular meeting was fairly contentious; but forcing everybody to meet got the cards on the table. And, once I felt enough information had been presented and all sides had been heard, I made a decision. That morning I decided that we'd shut the park and get the work started immediately, which would mean the repairs would take place during the winter months and be completed in time for people to use the park the following summer.

Decision-making would be easy if it were always a choice between good and evil or right and wrong. In the real world, leaders have to make decisions that are multidimensional, usually between two or more imperfect remedies, on criteria that encompass long-range goals and plausibility. In 1999, the contest for the Republican presidential nomination was gathering steam. Two men I knew and admire, both highly qualified to lead the country, were vying for the nomination. I had to make a choice.

John McCain has been a good friend for years. Because of what he endured as a prisoner of war for five and a half years in Hanoi, and all he has accomplished as a senator and man, he is a hero to me. The experience he went through can have one of two results—it can either crack you, or make you into a great man. In John's case, it was emphatically the latter. As I got to know him, I saw what a genuine person he was. In the months leading up to the campaign, we talked about his running for president.

I didn't know Governor George W. Bush as well. So I went to visit him in Austin to get to know him better and was impressed. By the summer of 1999 I concluded that he had a much better chance of beating Al Gore. For one, the Bush name unified the Republican Party right away. He went into the race with obvious support in two big, important states—Texas and Florida. I also felt close to his brother, Florida Governor Jeb Bush: I had campaigned for him, and he had helped me in the past.

The way Governor Bush ran his reelection campaign in Texas in 1998 showed broad appeal and made strong inroads among Hispanic voters. I thought he could be a crossover candidate unlike any other the GOP could produce. Further, Bush had command of what would be the key issue in the 2000 campaign—education. He devoted his attention to it as governor, and had done a good job. The art of being successful in presidential campaigns is figuring out the theme that will captivate people. Too often, candidates try to run the last campaign over again, but that's a losing battle. In 1992, Bill Clinton capitalized on repetition of his "It's the economy, stupid" theme. I thought the approach in 2000 should be "It's education, stupid," and Bush owned that issue.

Most important, I found Governor Bush to be a person of real substance during the time I spent with him. I knew the media would underestimate him, just as they had Ronald Reagan. This would be particularly true of the Eastern media, because Governor Bush doesn't speak in a way that suits their biases. The Eastern media mistakes pretense for substance and polish for smarts. Their habit of dismissing those who don't press those buttons usually works to such a candidate's advantage.

So although I was personally closer to John and perhaps would have supported him if he had had as good a chance of beating Vice President Gore, I told him that I was going to support the Governor—but that I would never say anything negative about him or participate in negative campaigning directed at him. Then I let George Bush know that he had my support. I told him I was a good friend of John McCain's, and explained why I had made my decision—that I thought he had a better chance of winning. I also told both men that if I could ever play any role in bringing them together, I would be happy to do so. In fact, Dick Cheney had not yet been mentioned as a vice-presidential candidate, and I thought Bush/McCain would be a terrific ticket.

Having made my decision, it was time to test it. As I began supporting Bush, some strain developed in my relationship with John. Whenever we talked, he would make half-teasing, half-zinging comments about my not supporting him. Then something happened that repaired that damage but created strain with the Bush camp. As the New York primary approached, there was a movement to keep Mc-

Cain's name off the ballot. The state of New York has Byzantine rules about getting on its primary ballots—there hadn't been a contested Republican presidential primary in twenty-four years—and some in the state GOP sought to protect Bush by keeping John off the ballot. I didn't think that was fair, and some of Bush's supporters interpreted my saying so as evidence of hidden support for John. It wasn't. It was just a straight, honest opinion. Additionally, I was convinced that Bush would beat McCain in New York and that that would be a better way to win.

They finally relented and put McCain in the primary. Immediately after that, whoever was running Bush's campaign in New York started to criticize McCain for having voted against breast cancer research. That's a big issue in Nassau and Suffolk counties, because the disease appears to affect women on Long Island disproportionately. I was asked to join in the criticism, which would have stung because I was at the time dealing with cancer myself.

I refused. First, the reason he had voted in the way they were referring to was that it was against part of a big Christmas-tree bill with a bunch of other items in it, so this vote had more to do with John's usual stance against overloaded legislation. I also thought negative campaigning was unnecessary. Bush was going to beat John McCain in New York, and there was no need for him to come out of it with a black eye for attacking a guy who had become a darling to the media, as well as to the independent voter, the exact voter Bush was going to need. John called to thank me. "I think you should be supporting me instead of Bush," he told me, "but I really respect you for not joining in the negative campaigning." For a while some of the Bush people were suspicious of me and whispered that my support might not be as strong as they wanted.

Afterward, I worked hard for Bush, and I think in the end his people respected me for my decisions. I know John did. It was like walking a tightrope, but it was an honest tightrope. Governor Bush went on to win the primary in decisive fashion.

BATTLING CANCER

One of the toughest series of decisions I ever had to make occurred during several extraordinary weeks in the spring of 2000. Decision-making weaves together the threads of all the rules for being a leader, so I'm going to explain at some length the interconnected decisions I made during that time. As some were literally life-or-death matters, and others had time limits associated with them, this volatile period provides an ideal examination of how I make decisions.

On Wednesday, April 26, Dr. Alexander Kirschenbaum of Mt. Sinai Hospital called me and said the five words nobody wants to hear: "Your biopsy results are positive." For a second, that sounded all right: I tend to associate "positive" with good news. Then the weight of it hit me. I had prostate cancer.

Nineteen years earlier, my father had died of the disease, at 73. This form of cancer kills about 37,000 Americans a year, so regular blood screenings for prostate specific antigens (PSA) are recommended for any man over 45. Those at higher risk, such as African Americans or those with relatives who have had the disease, should seek annual tests after 40.

In my case, early detection came as the result of a general physical. I have a degenerating vertebra at the top of my spine that bothers me about every five years. It was acting up—I was campaigning hard and feeling tired. On Thursday, April 6, I went for a physical and was given a PSA test and a digital rectal exam while I was there. I had no symptoms, so it was not as though my doctor suspected anything. In fact, he said, "Before I examined you, I expected you to show some high blood pressure, since you're under a lot of tension. It's remarkable, but your blood pressure's fine, and your prostate feels normal. Everything looks great."

The next day I was driving to a fundraiser at the Binghamton Country Club, in western New York, about three hours west of the city. I got a call on my cell phone from the doctor, who said my PSA test was in the questionable zone—high, but not very, and most likely nothing to worry about. He was leaving on vacation for a week, and said that he would arrange for more detailed tests with a urologist when he returned.

Judith was in the car with me. At that point, she was working for Bristol-Myers Squibb, the pharmaceuticals corporation, and knew just about every doctor in New York. Quietly, I explained what I had been told. There were others in the car and I didn't want anyone to know. I said, "Judith, we'll be back late tonight, after midnight, and I want to see a doctor tomorrow." She reminded me that the next day would be a Saturday and I said, "That's okay. I want to get started right now dealing with this. I don't want to wait."

Judith phoned a good friend of hers, Burt Meyers, an expert in infectious disease at Mt. Sinai Hospital. I knew him, too and he ended up being an advisor after the attacks on the World Trade Center. I told Judith to ask Burt to recommend a urologist and said, "It's okay to tell him what this is about." The next morning I went to see Dr. Kirschenbaum and he put me on ten days of Cipro, the drug that was to become famous during the anthrax scare. I asked, "Alex, can't we do the biopsy right now and find out?" He said, "No, because a modest elevation like this is often caused by an infection. The Cipro will do away with any infection." PSA can be driven up by many things, even an irritation of the prostate gland, so an elevation doesn't necessarily indicate cancer. After ten days on Cipro, I went back for another PSA test. A lower reading would indicate that there was an infection and not possible prostate cancer.

I remember exactly where I was when Dr. Kirschenbaum called me back with the results. I had gone to an evening Mass with Judith and Tony Carbonetti for Holy Thursday at St. Vincent Ferrer Church on Lexington Avenue, then on to Gino's restaurant just down the street. As we were eating dinner, my cell phone rang. My PSA was still high.

Judith took over with Dr. Kirschenbaum on the phone, getting the information I needed. By this time she had already done a lot of research about prostate cancer on the Internet, about percentages and chances. I had begun thinking about my treatment options, in case it was cancer. I scheduled a biopsy for early in the morning on Tuesday, April 25, right after Easter. Judith had told me that parts of the cancer can sometimes be missed in a biopsy, so I asked them to take the maximum number of samples. When we arrived at Mt. Sinai, there was a reporter outside, who asked me what I was doing there. I have no idea if he just happened to be hanging out there or if someone tipped him off to my arrival.

On April 26, at four P.M., I was sitting in my office at City Hall when Dr. Kirschenbaum telephoned with the fateful five words. After explaining some of the issues, he asked whether I'd prefer to meet him in person. I certainly would have, but I was reluctant to go to his office because the press was already calling my office to ask why I'd gotten a biopsy. Dr. Kirschenbaum suggested meeting me at Gracie Mansion. At about six P.M., he came over and went through a description of the biopsy findings. He did a drawing of the prostate and showed me that the cancer was found in one area but not the other, reviewed my treatment options, then explained how I should pursue a decision.

My head was swimming, but there was no time to digest what I was being told. I had to cut our meeting short to greet the Consular Corps. I found myself making a speech and posing for a hundred photos with diplomats just outside the room in which I had learned that a deadly cancer, the same disease that had killed my father, had been found in me. I returned to talk to Dr. Kirschenbaum some more and he told me he needed to take some additional tests.

This was the most frightening part, because it would determine whether the cancer had spread beyond my prostate. The doctor told me, "From what I can see and feel, I'm virtually certain that it hasn't."

"What does 'virtually certain' mean?" I asked.

He said, "Well, let's say there's a one percent chance."

The minute I heard that, I thought, "How do I know I'm not the one percent?" On the day that you're told you have cancer, you don't feel like a lucky man. I asked him to schedule the tests for the very next day.

I couldn't spend too much time feeling sorry for myself. There had been the photographs to take, the Consular Corps speech to give, then a preview of a play that I had promised to attend. In a way, resolving to do those things minutes after learning I had cancer was the first "decision" I made. I wasn't going to let the disease take over.

At the time, I had been gearing up for months to run for the seat being vacated by Senator Daniel Patrick Moynihan. I had raised considerable funds and was looking forward to what was shaping up to be an exciting race against Hillary Clinton. At the same time, my personal life was entering what can be described with some understatement as an "interesting" phase.

Any prostate cancer patient faces one immediate decision regarding treatment. There are three basic options: surgery, radiation, and hormone therapy. Surgery, known as "radical prostatectomy," removes the entire prostate. Those who choose radiation face three additional options. They can blast the area with external-beam radiation, target the precise area of the tumor with proton radiation, or implant radioactive seeds. Some men also choose hormone treatments to slow the production of testosterone. This can be used as a stand-alone method or in conjunction with the other treatments.

Each method has its pros and cons, with various side effects and levels of effectiveness. Many factors must be considered, such as the size and aggressiveness of the tumor, and the age, lifestyle, and overall health of the patient. Many prostate cancer patients find the decision on treatment agonizing.

Contemplating a decision about dropping out of the race for the Senate was clouding my decision about how to deal with cancer. Without consciously realizing it, I was trying to evaluate my treatment options with one eye on the Senate race. I'd catch myself thinking, "Well, if I get the surgery and am out for six weeks, then I'll be back by September. I'll spend July and August recuperating, and I can't do any fundraising, and I'll miss this event and that debate."

I would start thinking about what would happen if I didn't recuperate in time. I was concerned that I couldn't campaign 18 hours a day. In a campaign, my basic style was to wear down my opponent, and I realized I would not be able to do that. And then, of course, all the projections about side effects were based on percentages. When dealing with the side effects, some people recuperate easily. Others take months, held back by urinary problems, fatigue, sometimes simply by the pain involved. Suppose I fell into that category?

Radiation treatment had odds and side effects of its own. These were likely to limit me. Even though I was leaning toward radiation over surgery, I started thinking, "Well, maybe I can stay on Lupron longer and delay whatever treatment I choose until after the election." The doctors were telling me I didn't need to take immediate action, but when I asked whether it was advisable to put treatment off for six months, they flat-out said I shouldn't.

There was a ridiculous amount of media speculation at the time, focusing on what treatment I'd choose and how it would affect my run for the Senate. There was a soap opera quality to the coverage, and it became disturbingly easy to forget that it was a man's life being discussed so cavalierly. I quickly stopped reading it. First of all, a great deal of the coverage was wrong. Reporters were talking about me to doctors I'd never even met. Second, the saturation coverage was becoming chaotic, because of the national interest in the Senate race. Reporters tried to follow me to Baltimore, where I was consulting with doctors at Johns Hopkins. Others tried to get my health reimbursement records to deduce which specialists I was seeing. People were calling hospitals all over the city to see whether I'd spoken to them. Television networks wanted to follow me to my treatments and asked if I'd be willing to have a camera come with me to my MRI and other extremely private moments—even a digital rectal examination.

Although I was accustomed to being in a fishbowl, the intensity of the scrutiny was really beginning to affect my judgment, and my ability to focus on the medical options.

I had a gnawing feeling that it was wrong to allow the Senate race, as important as I thought it was, to affect decisions about my health. I took advice on the topic from all sides—from people who desperately hoped to see me outpoll Hillary Clinton to those who cared only about my well-being. The advice that rang the strongest was from Ken Caruso, who remained a close friend after having served as an assistant when I was U.S. Attorney. Often, when I seek multiple points of view, one person's take comes to represent the position that I end up selecting. In this case, it was Ken who crystallized my thinking.

He had been away in England, so he wasn't involved in the daily soul-searching that I was doing. He came to visit me at City Hall on May 18 and didn't hesitate to set out his opinion. "I'm just going to give you a perspective from somebody who's been reading about this in the newspapers from far away," he said. "I don't care if you're a senator or a mayor or anything else. You can't do anything unless you live, and are healthy. You're my friend. Put your health first." I decided to make my health my main concern, and to do so with a clear head I couldn't run for the Senate.

As soon as I agreed with that priority, other decisions fell into place. My first decision was that I would include hormones in my treatment.

Just making this decision provided a great degree of psychological peace. Secure in that knowledge, I could turn my attention to the other decisions. I had already begun taking a pill called Casodex, which began the process of reducing the testosterone in my body by shutting down the valve that led to the prostate. This served as a precursor to my first Lupron shot, since it ensured that the prostate wouldn't be flooded with the Lupron. The monthly injection of Lupron shrinks the prostate by shutting down the production of testosterone, the principal male hormone. That's valuable because when you're first diagnosed, you think the cancer is taking over your entire body. Knowing that the growth has been stopped allows the patient to make decisions about future treatment with a clearer mind—you don't feel as if the cancer cells are subdividing and attacking every second that you spend considering other treatment options. (Lupron alone is not a viable treatment for most prostate cancer patients. The majority of researchers view it as a temporary cure, so except for much older men it is generally not used as a single treatment.)

I was leaning toward radiation, but was still considering surgery—I'd say it was 60/40. But because I prefer not to make decisions until I have to, I decided that I would take the Lupron so that I didn't have to rush to judgment. Since radiation takes a few months to prepare for anyway, taking the Lupron would be that preparation for me, if I chose that option. And if I wanted to go into reverse and have surgery in July or August, the Lupron wouldn't be necessary, but wouldn't hurt.

On the morning of Friday, May 19, without telling anyone except Judith, I went to get the Lupron injection—a deep shot into the muscle of the backside. Later that day, following the literal and figurative shot in the ass, I announced that I was not going to run for the Senate.

Once I was on the Lupron, it took a while to be comfortable choosing my exact course of treatment. But now, with the white light of the Senate race no longer blinding me, I could make the decision more privately—not totally so, but with a modicum of solitude. During the course of the injections, my prostate was examined several times to determine if the Lupron was continuing to reduce the size of it. Once it had been shrunk as much as it could—which took three months—it was time for the next phase.

To clear my head during the period before I'd be ready for radiation, I took a month off from my immersion in the study of prostate cancer treatments. I wouldn't say I emerged "rejuvenated," but I was as refreshed as a pre-cancer-treatment, Lupron-taking mayor of a major city can be. Judith and I went back to several of the doctors and reinterviewed them. We discussed surgery and the various radiation options—internal seeds, external proton blasts, some combination of both. I spoke to Dr. John Blasko, who along with Dr. Haakon Ragde had developed the whole non-surgical transperineal seed implantation treatment in Seattle. I met Christine Jacobs, the CEO of Theragenics Corporation, which manufactures the seeds. She in turn put me in contact with specialists all over the country. When I rang Dr. Kirschenbaum after speaking to all these doctors, he said, "Tell me everyone you saw and I'll tell you which course of treatment each doctor advised." I mentioned a dozen names and, sure enough, he nailed every single physician's recommendation. Having considered all the options, I decided on using both seeds and external radiation, because I wanted to make sure I did everything I could to kill whatever cancer cells lingered there.

Ultimately, that option suited me better than surgery, which, while it removes the cancer from the prostate, doesn't guarantee that other cells may not be lurking just outside the treated area. There was a risk that I would have had to return for radiation later, and they couldn't have given me as much of that—once the prostate is missing, the amount of radiation has to be reduced. So I opted for putting the seeds inside the prostate, to provide the maximum likelihood that the cancer was killed.

I selected Dr. Richard Stock at Mt. Sinai to do the implantation. That choice illustrates an interesting point about management. Dr. Stock was younger than most of the other doctors I'd seen, but I chose him because I find that the generation that succeeds the originators of an idea will often take it to a new level, to make its mark. In this case, the originators of seed implantation would do a scan of the prostate and determine where to place the seeds before the surgery. The next generation, however, was looking to plant the seeds not entirely from a previously made scan but in real time, reacting to what they found when they went into the prostate. It reminded me of how each of my Police Commissioners improved on the innovations created by his predecessor.

I decided that after the implantation I'd supplement the seeds with twenty-five external radiation treatments—five a week, for five weeks—both to continue to kill the cancer cells inside the prostate and to provide a perimeter of a centimeter or two beyond where the cancer was found.

Early on the morning of September 15, 2000, I arrived at Mt. Sinai Hospital for surgery. In the operating room were Dr. Stock, Dr. Kirschenbaum, and a host of assistants and nurses. I shook hands with everyone. Considering the gravity of the situation, it felt surreally like a campaign. Next, I was given a preoperative dose of sedative and a spinal anesthesia. With all these young people in the room, I was slightly self-conscious to be exposed like that. As the sedative started to take effect, I lay down, and as I entered a half-sleep saw a huge television being wheeled in. There had been so much speculation surrounding my treatment that it had even been suggested that I allow the procedure to be broadcast, a notion I of course rejected. Seeing that television, I thought, "Oh no, I'm going to be in the altogether on New York 1—someone sold me out!" Just as I was finally drifting off, I recalled that the television screen was used to do the surgery. Relieved, I faded into oblivion. Two hours later, Dr. Stock woke me to tell me the operation had gone perfectly.

I've made business, professional, and political decisions this way all my life. It was similar to deciding how to sell the city's OTB operation, or how to run the coal company I was assigned to manage when I was in private law practice. In each case, I tried to construct the freedom and the time to make the most informed decision possible.

At the same time, I was ready to act on much less notice, had that been necessary. If the doctor had told me on that fateful Wednesday that I had cancer that was spreading rapidly and recommended that I have surgery the next day, then that's what I would have done. I wouldn't have delayed. But this was a different kind of decision. Every doctor assured me, and I knew from my own reading, that mine was a slow-moving cancer. Even had I done nothing, I'd have had some time to decide without worsening my prognosis.

Being mayor actually helped me get through these months, because I had responsibilities—still had people who depended on me. It also got me out of my own head and kept me from wallowing. I believe strongly that you never should be dishonest with yourself. You face your fear. The other benefit about my being open about having cancer was that the support I received was a source of great strength. Many people diagnosed with cancer feel that they have to hide it—that it will feel less real if no one knows about it, or that their employer will hold it against them, or that their friends will pity them. In fact, the fear gets worse by being hidden. If you can say, "I'm afraid to give that speech," "I'm afraid to make that decision," "I'm afraid to deal with cancer," you can start dealing with it.

In my case, I relied on people close to me. Judith Nathan and Denny Young were enormously helpful. Beth Petrone, Kate Anson, Sunny Mindel, Tony Carbonetti, and Manny Papir (Deputy Chief of Staff) stood by me, at work and personally. The police officers on my security detail also helped—they're the ones who went with me at seven A.M. for my radiation. And I was grateful for the kind words from thousands of people who called or wrote me. In fact, I was in the car on 86th Street, turning onto East End Avenue, when Hillary Clinton called to offer sympathy. Many people who contacted me had dealt with prostate cancer and had advice—including several well-known figures who had never publicly disclosed having had the disease.

No matter how open one is about a life-threatening illness, ultimately you face it alone. People can help you deal with the symptoms, sympathize with the effects of the treatment, but no matter how much support you have, there are still nights when you suddenly wake up, frightened. The way I face fear is by feeling it, acknowledging I'm feeling it, and then assessing my options. Prostate cancer is a frightening disease. But at least there are options for dealing with it.

Although I was honest about what I was going through, there were many private details that I kept to myself. One's sense of privacy and sensitivity to how others will receive the news dictate how much you should share. Some of my staff must have known what was happening, but I didn't talk about it. However, I do recall one time when I was on my way to a campaign event for New York State Senator Guy J. Velella up in the Bronx. The press was attacking him for being under investigation by the Manhattan District Attorney, and he needed me to stand by him. I was feeling sick throughout that day, and as soon as I got in the van I knew I shouldn't have. About three miles later, we pulled over so I could jump out of the car and I got sick all over the street. I was very embarrassed. But I washed up as best as I could and went on to the event. We rode around in a truck, and as I waved to the crowd I was sure I was going to faint. But having to perform—being needed—got me through. Later on, I thought of my fight with cancer as basic training for September 11.

I tried to keep a stiff upper lip, but there were other times during which the aftereffects were difficult. Oddly enough, there was so little pain during the first two weeks that I began to wonder if perhaps the seeds weren't powerful enough. I knew from my research that there was supposed to be a burning sensation, but I barely felt anything. I called Dr. Stock to let him know, and he told me to give it a few more days. He was right.

On October 9, 2000, I marched in the Columbus Day parade with Senator McCain, and Representative Rick Lazio, who had taken my place in the Senate race. Stopping at a diner, I ducked into the men's room and was in such pain I could barely stand. I was afraid I would not be able to march in the parade. I hadn't taken a painkiller, but I knew I'd never last through the parade without something. I had been prescribed Vicodin. So I got it out of my bag, split the tablet in two, and swallowed half a Vicodin. Five minutes later, the pain was gone, and I was able to march.

Afterward, I went with John McCain and his staff to Little Italy for lunch. I drank a half bottle of wine, forgetting that I'd had the Vicodin, and soon enough we were singing away. What you learn from John McCain—and I'm sure this comes from his confronting death—is that you have to enjoy life while you can. I was determined to do the same.

I thought about my heroes and how they had handled illness or disability, at least when they were in public. When I did actually sit down and unburden myself about the fear and the worry, I turned to Judith. She was the one who took care of me the most. The first Yankees game Judith and I attended together was July 18, 1999. You probably already guessed she was a Yankee fan before we met, and the fact that David Cone pitched a perfect game was a harbinger of things to come. When Montreal shortstop Orlando Cabrera made the 27th out, I went totally nuts. At the ballpark, I happen to eat peanuts with the shells still on. It says a lot about Judith that she stuck with me after observing this controversial preference. With the cancer diagnosis less than a year later, I realized just how much everyone needs a partner to get through something like this. I don't know how I would have done it without her.

In addition to her compassion, Judith understands medicine. She got on the Internet, called her physician contacts for recommendations and advice, and analyzed the different medications. She accompanied me to virtually every doctor's appointment, and would go through the anatomical drawings and share her perspective. She would ask questions I wouldn't have thought of, and sometimes afterward I'd have her call the doctor because she'd understand the issues much better than I could. She accumulated a wad of notes about an inch thick, and would be my sounding board for all we learned. She helped figure out the changes in my diet (repeat after me: cooked tomatoes = lycopene, an antioxidant that researchers think may help prevent prostate and other cancers), and the vitamin and supplement regimen that I continue to take to prevent a return of the cancer.

All this helped tremendously. It also underlines the way I make my decisions—taking as much time as I can to consider as many angles as possible. A decisive leader can sometimes appear as though he never questions what his next move should be. Faced with tough decisions, I sometimes endure excruciating periods of doubt and soul-searching and, as I said, I always try to play out the results of each alternative. However, once I make the decision I move forward. Something clicks, and all my energies are applied to ensuring the decision works rather than fretting over whether it was the right one.

Today I derive a great deal of satisfaction in helping others with cancer, particularly with prostate cancer. I keep up on the research, and find it gratifying to give someone substantive information on how best to prevent, cure, or reverse the course of the disease. I can advise on a process of decision-making that takes as many of the factors into account as possible—odds of survival, severity of side effects, the probable consequences for one's family.

It helps to hold on to your sense of humor. Prostate cancer is specifically a man's disease. Because of the part of the anatomy it afflicts, and even the nature of the testing to see if one's got it, there's a natural tendency to make jokes. There's a blood test, which looks for an abnormally high number of prostate specific antigens, and there's a digital rectal exam, which is exactly what it sounds like. On the day I rang the opening bell at the New York Stock Exchange to launch a national prostate cancer awareness campaign, my Chief of Staff, Tony Carbonetti, let me know what he thought of the second testing method: "There's a tattoo on my rear end that says, 'Exit Only.'"

No matter what, people are frightened when they learn they have cancer. It's a daunting disease, and it's okay to be afraid—to wonder, "Why me?" But what's not okay is to do what so many men do and avoid being examined because they don't want to know.

Cancer is a particularly insidious disease. Because the cells in your own body are turning against you, it feels like a betrayal from within. Living in the world involves a certain degree of unavoidable risk. Anyone can be run over by a car or struck by lightning. But if you talk to enough cancer patients—and that's one of the best things someone diagnosed with cancer can do—you'll see that the temptation to avoid confronting it is nearly overwhelming. As with any big decision, especially one of life and death, you have to resist that temptation.

The feeling of betrayal that accompanies cancer expresses itself in a variety of ways. Every little ache and pain conjures a worst-case scenario. On the Sunday afternoon after the biopsy, I was with my son, Andrew, at Harbor Links Golf Course. I was playing particularly well (and that is rare) and we had reached about the fourth or fifth hole when I started to feel a pain in my back. I became convinced that the cancer had spread. Then I felt some pain in my fingers, and was sure that it was the cancer again. I started to wonder if I was going a little crazy. That's one of the reasons it's so important to keep in touch with others going through the same thing.

Five days after I was diagnosed, Howard Safir, my friend of twenty years, received the same news: prostate cancer. We spent a lot of time discussing our different options. I talked to his doctors, he talked to mine, and we compared side effects. Howard told me that shortly after his diagnosis, his toe started to hurt. After staying up all night from both the pain and the worry that the cancer was spreading, he went for an examination first thing the next morning. His doctor laughed, and told him, "Howard, if the cancer had spread to your toe, you wouldn't be standing there." It turned out to be nothing, and a day later the pain disappeared.

Relying on the companionship of others who have experienced it is critical as you put your life into perspective. I remember one of my weekly police meetings. I always sat in one of the red armchairs and Howard sat in the chair to my left. I'm looking at him and he's looking at me and we're both sweating. I realized we were having hot flashes together, and nobody else knew it. About two to three weeks after you begin the Lupron treatments, you experience these two- to four-minute sweating spells. Although the doctor tells you to expect them, the first few hot flashes really surprise you. Then, after a while, it's annoying, but you get used to it.

For many reasons, my life was very different following my battle.

Even more than any of the obvious changes, it left me with the philosophical perspective that comes from considering one's mortality. I honed my ability to compartmentalize the challenges I faced: the cancer diagnosis, the Senate race, the dissolution of my marriage, and—P.S.—I was also mayor of a vast and complicated city.

Just when I'd find myself sinking into self-pity, somebody would rush into the office to tell me a police officer or a firefighter had been injured in a building collapse or other life-threatening event. This would not only give me instant perspective, but focused me on whatever emergency had occurred. I canceled very few functions and appearances, and kept a work schedule every day, even if it needed to be abbreviated for the nap or two I had to take.

BE READY TO PULL THE TRIGGER WHEN TIME IS SHORT

Leaders must find a balance between speed and deliberation. One facet of making decisions involves knowing how to act when there's not much time to deliberate. In 1986, I was to try the Parking Violations Bureau case, one of the most important municipal corruption trials in the history of New York City. On my first day in court, the defense made a motion to change venue out of New York City, ostensibly because the defendants—politicians and bureaucrats—could not get a fair hearing before local jurors. They proposed several locations, such as Buffalo and Hartford. My assistants wanted to discuss among ourselves the merits of all the possible venues. I didn't. Even as they started conferring, I stood up and told the judge, "Your Honor, I agree. Let's change venue. It will remove any question of taint in the case."

My assistants were surprised, but my instinct told me that New York City—especially Manhattan, where this case was to be tried—was probably the toughest place to win a conviction. It's the greatest city in the world, but with eight million people it also has more screwballs than anywhere else. There's also a natural sympathy among jurors, however misguided, toward men whose names they've known for years. One has to remember that even notorious Gambino crime family boss John Gotti was acquitted twice by New York City juries.

The case was eventually tried in New Haven, Connecticut, with a jury from Hartford. As soon as the defense made their motions I realized why they were so eager to switch venues. Their counsel's strategy was dominated by the political sensibilities of the defendants, who took polls about everything. They determined the percentage of New Yorkers who had heard about the case, and the percentage who had already made up their minds. They had even taken polls about me, measuring my standing among New Yorkers.

What they failed to realize was that all that was needed to find an acceptable jury was that 10 or 20 percent of eligible jurors who did not know about the case and had not formed a conclusion. In New York City, that percentage is a lot of people, and there's a good chance that one of those screwballs would be selected. If you're the defense, all you need for a hung jury is one true contrarian—and you're likelier to find him (or her) in New York than in New Haven.

I realized that the defendants were approaching the case as though it were a political campaign. It was a strategic error. A trial lawyer picking a jury seldom identifies that one person who has gone through life not being able to agree with anybody. John Gross, who had been my colleague in the U.S. Attorney's office and my law partner at Anderson Kill, once tried a police corruption case where one juror would literally run to the men's room every time they went to deliberate, and refuse to come out. The judge had no option but to declare a hung jury. A second jury convicted on all counts after reasonable deliberation.

When I heard the alternate cities proposed by the defense, instinct told me each would be safer for us than New York. Agreeing to the defense motion before they had a chance to retract the offer helped us win a conviction.

The need for quick decisions, of course, is strongest in times of crisis. People are afraid and uncertain, and need to feel that someone is in charge. While the city was still coping with the aftermath of the attacks, anthrax spores were mailed to Tom Brokaw and other prominent media and political figures. The last thing New York needed was another reason to panic. Immediately, I made the decision that mail-openers were not going to be seen on television in the hazmat moon suits that were becoming increasingly common. That would have exaggerated the response. That's also why I went to the scenes of reported anthrax.

Even though leaders should take as much time as available to make decisions, the process of making the decision should begin immediately. If a decision is due in five days, the time to start researching and considering the matter is now, not four days on.

I was 26 when I became an assistant U.S. Attorney. I had a mustache—it was 1970. My then boss, Mike Seymour, would implore his AUSAs to "just do it." (This was many years before Nike used such advice as a slogan.) He always erred on the side of getting things done, and told us that if we pursued a course that always preferred action to hesitation we would be better lawyers, better people, and better everything else.

That's the precept I used as mayor. When something came up, we'd begin addressing it quickly, even as we debated and argued the best solution. I think that approach was one of the factors that gave the city a degree of confidence in its leadership. Sometimes, people just want to see issues being addressed, even if they don't always agree with the result. That's one of the reasons I held daily press conferences. Some told me that this allowed too many opportunities for controversy or for detractors, but I felt that when issues arose in the city it was vital to show that someone was at the helm.

USE CREATIVE TENSION

The fur could fly at some of the meetings of my top staff. I find debates enormously helpful, and would create them specifically so that I could hear more views on just about everything. I always make a better decision if I hear three or four different views. If those advocating those viewpoints do so forcefully and with passion, all the better.

You cannot generate heartfelt debate unless the participants believe that the outcome is not predetermined. If your staff knows that you'll defer to the higher-ranking person's opinion or choose the idea pitched by whoever's known you longer, they'll never develop their case to the degree you require.

City Hall Park, near the southern tip of Manhattan, dates back to the late 1600s and provides a magnificent nine acres of green space amid the world's most densely packed real estate. Unfortunately, the park began to feel the effects of neglect in the early twentieth century, as plans to repair it hit one snag after another. It even lost its centerpiece fountain, which in 1920 was shipped to Crotona Park in the Bronx. In my 1998 State of the City speech, I promised to restore the park to its former glory.

This involved a major renovation of more than $10 milllion. Not surprisingly, different members of my administration had different ideas for it. The Parks Department answered to Deputy Mayor Rudy Washington, and wanted to do it one way, while the Economic Development Corporation and others wanted to do it another. Everyone started taking sides, and it soon became clear that many opposed Rudy's plan. Further, they all tried the old trick of trying to get me alone to endorse one version or the other. I wasn't having it. I let them fight it out, and eventually decided that Rudy's was the way to go. People were upset, and I'd say the majority of my administration was surprised at what I chose. But in 1999 we reopened the park and it was better than ever. We even brought back the fountain.

One might suppose that the attacks on the World Trade Center would turn a staff of opinionated, habitual arguers into meek yesmen. Not so. By late September 2001, our morning meetings, taking place on Pier 92 (in a tiny room at a table covered with plates of bacon and sausage that, up till then, my staff wouldn't bring to a meeting in deference to my cancer-recovery diet), began to resemble the spirited intellectual street fights of the previous seven and a half years.

One of a hundred examples that came up regarded the flow of traffic in Lower Manhattan. To accommodate the heavy equipment working at Ground Zero and the tons of debris going out, the Holland Tunnel was entirely closed to regular traffic. The extra security at the other entrances to Manhattan, the roads destroyed and closed near the disaster site, and the destruction of the PATH train to the World Trade Center all combined to make traffic a nightmare. On September 26, we had it out.

The idea of forbidding cars with only one occupant from six A.M. to noon had been championed by Iris Weinshall, the Commissioner of Transportation. Joe Lhota seconded: "We have to do this. Traffic is snarled so bad that even the emergency vehicles are having a tough time."

Deputy Mayor Tony Coles disagreed: "I'm skeptical of HOV [high-occupancy vehicle] rules. There are other ways to discourage traffic, such as promoting the trains and subways."

Larry Levy chimed in, "Forbidding any cars says, 'You can't come.'"

Bernie Kerik added, "The restrictions send a mixed message. We're telling everybody they gotta come back to the city, get back to normalcy. Then, on the other hand, don't come back unless you have more than one person in the car."

Lhota fired back, "You've got to live in an outer borough to understand this. Your thinking is upside down here. Traffic's backed up to Suffolk County. The state troopers are literally getting under the cars with mirrors—it's taking thirty seconds per car. Iris gave me the exact number today. Between six A.M. and noon, sixty-five percent of the cars have one driver."

John Dyson, who had been a deputy mayor and was at this point looking at the city's economy in the wake of the attacks, sided with those opposing the restrictions: "Joe, you're going to strangle the economy of the city if you do restrictions."

Lhota retorted, "But subway use is down. We're actually seeing an *increase* in the number of cars."

Dyson: "Think about *why*. People remember Tokyo and sarin gas in the subways. You have to deal with what's going on in people's heads."

Coles: "Barring cars is really regressive. We should do incentives and other things, but it sends the wrong signal if we prevent anyone from entering."

I weighed in for the first time: "We've done such good work getting out the get-back-to-normal message over the last two weeks that we've almost fooled ourselves into not remembering that we *are* in an emergency. The Attorney General said we're in 'clear and present danger.' That's not code, that's plain as day. There's going to be anticipation as the President prepares to fight in Afghanistan. And then there's going to come a time when we actually strike. Both of those are points at which there could easily be attacks directed at the bridges and tunnels. That would be easier to handle with fewer cars."

Joe Rose, the city's chairman of the Planning Commission, added, "There are other mechanisms available, like congestion pricing" [raising the cost of entering during "peak" hours and discounting other times].

Lhota: "There are alternative ways into the city, too. Let's get the ferry system going better, and we might actually make the waterways an unintended third-party beneficiary."

I wrapped it up. "There's no perfect solution. If you don't do the restrictions, it's a traffic disaster and no one wants to come into the city. If you do the restrictions, you discourage certain people from coming, and you may still have a traffic disaster. Let's reassess this after we get the morning report from Iris. But for now, I'm in favor of trying her idea out for a week and seeing how it works. I don't think it's so awful to remind people we're in an emergency—we are."

The restrictions turned out to be successful in reducing traffic, while not proving overly onerous to all but a few commuters. People carpooled and made better use of public transport. As Joe Lhota had suggested, the ferry system did indeed pick up a lot of the slack and perhaps even reached the critical mass it needed to become a permanent option. As the crisis abated, so did the hours of restriction.

Sometimes the best way to stimulate the debate you need to make an informed decision is to take a step back. During the Cuban Missile Crisis, President Kennedy received some unconventional advice from his brother: leave the room. Bobby Kennedy advised the President that his aides had begun telling him what they thought he wanted to hear. Matters became so tense that each member of Kennedy's staff was afraid to back a decision for or against nuclear war in his presence. No one wanted to be accused of wrongly advocating getting tough or making concessions, of being too strong or too weak. President Kennedy left the room.

I did the same thing at times. During the campaigns, for example, I realized that we often got more out of the morning meetings when I wasn't there. Those present were more willing to say that the candidate—me—had screwed up the previous night, that I'd looked stupid on television or had handled a question badly. So I stayed away, and had Peter Powers or David Garth summarize the results for me.

HEAR PEOPLE OUT

Once you've made a decision, you must stick to it; but up until that point make it clear that you'll entertain changing your mind even on subjects that seem cut and dried.

When I became mayor, the current and next-year budget gaps made me determined to reduce city spending, for the first time since 1981, but I didn't want to repeat the mistakes made during the infamous fiscal crisis of the 1970s. So two areas were immediately off the table for spending cuts. I refused to make major reductions to the capital construction budget. When the city had made that error in the past, it had cost many times more to repair the basic infrastructure once it broke down than it would have had the city kept on top of the roads and bridges all along. The second area was the Police Department. The city was being destroyed by crime. Not only was I unwilling to cut the budget of the NYPD, I knew I would be adding to it.

In addition to those two areas, the percentage of the city's budget devoted to the public schools was established by a state law that required the city to give the school system a fixed percentage of the budget each year. I might be able to spend what I wanted overall, but I couldn't alter the portion that went to the schools.

Between capital spending, the schools, and the police, a substantial portion of the overall budget, then about $32 billion, was already committed. So I had to be relentless in cutting expenditures everywhere else. Each agency described the horrors that would occur if their budget forfeited a single penny, but the law stated that the budget had to be balanced, at the risk of the city's finances being taken over by the state.

On our first pass, we cut significantly from almost every one, including the Division of AIDS Services. Frankly, I didn't understand exactly what that agency did, and DAS was on the list that had been prepared by the Office of Management and Budget detailing exactly what it would take to balance the budget. The cuts would first be exposed in February's proposed budget, then I would invite the commissioners and deputy mayors in to argue their case. I'd make the final decision by the time we published the executive budget in May.

In fighting the recommendation to cut the AIDS funding, Deputy Mayor Fran Reiter, who had responsibility for that agency, made a passionate appeal, and constructed her argument with a three-pronged approach. First, she explained exactly what DAS did—how the department assisted people in finding aid from other sources, such as private charities. Second, DAS had the ability to reduce the amount and degree of incapacitation of New Yorkers suffering from HIV and

AIDS, so that some people would be able to become self-sufficient, which would also relieve the cost burden on the city. Finally, much of what DAS did was to find reimbursement from the federal government, and to some extent the state government, as well as private sources. If we left 'the DAS budget intact, it would not immediately help the budget, but the long-term impact would be substantial, from both a humanitarian and fiscal point of view.

Fran made an effective, logical argument, exactly as a good lawyer makes when presenting the reasons a judge should decide her way. By exercising the principle to Hear People Out, I'd won a new perspective on why DAS should have retained its funding. But this was also going to be a case of Decide through Argument. A difference in philosophy had emerged regarding the appropriate role of government employees. Abe Lackman (the Budget Director) did not believe we should have people on the payroll trying to acquire private and public funds at the same time as the city was reducing its staffing levels. He recommended major cuts to DAS, which he saw as an unnecessary expense—claiming that private advocates could more effectively pressure the same private and public sources of AIDS funding.

Fran argued that Abe's position was fine in theory, but that nobody would perform as effectively as DAS. Ultimately, that would mean people would not get the level of services they needed, and at the same time the city would have fewer dollars flowing in from the federal government and elsewhere. I agreed with her, and it worked exactly as she said it would. I restored the funding, and the city ended up getting about $100 million in so-called Ryan White funding every year.

This decision also demonstrates why it's important to surround yourself with strong, independent people. If Fran hadn't been willing to take on the rest of the administration, the funding would not have been restored. She also had to confront my initial ideological response, which was closer to Abe's opinion that this was better left to private groups, at least in a city as financially strapped as New York in 1994.

I preferred our internal battles to stay that way—internal. Presenting a unified front to the public was critical. There would always be those who disagreed with a leader's decisions. Letting the public know exactly where each member of the administration stood on an issue, and who was feuding with whom, only made it easier for those who sought to exploit internal divisions for their own advantage.

Because I preferred our battles to take place behind the scenes, I would sometimes be criticized for hiring people who were reluctant to disagree with me. In addition to being a misinterpretation of my management style, that criticism was an insult to the people I hired. The fact that they didn't advertise every disagreement with me was interpreted as deferential. I call it loyalty—to me, and to the city.

There's an instructive end to the DAS budget story that provides an insight into what New York City is like. A big group came in to protest at our supposed cuts for AIDS services. By this point, Fran had won that battle—we'd reversed the cuts and actually increased DAS funding. Peter Powers saw the scheduled protest on the morning's list and told me, "I'll go out there and explain that we're actually increasing spending; maybe they'll even say something positive about you." With all the cuts, we were going through one demonstration after another—here was a chance to share some news about a program we were *not* cutting.

I told Peter that if he went out there he had better bring a copy of the executive budget—the protesters would never take his word for it. So he went outside and showed the leader of the protest the budget, pointing out the increase. And the guy says, "Thank you very much, but, well, we're here, we'll protest anyway." The group proceeded to protest for an hour or so, yelling, "More money! More money!" Afterward, the leader sought out Peter and thanked him.

The DAS story was one of many times in which I was persuaded to change my initial position. So it's an interesting paradox. A leader has to be strong enough to make his own decisions, and stick to them even when they're unpopular; but he also must be self-confident enough to solicit opinions and change his mind without worrying that he'll appear weak.

At the beginning of my first term, I decided it was critical to the city's revival to reduce the number of sex shops. They were retarding the growth of other businesses throughout the city, particularly in Times Square. Joe Rose, my Planning Commissioner, had conducted a report that detailed how much economic activity the shops were costing the city. We made maps of where they were sited throughout the city, and started looking for ways to limit them, confident that we could use the report to justify zoning restrictions. My impulse was to use Joe's report to eliminate all or nearly all of them. Looking at the maps and seeing just how many sex stores would have to be shut, Joe Rose and Paul Crotty told me the proposal went too far. If we tried to close every shop, a judge might shoot down our entire plan, leaving us back where we started.

Joe and Paul made the case for creating a zone in Midtown in which the shops could stay open, which would not only satisfy potential concerns about oppressive restriction but would eventually give us what we wanted anyway. Since the proposed zone reduced the area available to sex shops—basically limiting them to non-residential areas—the rents in the other areas of Midtown would increase. Eventually, rents would rise even within the zone, making it too expensive for the sex shops—the free market would achieve what zoning rules couldn't. I decided that Joe and Paul were right, and we allowed the buffer zone. In the years that followed, whenever the sex shops took us to court, time after time the judges would cite this little buffer zone that we created in Midtown Manhattan as proof that the rules were not overly restrictive.

Not all decisions have the same process behind them. Some are based on objective statistics. Others are pure intuition. For example, Fran Reiter designed her DAS presentation specifically to satisfy my need for empirical evidence. She had her facts and figures at the ready. Other decisions, however, can't be supported by that sort of presentation. There might be insufficient time, or the proposal might be so innovative that data and statistics simply didn't exist. A leader shouldn't require that the value of every idea has to be proven elsewhere before embracing it—that would leave innovation out of the equation.

Important, complicated decisions require both statistical analysis and intuition. Statistics can provide the necessary data, but unless you apply your own intuition, gathered from your own experience, you are just a computer spitting out formulas. Take the decisions I made regarding prostate cancer. I based them on statistics and analysis from the best research available; but then I applied an intuitive, subjective layer about which treatment was right for me, and made the decision on my own terms, in my own time.

7

Underpromise and Overdeliver

The 1998 New York Yankees had what may be the best year for any team in Major League Baseball history. In some ways, it was a strange year. They lost their first three games, their slugger Darryl Strawberry developed colon cancer, and there was a ferocious brawl in Baltimore. But by the time they finished sweeping the San Diego Padres to take the World Series, they had amassed an overall record of 125–50, the most wins ever.

What if Joe Torre had started the 1999 campaign by announcing that the Yankees would win even more games than in 1998? By that standard, the season would have been a disappointment, when in fact the 1999 group was in some ways even more impressive. In addition to sweeping the World Series yet again (this time against the Braves), the '99 Yanks lost only a single post-season game, going 11–1 in the playoffs and World Series. Despite a record of "only" 98–64 in the regular season, they played their best when it mattered most. They had to face more than their share of adversity—Joe Torre's prostate cancer, the deaths of three players' fathers (Paul O'Neill, Scott Brosius, and Luis Sojo), and Strawberry's continuing health and legal problems—so that year's prize was perhaps even sweeter because it was less expected.

A leader must manage not only results but expectations.

On Wall Street, the expectation game has become an art form. Companies offer "guidance" to analysts who predict each quarter's revenue and profit numbers. The aim is to dampen published expectations by a few pennies per share so that the company can announce the actual results and look like it had a blowout quarter. The problem is that the company can cry wolf only so often before the investors build those extra cents into the analyst predictions. A company that analysts expect to earn $1.50 will have investors looking for $1.60. If the number comes out at $1.55, the company will say it "beat the Street" by five cents, but investors will perceive it as having fallen a nickel shy.

That's why leaders ought to be as accurate as they can be about projections and, if they're going to err, make it on the side of under-promising.

On July 12, 2001, I gave my final presentation to the New York State Financial Control Board. I pegged revenues for Fiscal 2001 at $40,640,000,000. For my next four years of estimates, I used:

Fiscal Year 2002: $39,698,000,000
Fiscal Year 2003: $39,713,000,000
Fiscal Year 2004: $40,976,000,000
Fiscal Year 2005: $42,228,000,000

Did I really think New York City wouldn't match 2001's revenue until 2004? Certainly not. But it was my policy to underestimate anticipated revenues, because it forced those who worked for me to contain costs. By assuming low revenues, I could forcefully argue against unnecessary expenditures and maintain a frugal culture, even during flush times.

Too often, in government and in business, organizations base their projections on best-case scenarios. A city will borrow substantially after a particularly healthy year only to find, when revenues unexpectedly sink, that it needs to ramp up taxes simply to cover its debt. Or a business will hire new staff and plush up its headquarters, even when its strong recent past cannot be relied on to continue.

There were occasions when it might have been to my political benefit to assume much higher revenues. In fact, that would have been justifiable, given the growth of the economy in New York City, especially during my second term. The boom on Wall Street and soaring property values did indeed fatten the city's coffers; but I consistently chose not to sweeten projected revenues, even when it would have allowed me to score points by committing more dollars to special interest groups. New York City's comptroller was running for mayor during much of the last year of my term. From time to time he would make a big point about the city's debt being too high. Compare New York City's debt to other cities, though, and we were in a comparatively healthy condition. As a percentage of revenues, New York City's debt in July 2001 was 14.1 percent. In Chicago it was 19.3 percent; Houston, 18.9; Phoenix, 23.2; San Antonio, Dallas, Detroit, Honolulu, San Jose, Indianapolis, Jacksonville, all higher than New York's, with only Philadelphia and Los Angeles slightly lower (13.7 and 12.9, respectively). Nevertheless, the comptroller put out reports making dire predictions. That's not the way bond agencies saw the city's debt level, and they understand such figures better than anyone—they have to, since their clients have billions riding on their assessments. From 1993 to the date of my July report, we were upgraded by both Moody's and Standard & Poor's (Baa1 to A2 and BBB+ to A, respectively).

If I had wanted to disarm critics on the topic of city debt—even though I knew they were wrong—I could have issued higher revenue projections. That would have shrunk our debt payments when expressed as a percentage of revenue. I refused to do so, because raising revenue estimates would have whetted the city's appetite for spending.

Besides putting a brake on the budget, there is another reason for containing revenue projections. Contained expectations allow for the unexpected. Less than two months after I presented those "low-ball" numbers to the Financial Control Board, the city's economy was shaken by an unforeseeable calamity—the attacks on September 11. Optimistic budgeting would have left the city's finances much more vulnerable to the damage of the World Trade Center attacks. As it turned out, closing the budget gap created by the disaster was difficult but manageable.

By its nature, budgeting requires one to predict the future. Holding expectations in line with results can be tricky. In other areas it is much easier: don't announce an initiative until the results are already in. Try it out, refine it, get at least a preliminary set of results—*then* announce the plan. It's much like the production of a play. When possible, producers don't launch a new show directly on Broadway. They start it out in another city, where it'll attract less scrutiny, and tinker with it for a while before the stakes grow too high.

Sure, there are times in government or business when the announcement of an initiative is an end in itself. There might be PR value in the announcement, and it lets people know what you think your organization can do. It shows that your expectations are high and that you're committed enough to those expectations to say so publicly. Occasionally, in order to challenge myself and challenge the people working with me, I deliberately overpromised, or at least gave the impression that I was doing so. Perhaps this chapter could be as aptly called "Promise Strategically." But my general rule has been to avoid mentioning what I've done until I've actually accomplished something.

Sometimes the expectations of others are beyond anyone's ability to manage. In professional sports, a player who signs a big contract with a new team is expected to perform instant miracles. That phenomenon is perhaps strongest in New York, with so much media attention and highly demanding fans.

After falling a few outs short of their fourth consecutive championship in 2001, the Yankees had a busy off-season, including the signing of first baseman Jason Giambi to a seven-year contract worth $120 million. Another move—acquiring Mets third baseman Robin Ventura—attracted less attention. The team opened 2002 with a three-game series in Baltimore. The Yankees took two of three games, but Giambi struggled, while Ventura hit two home runs.

I went to the Yankees home opener in 2002. Giambi had another rough game, and though the Yankees won, the crowd got onto him toward the end, shouting "Tino," the name of the player he replaced. It was silly. Here we were, only four games into the season in a sport where failing at only two of every three attempts would be a stellar performance. Ventura, on the other hand, was greeted warmly.

This was entirely about exceeding and falling short of expectations. Although neither player had asked for those expectations—it wasn't as though either had promised to hit a certain number of homers—the fans had different goals in mind. By a third of the way through the season, Giambi had clubbed 15 homers (including two game winners), knocked in 41, and was hitting .315. He was being cheered wildly—for fulfilling expectations—as was Ventura, for exceeding them.

Sometimes there's a strategic advantage, beyond managing expectations, of delaying any announcement of what you're up to. Just as a poker player tries to disguise his hand until he's called, often it's to a leader's benefit not to let others know what he's up to until the last possible moment. I adopted this philosophy when I was a U.S. Attorney managing several investigations at once. Prosecutors rarely announce investigations in advance—you want as much time as possible to gather your evidence before witnesses and defendants vanish or become forgetful.

As mayor, I found that my first Police Commissioner, Bill Bratton, and I differed in style. His was to announce programs with fanfare, for the purpose of improving morale and setting a direction; mine, to start a program, prove that it worked, do some fine-tuning, then announce it, and in that way sustain long-term change. When I decided to tackle the squeegee operators, for example, I didn't declare my intentions. I first planned the initiative, encountered resistance from the Police Department, and asked them to devise a program. When they came back with a workable solution, I told them to put it into action. By the time we made the program public, the announcement explained improvements that people had already begun to notice without being told.

One small risk of this strategy is that you'll lose some of the praise for the positive results. People could have concluded—and a few probably did—that the squeegee operators simply disappeared, and I came along trying to grab all the credit. Usually, however, there's plenty of time to take the credit once you know a program actually works.

In the first two months of 2001, the crime figures for the city were falling rapidly—no small feat, considering the progress we had already made in the first seven years. Much of that additional success had to do with the police going after people with outstanding arrest warrants—long a neglected area of law enforcement for busy cops. When after about two months that initiative started to show real results, the Police Department wanted to publish the figures. They were true believers in Compstat's accountability standards and understandably wanted to add "warrants served" as an additional category, as well as a point of pride. I decided it would be better to wait until we had four or five months under our belts. If the trend continued, then we'd be okay and could announce it as a success. Which is exactly what happened. If we'd rushed to unveil those early results but the trend hadn't held, right about that time we would have been fielding questions about the initiative's failure.

Managing expectations by first knowing what to expect was especially valuable in the area of welfare reform. In the mid-1990s, more than 1.1 million New Yorkers received some form of public assistance—about one citizen in seven. By the time my second term ended, the number was less than 500,000 for the first time since 1967. I believe that the social contract is reciprocal. For every right there's an obligation, for every privilege there's a duty. Traditional welfare—a check arrives with virtually no obligation—deprives people of that relationship. Either they don't have a sense of the relationship between privilege and duty and you haven't helped put it there, or they had it and you helped them lose it. The recipients don't feel connected to society, and the taxpayers fund a system that they feel finances a permanent underclass.

I studied this topic extensively during the period after the 1989 election. By the time I was running for mayor again, in 1993, my Senior Advisor Richard Schwartz and I had developed a comprehensive welfare reform program. Only a few years later, our idea sounds obvious—that it's patronizing and even cruel to hand over money without hoping for anything in return, as though the able-bodied recipients were somehow beneath the expectation that every other member of society embraces.

We believed that if the city was going to help the welfare recipient, then it had a right to ask for something in return. This was the genesis of the city's workfare program. As soon as I became mayor, I asked Paul Crotty, the Corporation Counsel, to research how far I could go in requiring people to work. I wanted to know if there was anything under federal law that prohibited me from requiring welfare recipients to do public works, as they had in Roosevelt's Public Works Administration. We've got a lot of work that needs to be done in the city. There were plenty of people getting welfare checks. Could we get them to do that work? Paul came back with a memo saying the law permits just that, within limits that amount to a function of minimum wage restrictions. Nobody had ever done anything like this in New York, and nowhere in the country had anything like it been tried on the scale I planned. In the 1960s, under Mayor Lindsay, the prevailing wisdom was to make the process of obtaining a welfare check as frictionless as possible. The idea was to make welfare "user-friendly." Not surprisingly, the one-page form that required only a self-declaration of need resulted in a doubling of the city's caseload.

We decided to expand the concept of workfare, an idea that developed with the America Works program. America Works was a private company that got performance-based contracts, receiving the bulk of their money if—and only if—they found a welfare recipient a job that the recipient stayed with for at least six months. The recipients attended orientation sessions and work-skills seminars, and America Works was on-site to act as a go-between should any problems arise with issues like punctuality and child care.

The liberal world was incensed about the fact that America Works would "make a profit from welfare." The company was tying its profit to getting people a job, though, and the concept appealed to me immediately. Those who weren't able or willing to find permanent jobs were expected to participate in the Work Experience Program, spending twenty hours a week doing work like cleaning the parks and answering phones at various agencies.

Richard Schwartz and I struggled with the scale of the problem. We knew that with more than a million people on welfare, we wouldn't find permanent jobs for everyone. So, rather than announcing we'd have a set number of people off the rolls by any particular date, we started implementing it, putting people to work. Only in March 1995, after we knew that the program could succeed, did we announce the Welfare Reform Initiative. A chart illustrating the decline in the number of welfare recipients from 1993 to 2001 would show March 1995 as the start of the downward trend. In fact, it took us over a year to unveil the program, making small improvements to it the whole way.

When I ran for reelection in 1997, there were about 300,000 fewer people on the welfare rolls than in 1993. Had I announced when I first ran that I was going to reduce the welfare population by such a figure, *The New York Times* would have written an editorial saying I was crazy, and that if I somehow did do that the city would be in chaos. The reality is that I thought I probably could do it—if not predicting the exact number, I certainly believed in the concept. But I never wanted to make any promises because I wasn't sure how quickly we could accomplish what we wanted, or what the number would actually be. Once we knew how to do it—we'd made sure there were systems in place to find people jobs and identify those who needed them—then we would consistently put out the statistics, and people began to understand.

Well, the numbers turned out to be impressive. More than 600,000 people left the city's welfare rolls during my administration—from 1,112,490 to 497,113—greater than the population of all but fifteen American cities (amazingly, the September 11 disaster increased the number of New Yorkers on welfare by only 1,200). Our program constituted a major social realignment, restoring for many thousands the dignity of the work ethic.

In addition to buying the time and space to hone new programs, another reason I liked to announce results rather than intentions is that I could pursue a strategy without waiting for a consensus to build around it. Every initiative has supporters and detractors. No matter how "positive" a plan seems, there's always a side that considers itself the losers.

The welfare reform initiative, for example, looks on the surface like one of those situations worthy of the hackneyed title "win-win." Recipients got the money they needed and the dignity that comes from work, taxpayers felt their funds weren't being thrown into the East River, and everyone in the city got cleaner parks and other services. Not everyone saw it that way. The people who make their living representing the "best interests" of those on welfare—what I've taken to calling the "compassion industry"—didn't like the plan. Nor did the politicians who thought that appearing sensitive to the downtrodden meant keeping them permanently dependent. If we had waited until everyone was on board, it never would have happened.

Paul Crotty was helpful in developing this leadership philosophy.

We stayed in touch after we'd both finished our clerkships with Judge MacMahon. When I became mayor, I hired him to be my Corporation Counsel—advising me on what's doable under city and state laws. Paul would emphasize that the leader should go ahead and lead—not in an arrogant way, and not without abundant input from others. But the fact is, a leader who fails to act until every group has been heard from, every concern addressed, every lawsuit resolved, is a leader who's abdicating his responsibility. That was already my attitude; I'd felt the same way when I'd been a prosecutor. Paul reinforced it.

A few days before I was elected to my first term, a man came up to me at a campaign event, looked me in the eye, and told me there wouldn't be a Republican mayor of New York City until hell froze over. Exhausted, I shook the guy's hand and promptly forgot what he'd said. Then, during January 1994, the first month of my term, there were twelve snowstorms. When I woke up on the morning of February 1 and it was snowing, I started thinking about this guy— maybe he knew something I didn't. Then, when there was no snow in the latter part of my administration, I began to think Republican policies and programs work even to reduce the amount of snow.

By February 9, the city was bracing itself for the worst snowstorm of an already tough winter. I wanted to be positive that we'd have enough uniformed personnel on hand to keep the streets free for snow-plow-ing—to tell people not to use the tunnels and stay off the bridges. I went to police headquarters. The counsel to the Police Department had advised the PD that I couldn't declare an emergency. I called Paul in the middle of the night, asking if that was correct. "Go ahead and de-clare an emergency," he told me. "If they sue, they sue, but you're the mayor. Do what you have to do." I declared the emergency.

PROMISE ONLY WHEN YOU'RE POSITIVE

This rule sounds so obvious that I wouldn't mention it unless I saw leaders break it on a regular basis. In the long run, grand rhetorical promises undermine a leader's authority. For a public official, a sweeping pledge to reduce crime by a specific percentage or create a certain number of jobs may get good news coverage for a day or two; but if the results fail to match the prediction, the leader leaves everyone with the fear that the word of the boss cannot be trusted.

The days after the World Trade Center attacks revealed several instances of this phenomenon. When it was understood that the planes had been hijacked, the Federal Aviation Administration immediately shut down all flight operations at U.S. airports at 9:40 A.M. (EST). Just five hours later—at 2:30 P.M.—the FAA said that air traffic would resume at noon on Wednesday, September 12, at the earliest. In fact, by Wednesday, the FAA allowed only a limited reopening of the nation's commercial airspace system in the days to come, to let flights diverted on September 11 continue to their original destinations. By four P.M. Friday, September 14, the FAA had restored just a few general-aviation flights.

The airlines wanted to assure everyone that life would quickly get back to normal. It was the right impulse. Indeed, I heeded it myself over and over during those chaotic first weeks—but only after I was convinced that what I was telling people would happen would actually happen. Often, someone who is being pressed for deadlines will sputter something out just to appease the people who want to know. I do my best to anticipate those questions; but when you don't know the answer, you've got to be honest enough to say so.

Transportation in Manhattan was snarled in the wake of the World Trade Center disaster. One of the suggestions we took (as detailed in Chapter 6) was to limit most of the crossings into Manhattan to cars with more than one occupant during the morning rush hour, and to close the Holland Tunnel entirely. The competing demands were compelling. On the one hand, I thought a quick return to normalcy was important. New Yorkers had been attacked, literally and psychologically. Many things people had taken for granted—like a manageable commute—assumed greater importance as they became not just a *part* of life but comforting reminders of a *way* of life. On the other hand, Lower Manhattan could not handle a normal day's traffic — truckloads of debris had to be moved out and heavy equipment moved in, and several streets and mass transit options remained closed.

This goes directly to the importance of not overpromising. Sure, I'd have liked to have set everyone's mind at ease by announcing, "Everything is fine, come on back through the Holland Tunnel." But the comfort that people would have felt from hearing that would have been undone as soon as they hit the traffic jams. People would have sensed that life was in fact far from returning to normal and, worse, would have lost confidence in their leaders.

The idea of not promising until I was sure I could deliver became a rule for me. The first time Bill Bratton and I put out crime statistics, I remember being apprehensive. I'd made crime reduction such a cornerstone of my campaign that I wanted to ensure we had something meaningful to report. So it was September of 1994, and we'd achieved what today look like modest gains with relatively crude techniques compared to what Compstat became. The Police Department was excited about the progress and wanted to release the numbers, but I kept holding back until I was positive that we weren't going to show a couple of good months only to be hit with a 20 percent increase the following month.

Finally, I became convinced that the gains were real, and we organized a press conference. Just as the Police Department came over to the Blue Room at City Hall to issue the statistics, I got notification that there'd been a shooting in a subway station in Grand Central Terminal. No one was killed, but it was a terrifying scene — and newsworthy, since it was a man in a business suit doing the shooting.

That wasn't the only occasion when, just as we announced improved numbers, some high-profile crime would occur. I was well aware how important — and interrelated — the appearance of crime reduction and actual crime reduction were, and focused both on the numbers and on the visible quality of life.

DON'T TURN A VICTORY INTO A DEFEAT

One of the reasons I dislike announcing expectations before I know the results is that in doing so, a leader risks turning a positive development into a disappointment.

When Rudy Crew was Chancellor of Schools, he promised that he was going to improve reading test scores by 5 to 10 percent. The schools had already been improving, so this may have seemed a modest promise, but the school system in New York City was still in such a state of disrepair that any improvement should have been warmly greeted. Well, scores did improve—by 3.6 percent. The press remembered the 5 to 10 percent promise. *The New York Times* reported it under the headline, "Student Math Scores' Gain Is the Smallest in Recent Years." What was actually a boost in reading scores, which could have helped the morale of a broken system, ended up deflated because it failed to meet expectations.

One of the duties of a leader is to let his staff know how he expects them to behave. Employees should be expected to use their good judgment, but not to divine their boss's ideas and preferences—they are owed clear communication about what the boss expects. My staff came to understand that as much as I relish statistical accountability, I didn't like specific numbers being promised before we had the evidence that those numbers were attainable.

The risk of turning a victory into a failure is more than just a matter of impression and morale. Sometimes a misguided prediction can actually do some harm. When I was running for re-election in 1997, I viewed the campaign as critically important. Naturally, I wanted to win, but I also wanted as big a plurality as possible as a mandate for all that I planned to accomplish in a second term.

On November 3, 1997, I opened *The New York Times* to see a quote from my pollster, Frank Luntz, "predicting his client would get at least 60 percent of the vote in tomorrow's election." The moment I saw it, I became concerned. I knew that his polls at that point were showing 62 or 63, so from Frank's perspective he probably thought he was being conservative in his prediction. But not only did his comment violate the principle of not promising until you're positive, it also may have reduced my turnout. Democrats who had planned to vote for me were reading that same story. They could easily decide to stay home or cast a sympathy vote for my opponent. Even avid supporters might decide not to go out of their way to get to the voting booth, since my own pollster had assured them of a decisive victory.

As fate would have it, I did well in that election, earning 58 percent of the vote and carrying four of the five boroughs. The percentage of blacks who voted for me quadrupled over my 1993 victory, and against a Jewish, female opponent, I received seven out of ten Jewish votes and increased my share among women from 46 to 54. In fact, four out of ten Democrats voted for me.

Frank's 60 percent promise became a smaller issue than I thought; but it was annoying when a few stories pointed it out amid the success—the *Times* called it an "impressive victory . . . though not quite the historic sweep that his advisers have been predicting."

I would have preferred Frank to have said nothing. The fact is, my loss in 1989 and my win in 1993 were both with a bigger percentage of the overall vote than the only previous Republican to be elected mayor of New York City, John Lindsay, in either of his elections (and for his second election he switched to the Democrat ticket).

I called Frank in, and told him, "I don't understand why the hell you did that." I told him not to repeat that ever again, and explained to him how damaging overpromising could be. As it happens, Frank Luntz is a hard guy to take to the woodshed, because he defuses anger by simply being truthful. Sometimes, people will start in with, "I really didn't say that" or "It wasn't me, I was misquoted." More often than not, that just gets you angry, because they *did* say that, and now they're insulting your intelligence. But Frank immediately said, "I did it. I was wrong. It was the dumbest thing in the world. I shouldn't have done it. I'll do anything I can to make this better."

It's the right way to handle a mistake.

Police Commissioner Bernie Kerik was one of my closest colleagues when I was mayor and is a good friend. So I was surprised when the *New York Post* reported that he had told columnist Jack Newfield that his goal for 2001 was fewer than 600 homicides. In 1993, the year before I became mayor, there were 1,946 murders. In 2000, there were 673. Obviously, we'd been making amazing progress. What if the final number for 2001 had been 601—nearly 70 percent fewer than 1993, even as the population grew, and a 10 percent improvement even over the 2000 numbers? I didn't want to turn that victory into a failure and the headlines to read "Police Miss Murder Goal."

Bernie knew as well as anyone how I felt about these estimates and he explained to me how that below-600 prediction became public. Part of holding a high-profile position, especially in New York City, is facing pressure from the media. For the sake of a good story, reporters will try to pit a commissioner against the mayor, or vice versa. The newspaperman Jack Newfield was doing an HBO special on the warrant squad, which as part of Operation Condor was having great success in getting dangerous people off the streets. Newfield said to Kerik that the numbers until that point projected a year with fewer than 600 murders for the first time since 1963. Kerik said, "It's early," "Let's hope so," "I don't want to guarantee a specific number prematurely," and so on. Then he added that he'd love it if the total were indeed under 600. So the next day's headline was: "Kerik KO's Killings—Bids to Keep Total below 600 for the First Time since '60s."

The Police Commissioner in theory is "bidding" for zero homicides. Ask any family member of someone who's been murdered whether that single homicide is acceptable. Before the press conference the next day, I spoke to Bernie and underlined why I didn't like to commit to a number. I further tried to dampen expectations by explaining to the press that we had to keep our hopes realistic. They asked Bernie again if he thought he could hit below 600 and he said, "I agree with the Mayor."

The next day's headline in the *Post*? "Kerik Goal Riles Rudy"!

That's leadership in the media spotlight. For the record, the 2001 homicide total was 642. That's a 4.3 percent decrease over 2000's 671, a real improvement by any standard, particularly considering the decline since 1993 was already more than 60 percent—except the hypothetical one planted in the public's mind. But by getting on top of it the first day—and by Bernie being so straightforward—we got the story back to being about the reduction rather than the promise.

After beating the Cleveland Indians in the 1995 World Series, the Atlanta Braves engraved "Team of the 90s" on their rings. That turned out to be their only championship win that decade.

8

Develop and Communicate Strong Beliefs

Great leaders lead by ideas. Ideology is enormously important when running any large organization. The people who work for you, those who look to you for answers, the media, even your rivals have a right to know how you see the world.

Strong beliefs are sometimes risky in modern American politics. That's because a politician who explains his beliefs to people takes two major risks—that the goals stemming from the belief cannot be achieved (in which case he'll be called a failure) and that too many voters will disagree. But leadership isn't about succeeding on every single initiative, nor about building consensus behind every action.

The importance of developing strong beliefs is one of the reasons I favor politicians who have accomplished something substantial outside the political realm. Those who have spent their entire life in politics often become spin artists rather than thinkers. They lose attention span. Young people who go directly into elective politics often lose the ability to think critically.

For any issue, you must first figure out the substance, considering it from every angle, getting it into your bloodstream, before deciding the position you want to take. Once you know where you stand, it's perfectly appropriate to present your view in the most favorable light you can. But don't first work out how to make a favorable case, *then* select your position.

There are three critical stages here. First, you must develop beliefs. Next, you have to communicate them. Finally, you must take action, a theme I develop in the next chapter, "Be Your Own Man." In this chapter I concentrate on the first two.

DEVELOP STRONG BELIEFS

The ideas that form the basis of your leadership can develop in a number of ways. Some come from your parents, as many of mine did. Others derive from friends, teachers, clergy, even rivals.

For the first eighteen years of my life, I had two main vocations in mind—medicine or the priesthood. Both satisfied a feeling that had been growing in me my whole life: that to be happy and fulfilled, I had to serve a greater cause—helping others. My father was always helping people, trying to find a job for a neighbor or taking a relative to the hospital. Although neither of my parents was particularly devout, they both felt deeply the Church's message of experiencing grace by giving to others. That commitment filtered down to me.

All through high school (at Bishop Loughlin in Brooklyn), I would discuss religion and notions of service with one of my teachers, Brother Kevin, and with my friend Alan Placa. At the end of my time there, I signed up to enter the Montfort Fathers (in Bay Shore, Long Island), a religious order devoted to serving in the poorest countries. Alan was going to join the Christian Brothers. I wasn't going to do anything halfway: if I was going to become a priest, I was going to help out the most underprivileged I could find. I remember thinking I would probably end up in Haiti or Africa. But then, as June turned to July, I realized I had a problem: my budding interest in the opposite sex was something that wouldn't be suppressed. I thought, maybe I'm just not ready. I enrolled in Manhattan College hoping that perhaps I'd be better prepared for celibacy after a couple of years.

In college, I entered the pre-med program. But as much as I loved learning biology, I liked ideas better than science. Alan and I even joked about putting out a shingle, "Philosophers at Large," renting ourselves out as rhetorical opponents by the hour. At the time, the only kind of doctor I thought of becoming was a surgeon, but however skillful and knowledgeable that calling was, it also seemed to me somewhat mechanical. My ideas were narrow, I suppose: I didn't realize how creative medicine could be. But I turned away from medicine; and as by this time I was already dating, I knew that a religious vocation was not for me. In its place, I began to view my love of debate as pointing toward a new calling—to the law, where I could indulge that enthusiasm to the full.

When I first started thinking about becoming a lawyer, I feared I might be swamped with rote memorization and obscure statutes. Nonetheless, I took some college courses in American history and in American Constitutional history, and realized that I had underestimated the subject. It still wasn't until law school that I saw how richly philosophical the legal profession could be.

Both in college and law school, my fascination with Western civilization blossomed. I came to believe that the great contributions of Western thinking—political and religious freedom, elected leaders, the importance of private property, a free economic system—shared a common root, all evolving from the idea of the dignity of the human being. It makes sense that a society that believes in the rights and value of the individual human being allows citizens to elect their leaders, to decide what to believe, to stake claims to better lives. What fascinated me about democracy was that it did not come ready-formed: it had to be invented.

That invention was predicated on ideas developed by the great religions. Judaism contributed the notion that God and man enjoy a dialogue, and this leads on naturally to the idea that individuals are worth the Creator's time, that they're worthwhile. For Christians, God actually *became* a human being. It's an extraordinary idea: we humans were so valuable that God wanted to walk among us. Christianity spread because other people saw what it did to the lives of Christians. When nonbelievers threw early Christians to the lions, they were stunned by the peace with which the victims accepted their fate. The early martyrs were a tremendous advertisement for the ideas of Christianity. In the same way, Martin Luther King's stand against racism and his use of non-violence were extraordinarily powerful witnesses to the dignity of human beings. It held a mirror up to Americans. It showed them the distinction they were making between their promise of equality and the practice of racism. I began to see law as a way of giving embodiment to the best ideas man has had.

Classical philosophy played a large part in the development of my beliefs. Studying the Greek philosophers, from pre-Socratic times on, excited me. Exploring the Roman legal system, which formed the basis for most of Europe's, then the English legal system, which provided the roots of our own, taught me how ideas built upon one another. It was a thrilling awakening.

Debates—those not from New York might have called them "arguments"—with lifelong friends like Peter Powers and Alan Placa further shaped my thinking. Bright people debunking your logic is excellent training for anyone testing the consistency and validity of their ideas. Looking for mentors early on is critical as well. Lloyd MacMahon, Mike Seymour, Paul Curran, Harold Tyler, and Bill Smith all influenced me, by their deeds as well as their words. Many of those with whom I worked in the Justice Department and in the U.S. Attorney's office also played their part. It was all a gradual process, but one that never stopped.

My goal as a leader was to apply my beliefs and philosophy to real-world situations. As mayor, I insisted that everyone on my staff should concentrate on the core purpose of whichever agency or division we oversaw. In politics, even more than in business, the reply to queries is far too often "Because we've always done it this way." My goal was to move the agenda forward with every action, to back strong beliefs with specific plans of action. A good example of this was the public school system.

The New York City school system was never really going to improve until its purpose, its core mission, was made clear. What the system *should* have been about was educating its million children as well as possible. Instead, it existed to provide jobs for the people who worked in it, and to preserve those jobs regardless of performance. That's not to say that there weren't committed professionals at every level within the system. There were, and that's the shame of it. Those with their hearts in the right place were the ones who suffered most.

Until I could get everyone involved to sit together and agree that the system existed to educate children, fixing little bits of it was symbolic at best. Band-Aid solutions can do more harm than good. The system needed a new philosophy. It needed to say we're not a job protection system but a system at its core about children's enrichment. All rewards and risks must flow from the performance of the children. If you took a broken system and repaired just enough so that it could limp along, you lessened the chance that a real and lasting solution could be reached. That's why I resist partial control over a project. The schools should be made into a mayoral agency—like the Administration for Children's Services or the Fire Department—so the city can enact real solutions.

My successor, Michael Bloomberg, made a deal to get partial control over the schools. By winning the right to appoint the majority of the school board, he gained control over policy. He could set the general direction of the system and hire chancellors who shared his goals. This is an advance and should help to improve the school system. I would have accepted this, as he did, and then pushed for more. The teachers still maintain effective "management control."

They retained tenure, defeated merit pay, and maintained the formula-driven funding with no flexibility to reward high-performing teachers.

Unable to get the control I felt was needed, I pressed for incremental change that would force the school system to make educating children its focus and create accountability at each stage of that goal. First, I got the superintendents—the managers who oversee the principals—to agree to accept merit pay and the end of guaranteed tenure. They then argued that results were difficult to achieve without the ability to reward and punish those under them. No kidding. We were then able to get the school principals to accept the same notion—that ending permanent tenure and accepting merit pay would allow them to perform their jobs more effectively. Obviously, without the same flexibility to reward and encourage good teachers there's only so much a superintendent and principal can do. But it's a start, and it set the stage for my successor's attempt to gain even more control over the schools.

I practiced the same discipline in examining the purpose of New York City's hospitals—asking why they existed. In most cities, about 5 percent of hospital beds at most were operated by the municipality. In New York, the number was 20 to 25 percent. That was one of the reasons health-care spending averaged about $4,720 per person annually in New York, compared to about $3,775 in the rest of the country. The hospitals were supposed to be about caring for the sick and curing the ill. Unfortunately, the politically powerful union that represented hospital workers thought the purpose of the enterprise was to employ as many people as possible. They didn't want a system in which the best nurse got a bigger raise than the worst. Increased productivity from the best performers might result in someone noticing the worst employees weren't carrying their weight.

The system had so many people working in it that I was able to reduce the workforce by 12,000 yet still increase performance. We had some hospitals with 20 percent more employees than needed. In the most ironic form of featherbedding, people were literally taking care of empty beds. I went back to core purpose, and by our concentrating on patient care, every measure we took helped performance—from finishing the year in the black over the last three years of my administration (after years of routine deficits), to full accreditation for all facilities, to cutting the waiting time for prenatal care in half.

Assigning too many people to a task significantly reduces the quality of performance. It's tempting to think, "There's no harm in having more than we need"—but staff hanging around uselessly encourages others to do likewise. Oversupplying personnel is of course supported anywhere with a heavy union presence, but this is not a benign thing. Would it be benign to add several more surgeons to an operation? Or pilots to a cockpit? Any system functions best when the right number of staff is used, and any excess money can be employed to rebuild the business and reward high performers. Further, a surplus of labor makes it much more difficult for the hard workers. Their performance either deteriorates, or they leave.

As with the school system, the hospitals had many excellent, hardworking employees. But the purpose of the hospital system as it stood was not to provide jobs and job protection, but to provide healthcare. Understanding that mindset and establishing my own decidedly different viewpoint were critical to future dealings with the system and its union leaders.

Some beliefs develop in a methodical way. Through trial and error, you come to realize that an idea you had was mistaken. The notion that changing your mind about an issue shows weakness is ridiculous. People should be ready to admit when there is evidence to make them change their mind. That's an indication of intellectual honesty, not of a lack of backbone. By the same token, once the evidence is in and you've come to a new opinion, you've got to be willing to articulate it and stick with it, even if it proves unpopular.

A good example of this came during my first administration. From 1990 to 1993, over 8,300 people were murdered in New York City. (By way of comparison, this is 1,500 more people killed during those four years than during all eight years of my administration.) Citizens were scared, and wanted their leaders to act. The concept of "community policing"—that is, if a citizen sees a police officer standing on the corner, he'll feel safer—became fashionable across the nation. A shop owner was supposedly more likely to tell friendly Officer Joe, who walked a beat and knew the community, about the criminals hanging outside the shop. It was a comforting theory, the kind of neatly packaged idea that played well politically. It also had some validity so long as it did not transform police work into social work.

Quickly, however, community policing enshrined as a precept of big-city political correctness. It allowed those who found police work distasteful a method of dealing with it as a euphemism. To these people policemen were at the core objectionable—the whole notion of cops made them nervous. By recasting them as quasi–social workers, cops were somehow defined away. But the police are not supposed to be shrinking violets. They are there to make sure people obey the law. They are authoritarian figures albeit operating within legal, constitutional restraints. But the idea was seductive, and until I became mayor even I accepted the "cop on the beat" aspect of it. That is, until we analyzed the statistics for each precinct using Compstat.

The reality is that community policing doesn't stop crime. There are only so many police officers any city can afford. Once a certain quantity of them are committed to standing on a corner in every neighborhood, the number who can be deployed to higher crime areas or added to task forces targeting specific problems is reduced. Another problem: it's not only law-abiding citizens who are reassured by knowing where this visible new police presence is. Criminals get a big kick out of the predictable, daytime beats of community police officers—it makes scheduling nefarious activities much easier.

The example that drove this home to me was the oft-repeated

request to provide a police officer on every subway train. That sounded like a good idea, and I even advocated it for a period of time. Then I learned that 65 to 70 percent of subway crimes were taking place on the platforms and at the stations, not on the trains. I realized that the cop-on-a-train idea would produce a scenario in which those being mugged on the platforms could wave at the police officers as they rode helplessly by.

That convinced me to focus on putting police not where they were wanted but where they were *needed*—and to use objective criteria in determining the need. The numbers are indisputable. Compstat proved that the rapid deployment of officers to trouble spots was the best way to fight crime. As much as I love to trot out the statistics, let's just leave it at this—murder, burglary, auto theft, and shootings all declined about 70 percent or more from 1993 to 2001. Once I was convinced that our approach was working, I stuck by it, even when people who'd grown accustomed to Officer Joe complained that he was now arresting criminals at night rather than shooting the breeze in the daytime.

RE-EXAMINE BELIEFS: THE POLITICAL ODYSSEY

My skepticism about community policing is an example of a strong belief I came to only after seeing the facts up close and realizing that they couldn't be disputed. The development of beliefs can follow a more winding path, an evolution that might not be applicable to everyone but is irrefutable to the person honest enough to acknowledge it. Sometimes these beliefs are inconvenient, even painful. They may lead you away from long-held positions and might even cost you friends. But a real leader, one who leads from a true heart and honest mind, won't deny an emerging belief simply because it makes him uncomfortable.

That's how I became a Republican.

My parents were conservative in their thinking, but my father was a Democrat because they were "for the working people." They both voted for President Eisenhower, and my mother even registered as a Republican. For a while, when John F. Kennedy emerged, however, first as a near–vice presidential candidate in 1956, then as a presidential candidate in 1960, they voted for him. Caught up in the Kennedy magic, my mother became a Democrat. I was only a teenager during the Jimmy Hoffa hearings in the late fifties, in which the labor leader was confronted by Bobby Kennedy. I followed it with great interest. Then in 1964 I worked on R.F.K.'s successful campaign for the Senate. Around that time, I was elected to the first elective office I ever held— Democratic district leader in Nassau County. I was 21 years old.

But the parties were changing, and so was I. When in 1972 I went to the polling booth, I voted for George McGovern only because I knew he was going to lose. I actually told friends that if I thought mine would be the deciding vote, I'd have gone for Nixon, but since I knew it wouldn't be, and because I was a habitual Democrat, I voted for their choice. But I felt strange about it. It was almost as if I were voting more from nostalgia than rational choice. I knew in my heart that I was no longer a Democrat. Voting for McGovern was part of the transformation in my politics. I shouldn't have voted for him. I didn't want to. His views on foreign policy were not mine. He didn't adequately understand the danger of the Soviet Union, or that America had to remain strong and could not keep demilitarizing and expect to challenge Communism. Yet he represented the majority view in the Democratic Party at the time.

A year or so later, I went down to the Board of Elections and asked for my registration card. I told them I wanted to change parties. Then as now, there were so few non-Democrats in New York City that the lady there barely knew what to make of me. She told me that I'd have to reregister, as though I'd changed my address. We got into an absurd discussion until finally she allowed me a new card. I went to fill out the application and when it came time to check off my political party I stalled. I wasn't going to check Democrat. But I couldn't bring myself to check Republican, either.

My best friend, Peter Powers, had been a Republican forever, and we'd debated politics our whole lives, always on opposite sides. I'd even written a liberal column for my college newspaper. Republican-ism, I thought, was only for rich people. How could I be one of them? I agreed with them on foreign policy, and on many law and order and social issues. However, other than Nelson Rockefeller, Republicans weren't perceived as sensitive to the poor and working class, whereas I strongly identified with the working people with whom I had grown up in Brooklyn and Nassau County. I looked at the registration appli-cation and went down the line. I couldn't check off Conservative at that time. I thought about checking off Liberal, but it felt too left-wing. So I checked off Independent. The process was under way.

From 1962 to 1975, Judge Harold R. Tyler, Jr., served in the South-ern District of New York—the same district in which I served as an assistant U.S. Attorney. In 1975, Tyler became Deputy Attorney Gen-eral, the No. 2 in Edward H. Levi's Justice Department during the Ford administration. At that point, I'd been in the U.S. Attorney's of-fice five years, and many of my friends had moved on, including a few to Washington.

I had never tried a case in front of Judge Tyler, but I knew him and wrote to ask if I could work on his staff. I wasn't sure how he would respond, but I was looking for a new challenge. He asked me to come to Washington for an interview—this in the summer of 1975. When he offered me a position as Associate Deputy Attorney General, I didn't even know what the job was, but I knew it would be an opportunity to see at a relatively high level how the federal gov-ernment operated. He said that he had one Associate Deputy, Togo West, but needed another, and wanted me to oversee roughly half the divisions that reported to him, mostly on the criminal side. Togo was a civil lawyer, handling the civil divisions, the budget, and many other areas. But this was a challenging time for the Justice Department. We were going through the Church Committee hearings—the post-Watergate intelligence gathering and investigations. We were establishing a new public integrity section, and creating an internal auditing and monitoring function.

So, with all the U.S. Attorneys, the United States Marshals, plus the Drug Enforcement Administration (which was in trouble at the time) reporting to Tyler, he wanted another deputy with experience in criminal prosecutions. I took the job, and for the first time in my life moved out of the New York City area. As soon as I started, Togo told me with a broad grin that my new office used to be John Dean's. I wondered if it had been bugged. I can visualize that whole room, right down to the fake red leather furniture. Sometimes I'd be working late and could feel the ghosts around.

I started meeting lots of people in the G.O.P., including my good friend Jay Waldman, who's now a federal judge in Philadelphia. He was the chief of staff to Dick Thornburgh, assistant attorney general in charge of the criminal division. It struck me how talented they were. They worked hard, and lo! they did care about people. The image I had of Republicans, as morally inferior to Democrats, came from being a prejudiced New Yorker, as opposed to real observation of the two political parties and the people in them.

Jay and I talked a great deal about both parties, and I concluded that the Republican Party was better for the country, particularly at the presidential level. I realized that Republicans brought more talented people into government, because the G.O.P. didn't carry the same obligations as the Democratic Party, and didn't have the same pressure to water down the quality of the people that they brought into government with symbolic appointments. There are so many pulls and tugs on any Democratic President, with the entire labor movement seeking substantial influence in job appointments and every special interest group that supported you lining up for positions. I'm not suggesting that Republicans come to office unbeholden; but their debts are not as often to people who actually want or need to work in government. A Republican President can draw from a talent base far less restricted than his rival's.

I had to overcome a significant prejudice against Republicans that develops if you grow up in New York City. Now that I've been on the receiving end of it, I see it more clearly. Endless numbers of people tell me I'm the only Republican they have ever voted for. Many of these folk are 60, 70 years old. Every once in a while during their lifetime, there must have been a couple of Republicans who were a little better than the Democrats, but they still couldn't vote for them. It was a gut prejudice. For me, it was more a process of admitting that my views were more in line with the Republican Party. So in 1976, I voted for my first Republican candidate for president, Gerald Ford, and then in 1980 for Ronald Reagan. That's when I once again changed my registration—from Independent to Republican—for good. It has been straight Republican for president ever since although I've made a few deviations for some other races.

The reason I go into this level of detail is not to pad the rolls of the G.O.P. (although www.rnc.org is well worth a browse). Obviously, there are plenty of decent, bright, good-hearted people of most political persuasions. The point is to show that beliefs are not always easy to come by or right in front of one's face. The path is often lonely, arduous, even painful, at odds with how one perceives oneself. But an intellectually honest leader leads from a place where true beliefs live.

COMMUNICATE STRONG BELIEFS

A leader must not only set direction, but communicate that direction. He usually cannot simply impose his will—and even if he could it's not the best way to lead. He must bring people aboard, excite them about his vision, and earn their support. They in turn will inspire those around them, and soon everyone will be focusing on the same goal; the effort will come from within, which always results in more forceful advocacy than if someone is just going through the motions to please their boss.

Expressing ideology is one of a leader's most powerful tools. Nowhere was that clearer than during the days following the World Trade Center disaster. I tried to explain the enormity of what had happened and hold accountable those responsible for the attacks. On Monday, October 1, 2001, I addressed the United Nations General Assembly Special Session on Terrorism. I wanted to set forth a principled statement of American objectives. The people in that chamber are accustomed to ambiguities. Most of the time, there's a good reason for that—world issues are complicated and seldom yield black and white solutions. This time, it was not ambiguous: we were facing absolute evil. I wanted to challenge the UN's refusal to take strong, uncompromising stands. Sometimes, standing up for what you believe is the only option. I made eye contact with as many of the members as I could, especially those from countries I thought most needed to hear it. These people live in New York City. They saw what had been done. This is part of what I said:

> On September 11, 2001, New York City—the most diverse city in the world—was viciously attacked in an unprovoked act of war. Thousands of innocent men, women, and children of every race, religion, and ethnicity are lost. Among these are people from eighty different nations. To their representatives here today, I offer my condolences to you as well on behalf of all New Yorkers who share this loss with you. This was the deadliest terrorist attack in history. It claimed more lives than Pearl Harbor or D-Day.
>
> This was not just an attack on the city of New York or on the United States of America. It was an attack on the very idea of a free, inclusive, and civil society.
>
> This vicious attack places in jeopardy the whole purpose of the

United Nations. Terrorism is based on the persistent and deliberate violation of fundamental human rights. With bullets and bombs—and now with hijacked airplanes—terrorists deny the dignity of human life. Terrorism preys particularly on cultures and communities that practice openness and tolerance. Their targeting of innocent civilians mocks the efforts of those who seek to live together in peace as neighbors. It defies the very notion of being a neighbor.

This massive attack was intended to break our spirit. It has not done that. It has made us stronger, more determined, and more resolved.

The bravery of our firefighters, our police officers, our emergency workers, and civilians we may never learn of, in saving over 25,000 lives that day—carrying out the most effective rescue operation in our history—inspires all of us. The determination, resolve, and leadership of President George W. Bush has unified America and all decent men and women around the world.

The response of many of your nations—your leaders and people—spontaneously demonstrating in the days after the attack your support for New York and America, and your understanding of what needs to be done to remove the threat of terrorism, gives us great, great hope that we will prevail.

The strength of America's response, please understand, flows from the principles upon which we stand.

Americans are not a single ethnic group.

Americans are not of one race or one religion.

Americans emerge from all your nations.

We are defined as Americans by our beliefs—not by our ethnic origins, our race, or our religion. Our beliefs in religious freedom, political freedom, and economic freedom—that's what makes an American. Our belief in democracy, the rule of law, and respect for human life—that's how you become an American. It is these very principles—and the opportunities these principles give to so many to create a better life for themselves and their families—that make America, and New York, a "shining city on a hill."

There is no nation, and no city, in the history of the world that has seen more immigrants, in less time, than America. People continue to come here in large numbers to seek freedom, opportunity, decency, and civility.

Each of your nations has contributed citizens to the United States and to New York. I believe I can take every one of you someplace in New York City where you can find someone from your country, someone from your village or town, that speaks your language and practices your religion. In each of your lands there are many who are Americans in spirit, by virtue of their commitment to our shared principles.

It is tragic and perverse that it is because of these very principles—particularly our religious, political, and economic freedoms—that we find ourselves under attack by terrorists.

Our freedom threatens them, because they know that if our ideas of freedom gain a foothold among their people it will destroy their power. So they strike out against us to keep those ideas from reaching their people.

The best long-term deterrent to terrorism is the spread of our principles of freedom, democracy, the rule of law, and respect for human life. The more that spreads around the globe, the safer we will all be. These are very powerful ideas and once they gain a foothold, they cannot be stopped.

In fact, the rise that we have seen in terrorism and terrorist groups, I believe, is in no small measure a response to the spread of these ideas of freedom and democracy to many nations, particularly over the past fifteen years.

The terrorists have no ideas or ideals with which to combat freedom and democracy. Their only defense is to strike out against innocent civilians, destroying human life in massive numbers and hoping to deter all of us from our pursuit and expansion of freedom.

The United Nations must hold accountable any country that supports or condones terrorism, otherwise you will fail in your primary mission as peacekeeper.

It must ostracize any nation that supports terrorism.

It must isolate any nation that remains neutral in the fight against terrorism.

Now is the time, in the words of the UN Charter, "to unite our strength to maintain international peace and security." This is not a time for further study or vague directives. The evidence of terrorism's brutality and inhumanity—of its contempt for life and the concept of peace—is lying beneath the rubble of the World Trade Center less than two miles from where we meet today.

Look at that destruction, that massive, senseless, cruel loss of human life . . . and then I ask you to look in your hearts and recognize that there is no room for neutrality on the issue of terrorism. You're either with civilization or with terrorists.

> On one side is democracy, the rule of law, and respect for human
> life; on the other is tyranny, arbitrary executions, and mass murder.
> We're right and they're wrong. It's as simple as that.

My goal was to lay out in plain language what America stood for and what we had to lose if we didn't defend our values. The opportunity to address the United Nations was enormously valuable.

The people who elected me needed not only the critical information regarding transportation, casualty counts, the anthrax scares, and the future of New York City. They were also entitled to know my ideas about what had taken place, and what was to come. That's why I didn't just give my speech at the U.N. and stand on ceremony elsewhere. People don't always like to hear ideas. Sometimes they'd rather hear platitudes. But what's easy is not always what's best.

On Monday, September 17, the New York Mercantile Exchange reopened for the first time since the attacks. Located just a block from the twin towers, NYMEX had lost several traders. The dust was still thick, and here we stood in a building that symbolized the very freedom the terrorists tried to take from us. Undaunted, the traders had returned to work, and here they were, looking to me for a few words.

I tried to communicate actual ideas. "One of the most unholy acts in the history of the world was perpetrated against the people of our city," I told them. "They chose their target deliberately—the towers of the World Trade Center—which stand as the most recognizable symbol of our city's status as the financial capital of the world. Free enterprise has been an important aspect of life in New York City since our earliest days. It is the engine of our prosperity. It has provided the means for generations of immigrants to achieve the American dream. It is something that you should be proud to be a part of."

What the terrorists were striking at were not just American buildings and American lives, but mostly American ideas. They were intimidated not only by our success but by our openness and freedom. The people who attacked us were threatened by three main aspects about our society. One was the democratic electoral process by which we chose our leaders. The second was religious freedom, which included the freedom not to be religious. Third was capitalism, and our success as a wealthy country, which included our success in leading people out of poverty. These were the antithesis of what the terrorists believed.

Whenever I communicated, I explained the overriding philosophy behind what I was saying. This way people could understand and agree or disagree with my thinking. My goal was to integrate even the simplest policy decisions into my basic ideas. But then, at every stage of my career I've tried to be as available and candid—some reporters call it "blunt"—as possible. And I've learned a few things about communicating strong beliefs.

BE DIRECT AND UNFILTERED

One of the great advantages of being New York City mayor was that I could communicate directly. Because it was such a visible job, I didn't have to be a slave to press coverage. A leader who cannot access the airwaves or draw people to a meeting risks having the media shape the public's impression of him. Someone with as high a profile as the mayor of a big city can create his own impression, and can ensure that the press becomes just another element that factors into decisions.

Any leader likes to have the media on his side—it makes the job easier and it plain feels better than being beaten up every morning. But when you run a large organization there will always be a bias toward presenting you in a negative way. It's not necessarily a personal grudge (although sometimes there's that, too, and it's fair to wonder why so many journalists consistently vote to the left of their audiences). Probably the majority of those who cover any government—and most corporations—have a bias against the organization. Their instinctive reaction is to assume, in any instance that's open to interpretation, that you must be doing something wrong, taking advantage somehow. You have to find some way to offset this bias. One of the best ways is to communicate your true message directly, without spin, spokespeople, focus groups, or TelePrompTers.

During the 1989 primary campaign, I was given some advice from a venerable local television broadcaster, Gabe Pressman—although he probably didn't even realize that he gave it to me. I had been put on the defensive by the campaign of my opponent, Ron Lauder. Gabe interviewed me and I explained my position. After the interview, Gabe told me: "Your campaign shouldn't keep you bottled up." He went on: "The more you explain things, the more people will understand what you're doing and why you're doing it. Just let people hear what you have to say, because you've good reasons for what you're doing—even though I don't agree with it all." Until that point, I'd had others in the campaign answer criticisms leveled at me. From that moment on I took to explaining my own positions in my own words.

When I first ran for public office, I thought public speaking would be no problem. I'd argued many cases and enjoyed doing so, especially in appellate court. I'd argued in the First Circuit, the Second Circuit, the Third Circuit, the Eleventh Circuit, the New York Court of Appeals, the two appellate divisions in New York City, even in the U.S. Supreme Court. I would often stay up all night preparing, and it never seemed like work. I had fared pretty well with juries and judges, even under withering attack from some brilliant adversaries and judges, and so assumed it would be easy enough with voters.

I started by doing what I would have done as a lawyer—learn as much as possible, prepping the questions reporters and political rivals might throw at me. What I hadn't realized was that there is a difference between the guy at ease with questions and the guy who's nervous, and it usually has nothing to do with how much one knows. It's about self-confidence.

With my speeches, I'd write some pages, others would look them over, and we'd slave over the exact language. I became a much better political speaker when I went back to what I used to do in court: master the material, organize it, then throw the text away and just talk. It now actually annoys me when people read their speeches. I want to hear who they really are, how they sound when they speak from the heart. Now, when I deliver an idea, I feel that I'm communicating more honestly because I'm not reading from a script, but conveying my real feelings directly.

Preparing for political debates presented another learning curve. Back in the summer of 1989, whenever I had time between campaign stops I'd go by the office of my media advisor, Roger Ailes. Roger had worked on George Bush's campaign the year before. He would prep me for the debates, stressing that I should always be on the offensive, always bringing the questions around to what I wanted to talk about. He'd videotape me as if he were a television moderator or my opponent. The lessons that I learned were enormously valuable, one particularly so. We were preparing for a debate with my primary opponent, Ron Lauder, and the event would be televised.

Playing the role of reporter, Roger said, "Mr. Giuliani, as a U.S. Attorney, you've had absolutely no involvement or responsibility of any kind for education. In fact, aside from going to school yourself, you don't know anything about education. Do you even have an educational plan?"

I replied, "Yes, I do, and let me tell you all about it. One, reform the board, two, do this, three, do that, four, do this . . ."

I finished, and Roger started clapping. "Hey, great answer," he said. "I agree with all those things. You get an A for education—and an F for communication. This isn't the United States Court of Appeals. Judges would remember those four points, and they'd write them all down. But people at home aren't sitting there with a scorecard. Education—immediately, what does that say to you? Children. You have two minutes. The way you answer that question is, 'I care greatly about children. I have my own. I've always loved children, and I care about them. And I realize that the future of our city is built around children. So the core of my concern about education will be to make the educational system exactly like that, built around the children.' That happens to be the truth, and the viewers can sense that. And it's a lot more memorable than your dissertation. If you have more time, *then* tell them your four points. Connect with people first."

Roger explained that every time a candidate is given a microphone, he's getting $100,000 worth of publicity. Done right, two minutes is enough time to communicate the philosophical underpinnings of your message. The details and the substance are vital: they have to be there or you'll be exposed. But there's a time to win hearts and minds and there are times for details, and you have to pick your spots.

As I was preparing for the debates, I was nervous, unsure if I knew everything I needed. Whenever I'd prepare, I kept piles of books and position papers nearby, determined to have the answer to every question at hand. Roger was disgusted. "Throw those damn books away. You already know more than you need to be a candidate, probably more than you'll need as mayor. Stop with all of this tax policy and crime policy and traffic policy. Do you think Mayor Koch knows all this stuff? Just get up on your feet, use the knowledge you already have, and you'll do a lot better." As usual, he was right.

He also taught me to communicate directly and with emotional honesty. When we shot our first few television commercials, I'd read them, as most candidates do. He told me, "Forget it. Just take your glasses off and start talking, and we'll get it right. If you feel angry, communicate it. Sad, communicate it. Mopey, communicate it. Let people know that you're a human being and the rest will take care of itself."

After the 1989 election, Mike Seymour put together a small group to advise me. He gave me a photocopied chapter from Arthur M. Schlesinger's biography of John F. Kennedy, *A Thousand Days*. I'd read the book already but this drove a point home for me. It detailed how on the afternoon of an important speech, JFK would take the afternoon off—swim, get a massage. For the 1993 campaign, I began following that advice as best I could, taking time to get into the right frame of mind before an important address.

The experience of that campaign helped change me as a political speaker. As I say, I had been effective in courtrooms. On occasion, law students actually traveled to hear my summations in big trials like the Friedman corruption case, and thought they were effective. But when I turned to politics, somehow I couldn't rise to the same level. All that memorization and careful emphasis held me back. I thought of every word as though it were written on the Washington Monument—everything I said had to be precise. With practice, I eventually achieved a certain level of ability, so that by the time I gave my inaugural address as mayor I was a decent, but far from outstanding, political speaker. (Luckily, my son, Andrew, about to turn 7, carried the show by running round the podium repeating my line, "It should be so and it will be so.") I couldn't understand it. I had evolved from nearly incompetent to mediocre to pretty good, but couldn't seem to hit the level I had achieved in court. I knew I could do better.

I started working with Elliot Cuker, who is both my friend and an actor. Elliot pointed out that I'd give 200, maybe even 300 short speeches a year. I'd go to a dinner, get up and speak. With little time to prepare, I'd be funny and relaxed, and the speech would convey ideas, and sometimes even be inspirational. Then, when I gave a really important address, I would become ponderous again, scripted, rehearsed. I knew Elliot was right, just as Roger had been, but I wasn't sure how to fix it.

The State of the City Speeches provided the transition to being a more effective speaker. The State of the City speech seemed too important simply to wing it. I used it for a deeper purpose—organizing and planning the entire year around it. I employed it the way Jack Welch or Warren Buffett did their annual report—to communicate directly with their shareholders the results of the past year and their plans for the year to come. Elliot convinced me that this was the speech I *least* needed to read. He maintained that some of the talks I gave at little groups where I didn't even know what the group did—those were the ones I ought to be reading, if I had to read any. The State of the City speech I should deliver from the heart.

"Rudy, you developed this, you created it. This is inside you!" Elliot then made another point. Speaking without a script or podium means taking a certain risk. That's exciting in any live performance. When you go see Pavarotti or Domingo, part of the thrill is hearing whether he hits the note. That's why live theater persists. The excitement of a speaker risking failure—taking the chance that he'll forget what he came to say or stammer and stutter the whole time—electrifies the audience. They tune in more and pay closer attention.

I knew he was right, but what if I forgot something? Elliot said, hey, if you leave it out, you leave it out—we'll print a comprehensive list of the main points to hand to everyone who attended. I protested that the press would then say I didn't believe in the point I hadn't mentioned as much as the ones I had—but by then I realized that I was straining for an excuse to hang on to the security blanket of a script. Elliot told me to forget about the press reaction.

The first time I did it his way was my State of the City speech in 1996. I had a script, which I put on the podium and used as an outline; but I left the podium, and walked around a little. The speech went over fine—although the press couldn't believe it: they literally looked for hidden TelePrompTers. Elliot told me to do away with the podium entirely the next year. Even then, with another year of speeches under my belt, I couldn't bring myself to abandon my crutch completely. For the entire three months of developing the State of the City speech, I practiced it the old way. Finally, on the morning of the speech, I said, "Get rid of the podium."

It was one of the most satisfying speeches I ever gave and a turning point. I communicated directly, without the artifice of a script or the distance of a podium. That's the first time I thought of myself as a truly effective political speaker and I really began to find giving speeches satisfying.

Delivering speeches is only one facet of communicating ideas. In 1993, in the interim period after the election and before I took office, my advisors and I decided on a new strategy. The dire straits of those days required drastic changes. Peter Powers, Cristyne Lategano (my then Director of Communications), David Garth, and I decided that we had to get into people's living rooms and explain what I was doing and why I was doing it. We knew that the first year would be tough. I had to fight for the hearts and minds of the people, to get them on board with my ideas, even though they'd be painful at first. I couldn't leave it to the media to explain. We knew the stereotype would be "Republican mayor, tough guy, hurting people. Why is he cutting all these programs, doing this, doing that?"

So we decided that I'd communicate directly with people and explain that even the best programs can't be funded by a bankrupt city. We'd been losing jobs by the thousands—313,000 between 1990 and 1993. I explained to a group of schoolchildren at one event that there was no point in working hard to graduate from school if all that awaited them was a bleak economy with no jobs.

All this resonated with people when I spoke to them one-on-one. I got my own weekly radio show on WABC, then added a second on WCBS once a month. I did weekly interviews on Fox, WPIX. I made as many speeches as possible, went to every dinner and meeting I could, sometimes to three community groups a night. New York City had a long tradition of seeing its mayors in the outer boroughs during election time and when there was an emergency. We instituted a policy of holding the monthly town hall meeting in a different borough each month, something I did for all eight years, missing only the month of September 2001. And I made that one up by doing two in November—in total I held 96 official town hall meetings, distributed roughly equally among the five boroughs.

This was all intended to allow me unfiltered communication,

where people could grill me and I could address their concerns directly. I would repeat, as often and as clearly as possible, the principles on which my administration was going to rest. During my first year, *Newsday* ran a photo of me sitting behind a microphone with headphones on and with the caption, "Air Giuliani." That headline became one of my favorites, because it was the first to pick up that I was deliberately trying to go beyond the newspapers, communicating directly to the people.

THE IMPORTANCE OF LANGUAGE

Words are enormously important to me. I love to read and I love language, the sheer pleasure of words in the right order. Choosing one word over another is an important act.

Frank Luntz, who did polling for my campaigns in 1993 and 1997, is brilliant about words. His main goal is to discern the best way to describe controversial ideas. He even has a way of measuring people's reactions to words. He puts focus groups in a room, and asks them to press various buttons as they listen to you speak, concentrating on what they like and what they don't like. When you say things like, "We care about children," the reading goes way up. With "You must *not* do this," it goes way down. As a trial lawyer at heart, I can see the value of such research. In a legal contract, a particular word can become the subject of a five-year litigation. When I was a young assistant, I often listened to tapes of bugged conversations, and knew that one word could be crucial in determining whether a crime had been committed. Did he actually say yes to knocking that guy off, or didn't he?

However, I have a contrary view about words. Only a few people in my administration understood, but I stuck with it nonetheless. Part of what I was trying to do was change people's minds, and if you want to accomplish that you have to stop pandering to them—even if that means using words they don't like.

A good example is the word "voucher." Luntz would present data proving that when discussing education policy, if I used other language to describe a voucher, people would have a more positive reaction. Had I told someone I was going to give them their money back and allow them to choose the school their child went to, 70 percent would agree that was a good idea. On the other hand, if I said I was going to provide a "voucher," then only about 40 percent agreed. The reason was that the word had been demonized—the United Federation of Teachers and the National Education Association characterized it as a threat to de-fund public schools. It had become a demonized word.

Nevertheless, I refused to abandon it, and still do. We're only going to win the battle for choice for parents when the word "voucher" loses its stigma. In using all the euphemisms, voucher advocates cede the battle, because behind people's fear of the word lies the contorted thinking that prevents voucher programs from being adopted. Those who oppose vouchers tend not to understand them. For those of us who believe in the concept, it's our job to defang the word, to counter the irrational reaction to it. The only way to do that is to say the word, to discuss it, to find out what people are so afraid of. And the more supporters say the word, the less its opponents can milk it for propaganda reasons.

This idea about words—about seizing the rhetorical upper hand—dates back to when I was a U.S. Attorney. During my first organized crime indictment, in 1983, I used the word "Mafia" during a press conference. The Italian civil rights groups complained bitterly, and wrote angry letters to me and to my bosses in the Justice Department. It turns out that there had been a long-standing prohibition on the use of "Mafia," codified in a memo from Attorney General John Mitchell dating back to the late 1960s. There was a fear that the twenty million Italian Americans who were not associated with organized crime would be offended.

I do feel sensitive about the pressures on Italian Americans regarding organized crime—it's a burden for them (and for me, too). But the more I thought about it, the more I decided that the way forward was not to be afraid of the word "Mafia," but to use it and explain what any reasonable person already knows: that the Mafia is made up of an extremely small percentage of Italians and Italian Americans. It's roughly the same percentage in which every ethnic group commits crimes. Ultimately, "Mafia" says only that Italians and Italian Americans are human beings. Once we acknowledge that, we take much of the mystique out of it.

Word choices carry enormous symbolic weight. That's the reason we changed the name on every "Welfare Office" to "Job Center." This mattered to me more than people realized. Part of my philosophical transformation to the G.O.P. was based on another idea wrapped in a word: "entitlement." During the 1970s, as a private citizen, I became convinced that New York City was being destroyed by the preaching of entitlement. A mindset had been established that locked people into poverty. It said, "Here are the steps out of the basement. We're going to close the door and keep you in that basement because we need you to vote for us, to make us more important, to cheer for us." That's what the word "entitlement" said to me, and it's another example of the power of language.

STICK TO YOUR WORD

Any leader is only as good as his word. When it comes to communicating beliefs and ideas, a leader's word is not only an emblem of trust but a critical device in spreading the message. One of the first fights we had in my administration was over the merging of the police departments. New York City had the NYPD, the Transit Police, who patrolled the subways, and the Housing Police, responsible for the public housing projects. It was an unwieldy bureaucracy, each with its own unions and contracts. More important, it wasn't the right way to protect the city.

A guy who sells drugs in a housing development is probably selling drugs in bars and in subway stations as well. Somebody who rapes in a housing development one day, then rapes in the hallway of a privately owned building the next and on a subway the next should not be pursued by three different agencies who answer to different bosses and may or may not share information. It also made for an inflexible police force. If crime dropped 20 percent in the subways and rose 20 percent in the housing developments, we weren't able to deploy transit cops in the projects. The system wasn't producing the best police work and it made labor negotiations extremely difficult.

From my days as a U.S. Attorney, I knew how talented the New York Police Department was. With access to the personnel and organizational leverage of all three forces, I was convinced we could create the best urban police force in the world. That belief was not just hometown pride. There are several reasons the current NYPD is so good. First, with a force of 41,000, the NYPD is larger than the entire FBI. It essentially boils down to economy of scale. The NYPD can do things that other police departments can't. If we need to bring 2,000 police officers to a scene to make sure a riot doesn't take place, we have the experience, manpower, and equipment to make it happen.

Another advantage is that New York City contains five counties. In south Florida, for example, Miami has its own police force, but then there's the Dade County force and all the other forces within Dade County. The same is true of Los Angeles and Chicago and most big cities—large cities located within even larger counties. In New York City, if a crime occurs in Brooklyn, there's no need to coordinate the efforts and assign jurisdiction. There's no Kings County police force trying to muscle out the NYPD or declining to share leads.

We were losing those advantages with the Housing and the Transit Police. Previous mayors had unsuccessfully attempted to merge the three police departments. The housing developments opposed it, the advocacy groups opposed it, the unions opposed it. The logic for combining them, however, was compelling.

First, we had to figure out how to do it legally. The precise maneuvers are detailed elsewhere, but in brief, we got the Housing Police on board but needed a different tactic for the Transit Police. They'd threatened to sue us, loudly announcing that they'd never join the NYPD. They basically dared me to do something. So I did.

The Transit Police were funded by a formula that called for the city, state, and federal governments each to contribute a certain percentage. I told the Transit Authority that we were exercising our cancellation rights. New York City was no longer going to pay its share, and if the Transit Authority wanted police on its trains they could pay for them without any subsidy from the city. They thought that when push came to shove I'd blink—that I'd never be willing to stand the political heat of the prospect of lawless subways. They were used to dealing with mayors who'd been elected with union support and couldn't bear the prospect of standing up to one of the more powerful ones. Faced with my threat to hold back from paying part of their salary and knowing I had arranged an alternative policing system, they became convinced I was serious and ultimately negotiated a merger with us.

We won a battle no one thought we could win.

Next, we had to win the confidence of those who opposed it. People read into the plan all kinds of motivations: that we wanted to reduce policing in minority neighborhoods, or reduce policing in housing developments. In fact, I increased policing in most minority neighborhoods—and the numbers proved to even persistent critics that those were the neighborhoods that enjoyed the largest reductions in crime—not *because* they were minority neighborhoods, but because they needed the most help in fighting crime.

I met with people from the housing developments who were angry at me for merging their police department and explained that I couldn't overcome every one of their criticisms right at that moment. I didn't have all the answers for their hypothetical worst-case scenarios, but told them they were going to thank me someday soon. Six years later, with 70 percent fewer murders a year, many people remembered these conversations.

The merger never would have happened if the Transit Police thought I was bluffing. Because they believed that I'd actually withhold New York City's share of the Transit Police funding, they decided to agree to the merger. And the best part is that just about everyone, from the cops themselves to the taxpayers to the people who ride the trains—everyone except those who commit crimes in the subways—ended up feeling better off.

During the early days of the first Reagan administration, the air traffic controllers threatened to strike. It would have brought the entire aviation system to a standstill. It was summer 1981, and I was the Associate Attorney General, the No. 3 person at the Justice Department. The strike had been threatened for some time, so the Justice Department had developed an elaborate plan to deal with civil actions and possible criminal actions in case of a strike turning ugly. We were prepared to mobilize the FBI and the U.S. Marshals Service to protect facilities, and I had coordinated several injunctions, one ready to go to federal court and others to various states.

On August 3, 1981, 13,000 of the 17,500 members of the Professional Air Traffic Controllers Organization (PATCO) walked off the job. President Reagan held a cabinet meeting. Attorney General William French Smith brought me along to explain our strategy, and Ted Olson, then in charge of the Office of Legal Counsel, came as well. There was much discussion and advice, but it was clear that the President had determined what he was going to do.

All of a sudden, just as the meeting was breaking up, President Reagan turned to the Attorney General and asked, "Don't they take an oath?"

Bill Smith replied, "What do you mean, Mr. President?"

Reagan said, "Don't all of these air traffic controllers take the same oath that everyone who works for the United States takes, promising not to strike against the government of the United States?"

Smith looked at me, and I looked at him. This was not anywhere in our legal research. I thought about the document I had signed, and now that the President mentioned it I recalled thinking that it was strange how there was indeed, in addition to the usual oath, a promise not to strike. I said I was sure the controllers signed that oath, because we all had. The President asked for a copy. I ran outside, called the personnel office at the Justice Department, and told them to get out an employment statement with the oaths on it.

I sent one of our attorneys to pick it up. At the same time the Secretary of Transportation, Drew Lewis, checked to make sure that the Transportation Department used the same form with their staff. It did. We showed the form to the President, but nobody could forecast what he was going to do. To this day, I still don't know how he knew about it, because, although the President takes the oath, I'm pretty sure he doesn't sign a form not to strike. But, as was proven time and again, President Reagan was much more knowledgeable than many people realized.

At eleven A.M., President Reagan held a press conference in the Rose Garden and announced that any air traffic controller who didn't return to work in forty-eight hours—by eleven A.M. Wednesday—would be fired. He said, "Let me read the solemn oath taken by each of these employees, a sworn affidavit, when they accepted their jobs: 'I am not participating in any strike against the Government of the United States or any agency thereof, and I will not so participate while an employee of the Government of the United States or any agency thereof.'"

Congress had made such strikes a crime in 1955, and the law was upheld by the Supreme Court in 1971. Nevertheless, federal employees were staging strikes all the time at that point, including recent ones by postal workers and by employees at the Library of Congress and the Government Printing Office. Even air traffic controllers had staged a "sick-out" in 1970. But here was the Great Communicator standing up there and reading from an oath that every one of those controllers had signed. It was a master stroke. President Reagan could have been a great trial lawyer. The entire press corps, always ready to fight with him, was eating out of his hand. Suddenly it was as if the controllers had been caught betraying their country: "They broke their oath," everyone murmured. "They broke their oath."

That night I went on *Nightline*, representing the position of the Reagan administration. Also there was Robert Poli, the PATCO president, who was a nice guy. We debated the merits and demerits of the strike, of striking against the United States, and his demands for across-the-board raises of $10,000 per year, full retirement after twenty years, and a four-day, thirty-two-hour workweek. During the debate, Poli suggested several times that Reagan was bluffing and would never fire the striking controllers.

It was a brutally hot night in Washington, and after the debate Poli and I were leaving the ABC Studio across the street from the Mayflower Hotel. We shook hands and I told him I was sorry his members were out on strike, and that I hoped there was a way to resolve this. Then I said, "I hope you take this in the right spirit. This isn't meant to posture or negotiate . . . but you're wrong. President Reagan isn't bluffing."

I asked him to listen for a moment and tell me if this rang true. "You've been negotiating for two weeks with a group of people representing the President. They're not sure what to do. Some have said to him the very things that you've said—that he can't follow through on this. But go back home tonight and look at a tape of his statement in the Rose Garden and look at his eyes. You'll see that you're wrong, that he's going to do what he said. Whatever decision you make, don't make it because you think he's bluffing. I sat in the room with him, I watched him decide, and I looked in his eyes. This is a very convinced man. And you're making a miscalculation if you think public pressure or union pressure will get him to change his mind."

Without putting it quite this way, Poli replied in effect, "Ah, you don't know what you're talking about, kid."

There were people in the cabinet arguing against President

Reagan's deadline. They said that he couldn't carry it through, and when he backed down it would be worse for his having bluffed. They were basically advising him to warn the unions, threaten them, but then not take a firm stand that he couldn't take back. The President made it plain that if he didn't draw the line this time he'd have little credibility the next. What happened if the FBI decided to go on strike? Or the Navy? It was a matter of principle. If you work for the people of the United States, you waive the right to strike. President Reagan was thinking ahead, deciding that he'd rather fight it out with the controllers, as devastating as that could have been, than with a law enforcement agency or the veterans hospitals.

President Reagan, of course, was not bluffing. He fired more than 11,000 PATCO strikers, and the government's contingency plans for running the air traffic system and replacing the fired strikers worked perfectly. This is why it's so important to mean what you say. With that stand, Reagan single-handedly stopped the pattern of unions illegally threatening the people of the United States. I believe he knew that by standing up to the union and meaning what he said, this was exactly what he would accomplish. That experience influenced me a good deal, and drilled home the importance of communicating honestly. Any leader engages in negotiations on a regular basis, and too often it's a world filled with posturing. That's why words are so important. People need to understand that you mean exactly what you say.

TAILOR THE MESSAGE TO THE LISTENER

One of a leader's responsibilities is to meet the needs of those he or she leads. The point is not to alter your message depending on the audience, but to present it so that it can be understood by whomever you're addressing. The goal should be to ensure your message gets through loud and clear to as many people as possible.

Sometimes the best way to get a message across is not to say anything at all and let your actions speak for you. On Saturday, August 4, 2001, a senseless tragedy occurred in the Sunset Park section of Brooklyn. An off-duty police officer, driving a van, plowed into 24-year-old Maria Herrera, her 4-year-old son, Andy Herrera, and her 16-year-old sister, Dilcia Pena, as they crossed Third Avenue. Maria was eight months pregnant at the time, and although a baby boy was delivered by emergency Caesarian section, he died immediately after. The police said that blood tests indicated that the officer had more than twice the legal limit of alcohol. He was charged with vehicular homicide and multiple other crimes.

As though those facts weren't disturbing enough, it soon emerged that several of the officers in that precinct regularly drank alcohol in their precinct's parking lot and frequented a nearby go-go bar that they had been told was off-limits. I was livid. Here we had many excellent police officers spending much effort reducing crime and building confidence in the city, and not only had these guys behaved like out-of-control teenagers, but one of them was accused of destroying almost an entire family.

Bernie Kerik matched my anger and disappointment note for note. By Wednesday, he had identified thirteen police officers in the precinct whom he was going to discipline. With the community hurting, I wanted to announce that action was being taken as soon as possible, but at the time he called me to tell me about the action he was taking, I was up at Gracie Mansion, where we were holding a barbecue to honor the employees of a city agency. Bernie offered to come uptown to the mansion, but I didn't think it would be appropriate to make the announcement amid a party scene. I told Bernie I'd meet him downtown and decided we'd open City Hall for it, rather than doing it at One Police Plaza, police headquarters.

The head of any large organization that draws regular media coverage should understand that what he or she says on television, radio, and in the newspapers is not just a message to the public but is also like a memo to their employees. They, too, watch television, listen to the radio, read the papers. I felt that speaking to the public, and to the media, from the seat of power in the city would send the strongest possible signal that this criminal behavior would not be tolerated, that anyone who broke the law would be held accountable.

The need to communicate clearly was never more compelling than during the recovery from the World Trade Center attacks. People were desperate for information—everyone from the guy driving to work through newly restricted tunnels to the suddenly widowed young woman whose children no longer had a father. The information had to be correct, but there were delicate questions of taste and sensitivity as well.

One of the issues we faced involved death certificates for city employees who were missing in the World Trade Center rubble. At a morning meeting a few weeks after September 11, Deputy Mayor Bob Harding mentioned that the city actuary had come up with the point that we were continuing to keep the missing uniformed personnel on the payroll. The actuary had suggested they should now be taken off, which would allow the city to start paying pension benefits immediately. It would also help mitigate situations in which, say, there was a missing employee with nineteen years of service. If we didn't establish guidelines, and the widow took a year to seek a death certificate, we wouldn't know whether she was entitled to a twenty-year pension, or less.

My first reaction to hearing this was outrage. How dare anyone propose that the city tell a grieving widow to sign a death certificate before she was ready. But, as awful as that sounded, the point was reasonable. At some stage, reality had to settle in and those who had lost loved ones needed to start the healing process. In fact, the benefits for the surviving spouse of a fireman who died in the line of duty average about $60,000 a year, tax-free, for life, plus a lump sum of over $1 million. The Twin Towers Fund and other funds provided even more money, as well as pro bono legal services, financial planning services, free counseling, camp for the children, and a variety of other benefits. So it wasn't a question of trying to get people to accept some low offer as quickly as possible. But it just didn't sit right with me, and I started telling Bob exactly where the actuary could stuff his charts and schedules. Then Tom Von Essen, the Fire Commissioner, spoke up. Tom has a wonderfully succinct way with words. "We can't tell a widow her husband's off the payroll," he said, "when she's not ready to say he's dead." I ended up rejecting Bob's advice and decided to give people the option of making up their own minds when they wanted to make that difficult decision.

Other ideas required more direct communication. At a press conference we held to announce the reopening of Stuyvesant High School—one of the gems of New York City's public school system, and located only blocks from Ground Zero—I took time to praise Harold Levy, the chancellor of the Board of Education. Now, I've had my disagreements with Levy, but giving credit where it's due is an important part of communicating ideas. I told the audience that the chancellor had been involved in every step of the process of getting the school tested for safety and reopened as soon as possible. I pointed out that Levy had come to every meeting, weighed the impact on the students, and had counselors in place, at the ready.

That got me thinking. I don't pretend to be a psychiatrist, but with people asking me for advice about what to tell children about the attacks, I used the opportunity to suggest that honesty and frankness were the best policy. Speaking specifically about the high-school-age students at Stuy High, I said that opening the school even though the kids would be confronted by the massive cleanup equipment wasn't a bad thing. "Children have to face this. It has to be explained in the right way, a sensitive way. But protecting them from the reality just hides them from what their life is going to be like as they grow up. My feeling is that you ought to deal with children honestly."

9

Be Your Own Man

As a federal prosecutor for over a decade, as well as during two spells in the Justice Department, I grew accustomed to people being angry with me. I thought I was doing a good job so long as that anger was coming from a variety of sources—white-collar criminals, mobsters, corrupt politicians, narcotics traffickers. It's not a popularity contest. And sometimes, the only way a prosecutor can tell he's doing a good job—taking the tough cases, pursuing sympathetic defendants—is when people aren't thrilled with him.

Elective politics, on the other hand, *is* a popularity contest. That doesn't mean a leader—of a company, a government, or any organization—should lead with his finger in the wind. In fact, the opposite is true. A leader is chosen because whoever put him there trusts his judgment, character, and intelligence—not his poll-taking skills. It's a leader's duty to act on those attributes. That duty is an extension of a lesson I learned from my father when I was a boy, one that has been reinforced a thousand different ways ever since: Be Your Own Man.

Part of that is communicating honestly and from the heart. When

I give a speech or appear at a function, I'm pretty much the same person that I am with my staff or my friends. That's why I did away with reading from a prepared text at a podium. I want the audience to see me and I want to see them—to be able to achieve an atmosphere that says, "Hey, we're just people."

There's a deeper application to all this. Being your own man—or woman, of course—means that you should never feel that you have to sacrifice your principles.

Politicians in New York City traditionally wear dual-purpose baseball caps—Yankees on one side, Mets on the other. I could never do that. I've been a Yankees fan my whole life, even though I grew up within a mile of Ebbets Field, home to the Brooklyn Dodgers. My father came from Manhattan and was a devoted Yankees supporter. After they were married, my mother made my father move to Brooklyn, which in those days resembled inviting a Hatfield to live on the McCoy family farm. My father, always unhappy about the move, decided that he would exact revenge against my mother and her entire family—all of whom also lived in Brooklyn and were devout Dodgers supporters—by raising me as a Yankees fan. He bought me their pinstriped uniform, discussed my Yankees baseball cards, and indoctrinated me on the greatness of Babe Ruth, Lou Gehrig, Joe DiMaggio, Red Ruffing, Bill Dickey, Waite Hoyt, Yogi Berra, and Phil Rizzuto.

If you were looking to instill character in a youngster (or perhaps some pugilistic experience), then having him wear a Yankees cap a few blocks from Ebbets Field was the way to do it. Non-baseball fans—or those who have never lived in Brooklyn—may think I'm exaggerating when I describe the danger of cheering the Yankees in Dodger territory. Not so. The reason my father taught me how to box was to defend myself against Dodgers fans. A civilized discussion about the relative merits of right fielders Carl Furillo and Hank Bauer could turn bloody in a hurry. I was thrown in the mud and beaten up. I hesitate to tell this story because people think I dreamed the whole thing, but it is literally true that I was nearly lynched. I have seen the spot many times since—it later became a gas station, but it used to be a field. I was 5 years old and playing in that field when four or five kids grabbed me, stood me up by a tree, and put a noose around my neck. My grandmother saw it all from her window and started yelling until the kids ran away. And it was all because I was wearing my Yankee uniform. Decades later, when I entered politics, I didn't disguise my allegiance, and ultimately I hope Mets fans respected me because they knew that I was being honest: I'm a real sports fan, whose lifelong loyalties don't evaporate when expedient.

SET AN EXAMPLE

You cannot ask those who work for you to do something you're unwilling to do yourself. It is up to you to set a standard of behavior.

In the eight years in which I was mayor of the biggest, most complicated city in America, despite being in the jurisdiction of legendary prosecutors from the Southern and Eastern Federal Districts—Democrats appointed by President Clinton and Janet Reno—every single investigation that led to charges against any of the 250,000 city workers was begun by my own Department of Investigation.

The importance of setting an example is one of the reasons why I made such a big deal of paying my own way.

The principle applied when I ate at restaurants. I realized that a free cup of coffee and cheeseburger from a diner owner who voted for me was unlikely to compromise my integrity (although it would compromise my cancer-recovery diet). The owner would know that he wasn't going to get preferential treatment just because he'd treated me to a meal, and arguably there's nothing immoral—certainly nothing illegal—about accepting a gift from someone who expects nothing in return. When a proprietor flat-out refused to give me a check, I left enough money to cover the cost—and a nice tip.

Sometimes, though, I carried it to extremes. My friend Jon Sale was my law school classmate before he went on to serve as counsel on the Watergate impeachment inquiry and is now a well-respected criminal defense lawyer in Miami. He loves to tell a story about a double date I went on with him and his wife, Jane. This would be about 1990—I was in private practice after having run for mayor. The four of us were staying overnight in New Jersey. We were out late after a party and wanted a bite to eat. We found a twenty-four-hour diner, had our dinner, and it came time to pay.

No check. I asked once more. No check. Again, "Please, we need a check." Still nothing. "Give me a check!" I started to argue with the owner of the diner, a big Greek fellow, insisting that he give us a check while he was equally insistent that he wouldn't. "You were a great U.S. Attorney. You should've been mayor." He was like the opposite of the soup guy on *Seinfeld*: "I love you, no check!"

I wasn't in any public office, elected or otherwise. This was New Jersey, too—not even my home state. But it bothered me. Finally I got to the cash register and said to the owner, "Look, you're making my life more difficult. Would you *please* just give me the check." Irate, he at last handed me the bill—$25. I ceremoniously reached into my pocket, only to discover that I didn't have any money—and had left my wallet, with all my credit cards, in the room at my hotel. So I leaned over and whispered, "Jon, give me thirty dollars!" By this time, he was laughing hysterically. "Yeah, this makes a lot of sense," he said. "Thanks for letting me pay for preserving your integrity." Afterward, I realized I was perhaps carrying my objections too far—a cup of coffee from a grateful diner owner wouldn't have compromised my principles and would have given him a lot of pleasure.

As mayor, I expected high standards from my cabinet and top commissioners. We inherited a city in extreme disrepair, and had ambitious plans for its future. I wanted to make the most of that opportunity. During that first year, I worked every single weekend. In eight years, I missed only one day of work through sickness—when I had surgery for treatment of my cancer. (It was on the day after that I marched in the Steuben Day Parade with George Steinbrenner and Representative Rick Lazio). During radiation treatment, I would come to work after my seven A.M. appointment, carry on until the afternoon, then take a nap. Sometimes, it was a two-hour, even a four-hour break, but I never missed a whole day and often resumed work in the late afternoon or evening. I took no weeks off, and my longest "vacation" was a single four-day trip after the 1997 election.

The point is not that one has to be a superhero. Like any other employee, a leader shouldn't work to the point where he is no longer effective, and should take time off as necessary. That amount varies from person to person. Many leaders enjoy their vacations, and I never begrudged President Reagan his breaks at his ranch or President Clinton his vacations in Hilton Head. Leaders need different routines to be effective.

However, no leader should demand from others something he's unwilling to give himself. I worked the hours I did because there was so much to do and because I love my work. But an equally compelling reason could be found in the degree to which it inspired those around me.

Peter Powers became my top deputy in 1994, and it was a comfort to have someone I could trust so completely as my right-hand man. Peter lives on Manhattan's Upper East Side, about a block from Gracie Mansion. We frequently had late-night meetings there, starting after dinner and going deep into the night. In a way, those meetings were reminiscent of the debates he and I had back in high school, college, and law school, often including our friend Alan Placa. The three of us would passionately argue the issues of the day, sometimes switching sides in the middle to hone our rhetorical chops.

Years later, Peter recalled one night's meeting. In saying good-bye at Gracie at about two A.M., I signed off with, "See you at the morning meeting." He told me he walked home thinking, "It's late and I'm tired. Couldn't my best friend of nearly forty years have said, 'Take tomorrow morning off' just this once?" A few hours later—say 6:30 A.M.—he gets up, still sore at me, rubs the sleep out of his eyes, and turns on the television. Right there, he sees me giving a live interview at the scene of some water-main break, and he actually muttered out loud, "How can I stay mad at that bastard? He works harder than he asks of anyone else."

Joe Lhota, who rose through my administration all the way to Deputy Mayor for Operations, had a similar take. Returning an email within five minutes, even at three in the morning, was standard operating procedure for him. Asked about what it took to succeed in my employ, Lhota said, "Simple. Get up five minutes before Rudy and go to bed five minutes after." Well, maybe simple, but not easy.

The most important element of setting an example isn't attitude or diligence, but performing some of the tasks that you ask others to execute. If you can do what the people working for you do as well as the best of them, your ability to lead is enhanced tremendously. That doesn't mean you have to be the best at everything. In a complicated system, that's not only impossible, it's undesirable—a leader needs the expertise of specialists and shouldn't undermine them or interfere. Leading any enterprise means that management duties will take up the lion's share of your time. Nevertheless, leaders shouldn't abandon the trenches to pay attention only to the "big picture."

When I was U.S. Attorney I would go to court and argue cases, including appeals. I tried the most difficult case rather than the easier ones, not only because I believed in my abilities as a prosecutor but because I knew that would help me run the U.S. Attorney's office. The U.S. Attorney's office represents the United States Department of Justice in court.

The reputation of the Southern District of New York has no peer, then or now. It attracts the brightest lawyers, and each is accustomed to being a star. It's a little like the Yankees. The players show up having excelled elsewhere. It takes a true leader like Joe Torre to get them to come together as a unit. It doesn't hurt that Joe is a former MVP, batting champ, and nine-time All-Star.[1]

U.S. Attorneys typically do not try many cases themselves, especially in large districts. Their leadership and management duties are so great that there's not time. Occasionally, the Attorney General asks the U.S. Attorney to handle a case personally. As Associate Attorney General, I would make it clear when the President or the Attorney General wanted the U.S. Attorney to do this. That happened only once to me as the U.S. Attorney. In late 1983, a group of British protesters filed a federal suit in New York, seeking to interrupt the scheduled deployment of nuclear cruise missiles in Britain. Represented by Anne Simon and Lyndon Johnson's former Attorney General Ramsey Clark, the plaintiffs were joined by two Democratic Congressmen, Ted Weiss of New York and Ron Dellums of California. President Reagan and Defense Secretary Caspar Weinberger were among those named as defendants. Attorney General William French Smith told me that he thought it would be a good idea to argue the case myself. I did, and the suit was ultimately thrown out.

---

[1] As a St. Louis Cardinal, Torre led the league in hitting in 1971, with a .363 batting average, and was that year's National League MVP, with 34 doubles, 8 triples, 24 home runs, and 137 RBIs. He won the Gold Glove as Milwaukee Braves catcher in 1965. But Torre's best all-around year as a player may actually have been 1966, in which he not only set his career marks in round-trippers (36) and slugging percentage (.560) but also did so while catching 114 games, which ties his one-year high at that grueling position. He also took 60 walks, while whiffing only 61 times, the best ratio of his career. That Braves team was extremely interesting from a leadership point of view. In addition to Torre, the 1966 roster included future Major League managers Felipe Alou and Hall of Famer Eddie Mathews, who managed the Braves briefly in the 1970s. Woody Woodward became the general manager for the Mariners, and Lee Thomas for the Phillies. It's been said that a CEO may be measured in part by how successfully he grooms future CEOs — Jack Welch at GE, for instance, ran a company in which many people matured into leaders of other companies, including Robert Nardelli (Home Depot), James McNerney (3M), Gary Wendt (Conseco), David Cote (TRW), Larry Johnston (Albertson's), John Blystone (SPX), and Larry Bossidy (Honeywell) — not to mention his successor at GE, Jeffrey Immelt.

As U.S. Attorney, I argued six appeals. I also took on other duties myself, as when I went to Arizona to take a deposition from Joe Bonanno. A year later, Bonanno refused to testify to the existence and structure of the Mafia. With William Kunstler as his lawyer, the legendary crime boss claimed his heart was far too weak for him to appear in court, and presented all manner of medical evidence to support that claim. We insisted on an opinion from our side's doctor, and had Tim Weld, a renowned cardiologist and the brother of former Massachusetts Governor William Weld, examine him. When Weld told us the 80-year-old Bonanno had one of the strongest hearts he'd ever seen, I again went to Tucson to argue that he should be held in contempt. Judge Richard Owen agreed: Bonanno served fourteen months for refusing to testify. And Dr. Weld was right—Bonanno lived another seventeen years.

For me, it was more a question of restraining myself from going to court as opposed to not wanting to step into the ring. The same was true during my time as Associate Attorney General in the Justice Department—I looked for such opportunities—and fulfilled a dream for any lawyer when I argued *Bell v. United States* in the Supreme Court.

There is no more powerful motivation for others than a leader who sets an example. Teachers, philosophy, inspirational speeches are all valuable, but setting an example is the most valuable of all. Appearing in court would send a message to the young assistant U.S. Attorneys who worked for me: "He can do what we do, maybe even better than we can. And we would like to be able to do it like him someday." That certainly had a powerful effect on me when I was an assistant. My boss, U.S. Attorney Paul Curran, tried cases himself, including tough ones, such as Carmine Tramunti, then head of the Lucchese crime family. What made an even greater impression on me was when I brought an indictment against Frank Waters, charging him with selling heroin and cocaine. Waters had been a federal narcotics agent who was involved with the French Connection investigation. Paul took it on himself, even though it was not the kind of trial that even U.S. Attorneys who liked to go to court liked to take on. Paul lost, after one of the only two witnesses vanished, leaving a single witness to carry the case—a former federal agent who himself had been convicted of narcotics trafficking; but he won the admiration of his assistants because he had had the courage to handle such a difficult matter himself.

I became U.S. Attorney in 1983. By 1985, I felt that I had the office near to how I wanted it to operate and was ready to lace up my courtroom gloves and try my first case as U.S. Attorney. And I had just the right one.

My office was knee-deep in one of its most important prosecutions. We had indicted eight leaders of organized crime from the major families of La Cosa Nostra. This was personally meaningful to me, not only because of my animus toward such criminals but because I was part of a team that had developed the case from the beginning.

The majority of what a U.S. Attorney handles comes along in the middle of the investigation process, after some other agency, such as the local police or the FBI, has done preliminary work. But the Commission case arose directly from my reading a book in my apartment in Washington, D.C. I dreamed up the tactic of using the Federal Racketeer Influenced and Corrupt Organizations Act (known to *Sopranos* fans by its acronym "RICO") to prosecute the Mafia leadership for being itself a "corrupt enterprise." The idea behind the act was that an ongoing criminal enterprise is more dangerous to society than any specific criminal, since the organization will continue even after individuals are jailed. RICO allows for the prosecution of those furthering the enterprise, rather than only those who commit the crimes that benefit it. Joe Bonanno had written his memoir, *Man of Honor*. It is a surprisingly good read, but Chapters 12 through 18 detail the entire structure of "The Commission." I realized that Bonanno's description of how the families were organized provided a roadmap of precisely what the RICO statute was designed to combat. As soon as I became the U.S. Attorney I was able to hoist Bonanno by his literary petard.

The case was a rare one in that I had it from the beginning, and was able to supervise the investigation throughout. Mike Chertoff (now Assistant Attorney General to John Ashcroft) was one of my assistants, and he took over the detailed preparation. Between us, we knew the material intimately, and had many hours of evidence on tape. I was sitting on top of this strong prosecution, feeling extremely confident, when all of a sudden along came a much tougher case.

On January 10, 1986, Queens Borough President Donald Manes was discovered dazed and slumped over the wheel of his car on the shoulder of the Grand Central Parkway. Manes, whose leadership of the city's most populous borough and its Democratic Party had earned him the nickname "King of Queens," was bleeding from a self-inflicted gash on his left wrist. He knew we were conducting an investigation that would rock the city at the highest levels, and had tried to kill himself before we reached him.

Geoffrey Lindenauer, a close friend of Manes's, was the deputy director of New York City's Parking Violations Bureau. With its huge flow of cash—all in small, hard-to-trace amounts—the PVB had been a hotbed of corruption for a long time. When an informant told us that he had paid bribes to Lindenauer, we saw an opportunity to put an end to the racket. We arrested Lindenauer on bribery charges on January 14.

By March, Lindenauer had rolled on his partners in corruption. He pleaded guilty to two of the thirty-nine counts against him and detailed with disturbing precision his chores as the bagman for Donald Manes. Lindenauer recalled the bribes paid by companies seeking contracts from the Parking Violations Bureau, reciting the various restaurants in which he accepted envelopes stuffed with cash, which he'd later split with Manes in the bathroom at Queens Borough Hall.

I had not yet indicted Manes, for two reasons. One, we were still hoping to flip him—if Manes would cooperate with the prosecution, we were sure he would have useful information. Second, Manes was at the end of his rope. I feared an indictment could push him over the edge. Within days of Lindenauer's guilty plea, Donald Manes plunged a foot-long knife into his heart in another suicide attempt. Tragically, this time he succeeded.

Lindenauer's allegations led to indictments of a former director of the PVB, Lester Shafran, and a real estate mogul who had been the Taxi and Limousine Commissioner, Michael Lazar. Further investigation resulted in yet further indictments. On April 9, it was Stanley Friedman's turn—New York City's premier king-maker and a confidant of Mayor Koch. Though he had been a deputy mayor to Abe Beame, Friedman had never himself been elected to public office; yet his power to anoint leaders was unmatched. He used his position as head of the Bronx Democratic Party, and the loyalty of appointees, to utilize a city agency as a racketeering enterprise.

Friedman was a lobbyist for firms doing business with the city. He was also the largest private shareholder in one of them—a company called Citisource Inc, which manufactured handheld devices to issue traffic tickets. We charged Friedman with attempting to bribe Lindenauer and Manes in order to land deals for Citisource. Despite the official charge, Friedman remained confident to the point of arrogance. He was sure he was going to be acquitted.

He was scheduled to go to trial at the same time as the Commission case, indicted along with Lester Shafran, Michael J. Lazar, and Marvin B. Kaplan, chairman of Citisource Inc. In this case, we had no tape recordings. The chief witness had severe credibility issues (not only was Lindenauer an accomplice, his past included various sordid untruths and misrepresentations). Most of all, the defendants had a very able defense team, headed by Thomas Puccio, with whom I've shared a friendly rivalry. Tom attended my wedding and years later, when his son tragically died, I was at the funeral. Though we were not particularly close, I respected him as an investigator and a lawyer.

By the time Manes committed suicide, I had become more directly involved in the PVB investigation. Once the press got wind of the investigaton, it began moving quickly. Puccio was fresh off a remarkable win in Claus von Bulow's retrial, and as Friedman's attorney was regarded as the early favorite. As the pre-trial motions began, the assistant U.S. Attorneys handling the courtroom motions, Bill Schwartz and David Zornow, were being pressured by the judge, Whitman Knapp, whom I knew well from the hearings he'd held as chairman of the Knapp Commission on police corruption during the *Prince of the City* cases.

As I have said, being U.S. Attorney often feels like being a baseball manager. It wasn't a matter of simply putting the "best" players in place as much as matching the *right* players to a given situation. I had to have the judgment and independence to remove people and transfer others where I needed them. One lawyer might be the right person to investigate a case, but somebody else better to try it. A certain kind of case might need a different assistant U.S. Attorney with a certain kind of personality—tougher, or with a better grasp of storytelling.

Schwartz and Zornow, both excellent attorneys, had never handled something of this magnitude or complexity, and it was my view that given the pressure to go to trial so quickly, the team needed the addition of a more experienced trial lawyer. As we moved ahead, I realized that a great deal depended on the way the case was tried. There could be no mistakes. I started thinking about who should lead the prosecution, and made a list of my assistants, starting with the most experienced.

One morning, I was in the shower, thinking what a tough break it was that I couldn't handle PVB with them because I was slated to try the Commission case. Then I remember getting myself out of my own head, so to speak, and looking at the problem purely as a manager. I tried to think of the office as though everyone in it, including myself, was simply a collection of talents and skills, without regard to who would prefer to do what.

As hard as it was emotionally to remove myself from a case I felt as close to as the Commission, once I thought of it from the perspective of whom I'd choose were I standing outside the situation, it didn't take me long to make up my mind. Looking at it as objectively as I could, I realized that the trial lawyer best suited for the PVB case was me.

Trials in which the main witness is an accomplice require experienced lawyers who understand how to get the most out of the case. Your witness is going to be ripped apart by the defense, and you have to reconstruct him or his testimony is worthless. Our witness in the Parking Violations Bureau case, Lindenauer, was due to testify about the bribes he helped to arrange. The defense was going to show on cross-examination that Lindenauer had taken bribes himself, had fleeced people under false pretenses by claiming a phony psychology degree, had taken advantage of women who had come to him for help, and had lied on official forms. Lindenauer would be under attack for days, and by the time he got off the witness stand nobody would believe him. But he was telling the truth, and we would have to spend the rest of the trial rebuilding our case with items of circumstantial evidence, little bits of information that corroborated everything Lindenauer had said.

What I now had to do was manage myself and say, "Okay, this is the right allocation of resources." I was even tempted to work on both cases, but realized that I had to devote myself to the PVB. Between that and trying to juggle my responsibilities as U.S. Attorney, my plate was more than full. I had to stop myself fantasizing about how it would have been to win a conviction in PVB, then turn around and convict the leaders of the five organized-crime families, all the while managing the biggest, most prestigious U.S. Attorney's office in the country.

It would have been nice. But part of any leader's responsibility is recognizing his limitations. Another part is trusting those who work for you. Wonderful as it might have been to try both cases, it would have been devastating—not just for me, but for the people of the Southern District of New York—to lose either because I couldn't dedicate my best effort. Mike Chertoff took over the Commission and I devoted myself to PVB.

On the day I showed up in court for the first time, the defendants made a motion to transfer the trial out of the Southern District. I agreed immediately, accepting a change of venue to New Haven, Connecticut. This was hardly convenient for me. My first child, Andrew, had been born that January, and it was difficult to be away from him. But I knew we'd have a better shot at winning in the new location.

I give such detail about this case because it was a critical step in the development of my thinking. Had I not tried the PVB, I might never have run for mayor of New York City.

The first time the idea to run seriously entered my head was during the trial. One evening I was walking on the green in New Haven with the rest of the prosecution team. It was a rare few minutes of solitude before we dove back into preparation for the case that seemed to occupy our every waking moment. As I walked, lagging a little behind the others, I dwelt on the sad, infuriating details of a scandal that was emblematic of everything wrong with New York City's government, and it occurred to me that I could do even more to fight public corruption if I were mayor. I thought, "I could straighten this out." I'm not even sure I knew what "straighten this out" meant. The idea was so embryonic at that stage that I didn't even formulate what I would be getting into. But the corruption, the decades of machine politicians owning different agencies of city government and running them for their own benefit, disturbed me on a gut level.

It was a fleeting thought. I had never run for public office. As a Republican, I was outnumbered five to one in New York City. And I loved being the U.S. Attorney. I put it out of my head and focused on the case in hand.

My son actually created a major incident at the Friedman trial—an episode that revealed something telling about how the defense approached the case. On the Wednesday a week before Thanksgiving, I summed up for eight hours straight. The next day, Thursday, the four defense lawyers summed up for the entire day. On Friday morning, I spent ninety minutes on rebuttal. Then the judge charged the jury and sent them out at about two P.M. that afternoon.

David Zornow and I both had babies back home, so on Saturday morning, our wives brought them up for the day. The jury was going to deliberate all weekend, in the hope that we could be done before Thanksgiving. We had to hang around the courtroom, even as we spent time with our families, in case the jury reached a verdict. That night's news in New York showed Zornow and me pushing baby carriages, and Friedman went crazy. He demanded that the kids and carriages be banned from the courtroom — they were influencing the jury.

That was symptomatic of the entire way the defense approached the case. No one on the jury was reading the New York newspapers. But the defense team was defending the case based upon what appeared in the papers and on television — approaching it as if it were a political campaign.

On the Sunday, another funny scene occurred. The jury was still deliberating and the Giants were playing Denver in a prelude to that season's Super Bowl. The jury kept asking questions, so I couldn't go back to the hotel to watch the game. There were television trucks parked in front of the building in case a verdict was announced. One of the crews invited me into the truck to watch the Giants. So I got in and who should be there watching but Michael Lazar, one of the defendants. I was wondering if I should be in the truck with someone I was trying to put in jail. I looked at him and he looked at me and I said, "Our part of the trial is over, right? It's in the jury's hands now." Together, we cheered the Giants as they squeaked by the Broncos on a field goal. Lazar then invited me to his birthday celebration for the next evening. I declined, thinking it might be a little uncomfortable.

By late Monday, we realized from some of the questions asked that a verdict was imminent. On Tuesday, the jury came back at about ten A.M. and told the judge they'd reached a unanimous decision. The odds were stacked against us. The press had played it as very close, harping on Lindenauer's credibility problems. But they consistently missed a lot of the corroborating evidence, and didn't understand the intricacies of the testimony. The press was expecting acquittals. So it was stunning when the jury found all four defendants guilty.

A couple of days later, at the Macy's Thanksgiving Day Parade, the thought of running for mayor occurred to me again. I was carrying Andrew on my shoulders and realized that people recognized me. I was accustomed to strangers occasionally waving to me—I had indicted the Commission case and prosecuted Mafia cases, and also been on television a fair deal, so I wasn't unknown. But this was different. Everybody seemed to know who I was and came up to shake my hand and thank me. I didn't appreciate what was happening at the time, because I had been up in New Haven during the trial and hadn't paid much attention to the coverage. I knew we were getting on television because I could see the crews outside the courthouse every day, but I wanted to focus on how the jury perceived the trial, not the reporters. Further, from the opening statements onward, the coverage from my point of view had been so one-sided that our joke was that, should we land a conviction, its headline would read "Friedman to Appeal."

DEFY EXPECTATION

In 1958, Lyndon Johnson wrote an article for *Texas Quarterly*, "My Political Philosophy." A line from it made an impression on me: "I am a free man, an American, a United States Senator, and a Democrat, in that order." You have to base your decisions on the allegiances that are most important to you. That's one of the reasons debates on campaign finance reform miss the point. I favor it, but in the final analysis money won't make an honest man dishonest or a dishonest man honest.

In politics, there's an outcry whenever an officeholder who has received campaign contributions from a particular industry supports a position perceived as favorable to that industry. The implication is that, say, the tobacco industry's contribution "bought" the official's support, or, at best, bought significant access to the official. I'd be the last person to say it never happens, but much more common is a company choosing to support those it views as sympathetic to its interests.

At any given moment during my administration, someone who supported me was angry because I didn't do what they hoped I would do. Not without reason did Thomas Jefferson describe the U.S. presidency as "a splendid misery" that involves "the daily loss of friends." Being mayor of New York is far from misery, but certainly involves decisions that lose friends. Ultimately, you have to be able to make the decision you think is the right one. If the people who supported you did so for the right reasons, they'll still be with you, even if in some instance you act against their interests. If they withdraw their support, you don't want them around anyway. There's no one thing you can do to establish the principle. All you can do is keep making decisions based on what you believe, and by your example, you'll demonstrate your independence.

I am a big admirer of Alan Simpson, a former senator from Wyoming. He has great wisdom and a remarkable sense of humor. Alan used to say that the main thing in politics is the integrity of the politician, and the willingness of the politician, once elected, to double-cross the people who gave him the money. "Double-cross" was a strong word to use, there for dramatic effect, but what he meant was that most of the people who give you money when you run for office agree with you. On those occasions when they don't, you've got to stick to your guns, even if you must disappoint—double-cross—a contributor.

The best way for a leader to set an independent tone is to establish that every decision, including those made by people who act on the leader's behalf, must be made for the benefit of the enterprise. As mayor, I told this to my employees over and over. It doesn't matter if you say no to someone who's my closest friend or biggest campaign contributor. I'll support you because I want you to make decisions on the merits.

In politics, defying expectation doesn't refer simply to contributors or lobbyists. Occasionally, your principles will differ from the official party line. Leaders of all kinds face similar situations, in which the expedient and convenient position does not match the one you believe to be right. True leadership requires choosing, in every instance, the position that allows you to sleep at night.

As a Republican mayor in a city dominated by Democrats, I was accustomed to (some would say delighted by) disagreements. Many of my philosophical underpinnings were not typical of New York City voters, and certainly at odds with the views of most of the city's elected officials and media. I stuck to my guns on every one—low taxes, small government, strong law enforcement, shrinking welfare rolls, privatizing services, results-based teacher evaluations, favoring competition, and believing in capitalism as a force for good.

There were also times in which my views varied from those typically held by my fellow Republicans. For example, I'm in favor of gun control. This is not because I buy into the idea that guns create crime: after prosecuting criminals for so many years, I understand that human beings do that. There will always be murderers and rapists and robbers who use weapons. But it's hard to dispute the idea that easy, unlimited access to handguns amplifies the effects and deadliness of crime.

I was in the Reagan Justice Department when the idea of a waiting period for the purchase of a handgun first came up. I was in favor of it, which was against the weight of opinion within the administration. What persuaded me more than anything else was a Canadian study that showed that a waiting period imposed in the late 1970s had cut suicides in half. For me, that fact alone underlined the idea that when someone needs to buy a gun "right this minute" he probably shouldn't have one.

I took no pleasure in opposing the prevailing opinion within my party; but I had to have confidence in my own judgment and resolve to stick with unpopular opinions. Other times, I defied my party's expectation simply because I believed it to be the right thing to do. I support a woman's right to choose. And on May 11, 1998, I proposed legislation that entitled same-sex couples to many of the same rights as married couples, such as continuing to lease an apartment after one partner dies. When I signed that into law, it became one of the nation's most comprehensive regarding domestic partnerships.

DON'T LET CRITICS SET YOUR AGENDA

In Verdi's *Rigoletto*, the Duke of Mantua muses to the courtesans about the fickleness of women: *"La donna è mobile, qual piuma al vento, muta d'accento, e di pensier."* (I am known to sing this without much provocation.) Basically, "The woman is fickle, like a feather in the wind, changing what she says, and how she thinks." Ironically, shortly thereafter in the opera a woman dies through misplaced loyalty to the Duke. Nevertheless, that expression can apply both to voters and the media, but a leader must not let critics set the agenda.

One of the toughest decisions I ever made involved my endorsement of Mario Cuomo in his 1994 campaign for reelection as Governor of New York. The reasons were complicated, but there was one important consideration that did *not* come into my decision. After I announced my support, I became a hero to the liberal media. They printed articles about how brave I was in backing a Democrat, how unique and independent. My approval ratings were among the highest I ever had. I never fooled myself about that. I knew that the only reason the papers suddenly loved me was that, this time, doing what I thought was the right thing happened to be the prevailing view in the media. The second I arrived at a result they didn't like, I'd be right back in the editorial doghouse.

For example, my decision to reduce funding for the Brooklyn Museum of Art after it displayed sexually explicit cutouts and a portrait of the Madonna defiled with elephant dung was hysterically opposed by the New York elite. The politically correct never envisioned that people could in good faith have a difference of opinion about whether public money ought to be used to desecrate a religious image. There was an important First Amendment issue at stake. I believed that the mayor should never have the right to stop anyone from making a statement of any kind. People have a right to free expression. If they were to create offensive art on their own property, using their own funds, and someone were to attack them for doing it, the mayor would be obliged to protect them, and so would the police. But I believe there is a difference between protecting someone's right to desecrate a religious image and being required to fund that desecration using tax dollars from the very people it offends.

When I read the press, I consider what they have to say, but always with a grain of salt. Elected officials too often let editorial boards determine their policies. This is also true of certain public companies that allow the media and brokerage analysts to dictate policy. It's better to figure out your policy through channels you've come to rely on and then, if the media or other outsiders happen to point out something you didn't think of, fine, it can always be changed or fine-tuned. Had I listened to prevailing opinion, we wouldn't have cut the $8 billion in taxes we reduced between 1994 and 2001, or built the ballparks in Staten Island and Coney Island that turned unsightly lots into vibrant, attractive sources of pride and economic activity in those communities. Nor would we have provided security for City Hall in the pre–September 11 period, for which we were ceaselessly criticized, as if I were doing it on some authoritarian whim. In fact, we enacted the security measures only after several warnings about possible terrorist attacks.

There are hundreds of examples like that. So, yes, you try to factor in the opinion of editorialists but not let them determine what you do or say. Often I make a decision knowing that I'll be criticized but feeling certain that I'll be vindicated. A leader has to have the confidence to think that his decisions will be proven correct. While trying to retain humility, you must accept that the reason you're making these decisions and other people are not is because, for now, you're in charge and they aren't. You do no one any good if, like Hamlet, you cannot carry the weight of your convictions. Yes, you must guard against arrogance; but if you're doing your job and putting your motives and conscience through their paces, accept that maybe you really do know better and can see a little further down the road than others.

10

Loyalty: The Vital Virtue

A s I entered my final semester at New York University Law School in 1968, I interviewed for jobs that would begin in the coming fall—and almost blew it. I had been considered for clerkships with several judges. Lloyd MacMahon, a federal judge in the Southern District of New York, called to offer me a job on the same day that I saw him; I told him I would let him know within twenty-four hours. I was excited by the idea of working for such a legendary figure, but I wasn't sure I ought to accept the offer outright, since I had other meetings scheduled.

I went to see my advisor at New York University Law School, Irving Younger, to discuss my prospects. Professor Younger used to play opera when we talked and make me guess the arias. He didn't mince words. "You don't make Lloyd MacMahon wait. You don't make Lloyd MacMahon think you're not grateful for an opportunity." Professor Younger told me that I would find Judge MacMahon demanding, perhaps the toughest boss I'd ever have, but he told me some other things, too. "You want to be a trial lawyer. MacMahon will teach you more in one year than you could learn in ten from anybody else. Although he'll require a lot, and he'll yell at you and hurt your feelings and annoy you, you'll use his training for the rest of your life. Call him back right away. Take the job before he rescinds the offer."[1]

So I called and left a message. He didn't come in until the next morning and I was worried. I was thrilled when he called me early the next day—I accepted the job and canceled my other interviews. Six months later, I walked into the federal courthouse in Manhattan—two blocks from City Hall. Professor Younger was right. My life changed forever.

The reason young lawyers seek such apprenticeships—which pay about half as much as jobs at private firms—is that they help one learn how trials really work. Rather than researching some tiny element of an interminable brief that's filed in a courtroom he never sees, a clerk actually gets to observe every element of a trial. So any legal clerkship is a learning experience, but this clerkship was particularly intense, both because of his demanding personality and because Judge MacMahon was by nature a teacher.

He had two law clerks. Paul Crotty was the senior clerk, and I started as the junior. It was just us and the judge, plus Millie Babino, his administrative assistant. My first salary was $6,900. By the time I left, I was making $11,000. I thought I was rich.

Judge MacMahon taught both by example and instruction, and instilled in me a feeling about public service that has never left me. He enhanced my already strong beliefs in loyalty, hard work, and high expectations while teaching me quite a bit about respect, too. To this day, I cannot bring myself to refer to him as anything but "Judge MacMahon." When I was in my forties and appearing before him as

---

[1] Professor Younger asked me to deliver the commencement speech in 1988 at the University of Minnesota Law School, where he and his wife, Judith, were both professors. I agreed to give it because I wanted to see him again, but he died before the spring was over. I gave the speech and felt he was there in spirit.

U.S. Attorney, I would see him in chambers and he'd insist, "Call me Lloyd," but I couldn't do it. He was always Judge MacMahon to me.

By that time, 1968, I had already run for office in college, won and lost, and had dipped a toe in politics by working for John F. Kennedy and later becoming a Democratic district leader in Nassau County, Long Island—the first elective office I ever held. However, it wasn't until I understood how effective a leader Judge MacMahon was—how he got those who worked for him to believe in themselves and accomplish more than they thought they could—that I started to think I might be capable of similar responsibilities.

Judge MacMahon would come back from court with a stack of files. He had a big office, and we would pile them high on the table in his chambers. He would sit with us and discuss his preliminary sense of each motion. He'd say, "I'll take these twenty and work on them. Let's go over the other thirty—Paul, you take fifteen and here are fifteen for Rudy. To the extent that I've developed one, I'll tell you my impression." We'd work our way through the pile—a patent infringement case, an admiralty case, a derivative claim for damages between the citizens of different states, a copyright case—all different areas of the law.

Sometimes Judge MacMahon would have made notes, and there were different levels of how certain he was about which way we should go. Some would be easy—"We're going to dismiss this; it's a ridiculous, silly motion." Other times he would say he wasn't sure and needed us to research it and come to our own conclusions. Then we'd all draft opinions, and he would debate us and poke holes in our thinking and our writing: "Make this clearer." "Be more concise." "Learn grammar."

Under his tutelage, we gradually learned how to write legal decisions. He explained how it was not that different from a legal argument, being essentially an argument one might have to use in the court of appeals. You're accepting one side of the case or the other, just as plaintiff or defendant had in their brief to the court—you defend that point of view. Judge MacMahon got us to think logically, in terms not only of deciding the case but also of buttressing our arguments and anticipating objections from the appeals court. "What's our strongest argument?" he'd ask. "Well, put that first. Don't begin with that subsidiary argument. We want to convince them right away."

Judge MacMahon decided all of his cases on the law, but when we were writing our opinions he understood that emotion colors the facts so much that we couldn't simply leave them out of an opinion. In other words, once you make the decision then your job is to present the facts in the light most likely to persuade. He constantly emphasized the importance of keeping things simple. He tirelessly explained the way good newspaper writers set up their stories in a pyramid—the main idea summarized in the first paragraph, details coming below in descending order of importance. The idea was to take something complicated and explain it so that people could understand it.

The cases went from the judge's table to our desks. When Judge MacMahon came in, he'd look at the piles and sometimes he'd say, "Production is down. We had fifteen motions in this pile and there are still twelve. I want this down to nine." Paul and I tried to attack the piles more strategically, because Judge MacMahon scheduled these meetings regularly and monitored our progress closely.

Despite this workload, and all his other commitments, Judge MacMahon spent a lot more time teaching than many judges. For example, one of his clerks covered almost every case. So I would be in court during certain trials, while Paul would be there for others. Whenever there was a really good case or a particularly good lawyer appearing, Judge MacMahon would bring both of us to court. "Forget about your work," he would say. "You can do it tonight or tomorrow. I want you to watch Edward Bennett Williams."[2]

---

[2]Edward Bennett Williams's cross-examination of Jake Jacobson in *U.S. v. John Connally* was actually turned into its own book. The introduction to that book was written by Irving Younger.

This was extremely generous, because a clerk's absence meant more work for him. On the other hand, he loved teaching. We would go back into the robing room, and he would ask how we would have handled the case we had just seen. "Would you have cross-examined on that issue? Would you have cross-examined at all? Would you have called that witness? Why did the lawyer take fifteen minutes at the beginning to explain the case? By that time the jury is zoned out. Those first five minutes, when the jury looks at you and wants to hear what's coming out of your mouth—that's the optimal opportunity to get them moving in the right direction. You've got to seize it. Don't save your best argument for last, when maybe only a third of them are listening."

He would even assign readings of his own cases, such as his legendary prosecution of mob boss Frank Costello. He would give his clerks transcripts to read and discuss with him, and you'd slowly develop your own style. When I began trying cases myself, I would go back to those cross-examinations, oral arguments, and summations and reflect on how weaknesses in them might allow me to argue my own case more effectively. After two years I left Judge MacMahon to become an assistant U.S. Attorney, and within a month was trying cases myself.

If Judge MacMahon had been asked what he was training Paul Crotty, Ken Caruso, Jim Duff, David Denton, or Rudy Giuliani or any of his clerks to be, he would have said it was to be a fine trial lawyer. Being able to communicate, being able to explain, being able to simplify. He expected a lot from lawyers because he saw them as professionals, from whom one should expect the highest standards. He was sometimes mistaken for an ogre because he gave the lawyers who appeared before him a hard time, but I always understood him, even when I was on the receiving end. He thought our profession so important that we didn't have room for errors, much like a doctor does not. Lawyers can seldom retrieve their mistakes, and it's not the lawyer who pays for them, either—it's the clients who do. So the high standards he set were born out of respect, not its opposite. Thus he would get angry when he saw shoddy performance. And he had a way with zingers.

If he saw a lawyer doing a bad job, he might call him to the bench and say, "Where'd you go to law school?" The lawyer would reply Fordham or NYU or Harvard Law. The judge would then tell him to demand his tuition back. If it was a really bad performance, he might say to the client (only after the decision had been rendered), "How much are you paying for this representation?" The client would sometimes answer with a figure or refuse to name an amount. And the judge would say, "Well, you deserve your money back." Or if an assistant U.S. Attorney was doing a particularly bad job—and this was tough, because a lot of them are just starting—he would say, "It's very difficult to experience a situation in which the United States of America is virtually unrepresented in this courtroom."

He was exceptionally well organized, always pressing, always expecting more from his staff than they suspected they could deliver. Yet he never asked others to work harder than he was willing to do. He underlined the importance of studying the methods of others and also of developing one's own style and beliefs. He foresaw problems and planned in advance how to handle them. He stood on principle. He understood the need to communicate and persuade, not just rule by decree. Little by little, Judge MacMahon was laying the foundation for the leader I hoped to become. He intimidated me, occasionally even exasperated me, but by the time my clerkship ended he was like a second father. Such a transition doesn't just happen—a leader has to earn it.

Judge MacMahon served as a lieutenant in the Navy during World War II, and when he took on a clerk it was with something of a boot camp mentality—break 'em down before you build 'em up. There was method to all this. A young lawyer doesn't land a coveted clerkship without having performed well in law school. There's a big gap, though, between that and the real world. Judge MacMahon's pressure was intended to shape the clerk's style to fit his own. By the time the rookie got the hang of working for him, he had learned about the law. Equally important, he also knew that any praise he might receive really meant something when it came from Judge MacMahon. Meanwhile, a team was being built—the junior clerk bonded to the senior clerk, who had already gone through the same ordeal and provided support, while Millie Babino supplied tips on staying out of the doghouse.

Judge MacMahon was an inspirational teacher, a powerful thinker, a wonderful debater. I admired him for many reasons. But the reason I loved him, and would have done anything for this man, was the devotion he showed those who worked for him. If you clerked for Judge MacMahon, he was your friend for life. You put in so much for him because you could see the strength of his relationships with those who came before you. He never failed to make time for former clerks and relished their achievements as their careers prospered. After leaving his office, many of his former apprentices— an impressive group, to be sure—seldom made a professional decision without first running it by the judge. In fact, sometimes when I'd go to consult with him, who would I see coming out of his office? My friend Paul Crotty, the second-year clerk when I arrived.

When in 1970 my clerkship ended, I didn't necessarily think about what I'd learned in terms of "leadership lessons." But the judge's influence was strong—so much so that by the time I found myself in leadership roles, I realized that his methods and ideas had entered my subconscious. In particular, I made loyalty my cornerstone.

EMBRACE THOSE WHO ARE ATTACKED

Another leader who established an impressive loyalty dynamic was Ronald Reagan. Someone who worked for him would get in some kind of trouble and Reagan wouldn't cave in to pressure to fire them (and as a result was criticized). I observed this when I served in Reagan's

Justice Department, and remember thinking, "He'll take political heat for us, so we'll take political heat for him." Reagan would risk his popularity because of his personal loyalty to people who had stood by him, helped elect him, worked for him. You cannot believe what that did to boost the morale of his organization.

When someone around me is unfairly attacked, I go out of my way to make that person more important. I spend more time with them, and if they are a member of my staff, I see if there's a way I can promote them or give a speech to show that person how cherished they are.

Just consider the alternative. A leader who distances himself from his staff at the first sign of trouble might save a few popularity points, but it's shortsighted. Eventually, no one wants to work for someone like that. The best potential people don't apply, knowing that should trouble arrive, they'll be left twisting in the wind. And those already on board don't feel the courage to act boldly—they'll walk on eggshells lest they earn the cold shoulder of a boss who cares more about the opinions of outsiders than about his staff.

Take the case of Jason Turner. As commissioner of the city's Human Resources Administration, he oversaw some of the most successful welfare-to-work initiatives in the history of urban America. Richard Schwartz and I had started my administration's welfare reform program, and we were about halfway to our goal, when Jason Turner came in. He spearheaded the transformation from welfare agency to employment agency, creating twenty-seven job centers throughout the city. It was a brilliant and successful metamorphosis, but it was also enormously controversial in liberal circles in New York. Jason had come out of the welfare reform movement in the Reagan administration, so there were those who were angry with him for that. And because he believed, as I did, in privatizing as many jobs as possible, even people who worked for the city were constantly shooting at him, hoping to get the Department of Investigation to investigate him.

One complaint concerned his supposedly favoring a private contractor, for whom his wife had worked several years before. After we investigated, it turned out she had never been employed by them. Later, there was a claim—by the city's comptroller, no less, who just happened to be running simultaneously for mayor—accusing Jason of favoring a different contractor altogether, a firm called Maximus. The appellate court dismissed the charge, unanimously concluding that "there was no evidence of favoritism . . . no evidence that Maximus was afforded unfair access."

Jason was the victim of those overly eager to find something to drive him out of city government. We had to work our way through each allegation, trying to determine if there was any truth to them, while at the same time not betraying someone I knew was doing a great job. Imagine what it would have been like to recruit a replacement for Jason had I ditched him—his successor would have been scared of his own footsteps. The one allegation that stuck was that Jason, who was from out of state, rented a room from his friend, who also happened to be his deputy. It was a technical violation, and to me wasn't even that, because the spirit of the rule was to prevent bosses from pressuring their subordinates into deals that unfairly benefited the boss. Jason had been paying the market rate for the apartment. Anyway, the Conflict of Interest Board fined Jason $6,500, he paid it, and was then castigated by the same people who'd been unsuccessfully looking for real wrongdoing.

I looked at the situation. I'd prosecuted government officials for real offenses—schemes to enrich themselves at the expense of the public, or that made them independent kings of private fiefdoms. Everyone who works for me knows how I feel about corruption. But I feel just as strongly about not being intimidated into abandoning those who deserve my support. Obviously, if somebody wasn't paying taxes or was shaking down subordinates for kickbacks, then he couldn't stay in city government no matter how loyal I felt, or how much I liked him, or how good a job he was doing.

In this case, Jason needed a place to stay for a year, paid a reasonable amount of rent to his friend, and there would have been nothing wrong with the deal had it not been for this rule which was there to prevent actual abuses. You have to make your own judgments about situations and not react on the perceptions of the media or your rivals. I decided that Jason had done nothing essentially wrong. However, I didn't simply tell him that and send him quietly on his way. I held a press conference and specifically detailed the capricious nature of some of the rules. Not only did Jason feel supported, but those who hounded him with the hope I'd fire or censure him saw that their hectoring had not worked.

Embracing those who are attacked serves two functions. First, it reassures those who work for you and those you want to recruit to work for you. You won't abandon them. You won't betray them at the first sign of trouble. Second, by showing the world that you'll hug a vilified employee that much closer, you remove the incentive to attack.

Standing up for those under fire was not a new idea for me. After my first tour of duty in the Justice Department in the 1970s, I accompanied my boss Harold Tyler into private practice at the law firm Patterson, Belknap, Webb & Tyler. One of the first cases I worked on involved an investor suing our client, *Barron's* magazine, its star columnist Alan Abelson, and his editor, Robert Bleiberg. The plaintiff, Dr. Robert Nemeroff, alleged that Alan was leaking negative information about companies from forthcoming columns he'd written, so that short sellers would profit when the stock dropped after his column appeared.

Now, Alan was and is a gadfly. He loved to point out the shortcomings of companies and poke holes in the stories that hype artists told to support optimistic valuations. He's a brilliant guy, and utterly honest. The action had just been filed when I came to Patterson Belknap. Bob Bleiberg, in particular, was outraged. He didn't want just to win; he wanted to vindicate his publication's integrity. At Patterson, Robert Sack did most of the firm's First Amendment work, but he wanted someone to handle the matter in court. He consulted Harold Tyler, and they agreed that the case would be perfect for me. But meanwhile Dow Jones, the publisher of *Barron's*, was thinking of taking it elsewhere, to a proven aggressive litigator, an Arthur Liman type.

I read the complaint, met with Abelson and Bleiberg, and carefully studied the records. I spent hours reading Abelson's columns and examining the trading history of stocks he'd covered and came to a preliminary conclusion that he was innocent. We had some good defenses that would disprove the charges, because the trading was inconsistent. There were more times in which short sellers *lost* money betting against stocks Abelson slammed. Sure, we could isolate the times that it seemed as if short sellers had profited immediately after a column of Alan's appeared; but there were other people with the same information Alan exposed.

I was excited to be assigned such an important case, and told Bob that I'd be happy to defend him and Alan, that it would be a great start for me. I met with them again, and told them how we would organize the defense. They seemed to like me and my ideas, so I began to put together a staff. At the time, I was working on some other cases with my associate, Renee Cohen (now Szybala). Renee was extremely smart and lightning quick, so I asked her to share the *Barron's* case with me. I listened to her ideas, and together we devised a strategy, becoming convinced that we had a good chance to win in the decisive fashion our client demanded.

We had our next meeting at the client's office to go over documents. Bleiberg said a few things, as did Renee, then Bob indicated he wanted to talk to me alone. We went outside. "I don't want some young girl working on this trial," he told me. "I mean, she's just out of law school, she looks like a kid. I want two or three of your more senior associates."

Bleiberg was a big man with a forceful personality—and I didn't want to risk losing the client. But I told him, "Look, I selected her.

She's with me, and if she's not working on the case, I'm not working on it." Bleiberg thought for a moment, then said, "Well, I wasn't even sure I wanted you."

I went back inside and started to gather our documents. I told Renee the meeting was over. I was in shock, but wasn't going to show it or back down. I started to walk out with Renee, who didn't know what was going on or why we were leaving. Abelson sized up the situation and said, "Stay, stay, stay." He started whispering to Bleiberg and they went off into a corner and whispered some more. Then they came back and Bleiberg said, "Okay, stay and finish up with this. We'll have dinner afterward, and we'll get to know you better." These are men who love to have dinner. By eleven o'clock that night they loved Renee.

That suit ended very successfully. Not only was *Barron's* completely vindicated, but the plaintiff and his lawyers were required to pay some of our legal fees for filing a malicious suit and trying to use the courts to silence a publisher. The case became a landmark for Rule-11 sanctions against those who bring lawsuits in bad faith. Bleiberg developed a close relationship with Renee, who went on to advise *Barron's* on avoiding libel issues and even on business decisions. When I stood by her it not only cemented our own relationship but also let our clients know that they could expect the same kind of loyalty: if I didn't turn my back on my associate when the chips were down, I wouldn't turn my back on my client, either.

Standing by someone who's under fire is one thing. Going to bat for someone who's done real wrong is something else. Unfortunately, the line between the two is not always clear. My policy is that the people who work for me deserve the benefit of the doubt. If it turns out they're guilty, there will be time to hold them accountable. But if you abandon them at the first accusation and they're later exonerated, you'll never wash away the smell of betrayal. You'll have lost the trust of that employee, and of those who have never been accused.

On July 3, 1992, Police Officer Michael O'Keefe confronted a wanted drug dealer named Jose "Kiko" Garcia in the Washington Heights section of Manhattan. A hand-to-hand struggle ensued, and when Garcia pulled a gun and threatened to shoot him, O'Keefe fired, fatally. After Garcia's death, witnesses claimed Garcia had not shown a gun, and the community sought to punish this officer. Mayor Dinkins visited Garcia's family and the city paid for his funeral. O'Keefe was a Little League coach and a Boy Scout who never missed Mass and lived in Queens with his mother. Garcia was an illegal alien with a drug conviction who had disappeared while on probation.

For four days, false allegations concerning O'Keefe were published in the tabloids without rebuttal from the Mayor or the Police Department. Neither O'Keefe's exemplary record nor Garcia's criminal past was brought to light, and that became the backdrop for a horrible riot in Washington Heights. Only *after* the violence did the facts start to emerge.

For years after that, cops would tell me how it felt when the Mayor did not stick up for O'Keefe. They vividly recalled the image of the Mayor on television, sitting on the couch with Garcia's family, promising to see that "justice" was served. As a grand jury conclusively determined, O'Keefe had behaved entirely appropriately— even heroically. Many who claimed to have witnessed the incident turned out to have either lied or not been in a position to see what they alleged. Further, there was an audiotape of the officer begging for help as he called the police dispatcher for backup. The Mayor never released that tape. By the time O'Keefe was cleared, the damage to police morale was done. Their boss had sided with a drug dealer over one of their own.

I took the story of Michael O'Keefe and Kiko Garcia to heart when I became mayor. In a city with 41,000 police and some 250,000 total employees, some would inevitably find themselves in trouble. I made it a point to give them the benefit of the doubt, and more than that, to support them. If they were proven wrong, I'd come down on them—hard, if necessary. The presumption of innocence, however, was not just something my employees were entitled to—it was critical to morale. And it was critical to the enterprise, too. That riot was the second in the city in two years. I vowed that if I became mayor, we would never let a riot break out. (In July 1999, a blackout killed the lights in Washington Heights. As many as 300,000 people were without power for eighteen hours and more, in 100-degree heat. I could not have been more proud when the neighborhood showed itself a model of peacefulness and neighborly goodwill.)

The principle of standing by those who are attacked is so important to me that I would deploy it even when my guy was wrong, so long as it was not illegal. I might have to take him to the woodshed in private; but that wouldn't mean I would leave him hanging out to dry in front of everyone.

When I was mayor, there was a City Council member named Lloyd Henry. I would not necessarily call him an ally, but he was a good guy. He also happened to be an Episcopal minister. Even in the middle of a political dispute, Henry was the kind of person who would say, "I'm praying for you." When I was diagnosed with prostate cancer, he went out of his way to come up and hug me, and let me know that he was indeed praying for me. He was the last person you'd want one of your staff swearing at—especially on videotape. But that's what happened.

Beacon schools, as I have explained, are specialized schools that serve as community centers beyond the school day, and get city funding as such. The idea is that a poor area can use the school as a social center, the way churches were used in medieval times. In April 1998, Jake Menges was the Deputy Chief of Staff to Randy Mastro, my then Deputy Mayor for Operations. As a City Council meeting dissolved into chaos during a discussion of beacon-school distribution, Councilman Henry suggested that one of my commissioners be subpoenaed. In the heat of the moment, Jake Menges yelled at Henry something along the lines of, "You just lost your fucking beacon school."

At that point, we didn't realize New York 1, the all–New York news channel, had caught this on tape. When I heard about the blowup, I did what I'd done many times when someone who worked for me was in a potentially difficult situation. I called Jake in and told him to tell me exactly what happened—and that if he didn't say what people thought he'd said, we'd fight it. But I wanted the truth. He said he'd lost his temper and admitted swearing at Councilman Henry.

No doubt, Jake should not have said this. Number one, he shouldn't have said it this way. Number two, it wasn't right to link the councilman's lack of support on another issue to his chances of getting a beacon school for his constituents. But to Jake's credit, he didn't hem and haw to me, and I respected that. He admitted it and was willing to apologize to Councilman Henry. What makes this a challenging area of leadership is that the transgression was real; it needed to be addressed. You don't hate the person for it, and the idea is not to disgrace him. So deciding how to address the situation takes judgment. Jake's dealing with it directly and honestly fixed the problem.

I had an extremely innovative Taxi and Limousine Commissioner named Chris Lynn. Cabs in New York were legendary for taking visitors "for a ride." Chris implemented the bill of rights, which posted in every taxi everything a rider was entitled to expect—a clean cab, a non-smoking driver, air-conditioning, knowledge of the city's streets, and so on. He put maps in the back of the cabs, and instigated language lessons for non-English-speaking drivers. He also came up with charging a flat fare to and from the airports, which reassured passengers that their driver wasn't milking them with gratuitous detours. He was very creative, and his programs were good for both riders and drivers.

Despite his good works, the press had it in for Chris. During his time in private law practice, he had represented some questionable defendants—drug dealers and other undesirables—and the press was always making suggestions that Chris had been too zealous in the way he defended such clients. While that had nothing to do with his performance as commissioner, the papers in particular wouldn't let him alone.

Occasionally, they'd find some juicy morsel to pin on him, such as the time Chris had a run-in with the operator of a private parking lot near Yankee Stadium. The more stories they wrote, the more I backed him. I wasn't going to let any newspaper choose my administration.

A couple of people in my administration told me I was backing Chris up too much, that I should fire him because he'd become a liability. It's possible they were right, but I kept thinking about something I had read years before in Ed Koch's autobiography, *Mayor*. He describes how one of his deputy mayors had let him down, then gleefully recounts how the man groveled for his job, begging forgiveness. It was not to be—Mayor Koch canned him, enjoying every moment, and even making fun of the man's Italian phrasing. He didn't take the rap for hiring his own deputy mayor, but instead blamed the search committee that recommended him.

I thought about that story as I contemplated the Chris Lynn situation, and decided there was no way I was going to cut Chris loose. I would reprimand him privately, rein him in. But I wasn't going to humiliate him. He continued to serve at high-level positions in my administration.

It's not enough for a leader to give and receive loyalty. For loyalty to mean something it has to be established as a culture throughout the organization.

Any large group is bound to have intramural rivalries, and if people are talented and driven, a number of them will think they're the smartest in the room. To a degree, that's a good thing. Competition often brings out the best. When competitive rivalries turn to sniping, however, a leader has to remind everyone that they are all working toward the same ultimate goals. It tests the loyalty of people to the organization.

Early in my administration, the city had problems with the

excessive numbers of street vendors. They were on every corner, choking pedestrian traffic and taking sales from the permanent, rent-paying, sales-tax-generating establishments. Some balance had to be struck, and I put Rudy Washington in charge of it. He was working on other projects at the time, and it was the opinion of some of my staff that someone else should be assigned this task. It was suggested that another of my deputies, Fran Reiter, might have more time to handle it. In addition, her specialty was community relations, and there was contention over where the vendors would be located. It was a relatively small issue, so I deferred to that judgment. After a couple of meetings of the new vendor-location panel, the press noticed that Fran was now in charge and wrote that Rudy Washington had been ousted because he had been screwing it up. Well, that was the end of that. I immediately put Rudy back in charge and took the heat from the press for making a mistake in reassigning that duty.

It pays to stick with someone in the face of public criticism. The carping eventually fades. The devotion you've earned by showing loyalty will last. Many times I selected people for jobs knowing that I'd be criticized for choosing them. Sometimes, the very reason I picked the person was what the critics didn't like.

I knew there'd be heat when I promoted Bob Harding to Budget Director in 1998 and deputy mayor after that. Bob's father, Ray Harding, was the head of New York's Liberal Party and a longtime political supporter, friend, and advisor. My view was that Bob was the perfect choice to negotiate the tough labor deals we were working on at the time—I wasn't going to choose a lesser candidate simply to quiet critics. But I also had an inkling that Bob would work that much harder, to prove that he *wasn't* chosen because of my relationship with his father. The result: he turned out to be one of my most dedicated, effective deputies.

A similar dynamic emerged when I chose Geoff Hess to be my Senior Advisor. He's the son of my longtime friend Mike Hess, so naturally some in the press argued his hiring was nepotism. Geoff was only 31 at the time, but he had already served for two years in my Legal Department as a top aide to Denny Young, so I knew what I was getting. When an article in *Newsday* questioned his hiring, I told people to judge him on his performance, and to judge me on mine. Not only was Geoff determined to prove he was up to the job, he felt he had the confidence and trust of his boss. He took on the task of expanding Compstat to twenty other city agencies and, along with Debbie Kurtz, a deputy commissioner at the Department of Correction, got it done in less time than I'd expected—even amid dealing with the crisis following September 11.

Such mutual loyalty goes a long way. Geoff and Bob were with the group of us who were trapped in 75 Barclay Street when the towers collapsed. During the weeks that followed, they were both there for me and for the city every moment of the day. Literally. Late in September, Geoff went home to his apartment after another twenty-hour day at the command center we'd set up on the piers. Apparently, Geoff is in the habit of unwinding by watching television in his underwear—hey, who am I to judge? Well after midnight, Geoff looked down and noticed that he'd clipped his cell phone, his beeper, and his Blackberry email pager to the waistband of his boxer shorts. He told me that at that point he said to himself, "Wearing three communication devices on my underwear—now *that's* loyalty."

YOU'RE NOT PAID TO BE ABUSED

Anyone who has attended a game between the Mets and the Yankees knows that New Yorkers are not shy about expressing differing viewpoints. Well, some of the town hall meetings I held as mayor made those interleague games sound like a string concerto at Carnegie Hall. That's fine—I was there to hear complaints, and as a native New Yorker I certainly appreciate directness.

However, there's a line between spirited discourse and hijacking an open meeting for selfish purposes. We had some contentious meetings, with yelling and screaming and demonstrating. One time, a group handcuffed themselves to the chairs, and had to be removed. So from the beginning I established a rule: you can ask any question you want. I will let you complete your question. I will not interrupt you, no matter how angry and upset I get. In exchange, you have to listen to my answer respectfully, without interrupting. And if you don't, you are first warned, then thrown out, because I won't let you disrupt the 400 other people there.

As mayor, I was obligated to put up with a lot of things, but not sustained abuse. Nor were my commissioners. It wasn't my sensitivities that I was worried about, but the tone of civility I strived to establish throughout the city. The town hall meetings were often held in schools. When people would scream and interrupt and bully, I would point out that we were in a school building and that this was no way to set an example. This sounds like common courtesy, but it was a revelation for New York City in 1994. The idea back then was that politicians should sit there and take anything that was thrown at them, no matter how crazy. In fact, that level of discourse was practically the primary idiom in the City Council. When I was in private law practice, Staten Island Borough President Guy Molinari came to see me for some advice on testimony he was preparing to deliver to the City Council. Guy had been a member of Congress and of the New York State Assembly, as well as a marine, so it wasn't as though he'd never been exposed to rough debate. After he testified, he called me up and said he'd never seen people behave like that in his whole life. "The names they call each other! They fight with you, they fight with each other."

I thought about a story Judge MacMahon had told me about presiding over the drug-trafficking convictions of Carmine Galante, the boss of the Bonanno crime family. Galante and several co-defendants went berserk several times over the course of the trial, shouting obscenities, throwing things, and rushing the bench. Judge MacMahon ordered them handcuffed and gagged, then went on with the trial. Years later, many judges still credited his handling of that trial with setting a tone that allowed them to maintain control over their courtrooms.

With Democrats comprising forty-five or at times forty-six of its fifty-one members, the City Council in New York City—basically the legislative branch to the mayor's executive branch—was not always warmly disposed to my office. My commissioners had been summoned to the City Council a couple of times and had been abused—subjected to screaming, histrionics, and name-calling. So, having developed a rule about not taking abuse at town hall meetings for myself, I devised a similar strategy for those who worked for me.

I told my commissioners, "If anyone treats you in an abusive way, you have my authorization—and my advice—first, to say, 'Sir, if you continue to yell and act in an abusive way, I'm going to leave. I'm not treating you that way, and you may not continue to treat me that way.' Then, if the abuse continues, you should walk out, knowing that you have my full support."

In May of 2001, Jason Turner appeared before a City Council committee. We were approaching the five-year deadline President Clinton had set in 1996 as a lifetime limit on federal welfare benefits. New York State was operating a safety net program for those no longer eligible for such benefits. Our plan was to use the expiration as a contact opportunity so that those who came to apply for the safety net could be coaxed toward self-sufficiency. In the process of taking their application, the able-bodied person who'd received welfare for at least five years would be shown the varieties of jobs available, introduced to training seminars, and otherwise steered in the direction of self-sufficiency.

The chairman of the committee, Councilman Stephen DiBrienza, had a history of yelling and carrying on with commissoners. DiBrienza took it upon himself to heap personal abuse on Jason, asking him whether those who hadn't got around to applying for state welfare after their five years of benefits had expired could move into

Jason's home. The commissioner politely asked DiBrienza to "calm down" and was met with an even more ferocious rant. At this, Jason and his aides stood up and walked out of the room.

The City Council has subpoena power, giving it the right to call a witness. The subpoena does not give it the right to abuse a witness. There were other occasions in which commissioners walked out of hearings because of abusive conduct. They did so knowing I'd go before a judge to defend them if it came to that.

The result was that my commissioners knew their principal was behind them. They could take bold steps without worrying that they'd be abandoned. This policy had a fringe benefit. When the City Council finally realized I wasn't going to allow my people to be mistreated, the hearings evolved into more sensible conversations about problems.

Refusing to let the people who work for me take unwarranted criticism came tragically into play in the wake of the World Trade Center attacks. The stunned silence of the first few days gradually gave way to business as usual—some papers raising questions about the police and fire families allegedly getting so much money. No one deserved this unraveling of their lives and family. If I had my druthers, every single surviving family member, whether those of the lowest-paid busboys at Windows on the World or of the seven-figure earners at Cantor Fitzgerald, would get whatever they need. But the fact is, as mayor, as chief executive of the city of New York, my first obligation was to those who signed on to work for the city. Again, the idea is loyalty.

With the charity that the city controlled, the Twin Towers Fund, I hastened to distribute the money. By Thanksgiving, we got $46 million to the families of the uniformed personnel killed in the disaster; by June 2002, more than $155 million had been delivered. I wanted to do all I could to honor my pledge to the families of those who worked for the city, and at least we could supply financial assistance. There were three other goals behind our rapid response. One was to pressure the other charities to move quickly. Second, to force the IRS to issue a ruling on how the recipients would be allowed to treat the money they received. Finally, to get the families the money quickly to make them feel that they were remembered during the holidays, a time when they might feel particularly alone.

There's a more obvious management lesson here, too. The question wasn't only "Who deserves what?" Dealing with the immediate crisis was part of the equation, but considering the future was equally important. Imagine the city's fate had the mayor not gone to bat for the firefighters, police, and emergency personnel who died. Who would have rushed into the next fire to save lives if he wasn't completely sure his family would be taken care of if he didn't make it out? What kind of people would join the Police Department if the mayor and the city hadn't shown we supported them in times of need? Showing loyalty to the people who had shown the city such remarkable devotion was both the right thing to do and the only hope we had to move forward.

In 1970, after two years with Judge MacMahon, I joined the Southern District of New York as an assistant U.S. Attorney. One of my early cases was a tax evasion and bribery prosecution assigned by sheer coincidence to . . . Judge MacMahon. On the other side was Lou Bender, a distinguished and experienced trial lawyer, specializing in the defense of complicated tax cases with high-profile defendants. I was 26, very green, and convinced that this case was well over my head. There were tape recordings of some of the evidence, but the tapes were ambiguous. It would be up to the lawyers on each side to argue for interpretations of the circumstantial evidence.

This was maybe my fourth trial. Up to that point, I had been handling the grab bag more typical for a brand-new assistant U.S. Attorney—an illegal still in Harlem, a stabbing on the high seas, a bank robbery: cases with five or six witnesses that no one could lose—or at least shouldn't lose.

My boss, Mike Seymour, was undertaking a backlog reduction program and pressuring all his assistants to take as many cases as we could handle. He kept a big chart in his office and would check off each case as it was cleared. All of us were getting cases that were too complicated, and we had to do the best we could.

Anyway, I showed up in court, and right away Judge MacMahon asked whether the defendants wanted him removed from the trial because I had been his law clerk. I was half praying that Lou would say, "Yes, Judge, please recuse yourself." I certainly remembered how demanding Judge MacMahon could be, and was far from keen about the idea of appearing in front of him, especially in a difficult case with an excellent opposing counsel.

I listened as Lou Bender said, "Judge, I know you. You're going to be difficult on everybody, but fair. And you'll probably be more difficult on him than me. So I don't want you to recuse yourself." And I was thinking, maybe I'll stand up and recuse myself. Maybe there was a graceful way to say, "Gee, it'd be better to avoid any appearance problem . . ." But there was no getting out of it. Everyone who knew MacMahon also knew he'd never favor anyone.

So we began the trial. I was prosecuting as hard as I could, and Lou Bender was defending as hard as he could, and we got to the last day of trial, a Thursday. I rested the government's case. Lou Bender stood up and astonished everyone by saying that he was not going to put on a defense. He was going to rely on what he described as the substantial inadequacies of the government's evidence. I was surprised. I had no idea what to do. I was entirely unprepared to deliver a summation.

Judge MacMahon told Lou Bender, Okay then, sum up—present your summary to the jury. Bender replied, Come on, Judge, at least give me until tomorrow. Judge MacMahon said, No, Mr. Bender, you knew you weren't going to put on a defense. So you're going to give your summation now.

So I said, Well, Your Honor, since I didn't know he wasn't going to put on a case, may I have until tomorrow to do my summation? The judge said, No, you may not.

Both Lou Bender and I sat there, stunned. We thought maybe if we presented a united front, let him know that neither of us would object if he gave us more time . . . He would have none of it. You're both going to sum up right now—the court has time, the jury is here, we're going to end the case right now.

This was all less than fair to my side, which had no way to know that the defense wouldn't present a case. But contrary to popular mythology, courtrooms are not always fair. So Bender stood up and gave his summation. He'd been at it for forty years, and could perform almost without preparation, and for all I know he may have at least sketched out his speech, anticipating Judge MacMahon's put-up-or-shut-up order. When he had finished I stood up. Normally a scrupulous preparer, I was flying by the seat of my pants—no notes, no outline, nothing. I did the best I could to recapitulate the facts for the jury and walked them through why they had to convict. Some ninety minutes later I sat down, and Judge MacMahon told the court that he'd charge the jury the next day. I returned to my office exhausted. This was my fourth or fifth summation, and I had no idea if it had even made sense, let alone whether I'd remembered all the points I needed to make.

Judge MacMahon died on April 8, 1989, just as my first mayoral campaign was gathering steam. I can now reveal something I have always withheld.

That Thursday night, around 9:30, I was sitting at my desk at the U.S. Attorney's office when I got a call from Joe, the courtroom clerk. Joe said, "I know that was very stressful, but, I've got to tell you, when we went back to chambers, Judge MacMahon was beaming with pride—popping the buttons on his vest. He said it was one of the best summations he'd ever heard. He trained you well. I don't know if you're going to win or lose this one, but he was bragging about you to everybody up in chambers. I just wanted you to know that, kid. Don't tell anybody I called you."

Joe hung up the phone, and the next day I won the case. In all our years of friendship after that trial, Judge MacMahon never said anything about it to me. My conversation with Joe was the only communication I ever had about that particular summation. But in a way, the rest of my career was based on it. From then on, every time I had a tough case I would think back to that one. I learned not to recite documents to a jury or an audience, but to digest the facts and deliver them in my own voice. But most of all, feeling that I'd impressed someone I admire as much as Judge MacMahon was a revelation. I never forgot how good it felt to have earned the loyalty of someone I so respected. It meant everything.

11

Weddings Discretionary, Funerals Mandatory

Chief Raymond Downey epitomizes the phrase "New York's Bravest." As leader of the Fire Department's Special Operations Command and rescue missions, Chief Downey is an important reason that New York City is the model for rescue response and preventive planning around the nation.

When the World Trade Center was bombed in 1993, Chief Downey headed the rescue operation. When the Murrah Federal Building was bombed in Oklahoma City, FEMA called Chief Downey to the scene, where he led the operation for sixteen days. As leader of the New York City urban search and rescue team, Chief Downey responds to floods and ice storms across New York State, and he helped alleviate suffering in the Dominican Republic following Hurricane Georges.

Chief Downey is a local hero, recognized as a national authority. But if you ask him about the most important work of his life, he won't talk about the awards, the daring missions, or even *The Rescue Company*, the book he somehow found time to write. Instead, he'll talk about the bonds of family.

The Downeys are a fire-fighting family. Two of Ray's brothers—Tom and Gene—also joined the Fire Department, and Ray's son Chuck is a lieutenant with Engine Company 317, and his son Jim is the captain of Squad Company 18 on West 10th Street in Manhattan. Of course, these 39 years of service in the department—and Ray's five children and seven grandchildren—have all been made possible by his wife of forty years, Rosalie.

Rosalie Downey has endured especially long separations while her husband mans the front lines. I remember seeing him after a building collapsed on Houston Street. Chief Downey had been on the job for two days straight and I asked him how he was holding up. He said that he was feeling fine, but hadn't had a chance to see his wife. I wrote a note on his behalf, asking Rosalie to please excuse her husband's absence while he served the people of New York City. On this evening, as we honor the extraordinary accomplishments of this great New Yorker, we also honor his wife for her steadfast support and devotion.

Chief Downey died on September 11, 2001, alongside 342 of his brothers. He gave his life as part of the biggest rescue in the history of America. Over 25,000 people were saved because of the courage, professionalism, and leadership of men like him. Reading this tribute breaks my heart. But the passage above isn't a eulogy, and I didn't say it at his funeral. In fact, I prepared these words for Ray and then used them as the basis for remarks I gave to Ray, his family, and a hundred or so of his friends and fellow firefighters some six weeks before his death.

Here's how it happened.

On Sunday, June 17, 2001—Father's Day—two teenage boys, playing around near a hardware store in Queens, knocked over a can of gasoline. The fuel spilled under a door and ignited near the store's many cans of flammable lacquers and paint, causing a massive, five-alarm blaze. Firefighters Harry Ford, Brian Fahey, and John J. Downing lost their lives in the ensuing explosions—a tragic day for three fathers, who had eight children among them.

I saw Ray working at the scene of that fire. He'd joined the FDNY in 1962, had a brilliant career, and there he was, at 63 years of age, still fighting on the front lines. Amid the disaster—in addition to the three fatalities, over fifty personnel were injured—I saw Tom Von Essen and he pointed out Chief Downey. Tom said, "I keep telling him to retire and enjoy his life, and he keeps refusing."

I thought about how outstanding so many of these men were, and what a shame it was that it took a funeral before the admiration of their colleagues and family was expressed. If Ray Downey retired after I left office, I couldn't ensure that he be shown the respect he had earned. Echoing my thoughts, Tom said, "He's probably going to be here long after we leave and no one's going to recognize all he's done." And then Tom made a suggestion: "Why don't we give him a party now?" I thought that was a wonderful idea and told him to start putting it together. He enthusiastically replied, "Great, we'll get a restaurant," but I suggested that we do it at Gracie Mansion. Tom put the whole event together in a couple of weeks (yet another example of the FDNY's rapid response time) and scheduled it for July 23, 2001. I wondered if maybe we should do it in October or November as part of the many farewells I'd be saying as I prepared to leave office. But we already had the date set, so we kept it in July, and it was at that party that I said the words that began this chapter. The next time I saw Ray working like that was at the World Trade Center.

Until September 11, Tom and I thought that the Father's Day fire would be the Fire Department's worst, at least during my time as mayor. Twice before, I had lost three firefighters in a single conflagration, in 1994 and 1998, but the fact that this was Father's Day was particularly poignant, and Tom and I said to each other during that fire that we hoped we wouldn't have to go through another such funeral in our remaining months. I only wish that had been the case.

On October 20, 2001, many of the world's best-known entertainers gathered at Madison Square Garden to honor the rescue workers and raise money for victims of the World Trade Center attacks. It was a superb show and featured many once-in-a-lifetime moments (my staff and I got a kick out of Adam Sandler's "Opera Man," which managed to rhyme "Giuliani" with "why must you be gone-ee?"). But the event that moved me most didn't feature any celebrity.

I was standing on the stage, preparing to address the crowd. Ray Downey's son Chuck reached up from the audience and grabbed my hand. He gave me a memorial bracelet, engraved with his father's name and "S.O.C.," for Special Operations Command. He asked if I'd wear it and I proudly did so.

Until the World Trade Center attacks made it impossible, I attended the funeral of everyone who died in the line of duty in New York City. Being there not only showed people how important their loved one was, but had a reverberating effect, underlining the importance of the survivors as well. It's a lesson I learned from my father, who defined himself by helping people when they needed him most. He used to take me with him to wakes and funerals when I was a little boy, and I sensed how much it meant to our neighbors and friends that he made the effort. My father drilled the message into me with his trademark tenacity: weddings are discretionary; funerals are mandatory.

I've followed this rule ever since, perhaps occasionally to the point where it's gotten me in trouble with those who value lighter occasions. I tend to deal with the difficult times in people's lives better than the happy occasions, maybe because I try to save my time and energy for when I'm really needed. Don't get me wrong—as mayor, I performed more than 200 weddings. I love to eat, I love music, I even enjoy dancing. But everybody likes weddings. Funerals are difficult. That's why one's needed, and why it means more when one shows up. The fun events—weddings, parties, fancy dinners—all these are wonderful. And they're important; a leader ought to join with people in enjoying those rewards for hard work and sacrifice. But when the chips are down—when someone you care about is struggling for answers or burying a loved one—that's when the measure of a leader is taken.

I never realized how significant a part of my life my father's lesson would become. I always wonder if I can live up to his ability to give to others. Up until September 11, I didn't think I'd ever go to more funerals and wakes than he had.

I took the importance of funerals to heart long before I became mayor. My old friend Sara Vidal is a wonderful woman. She claims the record for being the person kissed most by Rudy Giuliani, because every time I see her I give her a big hug and kiss. Sara's sister, Raquel Vidal, not entirely incidentally, was a longtime aide to my predecessor, David Dinkins. Both of them became dedicated workers on my mayoral campaigns, and I was extremely grateful for their support. After their mother died in 1989, I went to the funeral—held at an Episcopal church, much like the one I grew up next to in Brooklyn, before I knew there were Italian Episcopalians—and the simple gesture of showing up meant a lot to both sisters. The fervor of their support in the years to come, and the genuine warmth that developed between us, was a powerful lesson. It was a lesson repeated often. Victor Robles was a City Council member, a Democrat. We worked together and had our share of disagreements. After his mother died, I attended her wake and every single time I saw him after that he mentioned how much it meant to him.

It didn't take long for the lesson of showing up for the hard stuff to come into play once I became mayor. Thirty-five minutes into the New Year, and into my new administration, two police officers were shot on the roof of a housing project. I visited them at the hospital in those early-morning hours, and on the afternoon of my first day in office went to Staten Island to see one of New York City's firemen who'd been hospitalized fighting a fire the day before.

Police officers and firefighters are the most obvious city employees whose funerals require the city's highest representation. But transportation workers and corrections officers and everyone else deserve the same respect.

On Saturday, August 4, 2001, District Superintendent Michael Gennardo went to work as usual at a Sanitation Department garage in Brooklyn. He showed up an hour early, as was his custom, and with a lot of cash and wearing expensive jewelry, as was also his custom.

What was not the custom of this man who had served the city for thirty-one years, known to his colleagues as "The Philosopher," was to be met by a degenerate thug who robbed and shot him.

I had spent Friday night at my friend Ken Caruso's house in eastern Long Island. We had stayed up late talking—a couple old friends, and lawyers to boot—and so I slept until 8:30 Saturday morning, which for me is really late. We were planning to have a leisurely breakfast and I was scheduled to play golf at noon. Ken came up to my room and said Beau Wagner, one of the police officers on my security detail, was downstairs. I always know that's not good. I ran down, half dressed, walked outside, and Beau told me a sanitation worker had been shot. Serious condition, Brookdale University Hospital in Brooklyn.

I always have my bags ready to go. I put them in the car and told Beau to start heading back to the city. Ken had never seen this happen before, the leap into action required when some disaster struck. I told Ken, I'm sorry, I'm out of here. I may see you tonight, but I've got to go—a sanitation worker has been shot.

We rushed to Brookdale Hospital and joined Michael Gennardo's family, two of the detectives working on the case, NYPD's Deputy Commissioner, Joe Dunne, the chief of the department, Joe Esposito, and Sanitation Commissioner Kevin Farrell. I felt as though I'd communicated to these people how highly I valued showing up at the hospital, how important I thought it was to the families.

By the time I spoke to the family, Gennardo had died. I embraced them and expressed my sorrow. I explained how much we owed people who worked for the city, that we would provide for the funeral arrangements and ensure they got all the benefits coming to families of those who died in the line of duty. Financial worries are the tangible burdens the city can take off the shoulders of grieving families. The intangibles are what matter more. In most cases—not every case, because there are times when people are so sad that it actually makes it worse; but nine times out of ten—it makes people feel better that the boss put in the effort.

It was a strange, sad experience to be at Brookdale that day, as it turned out. I've often been there when cops have been shot, accompanied by the wonderfully colorful Jack Maple, who had been a deputy to my first Police Commissioner, Bill Bratton. That same August day, Jack died of cancer. And a few days later it was his wake and funeral that were mandatory.

For me, showing up for the hard stuff extended beyond supporting just those who devoted their lives to working for the city. On July 17, 1996, TWA Flight 800 exploded in midair just off Long Island, minutes after leaving for Paris, killing all 230 aboard. Owing to the way the airline handled the situation, I felt that the city had to assert control. After wrenching the manifest from the airline, I personally broke the news to a number of grieving relatives. We set up a family center at the Ramada Plaza Hotel near Kennedy Airport and my staff and I stayed there virtually around the clock. We provided divers, boats, and equipment for the crash site, counselors and security for the hotel and the airport, and the Community Assistance Unit was there to lend a shoulder and advise the families—many of whom were not from the New York area—on every aspect of their tragedy. Little did we know that this was the training ground for Rosemary O'Keefe and her staff for the family center they would have to create following the twin towers attacks.

The city seemed to have more than its share of plane crashes during the eight years I was mayor. Each had left from Kennedy with more than 200 people aboard: TWA Flight 800, Swissair Flight 111, EgyptAir Flight 990, and, as if the city hadn't endured enough, American Airlines Flight 587 crashed just two months after the World Trade Center disaster. The nearby Ramada Plaza Hotel was commandeered for all of these, and became known in my administration as the Heartbreak Hotel.

As I learned from those airline tragedies, the families of the passengers are in the most painful straits imaginable. Logically, they know that their loved one is dead, but until they see his or her name on an official piece of paper, explicitly stating that their father or wife or son or daughter boarded the doomed plane, the reality doesn't set in.

My policy of being there for the hard times was put to the test following the World Trade Center attack. The scale of it, the volume of families needing comfort and assistance, was without precedent. Unlike other catastrophes, this one threatened the city's very ability to function. And because it was immediately clear that this was a crime committed by a murderous terrorist group, with members and sympathizers still at large, we couldn't attribute the destruction to a random act and move on to the grieving and rebuilding phases. The practical imperatives of doing whatever possible to minimize the chances of additional attacks stood alongside the enormous needs of the affected families.

I soon began to focus on the importance of appropriately memorializing those who lost their lives, particularly those who had died trying to save others. By the morning of September 13, at the temporary command center at the Police Academy we had established, I turned my attention to the horrible reality of our dead heroes. I told the staff: "We're going to have at least thirty police officers and three hundred firefighters who will need to be buried. Most of them will want to have an individual family funeral for their loved one. Because of the sheer number, we're not going to be able to provide the same large funeral for each, as we normally would for uniformed personnel. But we need to be clear how much we value their bravery and sacrifice."

We had all been up almost constantly since Tuesday morning, but the brainstorming began immediately. Bernie Kerik quickly solved the problem of how to give recognition to individual families by proposing that we form a "mini-ceremonial detail" of NYPD, Fire Department, and National Guard members for every funeral. Then we turned to finding an appropriate site for a citywide prayer service we planned for the following week. Central Park, Madison Square Garden, and other likely spots were mentioned, but Yankee Stadium seemed to me one of the strongest symbols of New York. Sunny Mindel wondered about the "appropriateness" of a baseball stadium for such a somber occasion, but I pointed out that the Pope had said Mass there, which decided the issue. At a beautiful service a week and a half later, on September 23, tenor Placido Domingo sang "Ave Maria," one of my favorite hymns, and Bette Midler belted out "Wind Beneath My Wings."

The massiveness of the calamity affected every city agency. The Health Department had to monitor the air around the site constantly. The Transportation Department was rerouting traffic and helping to inspect cars as they approached the bridges and tunnels. Sanitation was carting hundreds of tons of new debris, and the Buildings Department had to rustle up space for displaced businesses and inspect damaged structures to ensure safety. The economic picture was vastly affected, and every social service agency seemed to have its hands full. With all my staff consumed by the tasks occupying each of their departments, some of our obligations could be expected to slip through the cracks. I don't like it when things slip through the cracks.

A few days after we'd moved into our new emergency command center at Pier 92 on the Hudson River, Claire Shulman, the Queens Borough President, sent a message to one of the morning meetings. Many of New York's uniformed personnel live in Queens, and Claire had noticed that no representative from my office was in attendance at a firefighter's funeral. The stunning number of deaths meant I could not attend every funeral; after this was brought to my attention, my staff waited for my reaction. The group seemed evenly divided between those who expected me to be furious and those who thought our pressing schedules served as an acceptable excuse. The former was correct.

There was not a single member of my staff who didn't exhibit maximum effort and effectiveness under extremely difficult circumstances, but this was unacceptable. I decided to establish a triage to make sure that a city representative attended every funeral, and I told everyone at that meeting that I expected them not just to attend, but to make their presence felt, speaking to and comforting the victim's survivors.

The logistics weren't easy. There were anywhere from half a dozen to twenty funerals a day—of which I tried to attend at least six personally. One morning in early October, I was at the Pier 92 command center preparing for the day's schedule. Judith's friend Marilyn Krone was watching me lay out the day when I realized that it resembled a battle plan in which one is trying to reach as many people as possible over the course of a day. You can't go from the Bronx to Staten Island and back again, so you work out a realistic plan to make as many as you can.

On October 8, for example, atop the multitude of obligations in the recovering city, there were six funerals on my schedule. One could make the case—and some did—that I should have left the funerals and memorials to others. But which entries on my schedule that day should I have canceled? One was the funeral for a police officer, only the second NYPD funeral I'd had the chance to attend since the disaster. Should I have crossed that off my list? Or perhaps the service for Donald J. Burns, Assistant Chief of the FDNY? As citywide borough commander, Burns was required to be at every major incident anywhere in the city during his twenty-four-hour shift.

Looking over the schedule on the morning of October 8, Tony Carbonetti and I were reminiscing about all the good people whose funerals were filling the day. He recalled how—Tony has a way with words—"some schmuck fire inspector" was going to give City Hall a citation for the tent we built behind City Hall for the first Yankees World Series parade. Donald Burns explained what we'd have to correct to avoid the embarrassing summons. So how about him, with thirty-nine years of service to the department under his belt—should I have skipped his funeral?

In fact, I didn't view the responsibility to attend these wakes, memorials, and funerals as solely my or my administration's responsibility. At my press conferences in the awful weeks and months after September 11, I would urge New Yorkers to attend funerals of those who had died in the disaster, and not only those for people they personally knew. On Saturday morning, I would get on WINS or WCBS to ask people to come to these ceremonies, and we put a schedule of them on the city's website and urged the newspapers to publish them as well. This was an attack on all of New York and the entire nation— and every family I saw welcomed all comers.

As I have already described, Beth Petrone has been my executive assistant for eighteen years. I performed the ceremony when she married FDNY Captain Terry Hatton on May 16, 1998, at Gracie Mansion. She'd spotted him a couple years earlier and asked to be introduced. They were soon inseparable. Beth and Terry fell in love from the first moment they laid eyes on each other. After they married, Terry would send Beth flowers, and sometimes he'd pick her up after work, hanging out on the sofa outside my office until she was ready to leave.

As head of the elite Rescue 1, Terry had been honored many times. Having awarded Terry several of his nineteen medals, I knew him before Beth did. I first met him at the scene of a diner explosion in Queens, where Terry had safely extracted a waitress pinned by slabs of steel and concrete. A chief's son, Terry was a firefighter's firefighter, and a gentleman as well—the kind of man I would like my son to grow up to be. Terry and ten of his brothers from Rescue 1 were killed in the World Trade Center attacks, fearlessly leading the rescue until the end.

Some of his tools and keys were found by the remaining members of Rescue 1, a small solace for a heartbroken squad. I brought those things to Beth at Terry's wake, along with part of his uniform. I remained at the wake a long time, taking in the articles and photos on posters devoted to this good man. I noticed a photo of Terry rescuing a child from a fire. He kept that photo in his locker as a reminder of the best part of his job, of why he risked everything to help people he didn't know.

His funeral was two days later, on October 4, at St. Patrick's Cathedral—a very special place. Looking around, I noticed Commissioner Von Essen. Terry lived in the house next door to the Von Essens, and Tom had watched Terry grow up. Tom's own son, Max, sang "Amazing Grace" to begin the service as his father looked on. My dear friend Alan Placa said the Mass. To see that beautiful church, packed with people who loved Terry and Beth—and with many simply there to show their respect—that's why I know how important it is to show up at funerals.

12

Stand Up to Bullies

y father was an excellent boxer. His poor eyesight prevented him from becoming the prizefighter he wanted to be, but at 6 feet tall and 150 pounds, he was fast and very tough. He understood the sport, and would describe fights to me in great detail, explaining the strategies and techniques of the great fighters, men like Sugar Ray Robinson, Joe Louis, Willie Pep, Rocky Marciano, and Jersey Joe Walcott.

In boxing, he said, the most important skill was to stay calm. This was the best lesson my father taught me, repeated endlessly—remain calm, especially when those around you are uneasy or troubled. He put it into my head that someone who stays unruffled has a great advantage in being able to help others, to control the situation, to fix it. The fighter who loses his cool the first time he's hit will end up on the canvas. If he remains calm, even while he's being hit, he can look for opportunities to hit back. My father started to teach me to box when I was a toddler and he continued instructing me throughout my teenage years. As a Yankees fan growing up only blocks from

Ebbets Field in Brooklyn—home to the Dodgers—I soon discovered that those lessons came in handy. In later years, my father would tell me that if I were ever attacked I should imagine myself back in the boxing ring—remaining calm and looking for vulnerabilities.

One of the leadership rules I've relied on dates way back to my very first lessons, and to the first bully I ever confronted. I'll call him Albert.

When I was a kid, my family lived on the upper floor of a two-story house and my uncle William's family lived on the first floor. Willie was my mother's older brother. He was my godfather—my middle name is William—and our families were particularly close because he was married to my father's sister, Olga. Uncle Willie was a New York City police officer, and in those days cops had to wear their uniforms both to and from work. He was a neat man, tall and thin—he looked sharp in his police uniform, and I was very impressed by him. Long after he retired, he always wore a jacket, and usually a tie. He was a quiet, shy man who liked to keep to himself, and would spend his off hours reading the paper under the tree in front of our house.

Next door lived another family, and the father was also a police officer. For some reason, my uncle disliked him—perhaps he'd been nasty or unfair to Uncle Willie. Anyway, this guy had a son named Albert, a big fat kid, two years older than me—I was about 5 and he was 7. Albert took advantage of his size to intimidate other children. He would knock them down and sit or roll on them.

My uncle used to read *Spring 3100*, the in-house police magazine. I loved looking at it—still do, in fact. I would pore over Uncle Willie's copy, at the pictures of wanted crooks and new police technologies, but only for so long—my uncle would always take the magazine back. One day he was sitting alone under the tree and my mother was nowhere in sight. He called me over. A copy of *Spring 3100* was by his side.

"You want this magazine, right?"

"Yes," I replied.

"You want it to keep?"

"Sure!"

"Beat up Albert, and I'll give you the magazine."

"What do you mean?"

Uncle Willie said, "Look, your father's been teaching you to box. Throw a couple of jabs like your old man showed you and Albert will start crying—he's a fat slob and bullies are never as tough as they seem."

I was reluctant, because Albert was much heavier than I was. But Uncle Willie showed me the magazine and let me hold it, before taking it back and repeating that it would be mine as soon as I got Albert to cry uncle.

A little while later, my own uncle was sitting outside in his usual chair under the tree, when I saw Albert up to his usual tricks, pushing other children around, all of them smaller than he. I don't remember exactly how it started. Did I challenge him? Did he pick on me first? Did I come to someone's rescue? All I know is that I found myself in a fight with him, just the two of us.

I started jabbing at his face—*boom, boom, boom*, exactly as I'd been taught—and they were arriving, nearly all of them. Albert never even landed a blow—or if he did I was too excited to notice. His nose started bleeding, a shiner was already appearing, and finally he started to cry, turned, and ran off home.

It wasn't long before Albert's mother marched over to our house, dragging him by the hand. She found my mother and paraded her son's bloody nose and black eye. I was a little animal, she announced. My mother was immediately outraged—but not in my defense. "Why did you do this?" she demanded. I could see my uncle just a few feet away, still there in front of the tree, and I looked at him, expecting him to come forward and admit that he'd put me up to it. Instead, he remained stock still, as if he had no idea what was happening.

"Albert was bullying people around and I decided to stand up to him," I told my mother.

She slapped me hard across the face, right in front of these people. My mother snapped, "Apologize right now, and I'm going to tell your father tonight. He's going to give you a real beating."

"I don't want to apologize," I managed to mumble. "He started it." For that I got a second slap, and she repeated her command.

I know when I'm beat. Albert was still crying, and I begrudgingly said, "I'm sorry, Albert." My mother made us shake hands, and ordered me to stay in for the rest of the day. I glanced at my uncle, and thought, at least he could give me the darn magazine. But I didn't give him up. I just went slowly up to my room. After about twenty minutes, his daughter, my cousin Evangeline, came to join me. She was carrying his copy of *Spring 3100*. "My dad wanted you to have this," she said. "Since you have to stay in all day." I looked out the window. Uncle Willie was still there, under his tree. He wasn't looking up at me or anything, but I saw him give an unmistakable nod—as much for keeping my mouth shut about our arrangement, I knew, as for whipping Albert.

My father came home that evening as usual, and my mother told him what had happened. I could hear them talking in the room next door. I had beaten up Albert, made him cry; I was getting a reputation and had to be straightened out. She told him that it was his fault for teaching me to box, and that he should now give me a licking I would never forget. He came up to me, but before he could adopt a suitable face of disapproval, he blurted, "You whipped Albert? God Almighty! He's two years older than you, and twenty-five pounds heavier!"

Now my mother really got angry. She started saying that my father was turning me into an animal, making me a bum. But I didn't get hit that night.

At other times my mother would try to get my father to spank me, and he would avoid it. Not long after the Albert incident, we moved to Garden City South, Long Island, so that I could grow up away from the influences that my parents feared could harm me. When my mother demanded that my father discipline me, he would take me off to the basement and pretend to whack me. My mother would stay upstairs, and never knew that my father spent the time teaching me how to box. On the Albert occasion, his reaction was too spontaneous to play that game. I told him how I jabbed and jabbed and he said, "Great! That's what I keep telling you—always go into a fight with a plan." But he would always emphasize: "Never pick on someone smaller than you. Never be a bully."

I have a visceral reaction to bullies. I can't tolerate it when a predator takes unfair advantage. That's the reason I brought such intensity to prosecuting the Mafia and corrupt government officials.

I've deployed a similar principle in situations that might not look at first like typical bully confrontations. Whenever someone who thinks he has the upper hand tries to force his views, I send a clear message that I won't stand for that kind of coercion. If an adversary in a negotiation threatens to go public with something they think will embarrass me, I tell them, "Okay, let's do it—we'll hold a press conference." If someone threatens to quit as a bargaining ploy, I simply accept their resignation.

For years, the diplomats of the United Nations thought they could park in the city wherever they liked. I challenged that assumption. The symbolic value came through loud and clear: if an average New York citizen isn't allowed to block a hydrant or double-park, then neither is someone working under the auspices of the U.N. To presume otherwise is arrogance.

The policy of forcing member nations to pay their parking fines was more than a token. Standing up to people who don't think they have to play by the rules is valuable in its own right, but also conveys a message to the community that being decent is not the same as being weak. Further, it was a matter of international diplomacy, even of foreign policy. It's the Broken Windows theory applied to international affairs: letting a nation get away with not paying small fines only encourages it to renege on larger responsibilities.

One of the statistics I tracked in the weekly meeting with the Police Department was the number of crimes committed by diplomats. Often, there would be offenses—wife-beatings, sexual abuse of children, fights and assaults—committed by diplomats specifically assigned to the U.N. Well, a member nation that can't discipline someone who commits domestic violence can't administer a country according to the rule of law.

In spring 1997, the American ambassador to the U.N., Bill Richardson, waded into the parking-fines controversy with guns blazing, announcing how he was going to collect on all the tickets. But he backed down as soon as he confronted resistance. One of the points I made to him, and made to the public, was that if you can get these nations to pay their tickets, you begin to bring them into some understanding and acceptance of the rule of law. Conversely, if they come to America and flout our laws, refusing to abide by some of the most basic rules of civilized behavior, then they're likely to do the same in their own countries.

So I believed the United Nations could play a helpful role. Instead of the usual fuzzy, romantic idea of all these nations confabulating, maybe we could actually accomplish something. If we got them to the stage where they organized themselves at least to pay their tickets, maybe they could start respecting other rules of law of a more substantial nature. I don't think that a corrupt or despotic state will suddenly be brought to order and decency by being persuaded to write a parking check; but the determination not to confront the issue, the toleration of lawlessness, defines deviancy in exactly the way that Senator Daniel Patrick Moynihan described when he talked about "defining deviancy down." I thought the enforcement of ticket collection would be an important way for the United Nations to accomplish its objective of creating more respect for the rule of law and ultimately encouraging stable governments that can be accountable for their actions. They never got it.

When I became mayor, I focused attention on transforming Manhattan's 42nd Street and the surrounding Times Square area. One of the best-known symbols of New York City had degenerated over the seventies and eighties. "Forty Deuce," as the street was known, was lined with sex shops. In the shadow of the New York Public Library, junkies patrolled Bryant Park, openly buying and selling drugs. (In fact, a significant amount of my drug arrests as the U.S. Attorney used to emanate from the park.) As visitors emerged from the nearby Lincoln Tunnel, aggressive panhandlers would greet them, demanding a handout in exchange for unsolicited windshield wiping. It was an ugly face for the city to display to the rest of the world. Worse, it was a signal to the city that its leaders were unable to control even the most visible civic spaces.

It was clear that Times Square was badly in need of transformation; but part of the reason I was so determined to turn it around was that I personally experienced the lawlessness of the area. In spring 1993, some friends and I were going to the theater on a Sunday afternoon. Though I had begun my second run for mayor, it was early enough in the campaign that I did not yet travel with police escort.

As I was sitting in my car on Broadway around 46th Street, I saw a young man run by. Then an older man ran after him. And I saw a woman holding her shoe and hobbling along after the first two. We were already late for the theater, so I told my friends to go on ahead while I tried to help. I ran into traffic and caught up to the second guy on Sixth Avenue—by which time he'd stopped and was trying to catch his breath before resuming the chase. He told me a mugger had grabbed his wife's purse and violently pushed her aside as he did so. He said he was trying to "catch the sonovabitch."

I told the man that whoever he was chasing was long gone, and that he should go back to comfort his wife while I called the police. I asked him if he got a good look at the mugger and could identify him. He said he did. So we walked back and found his wife, who was shaken up and crying. As we walked, I looked all over for the police—it was a Sunday afternoon in Times Square, and there should have been plenty around. We then called 911 and waited.

Fifteen minutes went by and not a single cop appeared. I stood there thinking, "This is absolutely nutty." Times Square is the place we tell people to visit. We want people to spend money at the theaters and restaurants, so we can put New Yorkers to work, but we don't make it safe. We should be sending a message to New Jersey and Connecticut and Nassau County and California and Florida and England and Germany: come to New York City, enjoy all it has to offer and spend a few hundred bucks here. It feels safe and it is safe.

Instead, the city made it obvious that we didn't care to protect visitors, to create a hospitable, civilized place. If we did somehow manage to tempt a visitor to New York, we'd do our best to tax them out of ever wanting to return; the hotel tax, for example, was 21.25 percent. Who paid the price for an unsafe and exorbitant city? Not the visitors, who could always go somewhere else, and did so in droves. Not the corporations that were unwilling to develop the area—they simply shifted funds to projects in other places. The victims of Times Square's decline were thousands of New Yorkers. As I waited for the police, I thought, "This has got to change."

Some of the biggest bullies I faced as mayor were a few of the heads of New York City's powerful labor unions. As a Republican and an advocate of smaller government, I ran without the endorsement of most of the city's unions. One of the benefits of winning without that support was that I was then free to do what I believed was best for New York. However, that was only one problem solved. Confident in their ability to bring the city to its knees with the mere threat of a strike, some union bosses threw their weight around, oblivious to what their demands might mean for anyone else.

By the time I took office at the start of 1994, I had been preparing my budget for months. We inherited a deficit and faced an even bigger debt for the fiscal year that would start in July. Preparing for the spending cuts and working out a budget reduction plan was difficult for me. I knew how hard it was going to be to assemble the political support needed to cut between $2 billion and $3 billion, but there was no alternative. The city was being strangled by runaway spending. Raising taxes—the knee-jerk reaction to every other recent shortfall—wasn't a viable option. Revenues were already beginning to shrink, as employers and residents alike fled for cities that didn't confiscate the lion's share of their earnings.

Most of the unions understood how dire the crisis had become. These people didn't just work for New York City; for many of them it was their home. Although the negotiations weren't easy, the city's unions largely believed me when I explained that frugality now would help us all in the long run—which is exactly what happened.

One group, however, didn't think they should do their part to help. In October 1994, the lawyers who worked for the Legal Aid Society went out on strike.

The Legal Aid Society provides legal services to the poor, including their primary mission—representing indigent defendants in criminal cases. The city has an obligation to provide such counsel, and we contracted with the Legal Aid Society to fulfill that obligation. If its lawyers didn't show up for work, criminal defendants would be deprived of their constitutional right to representation. In fact, judges can release offenders when they don't get lawyers fast enough, or are kept in jail for too long without a lawyer. The Legal Aid Society had gone out on strike at other times during previous administrations. Sometimes these strikes had gone on for months, risking dangerous individuals being set free by judges because they didn't have lawyers when they appeared in court.

When Legal Aid threatened to strike in 1994, I announced that if they carried out their threat we'd do whatever we could to cancel their contract. This wasn't just about the inconvenience and selfishness of their position. Once a lawyer undertakes a case, he or she is bound to see it through to a conclusion. A lawyer who takes on a client cannot stop representing that case without that responsibility being relieved by a judge, even if the client can no longer pay. There was an important principle here.

That still didn't stop the Legal Aid Society from going out on strike. I said, "Okay, in two days I will consider you to have broken your contract. We'll find other lawyers to do the work. And in the future the city will not do business with any organization that includes any lawyer who has walked out on their ethical obligation."

Exactly two workdays later, the lawyers went back. They spent the next eight years suing me and the city for violating their alleged rights. That suit continued after I left office, continues still, and given the nature of litigation in America will probably not be resolved for some time. But the important point is that standing up to them worked. The lawyers got back to their jobs and lived up to their contracts. During my administration, that two-day strike was the one and only that Legal Aid staged.

GO INTO A FIGHT WITH A PLAN

Toward the end of 1999, the city's Metropolitan Transit Authority began threatening to strike. It would have proven disastrous, occurring just as New York was hosting the world's biggest millennium celebration. The agency's contract was due to expire at midnight on December 15, and the bus and subway drivers were set to walk off the job. In New York State, the Taylor Law makes it against the law for public employees to strike—whether they have a contract or not. Nevertheless, previous mayors had habitually granted amnesty to strikers as part of whatever settlement package lured city employees back to work. Now, the MTA is a state agency;

its employees do not work for the city. But because New York City's citizens and visitors are the primary users of a public transit system that handles eight million people a day—about a third of the mass transit in the United States—the city would bear the great majority of the fallout from any work stoppage. That had been amply demonstrated in paralyzing strikes during the Lindsay and Koch administrations.

We had to stop the union action. The main reason a leader has to stand up to bullies is also the simplest: it's the right thing to do. But another reason is that I had to set a tone. As in the schoolyard, if you let someone take your lunch money on Monday, he's going to take it on Tuesday and Wednesday and every day until you let him know you'll put up a fight. If we allowed the union to cripple the city—or gave in to the MTA workers' demands under threat of an illegal strike—we'd be run over by every union with a beef.

We drew up papers to get an injunction preventing a walkout. We communicated with the legal staff of MTA, but were going to represent our own interests as well. The case was before Michael Pesce, the chief administrative judge for the Brooklyn Supreme Court.

My Corporation Counsel, Mike Hess, called Judge Pesce to explain the urgency of the situation. Everyone was already worried about Y2K, and Seattle even canceled its millennium celebration over fears of terrorism. New York did not need to be held hostage by a union playing on these anxieties to get what it could not obtain through proper negotiation channels. The judge immediately grasped the magnitude of the situation and asked Mike to come to his home for an emergency *ex parte* meeting.

Mike showed up at Judge Pesce's Brooklyn townhouse at around seven A.M. on December 15, 1999. It was still dark and cold outside. The judge greeted Mike in his bathrobe. A couple lawyers from my office and two from the state's legal department were already there. I had gotten to know Judge Pesce in 1996 when his fiancée, Bonnie Walters, who had volunteered to work for my campaign, and her mother died as passengers in the crash of TWA Flight 800 off Long Island. He became a leader for the interests of the grieving families. Judge Pesce loves to cook and welcome visitors to his home—even lawyers. He sat everyone down at his kitchen table with all these pans hanging everywhere, reviewed and then signed the injunction. Mike wasn't surprised, since a strike was clearly illegal, but I had told him that we needed more than that—would-be strikers might defy such an order, assuming the city would again sit back and do nothing. So we needed an order with real teeth in it.

Mike explained all this to the judge, who asked what he had in mind. Mike suggested that individuals who failed to show up for work on December 16 be fined $25,000 personally, with the fine doubling to $50,000 on December 17, $100,000 on December 18, and so on. In addition, the Transport Workers Union would be fined $1 million on December 16, $2 million on December 17, $4 million on December 18—and the judge agreed to it all. But no dollar amount would have meant anything unless the people on the other side of the negotiating table knew that I'd actually collect those fines. The potential strikers had to be convinced not only that they were acting against the law but that there was now an administration tough enough to make the fines stick. Later that day the union settled.

At the press conference to announce that a strike had been averted Mike Hess stood next to me. A reporter asked me how we'd arrived at the $25,000 figure. I asked Mike to answer and he started to go on about "lost productivity" and "punitive damages." I never found out how he arrived at the number. But it worked.

DON'T EXCEED THE PIG FACTOR

This rule is about not ruining a good thing. A common example of piggishness in the corporate world is business expense accounts. If I spend money to travel for business or take a work colleague to lunch, it is appropriate to charge those expenses to the business. The pig factor kicks in when someone overstates the cost of that travel or that lunch. Then the whole system is jeopardized. Taking more than what one is entitled to is a form of bullying. And it doesn't even have to be overt fraud. Sometimes people can overdo legitimate expenses. Soon enough, the company cracks down and imposes limitations that hamper even justifiable and reasonable expenses.

In government, the acceptance of gifts comes up from time to time. If they were not in any way involved in the exchange of business, there would be no problem, but soon enough people start to accept presents from those who have business before the government. Then they get bigger. Soon they're not really gifts at all, but bribes, and not long after that extortion by government employees. So a perfectly appropriate and important human practice—the giving of presents—changes from a beautiful thing to a tangle of regulations. All because people exceeded the pig factor.

The spectacular meltdown of Enron is a dramatic example of exceeding the pig factor. The accounting rules they employed to hide their losses from the public were utilized by many companies for a much more benign reason, but Enron abused those rules to such an extent that the company was bound to fail. As a result, businesses of all kinds will now face arduous restrictions on their accounting practices. A new and expensive layer of accounting will be added, a particularly burdensome expense since it's not devoted to producing anything, but simply a safeguard. And all publicly traded companies, whether they have been exceeding the pig factor or not, will have to play by the expensive new rules.

The irony of most situations in which the pig factor has been exceeded is that the people who do the exceeding may have gotten away with it had they been a few percentage points less excessive. Little League pitcher Danny Almonte, for example, would probably have never been revealed as an over-age 14-year-old had those who perpetrated the scandal instructed him to allow a run here and there. Instead, the manipulative adults got greedy. Danny's streak of not allowing a single earned run in three championship series games and for almost every game during the regular season led to the scrutiny that eventually uncovered the deception.

Whenever I approach a problem, I seek the solution that's most favorable but does not overreach. There is no fail-safe formula for knowing where that line is. Leaders seem to develop a sense of it. Those who can't don't stay leaders for long.

In the wake of the attacks on the World Trade Center, the great majority of New Yorkers—and all Americans—dug deep and pulled together in a way that inspired the world. But a few bad apples tried to take advantage of the situation.

At the morning meeting on September 28, Joe Lhota brought to my attention that as many as 250 tons of debris (of the 133,000 removed from the site to that point) appeared to have been diverted by organized crime. There's money in recycling steel and other metals, and the idea that gangsters might profit from the catastrophe outraged me. I told Joe to consult Ray Casey, the chairman of the city's Trade Waste Commission. At that point we had executed two search warrants, on Long Island and in New Jersey, but I wanted some arrests. Even though the amount of material involved represented less than a quarter of a percent of the total, there could have been human remains in those 250 tons. Shortly after, we arrested several carters and the problem ended.

DON'T OVERREACH

I also saw to it that my administration didn't overreach during this time of crisis. One example came early on—eight days after the September 11 attack. At the morning meeting on September 19, Budget Director Adam Barsky was explaining about emergency aid. The largest Federal Emergency Management Agency claim to that point was the $4 billion granted after the Oklahoma City bombing. Far more federal money was on its way to New York, but the exact amount was yet to be decided. Also unanswered at that point was what entity or entities would be the recipients. Nearly everyone agreed that New York City was the logical grantee, but regulations called for it to be the state. Adam said, "That's a problem. For one, the grantee collects a one-half of one percent administrative fee. On twenty billion dollars, that's a hundred million . . ."

I stopped that line of thinking in its tracks. "This is a much deeper conversation than the usual city vs. state stuff," I said, and explained that, instead of running around saying, "The city should get *all* the money," what we needed to do was come up with an accurate, intellectually honest figure. Otherwise we would look greedy. If we set an amount, as in "We need $12 billion" or whatever the number might be, then we left George Pataki and the state government room to maneuver without feeling that the city was overstepping its reach. This helped to make our requests realistic and I believe gave us the credibility to get what we needed and helped ease the way for the White House to get money to the city so quickly.

"Standing up to bullies" might sound like a glib call to be macho and assertive, but the truth is that such action takes a toll. One of the best reasons to let bullies know that you won't back down from a fight is so that it doesn't get to that point often. That's not just a theory— there were many times in my administration when an early confrontation led to far less fighting down the road. Here's an example.

At about 8:40 P.M. on Wednesday, July 17, 1996, TWA Flight 800 crashed into the Atlantic Ocean just past Long Island. All 230 on board the Paris-bound 747, which had taken off from Kennedy International Airport, were killed. My community response team and I got to the scene within an hour and had set up an assistance center at the Ramada Plaza Hotel near the airport to provide aid and counseling to family members. We sent police boats, divers, and emergency experts to the crash site, and stationed extra police at the Ramada and at Kennedy.

When we got there, the first thing we tried to do was obtain the manifest so we could be sure who had been on the plane. In every such crash, relatives cling to the hope that their loved one, for whatever reason, decided not to board the plane. Particularly in this case.

Airlines are required by law to compile a complete list of passengers on international flights, including full names, passport information, and emergency phone contact numbers. This information is supposed to be made available within three hours of any crash. In this case, by 11:30 P.M., TWA said 229 people were aboard. By noon the next day, they were saying the number was 228. Later in the afternoon, they put the number at 230. The original tally included three Rome-bound passengers; it turned out they weren't on the plane. I can't overstate how excruciating such mistakes are on families. Each misstatement opens a new false hope. Further, telling the world that an airline doesn't know who is on its planes is an open invitation to terrorists. In fact, the three-hour law was passed in 1990 in response to the 1988 bombing of Pan Am Flight 103 over Lockerbie, Scotland, attributed to explosives in luggage that had been checked onto the plane even though the owner didn't board.

I repeatedly demanded an accurate passenger list from TWA, but was given every excuse why the airline could not produce one—from the FBI having taken it to the National Transportation Safety Board having instructed TWA not to release the names. Both excuses were untrue.

I sensed that something was up when about four A.M. I received a call from the CEO of the airline, Jeffrey Erickson, from a plane heading for Kennedy. I told him that I needed the manifest. He replied that we would talk about it when he got to New York, that he wanted to "liaise" with me. It was such a solemn occasion that I suppressed what I wanted to say, but from the moment I heard the word "liaise," I suspected he was not my kind of guy. I don't agree to "liaise" with people I haven't met. But then I thought, well, maybe I shouldn't be so judgmental based on the use of one word.

By the next day, I was exasperated. I felt we were getting the runaround from the airline. When Erickson finally showed up, he addressed the families and the press at Kennedy Airport, speaking for under a minute. He refused to take a single question. He added nothing to what we already knew, and there was certainly nothing to "liaise" about. Such conduct in a crisis was even worse than being misled under normal circumstances.

On behalf of the families of the passengers—and with an eye toward future disasters—I decided to make my anger known. On several national shows and on all the local channels, I criticized TWA for caring more about covering itself than promptly notifying suffering family members. On Friday, I recorded my weekly WABC radio show from the Ramada, and said, "The upper management of TWA incompetently handled the notification process for the families. That continues to be exacerbated by their not telling the truth about what happened."

Three months later, Erickson resigned. But that wasn't the point. In a city the size of New York, disasters are inevitable. I wanted leaders of companies involved in future disasters to understand what was expected of them—clear, honest, timely communication. By refusing to keep quiet about TWA's behavior, I made sure the consequences of putting corporate needs ahead of human suffering were understood.

This is precisely what happened. In each subsequent crash during my administration—from Swissair Flight 111 to EgyptAir Flight 990 to American Airlines Flight 587[1]—those in charge of the information acted with compassion and professionalism. I would hope

[1]September 2, 1998, Swissair Flight 111 crashed off Peggy's Cove, Nova Scotia, going from Kennedy International Airport to Geneva, Switzerland; October 31, 1999, EgyptAir Flight 990 crashed in the ocean off Nantucket Island after leaving Kennedy International Airport en route to Cairo, Egypt; November 12, 2001, American Airlines Flight 587 crashed in Rockaway, Queens, on the way to the Dominican Republic.

that they learned from Erickson and TWA's mishandling of Flight 800. Swissair especially was the complete opposite of TWA.

My policy of standing up to bullies did not originate when I became mayor. In a sense, that's the fundamental mission of all prosecutors. They bring cases against people they believe have taken advantage of those weaker than themselves. And when they do so, the complaint doesn't read "Rudy Giuliani v. Fat Tony, Matty the Horse, Tony Ducks, Christie Tick, Nicky Glasses, Figgy, Jackie the Lackie, Joey the Clown, The Nutcracker, and Tony Ripe" (to list a few of the more colorful aka's of defendants I prosecuted). Instead, the plaintiff is "The United States of America" or "The People of the State of New York."

In the mid-1980s, my office spent many man-hours developing a civil RICO case to prove that the internal structure of the Teamsters Union had become so closely tied to organized crime that the union itself had become a racketeering enterprise. The case was being pursued in two places—in the District of Columbia and at my office, the Southern District of New York. There was considerable pressure on the Justice Department, and on Attorney General Ed Meese, not to bring the case at all. Teamster boss Jackie Presser was one of the few union leaders to back President Reagan, and as head of the country's largest union he carried a lot of votes.

Ultimately, the Justice Department gave the case to the Southern District of New York. Publicity about the case began even before we had filed it, and the opposition to it from politicians was immediate, overwhelming—and bipartisan. We had not even confirmed any case existed, and already four presidential candidates lined up to oppose it: Democrats Paul Simon and Jesse Jackson and Republicans Jack Kemp and Alexander Haig. Then, in December 1988, 240 members of Congress sent a letter to President Reagan insisting that I be directed not to file the case. I don't remember if they demanded that I be fired, but at the very least they wanted me off the case, hoping my successor could be made to back down.

It was intimidating. No one thought we could win, and some of the most powerful people in America didn't hesitate to make that plain. The Teamsters were too large, too powerful. There was one very important exception—Vice President George H.W. Bush, who refused to join the bandwagon. Even though he, too, was seeking the presidential nomination, he publicly stated that he would not interfere with the independence of a U.S. Attorney.

Despite a constant litany of complaints—that I was politicizing the effort, that I was misusing the racketeering statute, and so on—I deeply believed that this was a case in which millions of people were being squeezed for the benefit of a few corrupt leaders. First, there were the thousands of honest, hard-working Teamsters who weren't getting the leadership they deserved, but were instead stuck with people whose sole qualification was a willingness to get in bed with the mob. Second, the integrity of trade unions in general was sullied by the cravenness of a few bad-apple Teamsters. Third, everyone in America had to pay just that little bit more for the goods they bought, which were carted by trucks driven by Teamsters. If this "Teamster Tax" had been the result of savvy negotiations by a lawful union, so be it. But when that money funded no-show jobs and outright payoffs—let alone murders, bombings, and beatings used to ensure mob-friendly candidates prevailed in Teamster elections—everyone lost.

The Teamster case meant a lot to me. In the late fifties, at the time of the McClellan Hearings on Teamster corruption, I had been a young man on Long Island. Hearing Bobby Kennedy's withering confrontation with Jimmy Hoffa left a mark on me, at an impressionable time of life, and made me all the more determined to win against the Teamsters thirty years later, when the union's leadership was still infested with organized crime figures.

By the beginning of 1989, the case was coming to a head. In addition, I had many other prosecutions at various stages of development, and at the same time the idea of running for mayor was taking shape. It was becoming increasingly clear that I could make it a competitive race, while the reasons I wanted to run were more compelling than ever. I made up my mind. On the last day of January, I left the U.S. Attorney's office—but not before I had tied up the loose ends against the unions and knew it would be in good hands with the interim appointment of my Executive Assistant Benito Romano, as acting U.S. Attorney. On March 14, the Teamsters signed plea bargains consenting to the government supervision and court-appointed overseers we had asked for, and the members got a little more democracy, as national officers would now be elected by direct vote.

Being mayor of New York City was extremely challenging, especially during the last few months of my second term. But even the responsibility of being mayor was somehow different from the weight of the decisions of the U.S. Attorney's office.

I loved that job as much as I loved being mayor. It was totally fulfilling. However, I'll never forget how I felt on the first day of February. I woke up as though a great weight had been lifted from my shoulders. I felt like a regular person again. I realized that all that fighting, all that standing up to bullies, had worn me out. As U.S. Attorney, the responsibility of deciding whether to indict people weighed on me heavily. With every indictment, I would wrestle with these almost religious questions: What was fair? What impact might an indictment have? On February 1, I thought, Well, now somebody else is going to have to stay up at night and think about all that.

Standing Up to Bullies is not easy. The reason you do it early and resolutely is so you don't have to do it more than you should.

13

Study. Read. Learn Independently

My mother, Helen Giuliani, exerted tremendous influence on my education. She loved to teach. She had graduated first in her high school class and would have gone on to be a teacher, but with the Great Depression looming and her father already dead, she had to go to work to support her family. Instead of a class to teach, she made me her special student.

Before I can remember, she gave me lessons. She was particularly fond of history and instilled in me a strong belief that knowing about the past would reveal the whole story of the world. She would read aloud to me, encouraging me to use my imagination to picture different scenes. She would transform a simple drive through Long Island into a lesson, urging me to envision what it would have looked like when Native Americans inhabited the area and how it changed when Columbus arrived and settlers followed.

My mother adored books, viewing them as a source of great enjoyment rather than a chore or tool. She planted the idea that a book could take a reader anywhere, that anything could be mastered if one read deeply enough. She used to tell me that reading a book could take you on vacation. She went to the Pacific Islands reading James Michener's *Hawaii* and visited Tuscany by reading Irving Stone's fictionalized biography of Michelangelo, *The Agony and the Ecstasy*. I couldn't wait to take a history course in school. When I did, I treasured my textbooks and would touch and smell them, fascinated with the worlds depicted inside. I still like the look, feel, and smell of books. In my early days of schooling, I hewed to my mother's strict schedule of homework first, play later. As I grew older and discovered baseball and girls, I naturally resisted that discipline, but even as I found excuses to put off studying, and would resort to cramming just before exams, the love of learning was still there. Sure, there were certain subjects that bored me, and other academic chores I didn't relish. But by and large my mother created a great love of acquiring knowledge, an excitement about learning new things.

She taught me an educational strategy, too—whenever I wanted to learn something, I tried teaching it to myself. Over time, I developed the romantic notion that one can find secret solutions in books. I intensely read about every subject I undertake, and I do so with the conviction that I will learn things about it that nobody else knows.

TEACH YOURSELF FIRST

My son, Andrew, became interested in golf in the late 1990s. Craving the action and physicality of the sports I grew up on, I had never really taken to what seemed like a very slow game. Every time I found myself trapped on a golf course, I would cringe at the endless rules. It's hard enough just to hit long and strong without the frustration of adding strokes when your ball's in the water or cruelly lips out after a seemingly perfect putt. So I couldn't figure out the magical spell this exasperating game held over millions. To make matters worse, Andrew kept urging me to play with him. I finally relented and in the spring of 1998 we played nine holes together at Dyker Beach in

Brooklyn, a public golf course. Andrew was so rigid about all the rules that when he asked me how soon we could play eighteen holes, I told him never.

Then a flight cancellation led to an unexpected few hours of downtime during a political trip to New Mexico with my friend and colleague Randy Levine and others. We were thinking about touring Santa Fe. But Randy urged us to play nine holes of golf.

Reluctantly, I agreed. On the very first hole, Randy saw me struggling with my swing, with the golf ball flying all over the place. "Rudy," he said, "this isn't the PGA Tour—we're here to have fun. If you miss-hit your drive, tee up another ball." Suddenly, it became clear to me: golf is supposed to be pleasurable, not a torture. I was hooked (as was the ball). I had caught the strange fever that has driven so many people to spend endless hours knocking a dimpled rubber sphere into a small hole hundreds of yards away.

Soon my weekend games with Andrew became not just an excuse to spend time with my son but a true pleasure, a rare few hours away from the challenges of running the city. Once I realized my interest in golf would last, I did what I always do when I take up something new—I read a dozen of the best books I could find. *Golf for Dummies*, by Gary McCord, was the first I digested. *Dave Pelz's Short Game Bible* taught me to think about golf from the cup out, working on my putt first, then chipping, then pitching, and finally driving. And I read the classic *Ben Hogan's Five Lessons: The Modern Fundamentals of Golf*, which lays out the basics of the swing in clear, encouraging terms. As my game improved, I added videotapes as well. I started to instruct Judith and discovered that I'm a better teacher than player. Now I'm coaching Caroline as well, and am proud to report that she recently smoked the ball over the water at Maidstone in the Hamptons, about 140 yards into the center of the fairway.

I approached other hobbies the same way: when I resumed smoking cigars, I sought to learn as much as I could about the history and manufacture of this exquisite vice. When I was the receiver of the coal company in Kentucky, one of the guys there, Andy Adams, owned horses and would talk about them. This was 1978, the era of Triple Crown winners Seattle Slew and Affirmed, and I got interested. I bought Andrew Beyer's *Picking Winners*, and pored over his tables for converting speed at different length races (i.e., "Six furlongs in 1:13 = seven furlongs in just over 1:26") to deduce which horses might offer better odds than the market reflected. I would go to Saratoga to put my research to the test, as well as get permission to stand right by the track so I could take photographs as the horses galloped around the turn.

When I was a sophomore in high school, my music teacher would discuss the coming Saturday's radio broadcast of the Metropolitan Opera. Like most teenage boys I had no use for opera. But through my love of history, I was intrigued with the comparison between Napoleon's and Hitler's similar miscalculation of invading Russia. Then he played Tchaikovsky's *1812 Overture*, pointing out how the themes combined the *Marseillaise* with Russian folk tunes until the latter finally prevailed in a climax with the cannon. That Saturday, I went to buy the latest rock 'n' roll hit, and noticed a recording of the *1812 Overture* showing a picture of Napoleon fleeing Moscow on horseback. It was on sale for 99 cents, as was Handel's *Julius Caesar*. In school, we were reading the Shakespeare play it's based on, so I bought both. Then, just as I was leaving the shop, I saw a recording of *La Traviata* with Toscanini as conductor, and the singers Licia Albanese, Jan Peerce, and Robert Merrill. The guy at the store told me that I should get that, too, and I had just enough money to cover all three. I went home and soon I was hooked.

To enjoy opera, you have to work at it. As with golf, people can get discouraged by the amount of time that has to be invested. But the rewards are enormous. And like everything I grow interested in, I read about opera. I did the same again to a greater and more serious extent when I was diagnosed with cancer. I learned as much as I could about the disease in general and prostate cancer specifically — so that I could understand what I was being told and could form my own opinions, and see whose advice best reflected my own approach to recovery.

While I was U.S. Attorney, one of my most complicated, adversarial, and high-profile prosecutions involved Michael Milken, whom I investigated for securities fraud, which resulted in his 1989 indictment. Although I had left office by the time Milken finally pleaded guilty, the investigation engendered a great deal of animosity toward my assistants and me. So it was a sad, strange coincidence that it was prostate cancer that reunited us years later.

Michael Milken fought the disease ferociously—in himself and as the founder of CaP CURE, the largest private funder in the U.S. of prostate-cancer research. After I was diagnosed, Milken called me. Having survived prostate cancer, he was emerging as an authority on the disease, as well as an extremely effective advocate. Michael's not a doctor, nor a scientist, but his knowledge of prostate cancer was extensive. When we met, my immediate impression was that he was dealing with his cancer the way he dealt with making billions of dollars for himself and his clients—zealously, and totally focused. For example, he didn't just make a half-hearted effort to "eat right." He hired a chef to prepare vegetarian substitutes for the bacon-and-egg and Reuben sandwiches that had been his mainstays, and he shared his knowledge with others. (Speaking of books, Milken and his chef put out a terrific book of recipes, *The Taste for Living Cookbook: Mike Milken's Favorite Recipes for Fighting Cancer*.) By developing his own independent knowledge, Milken not only faced up to a deadly disease but is doing a great deal to help others do the same.

DON'T LEAVE IT TO THE EXPERTS

Any good leader must develop a substantive base. No matter how talented your advisors and deputies, you have to attack challenges with as much of your own knowledge as possible. That does not mean a mayor must know more about disease than his health commissioner or more about the intricacies of municipal finance than his budget director.

The head of a restaurant company might not be a master chef, and plenty of airline executives are not qualified pilots, let alone mechanics or baggage handlers. But a leader should have independently acquired understanding of the areas he oversees. Anybody who's going to take on a large organization must put time aside for deep study.

At best, the leader of a complicated system has expertise in one or two departments. I had been the third highest official in the Justice Department and the U.S. Attorney in the Southern District of New York, so as mayor I felt confident that I knew at least enough about law enforcement to contribute meaningfully right off the bat. But I wasn't an expert on disease or welfare or tax policy. The reason I recruited experts was to benefit from their knowledge and ideas; but I didn't rely on these people blindly. My job as leader was to make the pieces fit in the way that best served the overall enterprise. Even the best-intentioned expert will not know if his heartfelt recommendation to tackle a problem clashes with or undoes the approach chosen by another manager. So I had ideas and a guiding philosophy as I delved into areas, but beyond that it was my responsibility to develop real working knowledge.

Developing your own expertise is not simply something you ought to do because it's your duty (though it is), or even because it's fun to know how things work (it's that, too). It's also the best way to weed out the biases and pretensions among those who want to influence you. Say somebody—a manager at your company, the press, or an influential investor—is trying to blow something past you, confidently expressing that "everyone knows this is how so-and-so is done." You've got to learn enough about the fundamentals to know whether that's even true. It helps you distinguish between authentic and make-believe experts, the truly competent and the ideological knee-jerkers. Having your own knowledge gives you a frame of reference, helping you decide whether or not to trust the advice someone is giving you. Knowing the fundamentals helps you from being conned.

The truth is, you can't fake expertise. People pick up that kind of pretense right away and will take advantage of your ignorance or dismiss you outright as a dilettante. But when they know you do your homework and expect you to bring your own knowledge to the table, they're less likely to try to mislead you. You'll notice your staff showing up at meetings better prepared, putting more care into their presentations.

Finally, there's a psychological angle that goes back to those history lessons my mother gave me. Although I may not be able to prove it scientifically, I believe that if you read enough about something, you're going to unravel its mystery, and will ultimately understand the fundamentals in a deeper way than simple observation would provide. Then, if you have an inquiring mind, you can apply yourself to that subject and have success in ways not experienced even by those who have spent much more time on it. It doesn't always work that way; but more often than not a bright person who hasn't become shackled by bad habits or a "That's the way it's always done" philosophy can be a catalyst for change.

During the weeks following the World Trade Center disaster, when "free time" did not exist, I carved out hours to learn more about the issues that had been forced upon the city, to seek out sources of both knowledge and inspiration. When I read, I'm a devoted underliner. Shortly after September 11, Judith got me a copy of Yossef Bodansky's *Bin Laden: The Man Who Declared War on America*. Soon it was covered in highlighter and notes. I met with Bodansky to discuss his book and sat down with Henry Kissinger to talk about world terrorism and get his perspective on its history and ramifications.

This approach to mastering a subject was not new for me. By the time I joined the private law practice Patterson Belknap in 1977 I'd already experienced success as a lawyer. But I had never been in private law practice and had been out of law school for nearly eight years. I realized I'd be entering the civil area of the law, which I hadn't been involved in since my days as a clerk. So I went out and bought the relevant texts—on antitrust law, civil procedure, commercial paper, the works—and read them cover to cover.

Judge MacMahon used to observe that the great excitement of being a lawyer, particularly a litigator, is that you become expert in a whole range of subjects. He had textbooks all around his chambers— on chemistry and biology and so on—and would bone up on whatever field was germane to the case before him. Even if you forget it all after you finish the case, it's still fun to learn.

All this reinforced my habit of buying books, to read up on whatever challenge I was facing. Having my own independent knowledge of a subject has helped me run organizations that I didn't understand before. When I was appointed receiver of a bankrupt coal company in Kentucky, for example, I didn't even know what a coal mine looked like, let alone the market dynamics of the energy industry. Not surprisingly, there's a shortage of books on how to run a coal company; but I did find several good volumes on the structure of oil companies and on the energy business in general. By the time we took the company out of bankruptcy a few years later, I knew a good deal about that business.

A good trial lawyer learns about the subjects of his trials in a particularly useful way because he's got to know them well enough to explain them to others. A criminal lawyer walking a jury or a witness through the basics of DNA testing doesn't have to be a great scientist, but he does have to understand the scientific principles well enough to make the testimony come alive for a jury or a judge. That kind of knowledge can't be delegated. Just like employees, investors, customers, coworkers, and competitors, juries can smell a lack of authority. As usual, I turned to a book. *How to Write, Speak and Think More Effectively*, by Rudolf Flesch, came in handy time and again as I sought to master the art of communication.

There's a reason I mention DNA in the context of the importance of developing one's own substantive knowledge base. On August 26, 1999, the body of Vivian Caraballo was found on the roof of an apartment building in Williamsburg. She'd been strangled with a piece of cloth. Less than a month later, Joann Feliciano was found on a different Brooklyn rooftop, strangled with sneaker laces and speaker wire. Within a year, six Brooklyn women were strangled by what was clearly the work of a serial killer.

On August 5, 2000, the NYPD charged a 31-year-old panhandler named Vincent Johnson with four counts of first-degree murder. The hunt for this vicious killer is not only a story about excellent police work. It also shows how a knowledge base can make a critical difference; in this case, life or horrible death for those Brooklyn women.

The Brooklyn North homicide task force had taken a hard look at several suspects over the course of the murders. After one of them, a homeless man, was cleared when his DNA did not match evidence collected at the crime scenes, he struck up a relationship with Steven Feely, one of the detectives on the case. He told Feely about a fellow homeless man, Vincent Johnson, a drug addict who frequently talked about tying women up, raping them, and killing them. Showing impressive initiative, the man even called the detectives after he spotted Johnson walking over the Williamsburg Bridge and followed him until the police arrived to make the arrest.

Johnson incriminated himself in statements to the police but denied the rapes, refused to reiterate his statements on videotape, and eventually clammed up and demanded an attorney. More important, he refused to provide a DNA sample, which the detectives felt sure could link the killer to the crimes. Detective Feely then recalled telling Johnson not to spit inside the precinct house and remembered that the reason he'd warned him was that Johnson had previously spat on the street. Feely ran outside and collected the spit off the ground. It was then tested by the medical examiner. When the DNA in Johnson's saliva matched the DNA found at the crime scenes, the case was over. Johnson is now serving a life sentence without possibility of parole.

The same year that Johnson was taken off the streets, police arrested 25-year-old Arohn Kee in Miami after he had fled there with a teenage girl. The NYPD had detained Kee a month earlier in New York for a misdemeanor theft. Detectives suspected that Kee was responsible for a string of murders and rapes that had occurred in Harlem over the previous seven years. While in custody, Kee refused to give a sample for testing. He declared himself a Jehovah's Witness. Detectives then furtively obtained a sample of DNA from Kee—from saliva he left on the rim of a coffee cup in his cell. Police matched the DNA to samples from the crime scenes, but by then Kee had already left the city. A SWAT team arrested him and freed the teenage girl unharmed.

Kee was eventually convicted of the murders of three young women and the rapes of four others, and was sentenced to 400 years in prison. The prosecutor said that Kee was "the closest thing to pure evil" he had seen in 15 years on the job.

We caught those murderers and many other criminals—and also exonerated some who were falsely accused or suspected—because New York City analyzes more DNA than anywhere else in the country—almost three times as much as the FBI. Police Commissioner Howard Safir was the first to impress upon me the importance of DNA. Deputy Commissioner Maureen Casey was an expert on DNA and made our ability to process and analyze it state of the art. I strongly believed in DNA's potential to revolutionize law enforcement. And the reason I believed that is that I studied it.

When Matt Ridley's *Genome* came out in early 2000, I was already an enthusiastic supporter of DNA's usefulness to law enforcement. I gave the book as a Christmas present to many of my staff because I wanted them to share my enthusiasm. We'd been testing and storing suspects' DNA for about three years, but that book in particular features a clear description of the genome and the science behind DNA. If I can understand it, anybody can. Most important, the Police Department understands it. That's the point of getting this information into your bloodstream. It's one thing to tell a police officer by rote to swab someone's mouth, quite another to establish independent knowledge of what DNA is and how it works. Then, when surprising circumstances emerge—a fortuitous expectorate or a bloodstained bandage—those who work for you can act on their own initiative.

After the attack on the World Trade Center, we would soon become the world's largest user of DNA technology. That may be an unforeseen benefit that emerges from the attacks: because we will have carried out more genetic analysis than anywhere else in history. It will dramatically enhance our ability to use DNA for identification. Even so, I would never have imagined, reading *Genome*, that one day I would be sitting with the NYC Medical Examiner, Dr. Charles Hirsch, hearing him explain that in the immense disaster of September 11, identifying most of the victims would come down to looking for microscopic cellular remains.

At 2:30 in the morning on September 12, 2001, I arrived at my friend Howard Koeppel's apartment, where I was spending most nights. I watched some of the news coverage with Howard and Beau Wagner, one of the detectives on my security detail, and finally headed to bed around three. Next to my bed was a copy of the soon-to-be-published Churchill biography by Roy Jenkins, which I was reading sporadically. All day I had been thinking about London during the blitz and mentioning that as I made my way around the city. I urged New Yorkers to be as brave as the people of Britain.

Although I kept the television on all night, I also read until about 4:30 that morning, particularly the sections about Churchill becoming Prime Minister in 1940, selected mostly out of desperation, with his own party still doubtful about him. That led right into the Battle of Britain and how he kept up the courage and determination of his people as they were attacked day after day, night after night. I took strength from how he handled those dark hours with endless optimism. By the time I finished the biography I wanted to read Churchill in his own words. Joe Lhota gave me his copy of Churchill's *Their Finest Hour*, and for a couple of weeks in early October it seldom left my side.

Political biographies have long been on my reading list. John F. Kennedy's *Profiles in Courage* made a huge impression on me when I read it as a teenager (as an adult, whenever I'd hear a politician say something particularly pandering, I would muse, "Doesn't anyone want a chapter in *Profiles in Courage* anymore?"). I consumed biographies on Lincoln and Washington with the same enthusiasm I had for those on Ruth, Gehrig, and DiMaggio. My interest in Winston Churchill was deeply rooted by the time New York City was attacked. I'd read quite a bit by and about him at different points of my life—in school, of course, but also after I'd lost the mayoral race in 1989. The city was falling apart, begging the mayor to do something about the crime wave, epitomized by the memorable front-page headline in the *New York Post*: "Dave, Do Something." He basically told people nothing could be done. I started thinking about Churchill then.

On May 10, 1940, Hitler's armies blitzed the Netherlands, Belgium, and Luxembourg. On May 12, he invaded France, trapping about 200,000 members of the British Expeditionary Force. On May 26, the British rounded up every vessel imaginable—warships, ferries, fishing boats, pleasure boats—and sailed across the Channel under heavy fire to get them out. The motley fleet landed at Dunkirk's beaches and piers, grabbed as many people as possible, and scuttled back to Dover. On June 3, Hitler bombed Paris. And on June 4, just as the evacuation of Dunkirk was ending, Churchill stood before the House of Commons:

> We shall go on to the end, we shall fight in France, we shall fight on the seas and oceans, we shall fight with growing confidence and growing strength in the air, we shall defend our island, whatever the cost may be, we shall fight on the beaches, we shall fight on the landing grounds, we shall fight in the fields and in the streets, we shall

fight in the hills; we shall never surrender, and even if, which I do not for a moment believe, this island or a large part of it were subjugated and starving, then our Empire beyond the seas, armed and guarded by the British fleet, would carry on the struggle, until, in God's good time, the New World, with all its power and might, steps forth to the rescue and the liberation of the old.

Suppose Churchill had walked out from 10 Downing Street during the Battle of Britain and said, "There's really not much we can do about this." There must have been times when he doubted. Germany had occupied virtually all of Europe. America wasn't responding, at least not in the way he wished, and Roosevelt seemed unable to bring his people around to enter the war. The British were there, alone, bombarded by a Luftwaffe whose capability hadn't even been tested. Suddenly, the impregnable island empire was being invaded from the air—something that had never happened to England. Its cities, its civilian population, were being bombed on a daily basis.

We know now that Winston Churchill was clinically depressed. And yet, despite the times he felt "the black dog," as he called it, he always managed to inspire confidence and hope within his people. He and his cabinet would have their meetings in bunkers and sometimes they'd have to head for deeper, safer quarters right in mid-session. But when the bombings subsided, he'd wander the streets, doing what he could to help, calming people with his presence and courage.

I don't know why Churchill came to mind during the early 1990s when crime, job depletion, and welfare dependency all conspired to make New Yorkers feel victimized and hopeless. But that was when I knew for sure that I would again run for mayor in 1993. I talked about Churchill in a few speeches, and would apologize because it could have sounded grandiose. I wasn't comparing myself to Churchill; but his words were too inspiring to ignore. Above all, it was a way of thinking.

So there was a method to my day on September 11. I couldn't tell people, "Be brave," unless I was willing to walk the streets, or not to panic over anthrax unless I was willing to go to the places where it was suspected. That is what the optimism of leadership is about. Once the leader gives up, then everybody else gives up, and there's no hope. In my case, there were many times, especially in 1994 when I inherited billions in deficits, that I was unsure our plans would succeed. But I wasn't going to announce, "We're trying this cutback and that crime reduction technique and I *think* it might work." I had to believe and have faith.

It's up to a leader to instill confidence, to believe in his judgment and in his people even when they no longer believe in themselves. Sometimes, the optimism of a leader is grounded in something only he knows—the situation isn't as dire as people think for reasons that will eventually become clear. But sometimes the leader has to be optimistic simply because if he isn't nobody else will be. And you've got at least to try to fight back, no matter how daunting the odds.

Luckily, most leaders, from executives to mayors, aren't forced to worry about military action or the wartime safety of their citizens. However, when my hometown was attacked from the air—a few blocks from my office, a few miles from my home—and thousands of New Yorkers were killed, including hundreds who rushed to save others, I felt grateful to have studied the life of such a leader. The inspiration and encouragement I derived from reading about Winston Churchill was there when I needed it.

14

Organize Around a Purpose

Elisa Izquierdo was born on February 11, 1989. She was a beautiful baby, despite the fact that she arrived underweight and addicted to crack cocaine. She had been conceived in Fort Greene, Brooklyn, at a homeless shelter where her mother stayed and her father was a cook. The social workers at the hospital, horrified by her low birth weight, assigned custody to Elisa's father, and did the right thing: they notified the Child Welfare Administration.

Gustavo Izquierdo became a conscientious father, raising Elisa on his own into a delightful, happy girl. He attended parenting classes, braided her hair every day, and made his daughter the focus of his life. A Greek prince, charmed by Elisa, paid for her tuition at Brooklyn Friends School, the local Montessori. Meanwhile, Elisa's mother was struggling with drug problems and an abusive new husband. She petitioned for and was granted unsupervised visits with Elisa, which the little girl soon came to dread. Elisa told her teachers at Montessori that her mother locked her in a closet when she visited.

When Gustavo died of cancer in 1994, his relatives fought for custody of Elisa. However, her mother's lawyer, from the Legal Aid Society, claimed that the society's own caseworkers had visited the family and determined that Elisa would be better off with her mother's family. The Child Welfare Administration also approved the girl's mother, telling the court it had been monitoring the family for a year. The judge agreed, ordering Elisa to the home of her mother and stepfather, even though he was just back home after having served two months for stabbing Elisa's mother seventeen times.

On November 29, 1995, I attended Elisa Izquierdo's funeral. Her pretty dress and the flowers placed around her head in the casket couldn't obscure all thirty of the circular marks left on her body by blows from a hand wearing a ring, and the wounds on her head from being beaten against a concrete wall. Her mother told police that she had forced Elisa to eat her own feces and had mopped the floor with Elisa's head. The police discovered that she had been repeatedly sexually assaulted, and several neighbors said that they had called authorities several times about the family, having seen the children wander around in the middle of the night as the mother sought crack. Elisa had been suddenly removed from her school, without explanation. When she would scream and beg, her mother turned the radio louder.

Elisa would have been 7 in two months. At that time, my daughter, Caroline, was 6. It's inconceivable that someone could do such a thing to a child. I felt responsible for the death of this beautiful girl, but I have had to accept that government cannot substitute for parents. We can't be everywhere, and that's not even the goal. That doesn't mean my heart doesn't hurt to this day for Elisa Izquierdo.

The CWA had at least six encounters with Elisa, beginning with her birth as a crack baby. Nobody at CWA wanted this tragedy to happen; but she was under the care of the CWA, and we didn't do as much as we should have done to take her away from the mother, or check up as much as we should. The system failed.

Whenever I considered an agency, I tried to look at its core purpose and direct every decision based on how well it helped advance that purpose. Looking at the mess at the Child Welfare Administration, I asked myself, What's the mission here? What are the goals? I assigned Howard Wilson, commissioner of the Department of Investigation, to look into what we could do. He and I had been U.S. Attorneys together, and he worked for me when I headed the U.S. Attorney's office in the Southern District of New York. Now, Howard Wilson is relentless. Despite a lively sense of humor, if he detects something amiss, he is ferocious at uncovering it. He'll tell anyone, including the mayor of New York City, the unvarnished truth, regardless of the consequences. I asked him to find a better way to administer services to children in New York. I wanted him quietly to approach experts and those with experience in the field. And I wanted it done right away, before another Elisa Izquierdo needlessly suffered.

The CWA was just one division within the sprawling Human Resources Administration, which also handles welfare, AIDS services, job placement, and a myriad of other functions. New York City did not have a single entity devoted to children's safety. Howard issued a blistering report. He concluded that the city should sever CWA from HRA, making it a freestanding agency with its own budget.

I immediately embraced the idea. It perfectly suited my philosophy of identifying the core purpose of an organization and aligning the resources and focus along with that purpose. I had already suspected that policies for the protection of children were dictated more by expediency and preserving jobs for adults than the best interests of the children. When the subject of abuse first became a national issue, Americans were so horrified that the government began grabbing children from their homes at the first sign of trouble. That tactic tended to wreak further havoc on struggling families. After a predictable backlash, a philosophy focused rigidly on holding families together set in—sometimes putting children in harm's way. I didn't want to pick a particular "style" of handling the issue, but rather to organize an agency that would protect children. In some cases that would mean intervening to separate a child from a dangerous home and in others giving a family the support it needed to stay together.

One of the problems that emerged from Howard's analysis was that money we had earmarked for children had been siphoned off at HRA in a misguided effort to offset cuts we had made to the welfare budget. We needed a separate agency, so I could look at it directly. The founding of the Administration for Children's Services (ACS) was a perfect example of how administrative structure makes a vital difference. The fact that it began life buried within HRA was a big mistake. That we planned to make it independent and give it stature and prestige and have it report directly to the mayor was critical. The point was to create an agency with a single purpose: to protect children at risk. All of the other decisions would flow from that objective and only that objective.

At the end of the day, however, all this would have meant nothing if the wrong leader were in charge. Had we selected someone inadequate, ACS would have a better organizational structure, the value of reporting directly to the mayor, and a handful of good intentions. But with a patronage commissioner, none of those changes would have amounted to anything. We knew that no matter what, we couldn't protect every single child, but by appointing a talented, passionate, and effective manager, we would fulfill our responsibility to do the most that we could to protect children. Leadership is more important than systems or strategies or philosophy. Unless we could identify a gifted manager who was also a true reformer (and a compassionate one at that), the new agency wouldn't succeed. The phrase that kept coming to mind was that we needed a prosecutor with a social work degree. But I couldn't come up with the right choice.

Howard mentioned that our good friend Nick Scoppetta had approached him to say he'd been contemplating a return to city government after years in private practice. Nick had performed with distinction at all levels of government, as a crime-busting federal prosecutor and Knapp Commission investigator, and as deputy mayor to Abe Beame, and had even represented Sydney Biddle Barrows, the "Mayflower Madam," in private practice. He's also been a tireless advocate for the protection of children. When Nick was five, he and his two brothers were placed in New York City's foster care system. While he was taking night classes at Brooklyn Law School, he spent his days investigating abuse and neglect complaints for the Society for the Prevention of Cruelty to Children. Later, he was the president of the Children's Aid Society. In fact, my first visit to City Hall was to watch Nick be sworn in by Mayor John Lindsay, who had appointed him to be the city's Commissioner of Investigation.

I asked Howard to have Nick come in to see me. I didn't tell Howard what I wanted to discuss with Nick—just to make the appointment. I'm sure that they both assumed I was bringing Nick in to talk about a deputy mayor position. Just before Christmas, Nick came in and we talked and talked, reminiscing and discussing other issues in city government. Because of the holidays, things were quiet in City Hall, and I was grateful for the time to sit with an old friend over a cup of coffee.

Finally, I told him, "Nick, I'm going to create a separate agency, exclusively for children. It's going to have a budget of more than 1.7 billion dollars. And I would like you to consider running it. Like the Police Commissioner and the Fire Commissioner, you'd report directly to me. You will be at the morning meeting every day and you'll be able to tell me all the things we need to do to make this agency work." Nick was surprised, even stunned. But just as I had known as soon as Howard said Nick's name that he would be perfect for the job, Nick also knew that it was a challenge he had to accept.

We met a few more times, and from those meetings the structure of the agency emerged. The more I learned about how badly CWA was being run, the more convinced I became that this was a matter of life and death. I didn't want to waste any time.

With its $1.7 billion budget, the new agency would be the city's fifth largest—nearly twice the size of the Fire Department. The City

Council didn't want to do it. And we faced the usual reluctance to change from the HRA bureaucracy. I didn't care; I knew this was the right thing to do. On January 11, 1996, six weeks after Elisa died, I signed an executive order that separated the operations of CWA from HRA, and renamed it the Administration for Children's Services.

After Nick took the reins, we saw exactly how deep the agency's troubles ran. When it was part of Human Resources Administration, one deputy commissioner ran CWA's entire operation. That person was in charge of almost $2 billion but had virtually no authority. The deputy commissioner had to report up through many layers of bureaucracy before anything hit some other deputy commissioner's desk, after which it might make it to the commissioner's desk. The CWA deputy commissioner couldn't develop better training programs—or even get the desks and computers the office desperately needed.

To hire somebody, you went through several layers within HRA, went over to the Office of Management and Budget, then took the request over to City Hall. The person in charge of CWA had no control over that process, nor any way to make it happen quickly. When Nick took over, he discovered hundreds of fully funded positions for caseworkers that hadn't been filled. An unfilled caseworker position isn't just some number on a chart. It's a visit to a troubled home that never gets made, a child screaming for help who's never heard. It was demoralizing for caseworkers, and the burnout rate at CWA had been ruinous.

I decided before I even asked Nick to take the job that the new commissioner would report directly to me. Most agencies in city government report to one of the four deputy mayors. In creating ACS, I wanted to put children at risk on the same level as the Police and Fire Departments, so that I would hear about their problems daily—at the morning meeting.

Nick set about shaping the new agency, creating commissioner posts for foster care and preventive services, for management and planning, for child care/Head Start (which includes Child Care and

Head Start, Day Care and Head Start), and for legal service, among others. There had never been lines of demarcation like that. The department has 300 lawyers who go to court on behalf of abused children and other legal matters, and they had never had anyone in charge. There was not even a budget department. Seven thousand employees, but no personnel department.

Not surprisingly, this was not the first initiative to bring about changes in the way New York protects its children. Every time there was a highly publicized child fatality, there'd be public outcry about reform. Whoever was mayor would respond by changing the name of the agency—so Special Services for Children had become the Bureau of Child Welfare, which in turn became the Child Welfare Administration. This time, it was a whole new organization, not just a name change. It quickly became apparent we'd created an entirely separate, independent agency with its own management structure.

The results speak for themselves.

Our efforts to find permanent homes for New York children resulted in 21,000 adoptions from 1996 to 2001—a 66 percent increase over the previous six years. The amount of child support collected from deadbeat parents more than doubled during my tenure, the number of children in foster care fell about 40 percent, and for the first time ever the city provided more children with at-home preventive services than with foster care. ACS hired 1,700 new caseworkers, with raised eligibility standards and salaries, and from 1992 to 2000 the average caseload for these workers fell 41 percent—more than ten kids each. We also built a new $67 million ACS Center on the old Bellevue Hospital campus on the East River. And in 2001 the voters overwhelmingly approved my charter commission's proposal to make ACS a permanent stand-alone agency.

My interest in avoiding the pitfalls of organizational confusion began years ago, when I was the U.S. Attorney for the Southern District of New York. That's when I began to develop an approach to managing based on organizational structure.

The first question is always, "What's the mission?" Ask yourself what you'd like to achieve—not day-to-day, but your overarching goal. Then assess and analyze your resources. At my U.S. Attorney's office, the goal wasn't a certain number of arrests or a specific number of high-profile cases. It was to reduce crime by prosecuting criminals over whom the federal government had jurisdiction. That inspired me to think about the job thematically. Instead of going after particular criminals in random fields, I wanted to show that entire criminal pursuits could be attacked—organized crime, municipal crime, drug dealing, white-collar crime. It also meant not just making use of my own resources, but thinking about how best to integrate them with outside resources.

Consider organized crime. Checking it against our mission statement reveals that prosecuting its leaders was obviously worthwhile. The goal was not just to tot up a number of arrests and score convictions, but to eliminate some of the organizations—a far broader purpose. So first we looked at the resources available to us.

We had meetings to discuss all available laws; we contacted the FBI to see what they knew and reached out to the NYPD to ask how they were approaching the problem. As we spoke to different law enforcement agencies, I thought about the scope of the mob's businesses. It occurred to me that instead of knocking out convictions one by one, using crimes that had been discovered either by my office or the FBI or the NYPD, we could do more damage to the crime organizations by consolidating the accusations. Until then, cases like that—known as "RICO cases" to all fans of *The Sopranos* (I'm proud to say Tony Soprano singled me out as the person he'd least like to see cloned!)—hadn't been used to dismantle entire crime operations. Although it had been around since 1970, the RICO statute was rarely used and, even when it was, prosecutors based their cases on convicting individuals who acted as part of a particular racketeering operation, rather than for belonging to an organization whose central purpose was racketeering.

No one thought it could work. First, we spent years gathering evidence, subpoenas, wiretap orders, witnesses, and informants—and listened to so many hours of wiseguys on tape that I compulsively begin my speeches imitating them. All the while, I maintained my belief that we could strike at the heart of organized crime by analyzing it as a system instead as a collection of individuals. Finally, it all came together. In the span of a less than a year, we won major convictions, all under RICO:

- The Colombo case, which convicted nine members of a major Mafia family.
- The "Pizza Connection" case, in which a year-and-a-half trial resulted in the convictions of almost thirty men, including a head of the Sicilian mafia and many other mafiosi, who used a network of pizza parlors to distribute tons of heroin.
- Our crowning achievement, the Commission case, in which we convicted eight leaders from four of New York's organized crime families; each was sentenced to 100 years. (One of those convicted in this case, Tony Salerno, was the funniest mob figure I ever prosecuted. In fact, I almost regretted having to put him away, especially after I subsequently prosecuted him for crimes that added thirty years to his sentence, which he found quite redundant. For example, on being told that my assistant was prospering in the wake of the Commission prosecution, he replied: "Well, you give him a little message from Fat Tony. You tell that son of a bitch he owes me a thank-you note.")

Even more innovative than the use of RICO was that of RICO's civil component. I put together a group with the sole purpose of depriving the organized-crime enterprise of its financial means. The idea was similar to the Justice Department's current pursuit of the financial assets and systems of terrorist networks. It became clear that no matter how many mobsters we locked up, so long as the institutions that generated their profits were allowed to stand, new crooks would emerge to replace those we put away. So we used the civil provisions of the RICO statute to seize control of various carting companies, the Fulton Fish Market, and Umberto's Clam House, which had come to prominence days after it opened as the scene of Crazy Joe Gallo's assassination. (After we seized Umberto's, the legendary Murray Kempton wrote that the integrity of the restaurant's finances might have improved, but the food was awful under the federal monitor. Yet another indication of the value of privatization.)

Thus, finding the right organizational structure starts with a mission. Then you have to identify your aims, and what you should do to achieve them; find the right people for the job; and constantly follow up to make sure everyone is sticking to the original purpose, that no one's taken over your team and sidetracked them.

In some cases, the idea of aligning the organization with its purpose carried directly over from the U.S. Attorney's office to City Hall. One of the most important cases I prosecuted involved municipal corruption at the New York City Parking Violations Bureau. People sometimes dismiss corruption as inevitable, but their cynicism is frequently a response to the weakness among leaders to challenge corruption. I came away from that case convinced that part of what allows municipal corruption is the very structure of government. Many agencies that are not run by numbers and finance people still manage vast sums of money. This can be an invitation to mismanagement. In addition to the Parking Violations Bureau, there had been scandals under previous administrations within the Department of Transportation. To my mind, the agency in charge of collecting taxes should also be in charge of collecting as many fees as possible. Thus I reorganized all the PVB's fee-collecting under the Department of Finance, which had the experience, financial acumen, and integrity monitoring suited to money collection. Purpose and system became one.

There's a reason I picked the story of ACS to illustrate how strongly I believe in the importance of establishing an organizational structure.

It demonstrates the importance of aligning system with purpose. Two other management ideas are also at work here.

One comes from the importance of a "seat at the table." The fact that Nick Scoppetta reported directly to me meant that he could cut through red tape and take his agency's concerns directly to the mayor. It also demonstrated to others at the morning meeting how strongly I felt about this issue.

I took the same approach to reflect the significance of the Budget Director. In any large organization, the person looking after the budget is vital. Nothing that government, a corporation, or any other institution does can be accomplished without touching the budget in some way. It's a difficult job, mainly comprised of saying "no" to everyone, and it takes someone with toughness and tact. Yet under previous administrations, the director of New York City's $40 billion budget had been relegated to a lesser status. He reported to a deputy mayor, with a string of intermediaries between his office and his boss's.

Even before I became mayor, I made a point of studying the city's budget line by line. I believed that no one could truly understand the city without deep knowledge of how it spent money. When I took office, I was surprised that the Budget Director was buried on the organizational chart and remedied that, elevating him to report directly to me. That accomplished two goals. First, I could stay on top of everything that concerned how the city spent its money. Second, everyone else at the morning meeting got the message—when they saw the Budget Director there, they knew I was taking a hard look at expenditures.

I employed the same rationale in making my Commissioner of the Department of Investigation part of the morning meeting. I was criticized for that. Some felt that seeing the heads of the agencies he was supposed to investigate would compromise his independence, or that having him there might put a chill on people's willingness to speak freely. But I did it on purpose, for much the same reason that I had Nick Scoppetta there: to elevate the importance of the position and to send a message to everyone else that I recognized that importance.

Under Howard Wilson, and later Ed Kuriansky—both of whom served with me in the U.S. Attorney's office—DOI didn't simply respond to allegations, as it had in the past. Instead, the agency ran an aggressive internal anti-corruption operation, conducting stings and integrity tests. The message came through loud and clear: a city employee who took a bribe, rigged bids, arranged a sweetheart deal, or solicited kickbacks went straight to jail.

I asked Howard Wilson to probe the way the Child Welfare Administration was functioning. The Department of Investigation had traditionally been used to root out internal corruption—sniffing out bribes and tax problems among those who worked for the city. In the past, DOI had not been deployed to conduct management reviews for efficiency, effectiveness, and competence.

CHART IT, UNDERSTAND IT

I love to visualize charts, so much so that my staff would jokingly call me "Chart Boy" when they thought I wasn't listening. (Note: I'm always listening.) Whenever I considered a problem, I envisioned a chart that represented how we'd attack it—who would play what role and how the solution would flow. In a system as complex as New York City, it was clear there would be chaos if we didn't rely on sophisticated organizational charts, with all those wonderful lines showing who reported to whom. Charts also allow for accountability. If there's a problem in an agency, everyone can see exactly who oversees that agency, and who oversees that person as well—there's no way to duck the problem, no matter how high above it someone sits on the chart. Organizational charts are not simply maps of how things work. When used correctly, they're creative problem-solvers.

As fond as I was of these charts, I encouraged my staff to think outside those lines as often as possible. When I asked Howard to analyze the CWA, I wasn't worried about his title or the official mission statement for his department. All that mattered was getting the sharpest person available to turn a critical eye on a pressing problem. I frequently asked people on my staff to handle things beyond the parameters of their job description. To be sure, some employees are unnerved by the prospect of challenges in unfamiliar areas, but because people who worked for me knew that "it's not my job" was never the right answer, a surprising number of these experiments yielded unconventional solutions invisible to staff much more familiar with the terrain.

I certainly relied on the hierarchy in which the deputy commissioner answered to the commissioner who answered to the deputy mayor who answered to the mayor. You've got to impose a structure to bring order to what could easily become chaos. But I also insisted that those who worked for me feel free to come directly to me. I believed both in having a highly organized system and in subverting it whenever the right idea or situation presents itself.

Occasionally, one of my deputy mayors would get annoyed if someone in an agency that reported to them came directly to me. I'd always tell them that anyone, especially someone at the commissioner or deputy commissioner level, should be able to tell me what they're thinking.

Asking Howard Wilson to analyze the children's services is an example of what business schools call "highest and best use" of employee time. Some leaders are reluctant to break free of the "org chart," because managers can be counted on to fight over reallocation of "their" employees or other resources. One of the best ways to counter this is by underlining the supremacy of doing what's best for the company, and not just saying it but meaning it. Showing a manager that you appreciate his finding a way to get by without a valued member of his group goes a long way.

Another way I broke through bureaucratic gridlock was by assigning someone on my top staff no specific portfolio. As soon as I became mayor, I sensed how easy it would be to get mired in the "crisis of the day," as is so typical of any bureaucracy. "Oh my God, the press is calling, what are we going to do?" "The computers are all down—what now?" There was always some catastrophe—a building collapse, a major accident, a big fire. These had to be dealt with, but focusing on the disaster of the moment could have jeopardized long-term initiatives.

To address this, I created a new position called "Senior Advisor to the Mayor," a role that's been retained by the new administration. The job of the Senior Advisor was to keep initiatives moving. Richard Schwartz was the first to hold the post, followed by Tony Coles and then Geoff Hess. All three excelled at seeing the big picture—and because they weren't in charge of any specific department, they could coordinate action across several agencies without the usual fears of encroachment.

Another person who understood intuitively my organizational philosophy was Joe Lhota, who joined my administration in April 1994 as chief of staff to John Dyson, my Deputy Mayor for Economic Development. Joe was a rarity in New York City—an ideological Republican. He was also something of a rarity in my administration, in that he was an M.B.A. with a background on Wall Street, so he stood out among all the lawyers. He immediately showed leadership skills. By December, I asked him to become Finance Commissioner, who as the chief revenue officer for the city of New York enforced all the city's tax rules and regulations. A year on, he became Budget Director, then in 1998 was promoted to the second most powerful position after the mayor—Deputy Mayor for Operations.

When Joe was at the Harvard Business School, he designed an organizational chart of *The Godfather*. This was years before I knew him, but it turned out to be a prescient exercise—the *Godfather* movies provided reference points for jokes and wisdom throughout my administration. Breaking down the three films, there was the Godfather as chief executive officer, with two operating divisions run by Tessio and Clemenza. There was Tom Hagen, his *consigliere*, who was roughly equivalent to the mayor's counsel. Then there was Luca Brasi, who's much more of a force in the book than the movie. Brasi's value was that when he spoke to someone, it was understood that whatever he said came straight from the Godfather.

That's similar to how the mayor's senior advisor functions. It's an interesting role, because it cuts through what otherwise might be resistance to "interference" from someone outside the agency.

WHEN I DELEGATE, I DELEGATE

My organizational style was to be on top of as much as possible. While I expected my commissioners to run their agencies and take responsibility for their performance, I also insisted on being kept abreast of results and initiatives.

As a candidate, I learned I didn't have that luxury. There simply wasn't time.

In 1989, former New York State Attorney General Louis J. Lefkowitz, who was then in his 80s, came out to campaign with me one day. Louis Lefkowitz had run unsuccessfully as a Republican for mayor of New York City back in 1961, so he knew the uphill battle I'd face. I was sitting in campaign headquarters going over a position paper when suddenly he grabbed me by the arm and said, "Look, son, every minute you spend here you're not getting any votes. The people here are already going to vote for you, and if they don't they're crazy to be here. So get out and into the streets. Those are the people who we have to convince." That's when I realized I had to create an organizational structure different from the one I used as U.S. Attorney.

Back then, and later as mayor, I was the CEO. As a candidate, I was the front guy, the product. The campaign manager was the CEO. By 1993, I had taken that lesson to heart. Those who wanted to step forward with ideas for the campaign came to Peter Powers, not to me. Peter would talk to everyone, get their ideas, and weigh them. He and campaign consultant David Garth would fight it out and make the decisions. Occasionally, I'd veto a commercial or pick one event to attend over another, but mostly I let them do their jobs. Often, I wouldn't even come in to the campaign headquarters.

At the end of the night, if I had any energy left, I would often show up at David Garth's office on Park Avenue at eleven o'clock or so. We'd spend the next two hours going over position papers, strategy, and commercials. So I wasn't able to abandon control completely, but there were plenty of nights I was so wasted, I'd say, "I hired good people to do good work—I'm going to sleep."

Four years on, when I ran for reelection, I took a more aggressive role in running the campaign. But I had the luxury to do that, since I was more refining my positions as a candidate than running as a newcomer. And even then campaign manager Fran Reiter really ran it.

In fact, that's one of the reasons I hired good people instead of yesmen. A leader wants someone who doesn't just kowtow but can step up to the plate. Throughout my administration, I made a point of giving press conferences with the appropriate agency's commissioner at hand. By the end of my time as mayor, people like Police Commissioner Bernie Kerik, Fire Commissioner Tom Von Essen, OEM Director Richie Sheirer, Deputy Mayors Joe Lhota and Tony Coles and Budget Director Adam Barsky were familiar faces to governmentwatchers. I employed the same strategy as U.S. Attorney. When I tried a complicated and lengthy corruption case in New Haven, for example, Denny Young ran the U.S. Attorney's office. I knew the place was safe in his hands.

SOMETIMES ADD, SOMETIMES SUBTRACT

There is no general rule about the size of a well-run agency. Sometimes it makes sense to combine sprawling departments, as we did when the Transit Police and Housing Police came under the umbrella of the NYPD. In that case, we had a strong agency that was functioning well and so had more deployment flexibility and could take advantage of the scale gained by the merger. When the merger proved successful, we later added school safety to the NYPD's purview.

Other times, the more sensible approach was to cleave an operation from an agency where it was languishing. By giving ACS a "seat at the table," with its own budget and commissioner, I gave it the power—and responsibility—to fix its own problems.

Any complex system will inevitably evolve in ways that no longer make sense when circumstances change. In a corporation, for example, the person in charge of manufacturing might, say, be promoted to a vice presidency for product design. Because of his expertise in making what the company makes, he brings the manufacturing department under his control. He moves on, leaving a department that produced excellent products but was invariably over budget. So he was replaced by someone whose expertise was in fiscal discipline. That person cleans up the budget and negotiates much more favorable contracts with vendors, but has no idea how to handle the day-to-day challenges of the manufacturing department. A leader has to be aware of mismatches like this.

The organization of systems was a top priority for me. One of the most important decisions I made was to organize an Office of Emergency Management for New York City. Even before I was mayor, I was convinced that the city had to reorganize its response to emergencies. New threats such as biological and chemical attacks and terrorist bombings made it clear that we could no longer have agencies individually respond to emergencies. The new "hybrid emergencies" required an overarching organizational structure that was equipped to coordinate many different departments.

A bombing, for example, might result in an awful fire, but it's also a criminal act and may additionally require a response from other agencies, such as Transportation, Buildings and Health. An attack of sarin gas would require intense coordination of the Health Department and the Police and Fire Departments. I decided there should be an overarching agency—an Office of Emergency Management, to coordinate and to plan emergency response. When I was elected, I began to formulate a plan for such an agency. With the assistance of the Police Commissioner and Fire Commissioner, we conducted a nationwide search for a Director, which is how we found Jerry Hauer, who was later succeeded by Richard Sheirer.

As much as having an overarching agency, the point was to establish a group whose sole function was to plan and coordinate for large-scale disasters. They would know in advance what agency would take the lead in the event of a hostage taking or botulism outbreak, which saves precious time should that crisis—or a similar crisis—occur.

For all emergencies, there was a designated incident commander, provided for in a document that had been circulated and approved by all relevant agencies and finally by me.

This enabled us to more fully utilize all the component agencies as well. With West Nile virus, for example, the Health Department was brought up to speed on crisis management, rather than limiting their operations to the usual issues that were already under their control. Bringing in other agencies also changed the focus from a strict law enforcement emphasis. Earlier, any and all emergencies were handled from the "war room" in One Police Plaza. Non-police emergencies, such as hurricanes and snowstorms, inevitably felt as though they were being handled by the police, in consultation with the relevant agencies. Having one command center—at 7 World Trade Center—allowed all the component agencies to work in tandem and allowed the agency with the most expertise to become incident commander. Despite the many successes the new department had—with the West Nile virus, the Y2K problem, and the Millennium Celebration—the City Council resisted making OEM a permanent agency. Finally, in 2001, we got on the ballot a referendum to make it a permanent agency and it was overwhelmingly approved by the voters.

Human nature being what it is, crisis brought out the occasional humorous moment. One day, during the heat wave of Summer 1999, which resulted in a blackout in the Washington Heights neighborhood, I had Sunny get Jerry Hauer on the phone. In my most officious mayoral voice, I told him I expected him to come up with a plan to air-condition the entire city.

"Um . . ." Jerry began. "Normally, we don't bring air-conditioning to the people, we bring people to air-conditioning."

"Jerry," I replied, "you've got to think outside the box. Haven't you heard about those geodesic domes? Put large ones over big portions of the city. Jerry, I want you to work on this, there's not much time."

"Okay Boss, I'll see what I can do." Later on, we kidded about this, but for a while there, he was pretty concerned about whether I was serious.

I was always reevaluating to ensure that departments hadn't evolved out of efficient or effective alignment. For example, many of the city's agencies used to have their own construction divisions. Say the Parks Department, the Police Department, and the Department of Transportation each needed a thousand benches. Three different departments would design benches, three different procuring departments would buy them, and three different departments would install them. Not only did the city have three times the people it needed, we also lost the bargaining leverage and operating efficiency that came from designing, ordering, and installing three thousand benches. I merged all the construction divisions of the various agencies into a single Department of Design and Construction. Not only did we save money, we operated more efficiently. An agency that's already handled requests for benches from two departments can be expected to take care of the third more smoothly than a division that's never dealt with them before.

Anyone leading a large organization risks losing a feel for the forest while managing the trees. I deliberated on the purpose not only of individual agencies, but of government itself. I'd go through the questions: What are we here for? What are the available resources? I believe that a city government's primary mission is to protect its citizens and provide an unfettered opportunity to excel. Thus I made public safety, child protection, health, and education one pillar of my administration, with job creation, lower taxes, and efficient, navigable systems the other.

The reality is that there's only so much a city government can do—or should do. A dollar spent on a benevolent-sounding program is a dollar not spent somewhere else. A good leader establishes priorities and sticks to them, backing them with resources to carry them out. Sometimes the best way to fulfill those priorities is to remove the distractions—and expenses—that keep them from being fulfilled. When I became mayor, I inherited a government that had developed a worldwide reputation for inefficiency and unresponsiveness. Several books had been written about New York having become the "ungovernable city." One of my immediate goals was to streamline the government to allow us to focus on our major priorities.

For example, I didn't believe that the city belonged in the broadcasting business. In 1995, we sold WNYC radio for $20 million and WNYC-TV for $207 million—not only did that put $227 million into the city's coffers, it also meant that taxpayers were no longer forced to subsidize stations they may or may not have enjoyed. The same reasoning was behind my decision to divest the city of its interest in the United Nations Plaza Hotel, which brought in $85 million plus annual property taxes.

On the other hand, I rejected the first offer the city and the Metropolitan Transit Authority got for the jointly owned New York Coliseum site. I certainly wasn't accustomed to saying no to $200 million, especially for an area (West 59th Street) that had long been neglected. However, I insisted on a plan that enhanced the beauty of the area and contributed to what I saw as its mission—a performing arts nexus, anchored by Lincoln Center. By insisting on organizing around that purpose, we eventually got: a) the gorgeous building we wanted (the AOL Time Warner headquarters), b) a new home for Jazz at Lincoln Center, and c) $345 million.

The organizational impulse was reflected in the way I used my most public policy-setting speech, the yearly State of the City in January. No area of leadership should escape constant reexamination to make sure it is aligned with the purpose. That includes speeches. Considering the State of the City speech each year, I believed the purpose wasn't simply to report whether the city was in good or bad shape. I wanted to produce a blueprint for what I hoped to achieve. I accomplished many of the goals I announced, but there were plenty of aims I was unable to get done, such as abolishing the Board of Education, which I called for every year. Successful or not, the idea behind the speeches was to set a direction for the city. I wanted to challenge my administration, the City Council, myself, and the voters and citizens.

I believed so strongly in organizing around a purpose, in the link between structure and action, that I considered plans to change the structure of the mayor's office an actual change of policy. I discussed the merger of the three police departments at my State of the City in 1995, just as I announced the formation of ACS at the State of the City in 1996. In the 1998 address, I brought the Department of Mental Health, Mental Retardation, and Alcoholism Services (DMH) into the Department of Health (DOH). Even in my final State of the City address, in 2001, I was in full organization mode. I explained how I planned to make both the Office of Emergency Management and the Administration for Children's Services permanent freestanding agencies. I said that we should merge the Human Resources Administration and the Department of Employment, to further the goal of turning HRA into an employment agency.

The organization chart is not simply a cold management contrivance. It's a living, evolving tool a leader uses to send a message—to those who work for him, and even to remind himself—regarding the organization's goals and priorities. It was a lesson I learned early in my career.

When Vice President Cheney was Chief of Staff to President Ford, he held seminars for all his counterparts in cabinet- and sub-cabinet-level positions. I was the Associate Deputy Attorney General to the Deputy Attorney General, Harold Tyler, and my senior colleague Togo West had left and not yet been replaced, so I was Tyler's de facto chief of staff. Dick Cheney invited about twenty of us into the East Wing of the White House and sat us down in a big sun-filled room. He gave us a two-hour lecture on how to be of most service to our principal. He had prepared all these mimeographed handouts on how to organize our principal's day and allow him the most time to make decisions. The two major lessons he imparted have served me well to this day.

The first lesson was the importance of protocol and the psychology of dealing with other offices. Dick told us, "The Secretary of State or the Secretary of Defense does not want to hear from me, Dick Cheney, 'You can't do this or that.' They work for the President of the United States, they don't work for me. But sometimes the President doesn't have the opportunity to tell them. So you have to work hard at establishing relationships with your counterparts in their offices. If the President has to say no to the Secretary of the Treasury and needs me to convey the message, I am better off delivering that message to the Treasury Secretary's Chief of Staff." That helped me in my job. When I needed to communicate with Dick Thornburgh, who was then the Assistant Attorney General, I realized that he worked for Ed Levy and Harold Tyler, not for me. I tried to communicate through Jay Waldman, Thornburgh's Chief of Staff. It made it much easier for me to understand how to convey whatever Harold Tyler needed to communicate without coming across as presumptuous.

The other important lesson I retained showed what a good thinker Dick Cheney is. A chief of staff has considerable influence over his principal's schedule and time. Cheney told us to make sure that everyone always felt they had access to the boss—and to be doubly sure that was the case when we disagreed with the position of the person needing access. "You're going to have a lot of times in which your principal has to make a decision, and there are three people on one side and three on the other. Go out of your way to make sure the side you don't favor gets a fair hearing. Otherwise, you create the impression in the organization that you steer decisions in the direction that you like, to suit your ideology and prejudices, not those of your boss. If instead you take pains to allow the other side to have their say, no one will accuse you of being unfair when it does come out the way you hoped."

Those lessons stuck with me. Both as U.S. Attorney and mayor, I never allowed my Chiefs of Staff to bottle up commissioners and not let them see me. And I reminded them that the head of an organized crime task force or Police Commissioner didn't want to be told no by the Chief of Staff.

I always strive to determine the purpose of an organization, then to set it up so that everything else flows from there. In struggling with the proposals regarding the future development and use of Ground Zero, I tried to analyze it from the point of view of purpose—what should the purpose of this site be for the future. Some wanted towers to replace those that were destroyed, others wanted the space devoted to a monument, and there were any number of ideas in between. After considering what would be the lasting legacy of the horrible event, I came to the belief that no matter what went up, form had to follow function.

In other words, Ground Zero had to be a magnificent monument, and that goal had to dominate the plan. Our approach to the site had to come from the heart, and that meant two objectives had to be honored. First, the pain of the victims' families had to be respected. They had to know that their feelings and wishes were being considered over what was in effect the final resting place for their loved one. Second, we had to have an appropriate sense of history. This was hallowed ground, on a par with any other American battlefield site—Bunker Hill, Gettysburg, Appomattox. It deserved the gravity of any monument, rather than a plaque next to a quickly reconstructed version of what it was before September 11. We had to put the purpose of the site first and let the rest flow from there. In other words, we had to act like leaders. As the decisions are being made about how to rebuild Ground Zero, it is very important that the city reserve maximum space for a memorial. The expansiveness of the space must dramatize the reality of the attack. Furthermore, it would be unthinkable to cover over the burial ground of so many. Ultimately, the way I come to this view is by trying to think about how others will view us a hundred years from now. How we handle this site is important to our future, and it needs respect, dignity, and understanding.

The advantage of doing it the right way instead of the expedient way also happens to be the only way to get the desired results. Playing out alternative scenarios—an approach from my days as a trial lawyer—here's how I reasoned it.

Suppose the city addressed the future of Ground Zero from the perspective of rebuilding its tax base and restoring the lost 25 million square feet of office space. There would be more than 3,000 devastated families upset by that decision. Then suppose you went and rebuilt the towers, which was the politically popular option. It was one thing to tell a pollster, "Put the towers back up, screw the terrorists," another to lease space and ask employees to work there. You could easily end up with a white elephant, with no one willing to work above the third floor.

There was a better way. Say to the families, "Your interests come first. You are our No. 1 priority." Then spend most of your effort deciding how to raise the most beautiful, soaring monument ever. Create something up to the standards of the world's great museums and memorials, such as the Normandy beaches or the Holocaust Museum in Washington. Imagine how compelling it could be. There would be videotapes, interactive exhibits, a place to recall the lives of the victims, exhibits about what terrorism was in 2001, how the country had largely ignored it, just as the world ignored Nazism. Judging from the number of people who visited Ground Zero every day for months after the attack, just to glimpse the sliver of the site visible from the perimeter, a memorial done the right way would resonate deeply. Three months after the disaster, we put up a viewing platform and people from all over the world stood in line for hours waiting to look at the site, before there was any memorial.

You would have achieved your economic development, restored your tax base, and done it in a way that would lend dignity and purpose to this place of attack and destruction. You can erect offices anywhere—they don't have to be where they were. By focusing on the purpose of the site—to memorialize the attack and its aftermath for eternity—you would not only have done the right thing, you would also have managed to address the economic hit, and without hurting anyone already suffering an unbearable loss.

15

Bribe Only Those Who Will Stay Bribed

The prosecutor in me needs to make clear that when I say "bribe only those who will stay bribed," I don't literally mean bribe. In any leadership role, one must deal with all types of people. Obviously, as often as possible, one should confine dealings to people one trusts completely. There are plenty of times when a leader is forced to deal with those he is not sure about, or perhaps whose company he doesn't even enjoy. You owe it to those who rely on you to deal with whoever is best able to serve their interests, but you have to set at least minimum standards. As Ronald Reagan put it, trust but verify.

There used to be a rule in politics, which I'm not sure exists anymore, and it's a shame that it doesn't: to rise in politics, you have to be a man of your word. You can be a liberal, a conservative, a radical, or a reactionary. You can even be a crook, but when you make a deal you keep it.

As a Republican mayor in a city with five times more registered Democrats, I dealt with people of a wide range of political persuasions. I hired many Democrats in my administration and worked well with New York City Democratic leaders such as former City Council Speaker Peter Vallone. We had major disagreements of a substantive nature. We even went to court and sued each other. But we became and remained good friends because I knew I could trust him to tell me the truth. That did not mean that he was always going to agree with me, but it did mean that he would be straight with me. If we made a deal, he held up his end of the bargain. I had a similar relationship with Queens Borough President Claire Shulman. Despite differences in ideology, we had much in common, and because she is honest and straight, we always worked together effectively.

Our collaboration on the issue of power generation for the city illustrates the point. The strain on New York City's electrical system every summer had us concerned, especially after a 1999 blackout left about 300,000 people in Washington Heights and Inwood without power for up to thirty hours. The infrastructure was old, and Con Edison had not made the investment that it should have. To force the issue, we threatened to sue the company, but I knew we didn't have much of a case and would lose, just as the city had lost before against the utility. Con Ed knew that, too, but because they didn't want to fight it out in court they agreed to commit over $400 million to improvements.

Even then, the city didn't have enough generating power and was forced to buy the difference on the open market. Just when you need power most, the market becomes the most competitive—if it's hot in New York it's going to be hot in New Jersey and Philadelphia and Boston. The New York Power Authority agreed to put in ten generators small enough not to require environmental review, selecting strategic spots in the city to do it. As ever, the locations were controversial, especially the one in Queens on the East River. We searched for an alternative. I met with the Power Authority, and my people from the Department of Environmental Protection met with their engineers, who explained that power plants were difficult to place.

They needed connection to the grid, connection to the water, available land, and so on. I didn't think they were blowing smoke and I could see the financial leverage that was going to be used against communities without enough power.

Well, Claire Shulman was one of those opposed to the East River plant. She pointed out that Queens seemed to bear more than its share of such facilities, and when we made it clear that we would not change our decision she and a local community group took the Power Authority to court.

I told her that I, too, would have preferred a public park or beautiful housing to a generator on the East River, but I also had to think about the 12,000 megawatts New Yorkers could consume in an hour on a hot day. With the additional generation, we'd be able to produce about 80 percent of that inside the city. We'd have first call on that power, and there would be far less chance of delivery breakdowns when we were that close to the source.

So we disagreed. I told Claire that I would have to file a brief siding with the Power Authority. She had strong feelings the other way, believing that the New York Power Authority was misleading the city. Before I announced my support for the generator, we met and I explained that I wasn't making this decision just to give her a hard time. At last she said, "Okay, you do what you have to do, you're the mayor of the whole city, but I'm borough president, and I have to fight for my constituents." Eventually the court permitted the plant to be built.

Then there were others, people I shared little in common with and whose politics were very different from my own. So long as they could keep their word, I could work with them and develop a mutual respect.

Bill Thompson was the head of the Board of Education during much of my administration and was elected comptroller after that. I did not agree with many of the things he did as president of the board. He opposed the reforms I wanted and was content to adopt the agenda of the United Federation of Teachers. But despite our disagreements Bill Thompson was a man of his word, and if he made a deal he kept it. There were several times when he agreed to vote with our side, and he would always stick to it, even after pressure was brought to bear. Other times, when he'd decided to vote against us, he would explain his reasons forthrightly. I often thought his reasons were wrong, but to his credit he didn't try to finesse us; that's why I always asked my two appointees to the board to support Bill for board president.

One of the best illustrations of this principle came not from New York or Washington but from the rolling bluegrass of Hazard, Kentucky. Despite the culture shock I experienced as a born-and-bred New Yorker, the months I spent in Kentucky provided some of the most valuable leadership lessons I ever learned.

A coal company called Aminex Resources Corporation had fallen into receivership after those who had recently acquired the company had essentially looted its assets. The bankruptcy case came before Judge MacMahon and he called me on Good Friday 1978. He needed someone to take over the running of the company and restore fiscal health. He knew that I had absolutely no knowledge of the coal business, but even more than an industry expert, he wanted someone who could sue to recover what had been stolen. Additionally, there was so much distrust and bitterness among those who remained at the company that Judge MacMahon decided the business needed an outsider whom he knew could be trusted.

At that time I had been at the firm of Paterson Belknap for about a year. I consulted the senior partners at the firm, such as Harold Tyler, Bob Patterson, and Bob Potter, and explained to them the opportunity. Judge MacMahon told me that if we accepted the assignment we would not earn our firm's full rate, but that if we managed to bring the company out of bankruptcy and make the investors whole, the bankruptcy court might award us a bonus. Some of the partners liked the idea and some did not, but they all agreed that since the judge thought I should do it, I should accept the receivership. I called

Judge MacMahon, and just like that, found myself in a very unexpected place: in charge of a coal company in the hills of Kentucky.

I decided right away to ask my partner, Joel Carr, to work with me because he had experience with many businesses and clients from oil companies. Then I set about learning everything I could about the business. The bituminous value of coal determines its energy potential—a higher value is longer-burning. The veins Aminex controlled were filled with relatively cheap coal and lacked sustained burning capacity. However, Dayton Power & Light, a nearby utility, had built a plant designed to process exactly that type of coal. It turned out that strip-mining is as much a construction business as anything. Part of the decision-making process involves the calculated risk of deciding where to make the investment in setting up elaborate equipment. You've also got to factor in the costs of remediation—an area that's 10 percent richer in coal but costs twice as much to restore to its original condition might not be economically viable.

When we got to Hazard, there were two former Aminex owners essentially running the place, Andy Adams and Buggy Cleamons. Both were two true characters—and having had the business damaged by outsiders, they were understandably leery of a New York lawyer coming to town. The first time we met, they decided to test me. Buggy took me up in his helicopter and was trying to rattle me, by having the pilot careen perilously close to the hills. I sat back and enjoyed the countryside. I knew that if I let them think they had frightened me, I'd never have the respect I needed to turn the company around. After that, we developed a friendship, with Andy and Buggy sharing their years of expertise in the business and providing links to the rank and file.

That turned out to be critical. The first big meeting we had provided a crash course in the importance of dealing with people who keep their word. Aminex was a non-union operation. Traditionally, the workers' pay was tied to that of the United Mine Workers. Those unionized workers had recently received a raise and our workers were demanding a similar hike. After studying our books, I knew that Aminex was in danger of not even making its payroll, let alone giving anyone a raise. Convinced of my ability to reason with anyone, I thought, "Let me talk to them." I asked Andy and Buggy to get the workers together in a room. I thought if I had an opportunity to explain the circumstances I could make clear that our only chance of survival was to keep working, and that there would be raises for them once we rode out the immediate crisis.

I entered the large equipment shed where everyone had gathered and some three hundred workers were warily waiting. A few of these guys held shotguns — not a comforting sign in an audience. I started explaining my plan for the company and was having a hard time getting across. This was no jury in federal court — these were men whose livelihoods had been jerked around by the former management.

After finishing my speech I asked if there were any questions. A man in front sat whittling a piece of wood with a knife, and he put up his hand. I called on him and waited anxiously. He delayed and finally said with a heavy accent, "You a Jew?"

I thought I had misheard him. "Excuse me?" "You heard me. Are you a Jew? It was them New York Jews took all the money out of this company." Here I am, this serious young lawyer, so I answered his question earnestly. "I'm Catholic, but some of the people who work for me are Jewish, and I expect them to be treated with respect here."

I went on for about fifteen minutes and the meeting went from bad to worse. Finally, some guy said, "You got a seal?" I had no idea what he was talking about. He repeated his question and suddenly Joel shot up and sprinted to the car, bringing back with him the large valise containing all our legal papers. He ran back into the room holding the documents from the SEC and Judge MacMahon that officially declared me the receiver. We showed the papers to this guy, who was clearly a sort of leader among the men, and he told us, "You fellers leave the room. I want to look at this seal and we'll all talk about it." After a while, that guy plus about a dozen others came into the office where my team had been waiting. He said, "We believe that you really were appointed by the court, that you're not lying to us. We want you to come back every week to tell us exactly how much money the company is making, and when we're out of the woods we want to start seeing our raise."

I assured him that I would, and told him that it would be better if I relayed that information to him and his group of twelve, and they could report it to the others. And that's exactly what we did, from 1978 to 1981, with my associate Jeff Sabin taking over the day-to-day management of the company. Not only did we bring the company out of Chapter 11, but we restored its financial health to the point where it was sold for a good price; the bankruptcy judge eventually awarded Paterson Belknap a bonus for our efforts.

All this was possible only because I was able to deal with people like Andy and Buggy and the guy who inspected the legal papers. Though our backgrounds were as different as could be (not to mention our accents), we each kept up our ends of the bargain and together we pulled that company out of the red.

Sometimes a leader has no alternative but to deal with someone untrustworthy. The only option is to lock up every detail in the clearest possible language, ensuring that it's all written, and that there are witnesses. You should do your best to limit the dealing to the minimum necessary to get the deal done. But even as you're making the deal, they'll be finding some way to weasel out of it. You've got to know when you're dealing with somebody who won't stay bribed so you can collect your end of the bargain up front.

Ronald Reagan exemplified the best way to approach such situations. His refusal to award trust that hadn't been earned changed the nature of our country's relationship with the Soviet Union. Over arms control, he insisted on verification; he wouldn't take the Soviets at their word because it would have been reckless to have done so. The Soviet Union wasn't entitled to that civility.

Reagan forced the Soviets to make concessions up front before the United States made any in return. We know we're going to live up to any treaty. We have laws and protocols that ensure it, and our culture demands it. That wasn't true of the Soviet Union. Reagan insisted on inspection mechanisms with teeth, of the kind that previous administrations might have refused to pursue to completion.

In politics, in business, in any organization, you must apply to institutional decisions the wisdom acquired from individual relationships, because institutions are largely just reflections of individual behavior. Sometimes in negotiations you want a particular result so badly that you become soft-headed about the likelihood of the other side living up to its end of the deal. You want a new house so much, say, that you don't heed the signs of a crumbling foundation. The same mistake can occur in business, in politics, in every organization. A leader may be desperate for a certain result, or he might be led astray by thinking of the headlines and the kudos for delivering them. Ultimately, he may announce a deal with someone who either can't or won't hold up his end of the bargain.

CAN THE PERSON DELIVER?

In the 1990s the United States felt it had to negotiate with Palestinian Authority President Yasser Arafat—but we needed to require more of him, not less, because he was somebody who wouldn't "stay bribed." He'd be given territory, but wouldn't do what he said he would, and would say he couldn't unless he got *more* territory. We would make concessions, as would he; we'd live up to ours, he wouldn't live up to his. He would promise to expel or arrest terrorists—then fail to do so.

For years, I had been saying that we were negotiating with the wrong person. Let me return to my earlier analogy. If you're buying a house and arrive at a price, you expect your new home to be delivered once you've met your side of the bargain. If it turns out that whoever takes your money does not represent the seller, you know you've been had. That's what has happened time and again with Arafat. We've repeatedly received assurances that he was no longer going to provide haven for terrorists, then discovered that in fact Palestine was a breeding ground for them. There were those in power in the 1990s who, instead of refusing to deal with Arafat, helped promote him for the Nobel Peace Prize! The situation had grown eerily similar to the 1930s, when misguided sympathizers refused to see the world for what it was.

In October 1995, the United Nations celebrated its fiftieth anniversary. I was proud of the progress New York had made and looked forward to showing off that improvement on a world stage. I assembled a group called the New York City Host Committee and raised about $2 million to sponsor several events, such as a dinner on Saturday night for all the heads of state at the World Financial Center— held in the Atrium, which was destroyed in the World Trade Center attacks. (It's strange to think that it was in the shadow of that Atrium that I last saw Father Mychal Judge, Pete Ganci, Bill Feehan, and Ray Downey alive.)

Although I was concerned the entire week of the anniversary, I made it a point not to convey my concern to the public; but with so many of the world's leaders assembled in one place, the security challenges were substantial. The dinner had some 160 people, all heads of state, deputy heads, or ambassadors. We had police boats in the harbor, helicopters in the air, even divers in the water—because the Center was accessible by a tunnel underneath the Hudson River, the divers were there to make sure nobody attached explosives to the sea wall.

The cornerstone event for celebration was a concert on Monday, October 23, at Lincoln Center's Avery Fisher Hall. I had selected Beethoven's Ninth Symphony—the *Ode to Joy* for a joyous occasion.

By the night of the concert, I was at last starting to relax. Everyone was safe, the city looked great, and our preparations were paying off.

So there I was, sitting backstage for about fifteen minutes before the concert, getting ready to make a curtain speech with Gillian Sorenson, the U.N.'s public relations director, and also the wife of Ted Sorenson, who had been a speechwriter for President Kennedy. All of a sudden, Randy Mastro and Bruce Teitelbaum burst into the small office. Randy was then my Chief of Staff and Bruce was his deputy.

"What's the problem?" I asked.

"Arafat is here."

I wanted to know how that could be true. This was a privately funded event. When we drew up the list of invitations, we specifically excluded the Palestinian delegation, as well as seven other countries: Cuba, Iraq, Iran, Libya, North Korea, Somalia, and Yugoslavia. We had even sent that list to the United Nations, to let them know where we stood. Showing that there was some honor even among despots, Fidel Castro had decided, "You don't want me, I won't come."

Arafat had apparently arrived at a different conclusion. Somebody had slipped him a ticket and now here he was. I looked up toward the sky. "Throw him out," I told Randy and Bruce. "He's not invited."

"We can't do anything about it now," said Gillian Sorensen. "He's already here."

I disagreed. "Tell him to get out. He's not wanted here."

Randy had been one of my assistant U.S. Attorneys in the Southern District and Bruce had been a practicing attorney before joining my '93 campaign, so they naturally thought like lawyers and began playing out the "what ifs." They asked me what they should do if he refused to go, whether they should have the police remove him. I said, "Here's what we're going to do. First, you two will approach his chief of staff and say Arafat isn't welcome here, would he please leave. I'll send John Fleming (a hulking detective from my detail) with you just in case. If Arafat declines, then I'll go over and ask him personally not to stay. 'The Mayor specifically says he does not want him here.' If that doesn't work, I'll try to get some of the other diplomats to explain how embarrassing it is that he's present when he knows he doesn't have a right to be. Okay, I won't have the police throw him out, but we'll just keep asking him to leave, and make it really uncomfortable for him to stay."

In addition to Bruce and Randy, two others on my staff were there, Manny Papir and Cristyne Lategano. The conversation went on, and someone pointed out that he was, after all, holding a valid ticket, regardless of how he had obtained it. Others thought we should arrest him if necessary. I didn't want that, but I also rejected the idea of our doing nothing.

As we debated, Gillian Sorenson was getting more and more upset. "You can't do this," she kept repeating. "You simply can't."

I said, "Gillian, I don't see why not. This is my event. I raised the money for it from private donors. These are my invited guests. Furthermore, a number of those donors will be outraged that we're spending their money to entertain Yasser Arafat. They'll go crazy, and they have every right to."

There was another element to what I was feeling. I hold a special contempt for Arafat. When I was a U.S. Attorney, I investigated the hijacking of the Italian cruise ship *Achille Lauro*. While the ship was at port in Alexandria, four members of the Palestine Liberation Organization walked into the main dining room and began firing at random, wounding passengers. Armed with AK-47s, handguns, and grenades, the terrorists herded the 400 people on board and separated them by nationality, placing American and British hostages in a makeshift jail of oil drums, which they threatened to set alight. They forced the captain to leave the Egyptian port and set sail for Syria, and demanded that Israel release 50 Palestinian prisoners.

One of the hostages was Leon Klinghoffer, a 69-year-old retired Jewish businessman from New York. Partially paralyzed by two strokes, Klinghoffer was confined to a wheelchair. The terrorists wheeled him away from his wife, shot him in the forehead, then dumped his body into the sea. I don't forget those who kill Americans. The man who ordered that operation, Yasser Arafat was responsible for that terrorist act. Now the U.S. was romanticizing him. I kept thinking—negotiate with him if you believe you have to, but don't let your guard down by making it appear he's like an elected leader of a democracy. It deeply disturbed me. At that exact moment, I believed he was still harboring terrorists.

All this was going through my head as Gillian Sorenson was repeating, "You can't do this to him!" I thought, "Can't I? This is a guy who ordered innocent people to be murdered." Gillian was now arguing that an ejection would create an international incident. That's what made up my mind. I said, "Well, maybe we *should* have an international incident. Maybe we *should* wake people up to the way this terrorist is being romanticized."

I told Gillian, "Enough. The discussion is over. I've made a decision, and that's what I'm going to do. Now let's move on." By that point, the program was already running late. Gillian and I were both scheduled to make some introductory remarks welcoming all these dignitaries. I said to Randy and Bruce, "I'm going up now to deliver my speech. Go talk to his people and see if he'll leave."

I approached the stage to make my remarks and as I waited in the wings I looked up. There was Arafat, stage left in the first tier of private boxes, sitting directly opposite Yitzhak Rabin's box—they were actually facing each other. I could see Bruce and Randy enter the back of Arafat's booth and was grateful that it was these two who had the assignment. They are among the toughest guys one will ever meet—not afraid of anybody. I could see them standing in the doorway, talking to one of Arafat's entourage. Then Arafat himself came out, shook Randy's hand, and extended his hand to Bruce, who wouldn't take it. Randy and Bruce were talking to Arafat's guy, who was talking to Arafat, and Arafat was waving his arms around. They were flapping his ticket in Randy's face and Bruce was saying (as he later told me) that he personally oversaw the invitation list and it didn't include Arafat. By now it was time for me to give my introduction. I came on center stage and started to speak, but still, out of the corner of my eye, could take in that Arafat was still up there, still in animated conversation.

I was soon finished, left the stage, and headed for my box. I looked over to Arafat's seat and could see that it was empty. I was hoping that meant our plan had worked, because I didn't particularly want to create a scene; but I was also thinking that maybe he had moved off into the hall to cook up a counter-strategy, or perhaps just gone to the restroom. So I went outside, and there were Bruce and Randy walking toward me. Arafat, I learned, had left in a huff, declaring he had been insulted, and that he was going to hold a press conference to condemn us. I wouldn't have had it any other way, and returned to Beethoven's Ninth Symphony.

By the next day, I realized that this had indeed become an international incident. *The New York Times* was calling for my head, apparently willing to make a one-time exception in its opposition to capital punishment. A story headlined "White House Condemns Giuliani" quoted a Clinton spokesman lamenting the incident "in light of the constructive role that Chairman Arafat has played in the Mideast peace process." A senior administration official called it "an embarrassment to everyone associated with diplomacy." That the White House would assert that Arafat had played a constructive role exposed the weakness of Clinton's foreign policy. He was unable to see the kind of person he was dealing with, and never held Arafat to any standard of responsible behavior.

This is not Monday-morning quarterbacking. The whole time I was running for Senate, part of my standard speech was that Clinton was going to hand the country over weaker than he got it. I pointed out that the military was weaker, underfinanced and underpaid, and that our intelligence services had been denuded and were not paying attention to terrorism. For instance, Clinton allowed Saddam Hussein to escape all inspections. Even after he bombed him for refusing to let inspectors do their job, the end result was that we gave up the inspections. It was absurd. We bombed the man, then lessened our scrutiny of him.

Now even Ed Koch, Gillian Sorenson's boss when she had been his liaison to the U.N., went on television to rip me apart, apparently forgetting that he had condemned Arafat as a murderer and had called the U.N. a cesspool—not my first choice were I hiring someone to teach me the subtleties of diplomacy. All this was a controversy I appreciated, because I felt so certain I was on the right side. As Arafat has showed his true colors ever more clearly in subsequent years, to the point where even former supporters can no longer excuse his inability or unwillingness to curb Palestinian violence, I have occasionally reminded people of that concert and the outrage that followed.

Some Americans are unable to face up to the fact that there really are evil people, people who do not share our values. The desire for peace—and the simplistic and misplaced guilt many have—create a tendency to make anyone who demands results and a high standard of behavior into some kind of Neanderthal.

To my mind, U.S. foreign policy on the Middle East lost any constructive agenda once we began believing that our involvement there was like some chess game, in which each side had to move its pieces one at a time and were roughly morally equivalent. I even hear such thinking now, in statements about how "both sides have to reduce the violence." That is true—but there are meaningful distinctions between the kinds of violence on each side.

None of this means that we don't negotiate with people who are maybe even evil. We may have no choice. But we shouldn't treat him the same way we treat Rabin or Peres or Barak or Sharon or Netanyahu. I admit that some of these men are my personal friends; but they all share roughly our set of values. You can negotiate with them. With Arafat you have to require him to deliver *before* you do. If you deliver first, he's going to make you deliver again and again before he holds up his end of the bargain, if he ever does.

There's a difference between a tough gentleman and a bully. The former may drive a hard bargain, may even refuse to come to terms; but when he gives his word he keeps it. And he doesn't show up un-invited on the assumption that no one will have the nerve to throw him out. That incident occurred in the fall of 1995, and by then Arafat had led on the United States several times. In late summer 1993, having been promised 50,000 guns and a "police force" in the Oslo Accords, Arafat still gave no indication that he seriously intended to cap the violence, nor was it clear he was in a position to do so.

There are some people who should be completely avoided. It's counterproductive to deal with them, and will just drag you down. There are many times in which leaders think they have to deal with someone who doesn't meet their standards, when the reality is that they can just say no. As mayor, I would meet with any constituency, visit any neighborhood, help any community: there was no group of people I didn't want to reach. But I insisted on dealing only with people who kept their word. In the end, that makes everyone operate at a higher standard.

PART

III

16

Recovery

Early on the morning of Wednesday, September 12, I appeared on the *Today* show to reassure everyone that New York City was still here. I said that we would not only overcome the disaster but set an example in how to show that Americans refused to be terrorized. And then I began as I'd begun every morning since I became mayor—with a morning meeting. Even with police escort, the roads in Lower Manhattan were difficult to navigate, but the morning meeting began at its usual time—8 A.M. My staff, many of whom had been up most of the night, gathered around the table. One by one, the deputy mayors and commissioners, joined by Governor Pataki and members of his staff, detailed the challenges of the agencies they managed. We listened to each report; I decided some issues instantly, debated others, assigned task forces to some, and selected others to be acted on later. It was not unlike the way Judge MacMahon tackled the stack of motions that accumulated on his desk, always pressing forward, making sure progress was made.

We contacted the military and FEMA to order 11,000 body bags, and could pause for only a second to reflect on the horrific meaning of what we had just decided. We expanded the frozen zone and started calling the business leaders whose workforces had been decimated.

I had members of my staff who know those firms well calling companies and isolating for me the ones that were hardest hit, so I could contact them personally. I called Howard Lutnick, CEO of Cantor Fitzgerald, whose firm on the top floors of the north tower had lost over 700, including Howard's brother, Gary. Howard was understandably upset during our call and I offered him whatever assistance he needed. I again spoke to Dick Grasso, head of the New York Stock Exchange, concerned that the city might be in for additional attacks and that the Exchange was a possible target. I reached Phil Purcell, the CEO of Morgan Stanley, at home. His company had lost hundreds of men and women. He told me that he hoped that they'd find many of their people, that the number of missing would be reduced. They were having some success reaching survivors as the first day and night continued.

There's a reason for that success, in addition to the bravery of the FDNY and NYPD. Following the bombing of the World Trade Center in 1993, Morgan Stanley's head of security, Colonel Richard C. Rescorla, had meticulously planned and drilled evacuation plans in the event of another crisis. Rick had been born in England but came to America to fight in the Vietnam War. When the attack happened, Rick was ready. He and his team went office by office with a bullhorn, rushing the investment bank's employees onto the elevators and out of the building. With 3,700 employees there, Morgan Stanley was the single biggest tenant of the World Trade Center. Because of the bravery and preparedness of Rick and his team, thousands of Morgan Stanley employees made it to safety on September 11. Tragically, six employees died, and Rick was one of them.

The bulk of my career had been spent as a prosecutor, which honed my investigative skills. You've got to put yourself inside the mind of the criminals you're investigating—in this case, terrorists.

After September 11, the skies were closed and New York City was being defended by jet fighters and gunboats. I no longer expected a plane or missile attack, but I was expecting individual bombings. An additional attack would have had a devastating effect on the morale of the city. I tried to expect the unexpected from what was clearly a shrewd enemy.

City government was functioning at the Police Academy on 20th Street between Second and Third avenues. The previous day, we had been in touch with the city's hospitals, making sure doctors, beds, support staff, and donated blood would all be available for the thousands of injured we expected to arrive.

It never happened. That Wednesday morning, Judith was the first to say to me, "You know, nobody is checking in." I asked her what she meant—then realized that we had recovered some people on Tuesday, but none after that. I got reports throughout the night, and we weren't taking anybody out. We kept the capacity in place, hoping, praying. It was a terrible disappointment. Those who were in the Trade Center mostly made it to safety—over 25,000 people were evacuated in one of the greatest rescue operations in history. Those who didn't escape before the buildings collapsed . . .

At Thursday's morning meeting, I told my team that I wanted to have a major prayer service. I thought it would be enormously valuable to have a priest, a rabbi, a minister, and an imam, to underscore not just the unity of our city but that people of all beliefs were among the murdered. Director of Scheduling Kate Anson noted that Imam Pasha, a friend with whom my administration had worked in the past, was traveling in Senegal and not returning until Monday. I said, "Well, get me an imam."

Another issue revolved around the grim details of burying uniformed personnel, the firefighters and cops. We already knew that hundreds had died. Normally, we would have put on an Inspector's funeral for every one, with bagpipes and uniformed service members lined up at attention to escort the casket. Because of the sheer numbers, we were afraid that would not be possible. It turned out that with the efforts of the ceremonial units in the FDNY, NYPD, and PAPD, we were able to provide it for all who requested it. Meanwhile, I wanted to make it clear how much the city valued their bravery and sacrifice. After much discussion, we settled on Yankee Stadium as a site for the service and decided to schedule it for the following Sunday, September 23, in order to provide more time for grieving relatives.

Next, we turned our attention to the family members of the victims. Space is not easy to come by in Manhattan. One of the most pressing problems was selecting somewhere thousands of families could seek information, assistance, and comfort. On Wednesday, Governor Pataki made available the cavernous National Guard armory on Lexington Avenue. I went there on Thursday, and there was a line of family members snaking out the enormous building and curling around the block. I talked with families like that of 23-year-old Brooke Jackman. With a father and brother both working on Wall Street, Brooke started at Cantor Fitzgerald as an assistant trader three months earlier. I sat with her family, holding hands in a circle around a table, and told them, "I don't think the city realizes yet what it's going to go through."

After they had left, I took off my glasses and rubbed my eyes. Under normal circumstances, I don't sleep much. Over the last forty-eight hours, I had barely slept at all. I sat in a chair and just said out loud, to no one in particular, "The pain is just immense. The pain is unbelievable. And the worst part of this is that these people are going to live with this for the rest of their lives, because the image of the planes hitting the towers will be repeated again and again."

As commissioner of the Community Assistance Unit, Rosemarie O'Keefe—"Ro"—had almost come to specialize in disasters. She had established family centers for each of the plane crashes that had occurred during my administration, as well as handling blackouts and numerous other calamities. At the armory, with thousands of people desperate for information that simply didn't exist, Ro could easily have been overwhelmed. She listed her most pressing requirements: "There's plenty of food and bottled water. But I need supplies so bad—a hundred more tables, chairs, fans, maybe a couple of dozen air conditioners, it's so hot in here. Five Xerox machines, and good fax machines, so that updated lists can be circulated more quickly."

The list she was talking about was the definitive register we were struggling to assemble; the goal was to detail everyone who was in the building and was either confirmed dead, injured, or unknown. A disturbing issue arose. Some deranged people had been posting inaccurate information on unofficial web sites, so that families were reading lists that said a loved one had been seen at a hospital receiving treatment, when in fact he or she never escaped the site. It was one of the cruelest acts I could imagine. Still at the armory, I called Mike Hess to ask about the appropriateness of putting the official list on the city's web site. It was a complicated problem and I tried to present it with a combination of legal reasoning and common sense.

"First, can we legally distribute and put on a web site the names of people in a hospital? Second, can we legally publish the list of people who have been found and are dead? Third, can we publish information about people about whom we have some information, but not necessarily enough for identification purposes?" As an example of this third category, I read from a list the police had given me. "Mike, some of this stuff is gruesome as hell. 'Unknown male, upper torso, salt pepper hair.' The problem is, how do you limit this to the people who really need to know?" Mike took over. Months later, I reflected on the fact that this was about forty-eight hours after he had almost died at the World Trade Center. Mike symbolized the ability to face death and still focus on what needed to be done to help others.

At the armory, Joe Allbaugh, the Director of the Federal Emergency Management Agency, was coordinating the response. Allbaugh is a huge man, his military crewcut sheared to a fraction of his square Oklahoma head. Rosemarie O'Keefe is a classic New Yorker—she wears her emotions on her sleeve. As we left Major Obregon's office, I noticed Allbaugh and O'Keefe, two apparently opposite types, give each other a long hug.

I then addressed the thousands of family members. People were scared, despondent, frustrated. The PA system barely functioned in the cavernous space, it was hot as hell, and my voice was starting to give.

"We don't have magic solutions," I began. "This is going to be a long process. It's not going to happen in a day or so . . . The people who are doing this—the police officers and the firefighters and the federal and state officials—are putting their lives at risk. We had buildings collapse yesterday. We had the danger of another today. So they can move only at a certain pace, otherwise we're going to lose even more . . . There's probably no one in New York who hasn't been touched by this. Like you, I have people in there I know, care about, and love. Like you, I want to get them out. I hope and I pray that they're alive. And if that's not the case, I hope and I pray that we can recover them so we can give them a decent burial and the respect and the honor they are entitled to. So please work with us, and we'll work with you."

Someone asked whether there were people in the hospitals who were alive but unidentified. I told him that it would be an extremely small number. I didn't want to give anyone false hope. As it was, thousands of loved ones were finally realizing that there wasn't going to be a happy ending. The horror began to sink in: if you're here in this armory, it's because your loved one a) hasn't contacted you and b) is not on a list of the known dead. The increasingly desperate questions that followed—Are there people who are alive and in hospitals with amnesia?—showed how sad it would be when it dawned on those concerned that tales of survival underneath 110 stories of concrete and steel would not be plentiful.

As soon as I realized we were not going to have many injured people coming to the hospitals, I set Judith the task of helping Ro and Richie organize the Family Assistance Center. Clearly, mental health counseling would be paramount, then there were a myriad of other needs, from DNA collection (to identify family members) to emergency financial help to child care.

My first impression of the armory was that it looked like Ellis Island in the forties—confusing, dark, and depressing. It was also extremely warm in there, which was uncomfortable on the families who were desperate for information and answers. I decided to bring in Jerry Hauer, who had been my first Director of Emergency Management, to evaluate the current space and also help decide on a new space. I met with the head of the Red Cross, Judith, Richie, and several others to discuss the needs of the victims' families. The Red Cross representative was adamant that the armory was inappropriate. Nevertheless, Ro felt that the families had already become attached to the place and would resist leaving. I asked Judith what she thought and she said, "It's a terrible place, but let's go slowly in making a transition."

I felt we had to act. I didn't want people to get too accustomed to the armory if we were going to move. We needed a viable alternative, so that there'd always be a place for family members to go for assistance. I asked Richie to come up with alternatives. We were already preparing to move the command center from the Police Academy to Pier 92 on the Hudson River. Richie suggested Pier 94, immediately north. I instinctively liked the idea of locating the Family Center so close to the center of government—sending a message about its importance and allowing us as much time there as possible.

Jerry and Judith told me that they wanted me to look at it, and if I agreed with them they'd work out a transition with Ro and that "going slowly" would mean only two or three days. I went to the pier and saw that all these companies had volunteers ready to start building and installing what would transform 125,000 square feet of emptiness into a functional, comfortable place for thousands of grieving families. IBM had donated computers, consultants from Accenture were on hand to make all the agencies work hand-in-glove, Cisco was there to build the computer network, and many other corporate executives and employees had rolled up their sleeves and were ready to do anything from wire computers to lay carpet. I said, "This is it. This is the place." A few days later it opened, and it remained the Family Assistance Center until I left office on January 1, assisting over 20,000 people during the crisis.

Late Thursday afternoon, I met again with the Medical Examiner, Chuck Hirsch, in his office at Bellevue Hospital. Dr. Hirsch collects African violets and had special lights in his office to support rare, delicate breeds. It was a reaffirmation of life in a place of death. He had told me on Tuesday how slim our odds of finding survivors alive would be, and that was turning out to be horribly accurate. Now, with the wounds on his hands still held together by the jagged stitches he'd sewn himself on Tuesday, he explained in greater detail how he was planning to handle one of the most complicated, difficult challenges of the crisis—the identification of thousands of victims, including many that had been reduced to "biological stains."

I left his office in Bellevue Hospital and walked past the hospital's load-in area. There were dozens of stretchers, each covered with body parts. The smell was overpowering. But the care Dr. Hirsch's staff displayed in managing this unimaginable undertaking lent quiet dignity to human life.

I headed back to the Police Academy, where I'd convened a meeting of twenty or so religious and civic leaders and my two predecessors to discuss the Sunday service and to plan the months beyond. Someone suggested that an indoor venue should be considered because even such an impressive gathering of those of the cloth could not guarantee the weather. Arguing for Central Park, former mayor Ed Koch mentioned that a million people attended the Simon and Garfunkel concert there. My Parks Commissioner, Henry Stern, who had also served under Koch, said, "We only told you it was a million." Cardinal Egan replied: "Well, if I could be a bridge over troubled water, I'd like to offer up my residence as a meeting place for this committee."

After that meeting, I walked back to my "office" in the Police Academy. Hundreds of phone calls had to be made, taken, returned. The day before, I had spoken to General Electric CEO Jeff Immelt, who arranged for many generators to be delivered down at the site, then mentioned that he wanted his company to make a contribution specifically to the families of the uniformed personnel who had been killed. I told him I'd work out how to make that happen. He said he'd send $10 million. I was startled—and grateful. I asked Jeff if he would make this presentation public so I could inspire others to make similar contributions. By doing that, he helped create the idea of the Twin Towers Fund.

Other business leaders began calling to ask what they could contribute. On Thursday, Rupert Murdoch called. He also wanted to contribute to a fund specifically for the families of uniformed personnel who died. He suggested that we talk to his son, Lachlan Murdoch, to nail down the exact amount. Mike Hess began assessing how much it would take to provide for the family of every lost uniformed personnel.

I delegated to Larry Levy the function of organizing these donations. By doing this, Jeff Immelt and the Murdochs helped create the Twin Towers Fund, which in less than a year had distributed $155 million to the families. The fund established the principle that all donated money would go directly to the families, with any administrative costs being paid directly by donors who specified that their funds cover those costs. Larry was thus able to honor the original purpose of Jeff and the Murdochs and the thousands of others who felt compelled to help the families of these very special heroes.

I decided to hold a press conference to see if we could encourage other companies to help. Dell and AOL outfitted the entire center with computers and telecommunications equipment. WorldCom contributed free phone service. Home Depot co-founder Ken Langone called the Police Academy, saying, "I saw someone on television say the city could use generators and batteries. You'll have a truck-load of each by tomorrow." Mike Bloomberg personally paid for the McDonald's nearest Ground Zero to stay open around the clock to feed rescue workers, gratis. (We were down at the site so much during the first weeks that my staff took to calling that McDonald's "The Four Seasons." I became intimately familiar with it because it was the only place around with a reliable private bathroom.)

The public craved information, the families were suffering, the security of the city had to be addressed, and the rescue and recovery operation needed to be organized. A million other questions needed answers. That Thursday night was in many ways the low point. The Medical Examiner's office, the grieving at the Family Center, the re-alization that no survivors were likely to be found, it was too much to bear. At the Police Academy were dozens of people in a room made to accommodate just a few. I needed time to think about more than the immediate crises, to consider the long-term organization. But there were so many people around, so many problems. I was making hun-dreds of decisions, one after another. Every once in a while, I would stop and say a short prayer: "God, I hope I'm giving the right answers."

Every single agency of the city was shaken by the attacks. The Fire Department, having lost 343 members, was perhaps most af-fected. The Police Department lost 23 officers, and was charged with awesome additional tasks, such as policing Ground Zero and helping to patrol all entrances to the city. The Port Authority police lost 37 of-ficers and 38 civilians, including Neil Levin, the agency's head. The Medical Examiner's office and Health Department identified the re-mains of victims and administered mental health treatment (a job made even tougher when anthrax showed up a month later). The Sanitation Department not only had to help clean up 1,642,698 tons of fallen buildings, debris, and mess—108,444 truckloads—but its big vehicles were drafted into service to block vulnerable spots. The budget office was thrown into turmoil, the Department of Citywide Administrative Services found itself ordering untold amounts of supplies (all needed immediately), the Economic Development Corporation had to persuade frightened businesses to stay in New York City. Even departments one wouldn't guess found themselves involved. The Trade Waste Commission was charged with ensuring that the destroyed towers weren't diverted into mob-controlled hauling operations, and the Department of Employment staged job fairs at which those displaced by the terrorist attacks were given priority.

The offices were outfitted with a few phones and the Police Academy staff did the best they could, but the place hadn't been intended to accommodate the entire city government, let alone the others whose help was needed. Governor Pataki and his staff were working overtime, and everyone from Secretary of Health Tommy Thompson to Joe Allbaugh was parked on the Academy's inadequate furniture. Food, water, and protective gear collected on each surface.

Around ten P.M. on Thursday I started feeling tremendous pains in my shoulder and all down my back. It crossed my mind that I might be having a heart attack. I thought, "It couldn't be. God wouldn't let that happen now." I briefly considered going to a doctor but realized that I couldn't—it would get in the media and be blown out of proportion. I said to myself, "I don't have time now to get sick. I can get sick later."

Judith noticed I was in pain and suggested a simple remedy. "Why don't you take a walk by yourself?" She found a back door that led to a fire exit. With my security detail keeping a discreet distance behind me, I walked through Stuyvesant Town, just a few miles north of the disaster. A few people waved, shocked to see me alone with my FDNY baseball hat. I made it to the East River. A ghostly calm hung over what ordinarily would have been the bustle of a glorious September evening. The smell and smoke were equally thick as they rose from the ashes of the smoldering towers. I thought about the challenges our city, nation, and world would face, and about the families who would spend infinite nights without a loved one.

A few weeks earlier, I had taken my daughter, Caroline, out to celebrate her twelfth birthday. Our schedule was dinner—irresistible Italian food at Gargiulo's on Coney Island—followed by a ballgame at KeySpan Park, the picturesque stadium the city had helped build for the minor league Mets team, the Brooklyn Cyclones. We took a boat there, cruising on that same river I looked out on now. I have a photo of the two of us with the sun setting behind Manhattan, the twin towers standing sentry in the background. I briefly recalled that the Cyclones were in a minor league world series and wondered about the outcome. Since I was 7, I probably had never gone more than a day or so without checking the baseball scores. Then I remembered there was no baseball.

Seeing the river as I walked had a powerful effect on me. I remembered my father learning to swim in the East River, and was comforted seeing it rushing by, as always. The street was still here, New York City was still here. They did this tremendous amount of damage, and yet the river—and the city and its people—were all still here. It was my obligation to be strong and think clearly.

Walking reduced the pain in my shoulder and back, so I realized I wasn't having a heart attack. Maybe I had pulled a muscle in my right shoulder, probably on Tuesday. And the pain could have been exaggerated by stress and lack of sleep. By the time I walked back I felt better—ready to make decisions.

I am often my most severe critic. When I screw something up, I step out of myself and look at the errors I've made and agonize over why I didn't think of this or anticipate that. During the walk, I realized that I needed to resist that tendency, which was already building. I said to myself, "I can handle this. I am handling this. This is what I know how to do. This is what I was trained to do—to take charge, and make sound, sensible decisions." This brief half hour of solitary meditation gave me an abiding feeling that I'd get through it. I then returned to making sure the rest of the city would as well.

On Friday, September 14, President Bush came to New York City. After the attacks, I thought it was vitally important that he come to the site. I knew that it would inspire the people working at the site. President Bush is at his best among regular Americans, who intuitively sense his sincerity.

It is easy to forget how tense the country was in the days following the attacks. The Secret Service and others around the President must have advised him that it wasn't safe to visit New York City so soon. With 41,000 police, 3,000 National Guardsmen, Secret Service, and other federal agents patrolling the area, we were able to provide for security against snipers. However, there were still fires burning all over Ground Zero, flaring up unpredictably, at extraordinarily high temperatures. Additionally, the buildings all around remained precarious, parts of them still falling over the area. It was inherently very dangerous and impossible to secure safety.

There was an additional element to my desire for a presidential visit. At the same time as a leader provides strength and inspiration to those he visits, he also draws strength and inspiration from them. I knew this from my own trips to Ground Zero. I would hug the guys who were working there, shake their hands and talk to them, and feel their determination revitalizing me, even as they told me how much the visits meant to them. I was confident President Bush would have the same experience.

On Friday morning, Governor Pataki and I boarded a military helicopter at New York's Port Authority heliport and flew through a thick fog to McGuire Air Force Base in New Jersey. It was just the two of us, with one security guard each, and we did not disclose where we were going. The President was flying to New Jersey directly following the memorial services at Washington National Cathedral. While we waited for him to arrive, I spoke to one of the Air Force colonels at the base. He detailed just how intricate a maneuver the terrorists had pulled off—implementing four simultaneous missions. All of the missions required each participant to be disciplined and display various specialized skills, and to have three of them work to devastating effect without communicating from plane to plane. He said he wasn't sure he could have done as well. The colonel left me with a chilling thought: *the terrorists are evil but intelligent—don't underestimate them.*

I have seen Air Force One at other times, but as I watched President Bush exit that plane on that day it was hard to contain my tears of relief. I thanked him and told him how proud I was of how he was handling the country in this crisis. "What can I do for you?" he asked.

I told him, "If you catch this guy, Bin Laden, I would like to be the one to execute him." I am sure he thought I was just speaking rhetorically, but I was serious. Bin Laden had attacked my city and as its mayor I had the strong feeling that I was the most appropriate person to do it.

The three of us helicoptered to the site. The morning fog had lifted, and for the first time I saw the disaster site from the air. Everyone who took in Ground Zero on television and later visited it was stunned by how much worse it was seeing it in person. Everyone who saw it on the ground and later from above spoke of how much worse it was overhead, where the immensity of the disaster could be fully comprehended.

I heard the President catch his breath. Quietly, he said, "Oh, my God."

President Bush waded through the rubble, talking to the crowd, and the longer he stayed, the more the rescuers welled up with spirit. As he spoke through a bullhorn from a makeshift platform, one of the workers yelled out, "We can't hear you." President Bush replied, "I can hear you. The rest of the world hears you, and the people who knocked these buildings down will hear all of us soon." He stayed much longer than planned. It was inspiring.

President Bush, Governor Pataki, and I got into the President's limo. As I was doing so, Bernie Kerik, Tom Von Essen, and Richie Sheirer piled in with us—no one asked them to, they just jumped in. Later, as we drove out, President Bush looked through the window at the firefighters, cops, and emergency personnel digging through the hunks of steel and concrete, searching for signs of life. He said to us, "These are the people who fight and win our wars. I could see the anger on their faces, the determination." As we drove up the West Side Highway, hundreds of people had gathered on the median and along the road in a spontaneous display of support that would extend for weeks. The liberal West Side of Manhattan embraced the Commander in Chief, holding signs saying "George, we love you" and "We support you, President Bush." I couldn't restrain the New Yorker in me and said, "I hate to break it to you, Mr. President, but none of these people voted for you. And only four of them voted for me and the Governor."

For months, we had in place an exercise in which we'd drill on our response to a biochemical attack, specifically practicing for the distribution of medication. The planned date: Wednesday, September 12. We had stored much of the materials for that drill at Pier 92. Pier 92 offered 125,000 square feet of open space and easy transportation to and from Ground Zero by way of boat and the West Side Highway. Moreover, because it was already in use by the military, the points of access were relatively easy to guard. Richie told me he'd pull some of his OEM guys to start setting up Pier 92 as a command center. My most optimistic expectation would have been that even a rudimentary replacement for the felled center at 7 World Trade would be seven to ten days. By Saturday morning, we held our first meeting there. It was completely ready.

I went to the Family Center on Friday evening and it, too, was already transformed. Every social service agency the disaster victims could conceivably need—from the ASPCA for victims' pets to the Salvation Army to an expedited application for food stamps—was represented. They had wallpaper and balloons, and bunting and flags donated by the Yankees. About 1,000 computers had been moved in. Ro and Judith had set up 130 booths so that families could bring samples of DNA and ask sensitive questions with a modicum of privacy. The first few families were already there, receiving help with forms and legal documents. The Family Center on Pier 94 was up and running, a formidable achievement.

That gave us the sense that we could do anything. I am not even sure we understood that this was happening, this growing confidence, but I could see it taking shape. If we could replace a $25 million Command Center in three days and in four days build from scratch a Family Center that would eventually handle some 20,000 people, we could manage whatever this crisis threw our way.

Putting the Family Center together so quickly taught me a lot about Judith. She and I had become very close when I went through prostate cancer and I saw how knowledgeable and compassionate she was. But that was a personal crisis. This was governmental, societal, massive in its impact and response. We had never worked together before. The truth is that she was ideally suited to the needs at the Center. In a purely volunteer capacity, Judith teamed with Richie Sheirer, Rosemarie O'Keefe, and Jerry Hauer to transform 125,000 square feet on a pier in the Hudson River into a shelter for the thousands who were the families of victims. She persuaded everyone she knew to volunteer—from friends who assembled couches to doctors that specialize in post-traumatic stress disorder. It was an eye-opener.

That evening, I went to a memorial for Father Judge. His funeral was scheduled for the next day, but because it was scheduled between Pete Ganci's (in Farmingdale, Long Island) and Bill Feehan's (in Flushing, Queens), I wasn't going to be able to attend. I had to go to theirs; after all, they were the No. 2 and No. 3 ranking officers of the Fire Department. The next few months presented too many awful scheduling dilemmas like this.

After the memorial, I ate my first real meal since breakfast on Tuesday morning. Until that night, we had been eating pizza, sandwiches, and junk food, all of which I'd avoided since my cancer treatment. Late Friday night, we sat down for dinner at the Manhattan steakhouse Frank's. Judith and I were joined by Joe Lhota, Bob Harding, and Kate Anson.

We sat at a table in the back. Through the south windows, we could see smoke billowing from Ground Zero. We ate family style — several big plates of food and everyone taking some from each. Frank's always has plates of pickles, radishes, pickled tomatoes, and hunks of blue cheese on the table. Having grown used to eating with our fingers, we devoured many plates of these appetizers, then had two bowls of mixed green salad with heavy blue cheese dressing on the side. We then had two trays of steak, with creamed spinach. Everyone remarked that it was the first time any of us had held a knife and fork all week — to this day, Tom Von Essen still says "Oh, look how fancy" whenever he sees me eating with utensils. We couldn't believe how hungry we were.

Normally, at a dinner like this, we would have had red wine, but this time we declined, apprehensive that any alcohol would knock us out after so little sleep. And my night was not over. I had to be at a meeting that wasn't on my official schedule. I didn't even mention it to my closest staff. The topic was biological and chemical warfare, which I feared would be the next terrorist move.

I had organized a seminar with experts and doctors who specialized in infectious diseases and biological attack, ensuring that the group included not just biological warfare experts but doctors who actually treat people. My thinking was that if someone unleashed a chemical or biological attack we might have to treat 100,000 people. So I wanted experts who had actually managed the most complex treatment situations and understood details beyond the science, like how do you quarantine people, and what do you tell the public?

I scheduled our first meeting for eleven P.M., specifically to keep it secret from the press lest word of it further unsettle an already rattled city. That's also why I held it at Gracie Mansion. The sight of these people—some of whom were well known in the scientific community as experts on biological attack—might trigger concern if they came to the Emergency Management Center. Richie Sheirer, Jerry Hauer, the Police Commissioner, the Fire Commissioner, Health Commissioner Neal Cohen and his assistant commissioner for infectious diseases, Dr. Marcelle Layton, OEM's Edward Gabriel, and Dario Gonzalez and I spent several hours with people like Dr. Burt Meyers, an infectious disease expert at Mt. Sinai School of Medicine, Dr. Martin J. Blaser, the Chairman of NYU's Department of Medicine, and Dr. Josh Lederberg, who had won the Nobel Prize.

We reviewed plans related to possible attacks involving anthrax, smallpox, botulism, and sarin gas. We established charts for each—how one would detect the first sign, how much time each individual would have to act once the symptoms appeared. How would each disease be delivered? What were the antidotes, and what was our stockpile of each? How quickly could we react? Richie had completed an inventory of supplies of each antidote and where the dosages were stored. Ironically, some of our supply of the anthrax-antidote Cipro had been stored in the Command Center in 7 World Trade Center. Knowing that we had lost whatever had been in 7 World Trade, I asked Richie if we were now entirely without Cipro and Doxycycline and the rest. He reassured me: "We prepared for this. We had already spread the antidotes throughout facilities in all five boroughs."

It was a sobering meeting. When it was over, Bernie said to me, "Boss, I'm not going to sleep tonight." When someone like Bernie says he's concerned, I know the situation is difficult. I stayed up several hours thinking about all the things that could happen. There's always *something* that can be done. After that initial meeting, we met every couple of days in smaller groups, to attract less attention, and were joined by people like Mt. Sinai's Dr. Alejandra Gurtman and Philip M. Tierno, Jr., Ph.D., author of *The Secret Life of Germs*. We honed our plans and practiced putting them into action; but I still continued to feel a tremendous burden of anticipation.

A leader should be anticipating all the time. Almost immediately after the attacks on the World Trade Center, it became clear that the terrorists were Arabs. On September 11, I urged people not to react against any particular community. By Wednesday, September 12, there had been scattered incidents of New Yorkers harassing or intimidating those believed to be of Arab descent. While anger was understandable, I made it clear that the city would not tolerate group blame of any kind. Anger should be directed toward individuals and terrorist groups, not at those of a particular religion or nationality. At a press conference that afternoon, I chose my words carefully. "Nobody should attack anybody else. That's what we're dealing with right now. We are dealing with insanity, with sick hatred."

I wanted to create a link in the public's mind between the prejudices that drove the perpetrators of these horrible acts and any subsequent crimes directed at people because of their ethnicity or presumed beliefs. At the same time as I was speaking to these issues, we were acting to monitor and enforce them. The Police Department added a Compstat category specifically accounting for bias directed at Arab Americans. Every day, Police Commissioner Bernie Kerik would tell me that number so we could track whether we had a growing problem on our hands and where in the city such incidents were occurring. We let people know that anyone who harassed or abused someone because of their ethnicity would be arrested. I believe those twin efforts—speaking out about the need not to engage in group blame, as well as letting New Yorkers know we wouldn't tolerate any sort of harassment—helped to reduce the risk of incidents of violence. The reason I was ready for this aspect of the crisis was experience from a crisis that had occurred more than seven years earlier.

I had been mayor only two months when on March 1, 1994, on the Brooklyn Bridge, an illegal alien from Lebanon named Rashid Baz fired into a school bus filled with Jewish students. Sixteen-year-old Ari Halberstam was killed and several others were wounded. Tension in the city, especially regarding Arabs and Arab Americans, was extraordinarily high. A jury was considering the fates of those who bombed the World Trade Center in February 1993. A week earlier, a Brooklyn man who had settled in Israel had killed more than two dozen Palestinians in a mosque in Hebron.

Immediately after the Halberstam shooting, before we'd even arrested a suspect, I told New Yorkers, "This act of evil is not the act of a people, but it's the act of a person or persons. Let's show America and the world that we can make that distinction."

In that crisis, I used a two-pronged approach. First, I had to make the Jewish community feel more secure and let them know that this was going to be handled as a top priority. We checked the intelligence services and the Joint Terrorism Task Force, and it did not appear as if there would be any additional attacks. However, the fear that there could be was legitimate and had to be addressed. We put out significant extra policing, and I stated that we were doing so. People could hear that on radio and on television, and they could see for themselves more police officers on the street. I said that we would do everything we could to catch the person who did it. We would break down every barrier and knock down every wall.

At the same time, I was trying to dampen the concept of group blame. Prejudice is largely about that. It's about taking the perceived wrongdoing of one or a few people, which can be either real or imagined, then applying it to an entire group. I asked people on both sides not to do that. America is built on equal treatment.

* * *

From my childhood days, I had trained myself to control my emotions when others became more emotional. My father had always told me to remain calm in a crisis. As others around me got excited, he said, staying deliberately calm would help me figure out the right answers. When a crisis occurred, it was my job to lead people through it. That certainly didn't mean I didn't have feelings. Of course I did. And it didn't even mean I couldn't show what I was feeling. Of course I could. Leaders are human, and it actually helps the people you lead to realize that.

What got to me was not always predictable. I would go to nine funerals and be able to handle them all, then at the tenth something would trigger a strong emotional reaction. I'd see a little boy holding his dad's helmet. A mother who had lost her only son. A brother giving a eulogy would say he had never told his brother he loved him. I would realize the emotions were welling up and I'd do my best to find some privacy and let them out. During those first couple of days, but also for the next three and a half months, I did my best to let out the sadness and anger within me during brief moments, in private.

On the Friday after September 11, Tom Von Essen approached me with a dilemma. He had lost 343 men, including many of the Fire Department's leaders. He wanted to promote people to take the place of those who were gone, but he wasn't sure it was the right time. On the one hand, he needed officers in place to run the department. On the other hand, promotions would send a signal to the survivors that we were assuming the people being replaced were gone. Many were not ready to accept that.

I agreed with him that we should go ahead, and told him to think of the promotions as field commissions. In war, when a regiment loses its officers, promotions can be made on the battlefield. I told Tom to consider it in those terms. On Sunday, September 16, we promoted 168 members of the department. We had to regroup. Five days of round-the-clock rescue work had resulted in not a single live firefighter being pulled from the wreckage. The department desperately needed structure. The 343 missing firefighters included five of the department's top officials, such as Pete Ganci, the department's highest-ranking uniformed firefighter, Ray Downey, who had led New York's team that was sent to Oklahoma City after the bombing of the Murrah Federal Building, and twelve battalion chiefs. We lost the oldest and youngest members of the department—Bill Feehan, 71, and Mike Cammarata, 22. Normally, the yearly promotion ceremony is a time for celebration. This time, it was an event of great sadness. We had no other option but to press forward. For me, that ceremony may have been the single most wrenching moment of the entire crisis. (My address from the ceremony is in the appendix.)

When it was done, I sat down and the tears just welled up. I did my best to contain them but I couldn't.

A big part of leadership is consistency—letting those who work for you and others you lead know that you'll be there for them through good times and bad. In fact, that's why on the same day as the promotion ceremony I found myself at, of all places, a wedding.

After September 11, the world was in shock. New Yorkers in particular did not feel like celebrating. Human beings have an innate need to mourn. Burying our dead is one of the oldest rituals, and grieving is part of what makes us a civilized people. The wedding I attended on September 16, however, was important not only to the morale of the city but to my own morale.

On August 28, 2001, a rookie firefighter named Michael Gorumba suffered a heart attack while battling a three-alarm blaze near his Staten Island home. I got to the hospital before he died and met Michael's mother, Gail, and his sister, Diane. It had been an exceptionally difficult year for their family. Gail's father, husband, and son had all died within ten months of one another. At the hospital, I asked Gail how she was able to handle it all. She told me that the only way to deal with the difficult times in life was to take full advantage of the joyous times. Diane's wedding was scheduled for September 16, and Gail was determined to go ahead with the event. Later, Gail told Tom Von Essen that her daughter had no one left to walk her down the aisle, and that she wanted to ask me if I'd do it, not really expecting the mayor would have the time for it. But when Tom mentioned it to me, I thought it was a great idea and was grateful to have been asked.

Of course, I didn't know then how challenging life was about to become. But a promise is a promise. And Mrs. Gorumba's advice— focusing on the positive— turned out to be helpful to me in dealing with the attacks. So, after leaving the promotion ceremony, I went to St. James Lutheran Church in Gerritsen Beach, Brooklyn. I often avoided wearing a tuxedo, sometimes going so far as putting a bow tie on a white shirt with a regular black suit. But for this wedding, I decided to take my tuxedo out and put it on in the basement of the church, and then I escorted Diane Gorumba down the aisle. Gail told me that day that she hadn't even considered postponing the wedding. Yes, there had been a tremendous amount of sadness in her life over the past year. But that's what life is, she told me—there are moments of great joy and moments of great sorrow, and you mustn't let the sorrow wash away the joy.

In a way, the wedding was a perfect opportunity to demonstrate what I'd been telling the city all week. Life must go on. At that wedding, the message got through—several fire trucks and hundreds of people from the community lined the streets. Before long, people would be using "Don't let the terrorists win" as a motivation for resuming normal activity. Back then, during the first few weeks, it was critical to remind people that their pain over what had happened was not all there was to life. We would fight those who had done this savage thing to us because we are a good people, with many joyous occasions awaiting us once the veil of tears had lifted.

On Monday, September 17, I went back to City Hall for the first time since the attacks. It was only a few blocks from the disaster site and had been badly damaged by the fallout—the phones were still out, and it was hard to breathe even inside the building. It would be weeks before government could return there permanently, but with the Stock Exchanges and many businesses about to attempt their first day open I wanted to contribute to a sense of normalcy. The meeting was more crowded than usual. I'd invited people like John Dyson, my former deputy mayor, and New York State Secretary of State Randy Daniels to advise us on economic recovery.

I had been thinking during the weekend. "Let's ask Cristyne [NYC & Company CEO Cristyne Lategano-Nicholas] to take a look at tourism projections. My sense is that the city's going to be very crowded during the holidays. Some people will stay away scared, but far more will come, to make a statement. And let's discourage traffic right now. If someone calls to ask for help with bringing in fifty buses from wherever, tell them what we really need is for you to bring those people in three months from now."

Bob Harding reported that the U.N. wanted its representatives to tour the site. I had already decided that as many people as possible should see Ground Zero, so the image in all its horror burned into their memory. Mike Hess said that law firms had been calling to offer pro bono services to the victims' families; I told him to check out their reputations before we allowed them into the Family Center. Geoff Hess mentioned that the city had already supplied 750 million square feet of office space to displaced companies.

I walked to Wall Street to open the New York Stock Exchange. The streets were closed to private vehicles, and by walking instead of driving I was showing the city that it wasn't such a hardship. On the way over, Tony Carbonetti recalled a scene from a few days earlier: a group of Con Ed guys had been looking for a gas leak when Sunny Mindel lit up a cigarette.

We passed St. Paul's Chapel, the place George Washington prayed after being inaugurated as the first President of the United States. I pointed out the building in which George Washington was inaugurated. "This was the first capital of the United States. All those buildings are in the Wall Street area. In addition to being the financial capital of the United States, it houses some of the most important monuments to our liberty, our democracy." We were walking on the same streets George Washington walked. There were armed vehicles all around and checkpoints manned by soldiers with M-16s. But the streets were still there and we were on our way to reopen the American economy.

At the Stock Exchange, the morning bell rang for the first time in six days. The market was down that day, but the fact that it opened, was orderly, and "only" plunged 684 points showed how resilient the city and country were. As Floyd Norris put it in the next day's *New York Times*, "Never before has a day in which the stock market tumbled so far seemed like a good day."

After the Stock Exchange, I headed to the New York Mercantile Exchange. Because it is located just northwest of the World Trade Center towers, the NYMEX suffered many casualties in the attacks. Throughout the crisis, I tried hard whenever I spoke to add context to my words. I didn't want to issue simple homilies about how strong we were or clichés about how we'd overcome. It was crucial to tell people what was at stake, what had been lost, and why we had been attacked. At the same time, people needed strength from their leaders. So instead of simply saying, "Let's get back to normal!" I tried to explain why that was important.

I told the traders, "This part of New York is the financial capital of our city, our state, our nation, and the world. It provides the resources for most of the growth for the rest of the world. We need you to continue doing what you're doing. Not that I understand what that is [one of the traders shouted "Neither do we!"]. But it's enormously important to the growth of our economy. It's important to the ability of the American economic system. That's the philosophical underpinning of the American political system: the idea that Americans will make choices about their lives, rather than having a totalitarian system determine it for them. The economic system is just as important as our political system."

Then the phones started ringing, traders started buying and selling futures, and after six days of silence, business at the NYMEX started to sound like it should.

Historically, the positions of New York governor and mayor of New York City often created conflicts. That's true even when both belonged to the same political party—the interests of the city and the rest of New York State are not always aligned (or perceived to be aligned). When he was governor, President Roosevelt pushed Jimmy Walker out as mayor, though both men were Democrats. Mayor Lindsay and Governor Rockefeller, both Republicans, were adversaries, as were Governor Cuomo and Mayor Koch, each of whom ran for the other's job. So it is perhaps not surprising that many thought George and I had difficulties. In truth, as Republicans our philosophies were remarkably similar and we agreed on most issues. By this point we had gotten well beyond my earlier support of Mario Cuomo in the 1994 election. George supported me in my 1997 reelection campaign and I supported him when he ran for reelection the following year.

Our relationship was cemented in 2000 when I was wrestling with the decision over what cancer treatment to pursue at the same time as I was contemplating whether to press on with a run for the Senate. I called George on the Friday that I announced I was dropping out of the race, to explain my reasons. Without hesitation, he told me he completely understood my need to focus on my health. He said, "Why don't you come up to my house over the weekend? Libby and I would like to spend some time with you, just talking."

The next day, I went to his house in Garrison, right on the Hudson. We had lunch and drinks and talked and talked, and that's really when we became close. He's a man with a big heart, who understands how to relate to people outside of politics. In a way, our relationship was best summarized by a skit we did on *Saturday Night Live,* in which we kidded each other about whether people meant the city or the state when they spoke about "New York."

Before September 11, George and I probably had the most constructive relationship between a mayor and governor in recent New York history. But as soon as the attacks occurred, we wordlessly formed an unshakable partnership. We never sat down and decided to do so—it just happened. Within hours of the first attack, I think we both realized that there couldn't be separation of any kind—the city needed the state, the state needed the city. A lot of times, whatever tension that did exist came from our staffs. They were bright, competitive people and very protective of their principals. George and I realized—again, without having to say this out loud to each other—that if we sat at meetings together, then our staffs would work with each other, rather than devising different agendas in different buildings. I thought the Governor was heroic in the way he responded, compassionate and kind. Further, he always put the interests of New York City first, seeing our interactions as a partnership, and he never attempted to pull rank.

Even more than usual, I used the morning meetings to organize city government. We simply expanded the number and size of them as needed. My staff would hold our regular meeting at seven A.M. in a small, secured office on Pier 92. After an hour or so, we would head upstairs to a large room at the pier that had been equipped with about a dozen long tables set up in a rectangle. From fifty to one hundred people attended those daily meetings, from all the city agencies, with additional representatives from state and federal agencies. Guests included many members of Congress, foreign leaders, Attorney General John Ashcroft, FBI Director Robert Mueller, and the Reverend Jesse Jackson. When needed, we would hold extra evening "morning" meetings. I managed the entire crisis this way. The mayor and governor and other decision-makers weren't hiding—we were exposed to anyone who needed an answer. These open, transparent forums not only cut through the insulation, they also encouraged those present to go back to their own agencies and make decisions without hiding from people.

At the morning meetings between early September and the end of December—sometimes three or four per day—we made literally thousands of decisions. Many of these were of a basic, keep-the-city-running kind. One day I told the group that I'd seen people within the perimeter taking photos or selling trinkets and that I wanted to devise a plan to challenge credentials and control the site. Another day we discussed how to handle a request to film Ground Zero by Al-Jazeera, the Qatar-based satellite news channel of the Arab world (we agreed to it, under conditions). We created procedures to expedite the issuance of death certificates to family members, and hundreds of lawyers volunteered to help with the paperwork. We came up with the idea for job fairs to help those who had lost their jobs. We contemplated the morale of the recovery workers. And each day we'd go over the numbers, taking pains to craft accurate lists of those dead and identified, dead and unidentified, or those plain missing. We tabulated the visitors to the Family Center so we could be sure to have enough resources in place, and the Police Department prepared its usual weekly report, supplemented with categories specifically for World Trade Center data, such as "Total NYPD injuries" (on October 11, it was 1,143), "Unidentified body parts" (6,132), and Death Certificate applications (1,533). With each challenge that we handled, we realized how effective we could be as a team.

New Yorkers are particularly adept at rallying in a crisis. Perhaps because of the city's size and complexity, it sometimes takes a really big event before New Yorkers show how strong they are. The bigger the challenge, the more they rise to the occasion, which actually makes it easier to lead.

At the morning meeting on Wednesday, September 19, Sunny Mindel mentioned that someone had suggested the city might want to take an ad thanking everyone for going back to work. Tom Von Essen erupted. "No way! We're through thanking. People should come to work. They don't need to be thanked. There are thousands of families suffering because they've lost someone who can no longer come to work. If you have to be thanked for showing up, stay home."

On September 24, I went to Marine Park, in east Brooklyn, to attend the funeral of Lt. Timothy Stackpole. Tim had five kids and a terrific wife, Tara, and I'd gotten to know him after a 1998 blaze that had badly burned him and killed two of his fellow firefighters. When I got to the hospital after that fire, he told me his mother had always warned him to put clean underwear on, but he'd forgotten to do so that day. Not only could he laugh just a few hours after nearly dying, he was determined to work his way back to active duty and did exactly that. Being at Tim's funeral alongside hundreds of devastated firefighters, with their white gloves and broken hearts, was very difficult. And the knowledge that there were more than 300 other firefighters who had died, and thousands of others, was unbearable.

Flying in the helicopter after the funeral, I saw a man standing alone, casting lures from the banks of one of the channels by the Rockaways. People don't necessarily associate Brooklyn with natural beauty and tranquillity, but the image of this man standing by himself provided a stark contrast to the tumult and sadness that had consumed the city over the past two weeks. Suddenly I had a desire to go fishing. Just to sit out there with a pole. But I know myself, and I know I don't have the patience. After ten minutes, I'd be wondering, "Where are those fish?" I realized I was crying a little. A minute later, I was fast asleep, right there in the earsplitting helicopter. I was awakened when my head hit the window as we landed on Manhattan's West Side.

* * *

On Friday, September 28, we found some of Terry Hatton's equipment. When I got the news, I was attending a funeral and was later due at a memorial service at St. Patrick's Cathedral for Marsh & McLennan employees. Earlier, the Medical Examiner, Charles Hirsch, had called me into his office to help identify Terry. I called Beth Petrone. In what can only be called a miracle, Beth had discovered she was pregnant only days after Terry was killed. On this particular day, she was uptown with her sister, Karen Malin; they were at her doctor's office. I thought St. Patrick's would be a good place to talk to her. I said, "Beth, on your way out of the doctor's, why don't you and Karen stop off at St. Patrick's?" I met her in the conference room behind the altar, and told her that I had found Terry. I told Beth that the DNA matching had yet to be performed, but that we should go over to his firehouse to see if we could get more items to assist in the identification. We went over to Rescue 1 together and talked to Terry's brother firefighters, showing them what we'd found and where we'd found it. When I left her and got back in the van, I couldn't contain my tears.

Now that the guys from Rescue 1 knew exactly where Terry's things had been found, they went back to that area to search for Terry's body. I was in Staten Island at a mass with Tom Von Essen when I got a call telling me that Terry had been located, along with more of his tools and some papers from his wallet. To Tom, Terry Hatton was not just a particularly talented and courageous firefighter, or just the husband of someone we all loved. Terry had also been Tom's neighbor from the time he was a kid. He used to baby-sit Tom's kids. Tom watched him grow up. Tom and I helicoptered to meet the M.E. and identify Terry.

For the first weeks after September 11, I had a pattern. I was spending nights at Howard Koeppel's apartment. I'd get in late and, if I wasn't too exhausted, shower. I barely slept. I would piece together what were essentially naps—forty-five minutes or an hour, always with the television on. Even if I was reading, I had it on, and I don't normally watch much. And always with my clothes laid out, ready for me to dress in two minutes. This pattern continued for about three months.

The only times I would feel myself relaxing were at sporting events—at my son's freshman football games on Saturday mornings, at Yankee games, and at a Jets game I went to with my daughter, Caroline. At some of Andrew's games, I was only able to stay for one half before rushing off, often to a funeral or another emergency. But for those few minutes I could surrender to the pleasure of watching my son play football. The world seemed innocent again, and I could almost believe that life would return to a time in which high school kids thought more about touchdowns and girlfriends than terrorists flying planes into buildings.

As for baseball, the first home games played by New York's two teams were unbelievably uplifting. As people packed into a public place to watch our nation's pastime, Shea Stadium and Yankee Stadium felt like places of spiritual worship more than sports arenas. The teams themselves seemed to sense how important they were to the morale of the city. After a difficult first half, the Mets began a late-season push that fell just short of taking them into the playoffs. Without anyone asking them to, the Mets played in hats bearing the logos of the NYPD, FDNY, and Port Authority Police Department. And the Yankees put the city on their backs, the way leaders do. At ballparks throughout the country, fans responded—at Comiskey Park, for example, fans held up a sign I never thought I'd see when the Yankees visited: "Chicago Loves New York." In the first round of the playoffs, the Yankees battled back from being down two games to none to beat the A's three games to two; Joe Torre took me out to the mound for the celebration and gave me a cigar. Then in the American League Championship Series they took on the Seattle Mariners, who had set the modern record for wins in a single season and won.

All New York remembers losing in the bottom of the ninth inning of Game 7 of the World Series, but the Yankees provided a memorable season—just when the city needed it most.

When I went to Arizona for Game 6 of the World Series—Saturday, November 3—I was hoping the Yankees would wrap it up, so I could fly back to start the New York Marathon the following morning. Traipsing through all five boroughs, it's a great event, attracting over 30,000 participants from all over the world. More than ever, the unity and symbolism of the race represented the endurance and spirit the city had shown in recovering so quickly. Instead, the Diamondbacks pounded my beloved Bronx Bombers 15–2, to tie the series at three games apiece. I had Andrew and Caroline with me and I figured we'd stay in Arizona for Game 7 of what was already one of the greatest World Series in history. I was beginning to look forward to a day off—maybe golfing with Andrew and taking Caroline to see some of the sights in Phoenix. I love Arizona. Almost anytime I was invited to anything in Arizona, I'd say yes. I grew up on Westerns and something about seeing cacti and all that desert really gets to me.

During the eighth inning of Game 6, I was handed a cell phone. It was Health Commissioner Neal Cohen. He told me that I should find a landline before he went any further. I know that's never good news. I went to an office inside Bank One Ballpark and Neal told me they had found anthrax on a videocassette box that someone in Tom Brokaw's office at NBC had sent over to my Chief of Staff, Tony Carbonetti. After anthrax had been found at NBC and elsewhere, I had quietly asked for our offices to be swept, and now these results had come back. Anthrax had gotten inside City Hall, into Tony's office—about twenty feet from my downstairs office.

I decided to fly back overnight, start the New York Marathon on Sunday morning, fly to Arizona in the afternoon, catch the game that evening, then return to the city in time to be at work by Monday's morning meeting. That would give me time to make sure the anthrax situation was under control—the last thing the city needed was an image of City Hall shutting its doors. So that's what I did. People thought I was crazy, but the truth is that I actually got more sleep on the plane trips than I'd had for weeks. The same was true in early December, when I joined Governor Pataki and Mayor-elect Bloomberg on a trip to Jerusalem, to show solidarity after the suicide bombings in the Ben-Yehuda pedestrian mall and the Sbarro pizzeria. As busy as I was during my last month as mayor, I thought it vital to support Israel, Jerusalem, and its mayor, my personal friend Ehud Olmert. Among the first to call me after September 11 were Prime Minister Sharon and Mayor Olmert. They offered any help they could, but even more, they offered a tremendous example of daily heroism—how to go ahead with life in the face of constant threat. And again, the flight to Israel and back afforded a rare opportunity to reflect—and to sleep.

On October 11, we held a memorial at Ground Zero to commemorate one month since the attacks. It was still too dangerous for regular citizens to visit. This was an intimate gathering for the rescue and recovery workers who had been toiling amid the piles of rubble, pulling out a friend here, a colleague there. It was exhausting and sad work. That so many good people had died was extremely tough to accept, but what was even worse was that all of this had been done on purpose. These body parts and bloodstains weren't the product of some colossal accident. They were evidence of a massive terrorist attack on the United States of America.

At the memorial, Rabbi Joseph Potasnik gave perspective to that reality. "The eye is composed of light and dark," he observed. "But you only see from the dark part."

Later that morning, Saudi Prince Alwaleed Bin Talal, one of the richest men in the world, was scheduled to come to Ground Zero. We had established a procedure for me to take people on tours of the site. They were first cleared by the White House and the State Department. The idea was to reserve my time for those who the administration thought were valuable to take there. Officially, we wanted to build support for our foreign policy. My view was that I was taking people to get them angry. I wanted them to see the horror of what happened and support what America needed to do to defend itself.

We consulted with the White House and the State Department about whether we should take the Prince there. We were advised that we should, because he was generally friendly to the United States, someone who had an open mind. The hope was that the site might have an effect on him and make him more favorably disposed to the actions we were going to take against Bin Laden and Afghanistan.

I had seven wakes and funerals to attend that day, for six firefighters and a cop: Firefighter Robert Parro, Fire Lt. Edward D'Atri in Staten Island, Lt. Stephen G. Harrell, Firefighter Carl E. Molinaro, Firefighter Jeffrey Olsen, Firefighter Joseph Mascali, and Police Officer Walter E. Weaver. I got into the helicopter to head to Long Island for the funeral of one of the firefighters and as soon as I boarded said aloud: "Jeez, I hope we're supporting the right guy. It's so hard to tell with all these factions."

In the month since the attack, I had accompanied many world leaders to the site. Without exception, seeing Ground Zero up close overpowered them, as it had me. When the German chancellor, Gerhard Schroeder, visited, he had tears in his eyes. Jacques Chirac, Tony Blair, and Vladimir Putin all were devastated—Putin whispered, as if to himself, "This could happen in Moscow."

When Prince Alwaleed arrived he was wearing an opulent gold robe and headdress, along with seven or eight aides in black robes. He gave me a cashier's check for $10 million, for the Twin Towers Fund. Looking at the site from the small podium, the Prince was saying the right things. He discussed how badly he felt and that he wanted to help the victims. He thanked me for my leadership and congratulated me on rallying the spirits of the people of the city. But something wasn't quite right. I thought there was a smirk to his face, which seemed to carry over to his entourage. He was the only visitor who was unmoved by what he saw. Despite my discomfort, I thought, "It's probably just me." I wondered if it weren't some latent cultural misunderstanding, but I didn't think so; that wasn't like me. And as angry and sad as I was, I'd been trying so hard to advise against succumbing to stereotypes. So I dismissed my discomfort and went to the first funeral.

Afterward, I got a call from Sunny. She told me that after I left Ground Zero, the Prince's entourage had passed out a press release calling the attack a "tremendous crime" and explaining that he'd made a $10 million contribution to the Twin Towers Fund. But his press release didn't stop there. "We must address some of the issues that led to such a criminal attack," Alwaleed's statement said. "I believe the government of the United States of America should reexamine its policies in the Middle East and adopt a more balanced stance toward the Palestinian cause."

My first reaction was to give the money back. I wasn't going to let anyone use a donation to a fund for the families of the victims as a way to criticize the U.S. government. Making the case that the attacks on the Trade Center were justified, or even understandable, was not a point of view I could accept. Nothing the United States has or has not done could possibly warrant what happened on September 11. Indeed, I believe that the moral equivalency theory helped to create the climate in which the attacks took place. Suppose we did change, say, our foreign policy to accommodate their demands. Then what? Should we stop allowing women to vote? Forbid the free exercise of whatever religion one chooses to practice?

We have to get through our heads that these attacks were different from a dispute over land or trade. These attacks were aimed at the ideals America stands for, the very things that make American democracy what it is. The murderous terrorists—and those who support them—are plain wrong, and we have to be confident about saying that.

Which of the seven men whose lives were memorialized that day deserved their fate? Lieutenant D'Atri, who coached his son's Staten Island Little League team, the Sal-Mar Studios Expos? How about Carl Molinaro, who was married four years earlier, after proposing via a sign pulled behind a small plane that said, "Donna, will you marry me?" Then there was Officer Weaver, who a few years earlier rescued a dog from a man he arrested for animal cruelty. He named that dog "Midnight." Were the terrorists justified in killing him?

Then I thought, "Wait a second, this is not my money. This is ten million dollars for the families of the firefighters and police officers." But in my heart, I still thought the right response was to reject the donation. I called Tom and Bernie and discussed it. Both had lost many comrades. Then I asked Beth Petrone, because I wanted a sense of how the wife of a firefighter would feel. The reaction from all three was that nobody would want the donation. They considered it tainted.

I rejected the donation. I put out a statement explaining my reasons, and after I did so, many victims' family members told me they were glad. A surprising number of them used the same phrase: "We don't want his blood money." Not a single person ever came up to me and said I should have kept it.

Later that same day, a group of advertising executives came to see me at City Hall. John Wren, CEO of Omnicom, led a team from BBDO into the Committee of the Whole room. John had been a good friend for some time. A couple of days earlier, I had asked him to come up with a campaign that would capture the message that the city was open to visitors. Everywhere I went, people were telling me, "I came to New York City because I saw you on television asking us to come." I thought if I could reach all the people who didn't watch television press conferences, we'd be able to lure even more people to town.

John and his team—which included Phil Dusenberry, who did much of the creative work for President Reagan's 1984 reelection effort, including the "Morning in America" campaign—had developed an idea that encompassed three themes. New York City has the best people, great places, and the "spirit of New York." They told me the tag line—"The New York Miracle. Be a Part of It"—then explained the campaign, acting out the parts accompanied by a small boom box. The idea was that well-known New York personalities would excel at unexpected things. An ice skater performing wizardry at Rockefeller Center turns out to be Woody Allen, Barbara Walters auditions for a musical, Yogi Berra conducts the symphony (and wonders, "Who the heck is this guy Phil Harmonic?"). The idea was perfect. It captured the soul of the city, the idea that people come to New York to fulfill their dreams. That's been true for hundreds of years. These clever, winning ads made the point that the spirit of New York would endure.

Another of the ads BBDO pitched to me was to feature an older gentleman running the bases at Yankee Stadium. After he slides into home, the cloud of dust reveals Henry Kissinger saying, "Derek who?" The ad people weren't sure Dr. Kissinger would go for it, but I was certain he would. Henry's a big baseball fan and an even bigger Yankee supporter. More than that, it would be on behalf of the city in which his own dreams had been fulfilled. When I brought Henry Kissinger to Ground Zero, he told me it was worse than anything he'd seen in Berlin after World War II.

All the people who worked on those ads donated their time. John Wren not only devoted his company to creating the ads in record time, he also persuaded the networks to air them either free or at greatly reduced cost. It was exactly that spirit—the spirit that flooded New York City with so many volunteers that we couldn't find work for all of them to do—that BBDO captured so beautifully.

It's hard to explain exactly how much St. Paul's Chapel means to me, because of both its history and its role in my own life. It is hallowed ground, consecrated as a house of God in 1766, and is New York City's longest continually functioning building. In April 1789, George Washington walked there along Broadway and prayed in the chapel after being inaugurated as the first President of the republic. There's a plaque to memorialize the pew he prayed in and an original painting of the Great Seal of the United States.

In the 1970s, when I started pursuing my interest in photography, I used to go to the graveyard behind the chapel to take pictures of the World Trade Towers. In the eighties, when I was U.S. Attorney, my office on the 8th floor had a strange, triangular shape to it. I couldn't see all the way down Broadway, but I had a clear view of St. Paul's. Faced with excruciating moral decisions—should I go easy on this guy, should that guy be indicted—I would stand and look at the chapel and be inspired by the thought of God's enduring presence in our city and country.

On September 11, the damage reached as far away as City Hall to the north and Battery Park City to the south, several blocks farther from the point of impact than St. Paul's. The chapel not only remained standing, but not a single window was broken, not a brick out of place. The place where George Washington prayed when he first became President of the United States stood strong, untouched.

I thought St. Paul's the perfect place to say my farewell as mayor. I have explained how at the time of my appointment the city was desperately in need of an infusion of spirit. More than any single thing, it was the attitude of the average New Yorker that needed improvement. I was more successful in some areas than others. After September 11, my belief that leadership matters—that who is chosen to lead and how he or she does so truly makes a difference—only deepened.

My last day was December 31, 2001. I was scheduled to leave for Florida for a short vacation before I re-entered the private realm to launch my consulting business, Giuliani Partners. I drove myself to work in a Police Department Humvee. For my last morning meeting, I began by thanking my staff for their excellent work. They know how I feel about them, so I didn't make a big deal out of it or deliver a long speech. "Our goal was to serve the people of New York City. Not ourselves, and not each other. I very much appreciate that service. We had a chance to prove ourselves after September 11th. Every single one of us passed that test. You did an absolutely great job on the worst day of the history of this city. You showed personal bravery and integrity. I thank you all." Then we got to work. If they hadn't been meeting with me every single day at eight A.M., some of my staff might have thought I'd take it easy on my final morning. Instead, Bob Harding discussed the two last-minute options for completing a deal we were trying to get signed with the New York Stock Exchange. Adam Barsky gave us projected tax revenues for the coming three years. Tom Von Essen frisked Paul "Hollywood" Sheirer, Richie's 11-year-old son who had shown up for the meeting. Bernie gave the final crime numbers for the year, and mentioned that on the official form for contact information — in case a successor needed to reach us — he had written "unemployed" in the space for business phone. Tony Coles brought up the idea of a memorandum of understanding with the Jets, indicating support for a West Side football stadium. When it was Denny's turn at the table, he said, "Good run."

The meeting broke up and I walked downstairs to my office. Almost all my effects were packed — the hundreds of baseball caps and other mementos. I left only my most personal stuff to carry myself, in a beat-up brown attaché case that dates back to my days as an assistant U.S. Attorney: my police badge with five stars on it, the medal I got for going into the 1992 fire at St. Agnes Church, a couple of particularly sentimental photographs. Then I left. I drove the Humvee through the narrow streets of Lower Manhattan to the New York Stock Exchange, where I rang the closing bell on the last day of the year and the last day of my mayoralty.

On January 1, right after attending Mike Bloomberg's inauguration, I went to Ground Zero — just to walk around with Judith, with no reporters or dignitaries or politicians. I wanted it to be the last place I visited before I left. I had been there hundreds of times in the three and a half months since the attacks. And yet, walking around the site that day, I felt tremendous anger, as raw and intense as when

I first saw the smoldering pile on September 11. Part of leadership is harnessing your passions in a way that serves your goals—my father's advice: stay calm. But another part of leadership is retaining your humanity. The anger I felt, and continue to feel, about the attacks on the World Trade Center is healthy. The challenge was to put it to work in ways that would make me a stronger, better leader.

Appendix A:
Before and After

The numbers tell a compelling story of how the leadership ideas in this book transformed life in New York City from 1994 through 2001.

PUBLIC SAFETY

In addition to reducing murder by two-thirds, overall crime fell by 57 percent, and shootings by 75 percent. There were nearly 1,200 fewer rapes in 2000 than in 1993, and police shooting incidents fell from 212 to 73. Robbery fell from 85,883 to 32,213. Burglary tumbled from 100,933 to 38,155, while auto theft plummeted from 111,611 to 35,673. The crime decline was citywide. In 1993, there were 92 murders in Crown Heights and 35 in Harlem. By 2000, those numbers were 35 and 5.

Emergency response time fell from 8:36 to 7:30—a minute that saved lives.

There was a miraculous 93 percent reduction in inmate-on-inmate violence in the city's jails. The television program *60 Minutes* visited the system's signature facility, Rikers Island, in 1991 and reported, "In 1990, there were more than 2,500 violent incidents at Rikers. Blood is a common sight." In January 2001, *60 Minutes* revisited the jail. This time, they reported, "Last year there were just 70 inmate slashings and stabbings—a dramatic drop compared to the more than 1,000 such incidents a decade ago."

In 1999, New York City analyzed more than twice as many DNA samples as the FBI.

Mandated zero-tolerance for drunk drivers resulted in the forfeiture of 4,000 cars.

Implementation of extensive anti-gun initiatives took 90,000 illegal guns off the street.

Organized crime was removed from key industries such as trash carting and food distribution, resulting in the effective repeal of the "mob tax." This saved local businesses approximately $600 million a year—equivalent to the largest tax cut in city history.

ECONOMIC DEVELOPMENT

Times Square revitalization included new projects and buildings such as the Disney Company, Morgan Stanley, Madame Tussaud, Condé Nast, and the Durst Company. NASDAQ headquarters relocated from Washington, D.C., to a state-of-the-art Times Square facility near a brand-new ESPNZone, MTV Studio, ABC Studio, and a WWF-themed restaurant.

More than 200 new businesses opened in Harlem between 1994 and 2001. The $300 million Harlem USA project includes well-known retailers such as Magic Johnson Theaters, HMV Music, the Gap, and New York Sports Club. Other projects included the neighborhood's first large supermarket, a mixed-use retail and office building on Lexington Avenue between East 125th and 126th Street, and the development of the West 116th Street Corridor.

New minor-league baseball parks opened in Brooklyn and Staten Island.

The Hunts Point Food Distribution Center opened in the Bronx, home to 14,500 jobs and approximately 750 businesses.

In 1994, there was not a single Home Depot—or big box store of any kind—in New York City. By 2001, there were more than a dozen.

Forty-one Business Improvement Districts developed throughout the City since 1994.

Jamaica Center, an $80 million project in Queens, will provide 500,000 square feet of mixed-use retail and entertainment space.

AOL Time Warner Headquarters at Columbus Circle will include a five-star hotel, retail, commercial, and residential space, and a new state-of-the-art facility for Jazz at Lincoln Center.

At the Brooklyn Army Terminal, renovation of approximately 2.6 million square feet of space now houses 70 tenants and employs 3,000 workers.

Digital NYC leased space to more than 80 growing businesses in 1 million square feet of space on sites in Harlem, Long Island City, the Brooklyn Navy Yard, Staten Island, and the Bronx.

Staten Island Corporate Park, a 400-acre property, includes the first hotel to be built on Staten Island in 25 years.

Renaissance Plaza, a new Marriott Hotel and office building, is the first new hotel in Brooklyn in 50 years.

Gateway Center and Gotham Plaza include two new buildings on 125th Street in Harlem—a combined 130,000 square feet of retail and office space.

In 2000, *Fortune* magazine named New York City the No. 1 place for business in North America—the second time in four years that New York has captured the coveted title.

Between 1990 and 1993, New York City lost 350,000 private-sector jobs; unemployment was 10.2 percent. From January 1994 through 2000, New York City posted its strongest seven-year job gain on record, creating more than 485,000 new private-sector jobs. By the end of 2000, the city's unemployment rate had fallen to under 6 percent. In October 2001, one month after the terrorist attack on the World Trade Center, the city's unemployment rate stood at 6.3 percent, nearly four full points lower than when I took office.

SOCIAL POLICY

- Began reforming New York City's welfare system two years ahead of federal reform efforts. Cut welfare rolls by approximately 60 percent, reducing the public-assistance caseload from more than 1.1 million in 1995 to below 500,000 in 2001—the lowest number of people on welfare since 1966.

- Transformed Welfare Offices into Job Centers, creating 27 facilities citywide. The city placed 151,376 welfare recipients with jobs in fiscal year 2001—more than ten times the 9,215 welfare recipients matched with jobs in fiscal year 1993.

- Introduced eligibility, verification, and review programs to guard against fraud and abuse.

- Instituted the Work Experience Program, in which 330,000 disadvantaged New Yorkers have earned benefits and gained work experience while performing important labor for the city.

- Reformed key elements of the city's homeless-assistance program; under the Employment Incentive Housing Program, helped homeless New Yorkers find permanent housing in the private market by providing rent-payment help for two years while the recipient becomes self-sufficient.

- Redesigned the city's subsidized child-care program to establish a single system for all eligible families, with continuity of child care as parents leave welfare for work.

EDUCATION

During the eight years of my administration, funding for the largest public school system (1.1 million schoolchildren) in the nation increased from $8 billion to $12 billion.

- Introduced Project Read, a $125 million annual investment in intensive reading training for students.
- Introduced Project Arts, a $75 million annual program that permanently restored arts education programs.
- Introduced Project Smart Schools, a $150 million program that installed more than 7,000 computers in classrooms and libraries, giving every middle school student access to a computer. Instituted a $31.5 million public-private program to fund 300-book libraries in 21,000 classrooms.
- Introduced Project Textbook, which doubled the $70 million allocated for current textbooks.
- Introduced Project Science, a $25 million program that offers special weekend science classes to eighth-grade and high school students who are in danger of falling behind in this crucial subject.
- Ended social promotion and expanded summer school.
- Restored over 50 high school athletic fields through the public-private partnership "Take the Field."
- Created the nation's first and most generous Charter School Fund to encourage educational opportunity.
- Abolished tenure for principals and established a system of performance-based pay.

Full-time teachers, 1993: $66,530
Full-time teachers, 2000: $79,924

Student-teacher ratio, 1993: 15.3:1
Student-teacher ratio, 2000: 13.8:1

CULTURAL AFFAIRS

Under my administration, the city gave more generously to its cultural institutions than even the National Endowment for the Arts, which funds organizations nationwide. In 2001, New York City contributed $134 million for operating and program costs, compared to the NEA's entire annual budget of $105 million.

Commitments of $240 million to Lincoln Center's $1.5 billion capital master plan, $40 million to Metropolitan Museum of Art improvements and renovation, $65 million to the expansion of the Museum of Modern Art, $26 million to the New York Botanical Garden in the Bronx, and $33 million for New York Aquarium redevelopment at Coney Island are just some of many examples of the city's investment in culture.

Completed projects were too numerous for a complete list, but included the Congo Gorilla Forest Exhibit at the Wildlife Conservation Society/Bronx Zoo, the New York Public Library's Science, Industry and Business Library, Alvin Ailey Dance Headquarters, the New York City Police Museum, the Heckscher Theater at El Museo del Barrio, and the Center for Jewish History.

Successfully lobbied the state legislature to remove the 4 percent sales tax on film and television production consumables (in 1996) and on consumables for theater production (in 1998).

CHILDREN'S SERVICES

- 21,000 adoptions during fiscal years 1996-2001, a 65 percent increase over the previous six-year record.
- Removed the Child Welfare Administration as a branch of HRA and created the Administration for Children's Services, the city's first independent child-welfare agency.
- Hired more than 1,700 new caseworkers and raised hiring standards and salaries.
- Implemented HealthStat, a program designed to identify children eligible for health insurance but not covered by any plan. From its launch in June 2000 through the end of 2001, HealthStat enrolled more than 150,000 adults and children in Child Health Plus and Medicaid.
- The foster-care population declined from 42,000 in 1996 to 28,700 as of August 2001, marking the first time the city ever provided more children with at-home preventive services than with foster care.

Between 1992 and 2000, child support funds collected increased from $159.5 million to $403.6 million.

Adoptions, 1992: 1,784
Adoptions, 2000: 3,148

Number of cases per caseworker, 1992: 24.2
Number of cases per caseworker, 2000: 14.1

FISCAL POLICY

Twenty-three city taxes were reduced or eliminated, including the unincorporated business tax, sales tax on clothing under $110, the commercial rent tax, and six reductions in the personal income tax. These measures have saved individuals and businesses more than $8 billion cumulatively.

The overall hotel occupancy tax rate was reduced from 6 to 5 percent, beginning December 1, 1994. From fiscal 1995 though fiscal 2000, consumers paid $100 million less in hotel taxes. At the same time, hotel occupancy rose dramatically while employment in the hotel industry grew 28 percent since 1993. In fact, the city collected $112 million *more* from the hotel occupancy tax in fiscal year 2001 than in the year before the reduction was enacted.

Conservative debt and investment policies were established: the city's debt service must not exceed 15 percent of city revenue or 20 percent of tax revenue, and floating-rate bonds must not exceed 20 percent of outstanding debt.

To encourage both public fiscal discipline and private enterprise, the administration reduced taxes by a cumulative value of $8 billion between fiscal years 1994 and 2001.

The growth of city spending slowed significantly. The average annual growth of city spending was 7.4 percent in the years 1983–1990, and 4.7 percent between 1991 and 1994. In 1995, there was actually a 1.6 percent decline in annual spending, and the average rate of yearly spending growth during fiscal years 1995–2001 was 3.7 percent, resulting in savings of approximately $9.9 billion.

In fiscal year 2001 (which ended June 30, 2001), the city had a $2.9 billion surplus, and the fiscal year 2002 budget lowered spending 2.6 percent.

The city payroll was reduced by more than 20,000 full-time employees, while adding to the ranks of teachers and uniformed police.

In July 1993, New York City's credit rating from Moody's was Baa1; Standard & Poor's and Fitch both gave the city an A-. By the end of my term, the city's credit ratings were stronger than ever—up to an A2 Moody's rating, an A rating with Standard & Poor's, and an A+ Fitch rating.

City tax revenue as a share of personal income, 1993: 8.8 percent
City tax revenue as a share of personal income, 2001: 7.4 percent

QUALITY OF LIFE

City-sponsored programs built or rehabilitated 73,090 homes and apartments. There was a net gain of 62,000 housing units between 1993 and 1999. With low-interest city loans, 22,937 privately owned low-income housing units were rehabilitated. The rate of home ownership increased more than 10 percent from 1994 to 2000, even as property values rose throughout the city.

An aggressive new adult zoning law bars sex shops within 500 feet of residential neighborhoods, churches, and schools.

The number of streets rated "acceptably clean" topped 85 percent from fiscal year 1998 to fiscal year 2001.

New York City acquired 2,038 acres of new parkland—the most since the Wagner Administration of the late fifties and early sixties. (Between 1990 and 1993, New York City acquired 372 acres of new parkland.) In 1993, only 69 percent of the parks were graded acceptably clean. In 2001, 91 percent of parks enjoyed that designation. Over 100,000 new trees and 2,000 "Greenstreets" were planted from 1994 to 2001.

Many parks were created, including the Hudson River Park from Battery Park to 59th Street, the Brooklyn Bridge Park, and the seven-mile Bronx River Greenway. Many other parks were restored, including City Hall Park, Madison Square Park, Union Square Park, Foley Square, Galileo Park (the Bronx), Green Central Knoll Playground (Brooklyn), the Forest Park Bandshell (Queens), Willowbrook Carousel (Staten Island), and the revitalization of the New York City Aquarium on Coney Island.

Tourism increased from 25.8 million visitors in 1994 to 37.4 million in 2000; New York City was named the best city in the nation to visit by Zagat's, the best sports city by *The Sporting News*, and the city with the best food by both *Travel & Leisure* and a CNN/*USA Today* poll.

City-owned vacant buildings, 1994: 1,862
City-owned vacant buildings, 2000: 633

Appendix B:
The New York City Fire Department Promotion Ceremony
Sunday, September 16, 2001

We gather on the day after the New York City Fire Department laid to rest three of its legends: Chief Ganci; First Deputy Commissioner Feehan; and our beloved Father Mychal Judge. Some may wonder why we're proceeding with a promotion ceremony during such a devastating time of loss. The answer is very clear: those who were lost and missing would want us to continue. They invested their lives and their love in this department. They gave their life for it. And it's out of a sense of profound responsibility to their memory that we must go forward.

I want you to know that the prayers of every single New Yorker, and I believe every single American, are with you. Your willingness to go forward undaunted in the most difficult of circumstances is an inspiration to all of us. It sends a signal that our hearts are broken, no question about that, but our hearts continue to beat, and they beat very, very strongly. Life is going to go on. Both the life of the city and the life of the department. We have very important work to do today, tomorrow, in the months and in the years ahead.

Winston Churchill, the leader of war-torn England who saw his country through the Battle of Britain with bombings every day, once said, "Courage is rightly esteemed the first of human qualities because it's the quality which guarantees all others."

Without courage, nothing else can really happen. And there is no better example than the courage of the Fire Department of the City of New York.

In the last great attack on America, the attack on Pearl Harbor, the first casualties were the members of our United States Navy. They wore a uniform like you do. In this war, the first large casualties are being experienced by the New York City Fire Department. The Navy regrouped, it fought back, it won the Battle of Midway and it turned the tide of the battle in the Pacific, after it had been devastated. The New York City Fire Department is being re-formed today. It reminds me of battlefield commissions during a time of war.

When I was very young, one of the earliest experiences that I remember is my uncle, my mother's younger brother, who was a firefighter in Brooklyn, being seriously injured when he was thrown from a ladder truck going to a fire, which was a false alarm. He broke both his legs and they thought for a while that he had broken his back and might not be able to walk again.

My mother would take me to visit him at Kings County Hospital. He was in tremendous pain, but one of my earliest memories was his talking about wanting to go back to work. It was the thing that got him through, the thing that sustained him. He would talk about how he loved his job. And even as a 5- and 6-year-old, I could figure it out. Here was a man who had broken both his legs and maybe his back, and he wanted to go back to the work he loved. And he did. He had a long career in the Fire Department, got injured twice more, and then retired as a Captain. And he was one of my early heroes.

So you're all my heroes. You have been from the time I was a little boy, and from the day that I became the mayor of New York City. And I'm heart-broken that we have to add so many, I don't know how many, to that memorial wall back there. I had hoped that there would be no more.

But we're going to take out of our hearts being broken the determination to make this city even more secure, to show to the cowards who wanted to destroy our spirit that, yes, they've taken some of our most precious lives, but they have not taken our spirit.

The spirit of democracy is stronger than these cowardly terrorists. Countries that live under a rule of law agree on being a democracy and respect and care about human life the way the firefighters of New York City care about human life. That's what we want. That's the future we want for our children, that's the future we want for the rest of the world. It's what America has always wanted. And it's something that you embody in a way that can be an example to America.

So I would please ask you to stand and join me in a round of applause to honor the men we've lost and the men that we're still searching for.

Thank you very much and God bless you all.

Acknowledgments

"Surround Yourself with Great People" is not only the name of a chapter in this book. It's a rule I've lived by my whole life. I've been extremely fortunate to find many, many great people to count on during my career. The City of New York employs some 250,000 at any given time. Of course I didn't personally know all of these people, but with very few exceptions, they earned my gratitude. Most could have chosen more lucrative careers outside the public sector. The same is true of the lawyers I worked with during two tours in the Justice Department and two stints in the U.S. Attorney's office. And then there are hundreds of family, friends, teachers, mentors, colleagues, partners, and even rivals, all of whom helped to develop my thinking about leadership.

Blessed with so many in my life, I undoubtedly omitted dozens of their names here. I apologize to those good people.

My first debt of gratitude is owed to my family. My parents, Harold and Helen Giuliani, their only living sibling and my hero, my Uncle Rudy, my many uncles, aunts, and cousins, my children, Andrew and Caroline. And of course, the special person in my life, Judith Nathan.

I wrote this book with Ken Kurson. But more than that, Ken helped me to analyze and understand even better the principles of leadership I had utilized throughout my life. He became a good friend and in the days after September 11 was by my side day after day and became a trusted and valued member of our team.

Throughout my school days, from elementary school through law school, many of my teachers and classmates left a lasting impression. The De La Salle Christian Brothers at Bishop Loughlin and Manhattan College, Brother Aloysius Kevin, Brother Gabriel Joseph, Brother Peter Bonventre, Irving Younger, Steve Hoffman, and Jiri Hovak all helped nurture my love of learning.

I have been privileged to answer to many terrific leaders. My first boss, Judge Lloyd MacMahon, taught me as much about leadership—and about life—as anyone. Presidents Ronald Reagan and Gerald Ford, William French Smith, Paul Curran, Mike Seymour, Harold Tyler, and Edward Levi all influenced me greatly.

I've worked with some amazing lawyers. No, really. Among the terrific attorneys I've had the pleasure of working alongside, in the U.S. Attorney's office, the Justice Department, and in private practice: Michael Mukasey, Bill Simon, Benito Romano, Jane Parver, Bob Paterson, Bob Potter, John Gross, Renee Szybala, Ken Caruso, David Denton, Jim Duff, Jay Waldman, James Rather, Howard Heiss, Mike Chertoff, Bill Schwartz, David Zornow, Jon Sale, Togo West, and Joel Carr.

As mayor, my staff was my second family. I am grateful for the contributions of all my Deputy Mayors: Peter Powers, Randy Levine, Joe Lhota, Fran Reiter, John Dyson, Rudy Washington, Tony Coles, Randy Mastro, Bob Harding, and Ninfa Segarra. All of us were joined at the morning meeting by Denny Young, Tony Carbonetti, Paul Crotty, Bruce Teitelbaum, Cristyne Lategano-Nicholas, Sunny Mindel, Tom Von Essen, Bernie Kerik, Richie Sheirer, Howard Safir, Bill Bratton, Larry Levy, Howard Wilson, Ed Kuriansky, Beth Petrone-Hatton, Kate Anson, Colleen Roche, Adam Barsky, Joe Rose, Mike Hess, Geoff Hess, Neal Cohen, Steve Fishner, Abe Lackman, Marc Shaw, and Nick Scoppetta.

My commissioners and agency heads served the city with

distinction. I join New York City in thanking Iris Weinshall, Jason Turner, Ray Casey, Rosemarie O'Keefe, Lou Carbonetti, Henry Stern, Jerry Cammarata, Michael Carey, Matthew Daus, Chris Lynn, Bill Diamond, Kevin Farrell, Bill Fraser, Tino Hernandez, Ken Holden, Richard Roberts, Richard Schwartz, Patricia Reed Scott, Herbert Stupp, Charles Hirsch, Marta Varela, Jane Hoffman, Schuyler Chapin, Joel Miele, Diane McGrath-McKechnie, Raul Russi, Jennifer Raab, James Hanley, Frederick Patrick, Jerilyn Perine, George Rios, Andrew Eristoff, and Martin Oesterreich.

Others in city government merit mention, including Joe Dunne, Joe Esposito, Eric Hatzimemos, Josh Filler, Fipp Avlon, Jerry Hauer, Matt Higgins, Carrie Karabelas, Marcia Lee, Tamra Lhota, Manny Papir, Jake Menges, Jack Maple, and Louis Anemone. I'm particularly thankful to the police who protected me over the years, including Beau Wagner, Patti Varrone, Freddy Garcia, Richard Godfrey, Billy O'Gara, John Huvane, Timmy Wilson, Teddy Samothrakis, Barry Brisacone, Stanley Ko, Sergio Conde, Willy Varella, Tibor Kerekes, James Feeley, Robert Reekie, Michae DiBenedetto, Angel Matos, Steve Bavolar, Eddie Castellar, Gerard Dragonetti, John Fleming, Billy Gleason, Michael Aponte, and Eric Deane.

I'm joined in various business pursuits by many wonderful people. Some of their names: Brad Grey, Jon Liebman, Harvey Weinstein, Mike Rudell, Eric Brown, Jonathan Burnham, Susan Mercandetti, Richard Cohen, Rebecca Myers, Timothy White, JillEllyn Riley, Kristin Powers, Devereux Chatillon, Kathy Schneider, Hilary Bass, Roy Bailey, Dan Connolly, John Wren, Julie Mendik, Janna Mancini, Sheila Gallagher, Ryan Medrano, Jay Weinkam, Matt Mahoney, Jackie Brisacone, Karen Malin, Ann Printon, Debbie Kurtz, Marc Von Essen, and Maureen Casey.

I'm blessed to have many terrific friends and supporters. An incomplete list includes Alan Placa, Howard Koeppel, Mark Hsiao, Regina Peruggi, Raoul and Myrna Felder, Jim Simpson, Elliott Cuker, Ted Olson, Carl Figliola, Joe Torre, George Steinbrenner,

Fred and Jeff Wilpon, Bette Midler, Larry King, Goalie Giuliani, Tony Bennett, David Letterman, Lorne Michaels, Cardinal O'Connor, Bill Weld, Arnie Burns, Willie Mays, Jim Kelly, Edward Weinfeld, Sidney Lumet, Adam Sandler, Bob Leuci, Richard Green, Imam Pasha, Rabbis Shea Hecht, Arthur Schneier, Moshe Sherer, Sholom Klass and Yehuda Krinsky, Susan Alter, Henry Kissinger, Ken Langone, Georgette Mosbacher, Bernie Mendik, Jerry Speyer, Ken Bialkin, Saul Cohen, Jack Hennessey, Whitney Nathan, Mindy Levine, Roberta Waldman, Whitman Knapp, Sara Vidal, Placido Domingo, Michael Pesce, and Louis Lefkowitz.

My battle with prostate cancer may not have turned out as successfully as it did without the knowledge and skill of Alex Kirschenbaum, Richard Stock, Valentin Fuster, Burt Meyers, Christine Jacobs, Peter Scardino, Howard Scher, John Blasko, and Haakon Ragde.

Finally, my career in politics has been enhanced by the good fortune of knowing George H.W. Bush and George W. Bush, John McCain, George Pataki, Mike Bloomberg, Peter Vallone, Claire Shulman, Guy Molinari and his daughter Susan Molinari, Frank Luntz, Ray Harding, Carl Grillo, Mike Petrides, Steven Perry, Richard Bryers, David Garth, Adam Goodman, Roger Ailes, Joe Bruno, Herman Badillo, Roy Goodman, Tony Seminario, Tom Ognibene, Bobby Wagner, Jr., Rita Mottola, Charles Kushner, Rick Friedberg, Kai Vanderlinder, Joe Spitzer, Sam Domb, Abe Biederman, George Klein, Bud Konheim, Ed Arigone, Jenny Esterow, James Nederlander, Stewart Lane, Billie Tisch, and Ed Kane.

Index